ACCA

PAPER F5

PERFORMANCE MANAGEMENT

P
R
A
C
T
I
C
E

&

R
E
V
I
S
I
O
N

K
I
T

BPP Learning Media is the **sole ACCA Platinum Approved Learning Partner – content** for the ACCA qualification. In this, **the only Paper F5 Practice and Revision Kit to be reviewed by the examiner**:

- We discuss the **best strategies** for revising and taking your ACCA exams

- We show you how to be **well prepared** for your exam

- We give you **lots of great guidance** on tackling questions

- We show you how you can **build your own exams**

- We provide you with **three** mock exams including the **December 2011 exam**

- We provide the **ACCA examiner's answers** as well as our own to the June and December 2011 exams as an additional revision aid

Our **i-Pass** product also supports this paper.

FOR EXAMS IN 2012

BPP
LEARNING MEDIA

First edition 2008
Fifth edition January 2012

ISBN 9781 4453 7994 4
(previous ISBN 9780 7517 9401 4)

e-ISBN 9781 4453 2419 7

British Library Cataloguing-in-Publication Data
A catalogue record for this book
is available from the British Library

Published by

BPP Learning Media Ltd
BPP House, Aldine Place
London W12 8AA

www.bpp.com/learningmedia

Printed in the United Kingdom

We are grateful to the Association of Chartered Certified
Accountants for permission to reproduce past
examination questions. The suggested solutions in the
exam answer bank have been prepared by BPP Learning
Media Ltd, except where otherwise stated.

Your learning materials, published by BPP Learning
Media Ltd, are printed on paper sourced from
sustainable, managed forests.

Contents

BPP LEARNING MEDIA

Question index

The headings in this checklist/index indicate the main topics of questions, but questions often cover several different topics.

Questions set under the old syllabus *Financial Management and Control* and *Performance Management* papers are included because their style and content are similar to those which appear in the F5 exam. The questions have been amended to reflect the current exam format.

Mock exam 1

Mock exam 2

Mock exam 3 (December 2011)

Planning your question practice

Our guidance from page xxiv shows you how to organise your question practice, either by attempting questions from each syllabus area or **by building your own exams** – tackling questions as a series of practice exams.

Using your BPP Learning Media products

This Kit gives you the question practice and guidance you need in the exam. Our other products can also help you pass:

- **Learning to Learn Accountancy** gives further valuable advice on revision

- **Passcards** provide you with clear topic summaries and exam tips

- **Success CDs** help you revise on the move

- **i-Pass CDs** offer tests of knowledge against the clock

You can purchase these products by visiting www.bpp.com/mybpp.

Topic index

Listed below are the key Paper F5 syllabus topics and the numbers of the questions in this Kit covering those topics.

If you need to concentrate your practice and revision on certain topics or if you want to attempt all available questions that refer to a particular subject, you will find this index useful.

Helping you with your revision – the ONLY F5 Practice and Revision Kit to be reviewed by the examiner!

BPP Learning Media – the sole Platinum Approved Learning Partner - content

As ACCA's **sole Platinum Approved Learning Partner – content**, BPP Learning Media gives you the **unique opportunity** to use **examiner-reviewed** revision materials for the 2012 exams. By incorporating the examiner's comments and suggestions regarding syllabus coverage, the BPP Learning Media Practice and Revision Kit provides excellent, **ACCA-approved** support for your revision.

Tackling revision and the exam

You can significantly improve your chances of passing by tackling revision and the exam in the right ways. Our advice is based on feedback from ACCA examiners.

- We look at the dos and don'ts of revising for, and taking, ACCA exams
- We focus on Paper F5; we discuss revising the syllabus, what to do (and what not to do) in the exam, how to approach different types of question and ways of obtaining easy marks

Selecting questions

We provide signposts to help you plan your revision.

- A full **question index**
- A **topic index** listing all the questions that cover key topics, so that you can locate the questions that provide practice on these topics, and see the different ways in which they might be examined
- **BPP's question plan** highlighting the most important questions and explaining why you should attempt them
- **Build your own exams**, showing how you can practise questions in a series of exams

Making the most of question practice

At BPP Learning Media we realise that you need more than just questions and model answers to get the most from your question practice.

- Our **Top tips** provide essential advice on tackling questions, presenting answers and the key points that answers need to include
- We show you how you can pick up **Easy marks** on questions, as we know that picking up all readily available marks often can make the difference between passing and failing
- We include **marking guides** to show you what the examiner rewards
- We include **examiners' comments** to show you where students struggled or performed well in the actual exam
- We refer to the **2011 BPP Study Text** (for exams in 2012) for detailed coverage of the topics covered in questions
- In a bank at the end of this Kit we include the **examiner's answers** to the June and December 2010 papers. Used in conjunction with our answers they provide an indication of all possible points that could be made, issues that could be covered and approaches to adopt.

Attempting mock exams

There are three mock exams that provide practice at coping with the pressures of the exam day. We strongly recommend that you attempt them under exam conditions. **Mock exams 1 and 2** reflect the question styles and syllabus coverage of the exam; **Mock exam 3** is the December 2011 paper.

Revising F5

All questions are compulsory so you must revise the **whole** syllabus. Selective revision **will limit** the number of questions you can answer and hence reduce your chances of passing. It is better to go into the exam knowing a reasonable amount about most of the syllabus rather than concentrating on a few topics to the exclusion of the rest.

The exam has been changed from June 2009 so that there will be **five** compulsory questions covering as much of the syllabus as possible.

Practising as many exam-style questions as possible will be the key to passing this exam. You must do questions under **timed conditions** and ensure you write full answers to the discussion parts as well as doing the calculations.

Avoid looking at the answer until you have finished a question. Your biggest problem with F5 questions may be knowing how to start and this needs practice.

Also ensure that you attempt all three mock exams under exam conditions.

Passing the F5 exam

Displaying the right qualities

- You are expected to have a core of management accounting knowledge from your previous studies eg papers 1.2 (old syllabus) or F2 (new syllabus)

- You will be required to carry out calculations, with clear workings and a logical structure

- You will be required to interpret data

- You will be required to explain management accounting techniques and discuss whether they are appropriate for a particular organisation

- You must be able to apply your skills in a practical context

- You must understand what numbers tell you about the performance of a business

Avoiding weaknesses

- There is no choice in this paper, all questions have to be answered. You must therefore study the entire syllabus, there are no short-cuts

- Questions will be based on simple scenarios and answers must be focused and specific to the organisation

- Answer plans will help you to focus on the requirements of the question and enable you to manage your time effectively

- Answer all parts of the question. Even if you cannot do all of the calculation elements, you will still be able to gain marks in the discussion parts

- Make sure your answers focus on practical applications of management accounting, common sense is essential!

Using the reading time

- Speed read through the question paper, jotting down any ideas that come to you about any of the questions
- Decide the order in which you are likely to tackle questions (probably easiest questions first, most difficult questions last)
- Spend the remainder of the reading time reading the questions in detail analysing scenarios, jotting down plans (any plans written on the question paper should be reproduced in the answer booklet)
- When you can start writing get straight on with the questions you have planned in detail

Gaining the easy marks

Easy marks in this paper tend to fall into two categories.

Calculations

There will be some relatively straightforward calculations at the start of the question and they will then probably get progressively more difficult. If you get stuck, make an assumption, state it and move on.

Discussions

The examiner has stated she intends, wherever possible, to separate discussion from calculations. This means that you should be able to gain marks from making sensible, practical comments without having to complete the calculations.

Discussions that are focused on the specific organisation in the question will gain more marks than regurgitation of knowledge. Read the question carefully and more than once, to ensure you are actually answering the specific requirements.

Pick out key words such as 'describe', 'evaluate' and 'discuss'. These all mean something specific.

- 'Describe' means to communicate the key features of
- 'Evaluate' means to assess the value of
- 'Discuss' means to examine in detail by argument

Clearly label the points you make in discussions so that the marker can identify them all rather than getting lost in the detail.

Provide answers in the form requested, particularly using report format if asked for and giving recommendations if required.

Exam formulae

Set out below are the formulae which you will be given in the exam, and formulae which you should learn. If you are not sure what the symbols mean, or how the formulae are used, you should refer to the appropriate chapter in the Study Text.

Exam formulae *Chapter in Study Text*

Learning curve
10

$Y = ax^b$

Where
- Y = the cumulative average time per unit to produce X units
- a = the time taken for the first unit of output
- x = the cumulative number of units
- b = the index of learning (log LR/log 2)
- LR = the learning rate as a decimal

Regression analysis
10

$y = a + bx$

$$b = \frac{n\sum xy - \sum x \sum y}{n\sum x^2 - (\sum x)^2}$$

$$a = \frac{\sum y}{n} - \frac{b\sum x}{n}$$

$$r = \frac{n\sum xy - \sum x \sum y}{\sqrt{(n\sum x^2 - (\sum x)^2)(n\sum y^2 - (\sum y)^2)}}$$

Demand curve
5

P = a − bQ

$$b = \frac{\text{change in price}}{\text{change in quantity}}$$

a = price when Q = 0

MR = a − 2bQ

BPP LEARNING MEDIA

Exam information

The examiner for this paper is **Ann Irons**, who replaced Geoff Cordwell from the December 2010 sitting onwards. Ann Irons has written several articles in *Student Accountant*, including one on how to approach the paper (September 2010 issue). Make sure you read these articles to gain further insight into what the examiner is looking for.

Format of the exam

Five compulsory questions of 20 marks each.

This format has changed from June 2009.

Time allowed: 3 hours plus 15 minutes reading time.

The examination will comprise a mix of computational and discursive elements.

Additional information

The Study Guide provides more detailed guidance on the syllabus.

December 2011

1   Short-term decisions; relevant costing
2   Divisional performance; transfer pricing
3   Budgeting; objectives of budgetary control; participative budgeting
4   Costing methods: life-cycle costing; learning curve
5   Variance analysis; material usage, mix and yield; activity-based costing

The December 2011 paper is Mock Exam 3 in this Kit.

June 2011

		Question in this Kit
1	Risk and uncertainty: decision rules; pay-off table	38
2	Pricing decisions: demand function: MC = MR; pricing strategies	27
3	Variance analysis: flexed budget; sales mix and quantity variances	67
4	Performance measurement: balanced scorecard; ROI and RI	70
5	Costing methods: throughput accounting	15

Examiner's comments. This paper consisted of five compulsory 20 mark questions.

The paper was 57% computational and 43% narrative.

The pass rate on this paper was slightly lower than the previous sitting. It was clear from marking that question 1 seemed to pose a particular problem for candidates, with the majority being unable to construct an accurate payoff table. Similarly, whilst many candidates were able to produce the flexed budget required for question 3, most were not able to tackle the discursive elements of this question. On the whole, question two was the best answered, although few candidates were able to calculate an optimum price and quantity for the product in this question.

While there were notable amount of really high marks (in the 70s and 80s) but there was also a significant amount of really low marks (many less than 20%). It looked like some candidates yet again had not revised some of the key areas. F5, by its nature, is a fairly challenging paper. It is a paper that requires a significant level of work in order to pass it. It relies on learning/revising a substantial number of management accounting techniques and then also being able to explain them and understand the impact of their results on the business. If you want to pass it, put some work in and use all of the resources available to you – past exam papers, Student Accountant articles, past examiner's reports etc, all of which are available on the ACCA's website.

December 2010

Question in this Kit

1	Variance analysis: sales price and volume; material planning and operational; labour rate and efficiency	66
2	Performance measurement: financial performance; non-financial performance	84
3	Linear programming: constraints; graph; optimal solution; shadow price	22
4	Costing methods: absorption costing; activity based costing	7
5	Budgeting: incremental budgeting; zero-based budgeting; public sector	46

Examiner's comments. This paper consisted of five compulsory 20 mark questions.

The pass rate on this paper saw a drop from previous recent sessions. I believe that the reason for this is primarily that candidates tried to question spot. So, for example, because linear programming came up in June 2010, the belief was that it would not come up again in December 2010. The lesson to be learnt is that you can't question spot in these exams. You have to make sure that you are comfortable with every area of the syllabus; otherwise you may be caught out. Anyone who watched the 'Examiners' Special' online in September would have got this message.

The paper was 54% computational and 46% narrative, since within question two there were a certain number of marks available for the calculations. On the whole, question four was the best answered, although there were still a surprising number of candidates uncomfortable with the area of activity based costing. In every question, the candidate had the opportunity to earn some easy marks quickly, and well prepared candidates attempted these parts first.

June 2010

1	Activity based costing: pricing strategies; marginal costing	5
2	Variance analysis: materials; labour; sales	65
3	Linear programming: optimal mix; shadow prices; optimal production plan	21
4	Transfer pricing: calculation of prices; discussion of pricing policy	76
5	Performance measurement: calculation; discussion of targets; budget manipulation	83

Examiner's comments. This paper consisted of five compulsory 20 mark questions.

The mix of narrative to numerical requirements was 47% to 53%. Most candidates attempted all questions and there was no evidence that the paper was found to be particularly time pressured.

December 2009

Examiner's comments. Under the recently introduced format, the paper consisted of five compulsory 20 mark questions.

Most candidates attempted all questions and there was no evidence that the paper was found to be particularly time pressured.

June 2009

Examiner's comments. This was the first sitting with a change of rubric setting five questions of 20 marks each.

Layout was still an issue but standards of performance assessment are improving. More candidates have more idea about what is expected when assessing the performance of a business.

December 2008

Examiner's comments. There was little evidence of time management issues but layout of answers was again mixed. Poor layout and untidiness is not acceptable. Standards of performance assessment improved slightly and the signs were encouraging.

June 2008

Examiner's comments. There was evidence of poor time management with some candidates spending too long on the linear programming question and writing copious amounts unnecessarily in other questions.

Preparation for the performance management question has to revolve around principles and techniques and students will have to be able to have original thoughts on the exam day. The scenarios will always be straightforward but an interpretation will be needed.

Poor layout is not acceptable eg excessive crossing out, unlabelled workings, no tabulation.

Candidates continue to struggle in the written (discursive) elements of the paper. Practice in writing skills is needed and an improvement in the techniques of commentary, assessment and the ability to answer the question set as opposed to merely demonstrating knowledge.

December 2007

Examiner's comments. There was no evidence of time pressure with most candidates completing the paper.

Many of those that failed did not have knowledge of target costing, did not understand budget revisions and could not interpret simple financial data.

The layout of questions was mixed, with the weaker candidates producing messy and poorly laid out work.

Pilot paper

Analysis of past papers

Covered in Text chapter		Dec 2011	June 2011	Dec 2010	June 2010	Dec 2009	Pilot Paper
	SPECIALIST COST AND MANAGEMENT ACCOUNTING TECHNIQUES						
2a	Activity based costing	5		4	1		1
2b	Target costing					2	
2c	Life cycle costing	4					
2d	Throughput accounting		5				
2e	Environmental accounting						
	DECISION-MAKING TECHNIQUES						
3	Cost volume profit (CVP) analysis						
4	Multi-limiting factors and the use of linear programming and shadow pricing			3	3		
5	Pricing decisions		2		1	5	
6	Make-or-buy and other short-term decisions	1				5	
7	Dealing with risk and uncertainty in decision-making		1				
	BUDGETING						
8	Objectives	3					
9	Budgetary systems			5			
9	Types of budget		3			3	
10	Quantitative analysis in budgeting	4	2			3	3
8	Behavioural aspects of budgeting	3			5		
	STANDARD COSTING AND VARIANCE ANALYSIS						
11	Budgeting and standard costing						
12	Basic variances and operating systems		3	1	2		2
12	Material mix and yield variances	5			2		2
13	Planning and operational variances			1		1	
13	Behavioural aspects of standard costing						
	PERFORMANCE MEASUREMENT AND CONTROL						
14	The scope of performance measurement		4	2	5	4	4
15	Divisional performance and transfer pricing	2	4		4		
16	Performance analysis in not-for-profit organisations and the public sector						

Useful websites

The websites below provide additional sources of information of relevance to your studies for *Performance Management*.

- www.accaglobal.com

  ACCA's website. The students' section of the website is invaluable for detailed information about the qualification, past issues of *Student Accountant* (including technical articles) and interviews with examiners.

- www.bpp.com

  Our website provides information about BPP products and services, with a link to the ACCA website.

- www.ft.com

  This website provides information about current international business. You can search for information and articles on specific industry groups as well as individual companies.

- www.economist.com

  Here you can search for business information on a week-by-week basis, search articles by business subject and use the resources of the Economist Intelligence Unit to research sectors, companies or countries.

- www.bbc.co.uk

  The website of the BBC carries general business information as well as programme-related content.

Planning your question practice

We have already stressed that question practice should be right at the centre of your revision. Whilst you will spend some time looking at your notes and Paper F5 Passcards, you should spend the majority of your revision time practising questions.

We recommend two ways in which you can practise questions.

- Use **BPP's Learning Media's question plan** to work systematically through the syllabus and attempt key and other questions on a section-by-section basis
- **Build your own exams** – attempt questions as a series of practice exams

These ways are suggestions and simply following them is no guarantee of success. You or your college may prefer an alternative but equally valid approach.

BPP Learning Media's question plan

The BPP plan below requires you to devote a **minimum of 30 hours** to revision of Paper F5. Any time you can spend over and above this should only increase your chances of success.

Step 1   **Review your notes** and the chapter summaries in the Paper F5 **Passcards** for each section of the syllabus.

Step 2   **Answer the key questions** for that section. These questions have boxes round the question number in the table below and you should answer them in full. Even if you are short of time you must attempt these questions if you want to pass the exam. You should complete your answers without referring to our solutions.

Step 3   **Attempt the other questions** in that section. For some questions we have suggested that you prepare **answer plans or do the calculations** rather than full solutions. Planning an answer means that you should spend about 40% of the time allowance for the questions brainstorming the question and drawing up a list of points to be included in the answer.

Step 4   Attempt **Mock exams 1, 2 and 3** under strict exam conditions.

Syllabus section	2011 Passcards chapters	Questions in this Kit	Comments	Done ✓
Revision period 1 *Specialist cost and management accounting techniques*				
Absorption and marginal costing	1	1	Answer this question in full as it provides good revision of absorption and marginal costing.	☐
Activity based costing	1, 2, 5	5	This June 2010 question tests ABC, absorption costing and pricing strategies. Answer in full.	☐
	2	7	Answer this December 2010 question in full.	☐
Target and lifecycle costing	2	9	Answer this December 2007 question in full.	☐
Lifecycle costing	2	10	Answer in full for an idea of how lifecycle costing could be tested.	☐
Throughput accounting	2	13	Answer this question in full as it revises limiting factor and contribution calculations as well as asking you to explain some elements of environmental accounting.	☐
	2	15	Answer this June 2011 question in full.	☐
Environmental accounting	2, 5	25	Part (c) of this question tests your knowledge of management accounting techniques that can be used to account for environmental costs. Answer in full.	☐
Revision period 2 *Decision-making techniques*				
Cost volume profit (CVP) analysis	3	16	This is a good test of the main elements of CVP analysis. Answer in full.	☐
Linear programming	4	22	Answer this December 2010 question in full as it gives you valuable practice at all aspects of linear programming.	☐
Pricing	5	27	Answer this June 2011 question in full as it has some testing calculations and makes you think about the practical aspects of pricing strategies.	☐
Short-term decisions	6	30	This is a good test of relevant costing principles and also includes a discussion on cost-plus pricing. Answer in full.	☐
	6	33	Answer this December 2009 question on shutdown decisions in full.	☐
Risk and uncertainty	7	38	This June 2011 question tests your knowledge of decision rules and pay-off tables. Answer in full.	☐
Revision period 3 *Budgeting*				
Objectives of budgetary control	8	41	Prepare an answer plan for this question. Each part could appear as a discussion part of a question involving calculations, for example on quantitative analysis or variance analysis.	☐

Syllabus section	2011 Passcards chapters	Questions in this Kit	Comments	Done ☑
Budgetary systems	9	42	Prepare an answer plan for this question.	☐
	9	43	Prepare and answer plan for parts (b) and (c) of this question.	☐
Budgets	2 & 9	45	Answer this December 2008 question in full as it covers both lifecycle costing and budgeting.	☐
	2 & 9	46	This December 2010 question tests your knowledge of zero-based budgeting. Answer in full.	☐
Quantitative analysis	10	50	Answer this Pilot Paper question in full.	☐
		52	Answer this December 2009 question on learning curves in full.	☐
Revision period 4 *Standard costing and variances analysis*				
Variance analysis	11, 12	53	Answer this question in full as it shows how various areas of the management accounting syllabus can be combined into one question.	☐
	12	54	Answer in full as this question provides excellent practice in the preparation of an operating statement.	☐
	13	61	Answer this Pilot Paper question in full.	☐
	12	63	Answer this June 2009 question on mix and yield variances in full.	☐
	12, 13	64	Answer this December 2009 question on material price and usage, and planning and operational variances in full.	☐
	12, 13	66	Answer this December 2010 question in full.	☐
	12, 13	67	This June 2011 question tests your knowledge of flexed budgets and sales mix and quantity variances. Answer in full.	☐
Revision period 5 *Performance measurement and control*				
Transfer pricing	15	76	This June 2010 question contains a mix of calculation and written requirements. Answer in full.	☐
Performance measures	14-16	70	This June 2011 question tests the Balanced scorecard, RI and ROI. Answer in full.	☐
		80	This December 2009 question tests your knowledge of budgetary systems and forecasts. Answer in full.	☐
		81	Answer this Pilot Paper question in full.	☐
		83	Answer this June 2010 question in full.	☐
		86	Answer this December 2008 question in full.	☐

Syllabus section	2011 Passcards chapters	Questions in this Kit	Comments	Done ☑
Performance measures	14-16	87	Answer this June 2009 question in full.	☐
		88	Answer this December 2009 question in full	☐

Build your own exams

Having revised your notes and the BPP Learning Media Passcards, you can attempt the questions in the Kit as a series of practice exams. You can organise the questions in the following ways.

- Either you can attempt complete past exam papers; recent papers are listed below:

	Pilot paper Question in kit	December 09 Question in Kit	June 10 Question in Kit	December 10 Question in Kit	June 11 Question in Kit
1	4	33	5	66	38
2	61	52	21	84	27
3	50	64	65	22	67
4	81	80	76	7	70
5		88	83	46	15

- Or you can make up practice exams, either yourself or using the suggestions we have listed below.

	1	2	3	4	5
1	2	3	8	10	11
2	19	23	24	29	30
3	43	26	44	48	49
4	53	54	55	56	57
5	68	71	72	73	77

Questions

SPECIALIST COST AND MANAGEMENT ACCOUNTING TECHNIQUES

Questions 1 to 15 cover Specialist cost and management accounting techniques, the subject of Part A of the BPP Study Text for Paper F5.

1 Preparation question: Cassiop

The following budget and actual data relates to Cassiop for the past three periods.

Budget	Period 1	Period 2	Period 3
Sales (units)	10,000	14,000	12,200
Production (units)	8,000	14,200	12,400
Fixed overheads	$10,400	$19,170	$17,360

Actual			
Sales (units)	9,600	12,400	10,200
Production (units)	8,400	13,600	9,200
Fixed overheads	$11,200	$18,320	$16,740

The value of the opening and closing inventory of the units produced is arrived at by using FIFO. The budgeted and actual opening inventory for period 1 was 2,600 units and its valuation included $3,315 of fixed overheads. The company absorbs its fixed overheads via a predetermined fixed overhead rate per unit which is calculated for each period. It is assumed that variable costs per unit and selling prices per unit remained the same for each of the periods.

Required

(a) Calculate the under or over recovery of fixed overhead for each period and indicate how it will affect the profit or loss.

(b) 'Absorption costing will produce a higher profit than marginal costing'. Explain why you agree or disagree with this statement, making reference to the data provided above as appropriate.

(c) Explain briefly why absorption costing is usually considered to be unsuitable as an aid for decision making. Justify your answer.

(d) Discuss the advantages and disadvantages of using the 'full cost' (absorption costing) method for dealing with the costs of internal services. Include in your answer comments on the motivational aspects of this method of costing.

Helping hand. Part (a) asks you to calculate under or over recovery of fixed overheads. What you need to do first is calculate the BUDGETED fixed overhead absorption rates for each period.

Then use these rates with ACTUAL production to calculate overhead absorbed. Compare this with ACTUAL fixed overheads to find over or under absorption.

Part (b) wants you to briefly explain marginal and absorption costing in particular how inventories are valued. You then need to calculate inventory levels in each period including opening inventory and closing inventory.

Use these inventory balances and the overhead absorption rates you calculated in part (a) to work out the effect on profit. See our table in the answer and work through this if you don't understand it.

You need to make at least five to six good points in part (c).

Finally, part (d) is another written answer asking for the advantages and disadvantages of absorption costing. You may need to refer to the Study Text if you run out of inspiration.

---

2 Linacre Co (FMC, 12/05, amended)

36 mins

Linacre Co operates an activity-based costing system and has forecast the following information for next year.

Cost Pool	Cost	Cost Driver	Number of Drivers
Production set-ups	$105,000	Set-ups	300
Product testing	$300,000	Tests	1,500
Component supply and storage	$25,000	Component orders	500
Customer orders and delivery	$112,500	Customer orders	1,000

General fixed overheads such as lighting and heating, which cannot be linked to any specific activity, are expected to be $900,000 and these overheads are absorbed on a direct labour hour basis. Total direct labour hours for next year are expected to be 300,000 hours.

Linacre Co expects orders for Product ZT3 next year to be 100 orders of 60 units per order and 60 orders of 50 units per order. The company holds no inventories of Product ZT3 and will need to produce the order requirement in production runs of 900 units. One order for components is placed prior to each production run. Four tests are made during each production run to ensure that quality standards are maintained. The following additional cost and profit information relates to product ZT3:

Component cost:	$1.00 per unit
Direct labour:	10 minutes per unit at $7.80 per hour
Profit mark up:	40% of total unit cost

Required

(a) Calculate the activity-based recovery rates for each cost pool. **(4 marks)**

(b) Calculate the total unit cost and selling price of Product ZT3. **(9 marks)**

(c) Discuss the reasons why activity-based costing may be preferred to traditional absorption costing in the modern manufacturing environment. **(7 marks)**

(Total = 20 marks)

3 Z Co

36 mins

Z Co supplies pharmaceutical drugs to chemist shops. Although the company makes a satisfactory return, the directors are concerned that some orders are profitable and others are not. The management has decided to investigate a new budgeting system using activity based costing principles to ensure that all orders they accept are making a profit.

Each customer order is charged as follows. Customers are charged the list price of the drugs ordered plus a charge for selling and distribution costs (overheads). A profit margin is also added, but that does not form part of this analysis.

Currently Z Co uses a simple absorption rate to absorb these overheads. The rate is calculated based on the budgeted annual selling and distribution costs and the budgeted annual total list price of the drugs ordered.

An analysis of customers has revealed that many customers place frequent small orders with each order requesting a variety of drugs. The management of Z Co has examined more carefully the nature of its selling and distribution costs, and the following data have been prepared for the budget for next year:

Total list price of drugs supplied	$8m
Number of customer orders	8,000

Selling and Distribution Costs	$'000	Cost driver
Invoice processing	280	See Note 2
Packing	220	Size of package – see Note 3
Delivery	180	Number of deliveries – see Note 4
Other overheads	200	Number of orders
Total overheads	880	

Notes

(1) Each order will be shipped in one package and will result in one delivery to the customer and one invoice (an order never results in more than one delivery).

(2) Each invoice has a different line for each drug ordered. There are 28,000 invoice lines each year. It is estimated that 25% of invoice processing costs are related to the number of invoices, and 75% are related to the number of invoice lines.

(3) Packing costs are $32 for a large package, and $25 for a small package.

(4) The delivery vehicles are always filled to capacity for each journey. The delivery vehicles can carry either 6 large packages or 12 small packages (or appropriate combinations of large and small packages). It is estimated that there will be 1,000 delivery journeys each year, and the total delivery mileage that is specific to particular customers is estimated at 350,000 miles each year. $40,000 of delivery costs are related to loading the delivery vehicles, and the remainder of these costs are related to specific delivery distance to customers.

The management has asked for two typical orders to be costed using next year's budget data, using the current method, and the proposed activity-based costing approach. Details of two typical orders are shown below:

	Order A	Order B
Lines on invoice	2	8
Package size	small	large
Specific delivery distance	8 miles	40 miles
List price of drugs supplied	$1,200	$900

Required

(a) Calculate the charge for selling and distribution overheads for Order A and Order B using:

(i) The current system; and
(ii) The activity-based costing approach. **(13 marks)**

(b) Explain the implications of switching to ABC for pricing of Z Co's products and suggest a suitable pricing strategy. **(7 marks)**

(Total = 20 marks)

4 Triple (Pilot paper, amended)   36 mins

Triple Limited makes three types of gold watch – the Diva (D), the Classic (C) and the Poser (P). A traditional product costing system is used at present; although an activity based costing (ABC) system is being considered. Details of the three products for a typical period are:

	Hours per unit		Materials	Production
	Labour hours	Machine hours	Cost per unit	units
			$	
Product D	½	1½	20	750
Product C	1½	1	12	1,250
Product P	1	3	25	7,000

Direct labour costs $6 per hour and production overheads are absorbed on a machine hour basis. The overhead absorption rate for the period is $28 per machine hour.'

Required

(a) Calculate the cost per unit for each product using traditional methods, absorbing overheads on the basis of machine hours. **(3 marks)**

Total production overheads are $654,500 and further analysis shows that the total production overheads can be divided as follows:

	%
Costs relating to set-ups	35
Costs relating to machinery	20
Costs relating to materials handling	15
Costs relating to inspection	30
Total production overhead	100

The following total activity volumes are associated with each product line for the period as a whole:

	Number of Set ups	Number of movements of materials	Number of inspections
Product D	75	12	150
Product C	115	21	180
Product P	480	87	670
	670	120	1,000

Required

(b) Calculate the cost per unit for each product using ABC principles (work to two decimal places). **(12 marks)**

(c) Explain why costs per unit calculated under ABC are often very different to costs per unit calculated under more traditional methods. Use the information from Triple Limited to illustrate. **(5 marks)**

(Total = 20 marks)

5 Brick by Brick (6/10) 36 mins

Brick by Brick (BBB) is a building business that provides a range of building services to the public. Recently they have been asked to quote for garage conversions (GC) and extensions to properties (EX) and have found that they are winning fewer GC contracts than expected.

BBB has a policy to price all jobs at budgeted total cost plus 50%. Overheads are currently absorbed on a labour hour basis. BBB thinks that a switch to activity based costing (ABC) to absorb overheads would reduce the cost associated to GC and hence make them more competitive.

You are provided with the following data:

Overhead category	Annual overheads $	Activity driver	Total number of activities per year
Supervisors	90,000	Site visits	500
Planners	70,000	Planning documents	250
Property related	240,000	Labour hours	40,000
Total	400,000		

A typical GC costs $3,500 in materials and takes 300 labour hours to complete. A GC requires only one site visit by a supervisor and needs only one planning document to be raised. The typical EX costs $8,000 in materials and takes 500 hours to complete. An EX requires six site visits and five planning documents. In all cases labour is paid $15 per hour.

Required

(a) Calculate the cost and quoted price of a GC and of an EX using labour hours to absorb the overheads.
(5 marks)

(b) Calculate the cost and the quoted price of a GC and of an EX using ABC to absorb the overheads. **(5 marks)**

(c) Assuming that the cost of a GC falls by nearly 7% and the price of an EX rises by about 2% as a result of the change to ABC, suggest possible pricing strategies for the two products that BBB sells and suggest two reasons other than high prices for the current poor sales of the GC. **(6 marks)**

(d)   One BBB manager has suggested that only marginal cost should be included in budget cost calculations as this would avoid the need for arbitrary overhead allocations to products. Briefly discuss this point of view and comment on the implication for the amount of mark-up that would be applied to budget costs when producing quotes for jobs.   **(4 marks)**

(Total = 20 marks)

6 Jola Publishing Co (6/08, amended)   36 mins

Jola Publishing Co publishes two forms of book.

The company publishes a children's book (CB), which is sold in large quantities to government controlled schools. The book is produced in only four large production runs but goes through frequent government inspections and quality assurance checks.

The paper used is strong, designed to resist the damage that can be caused by the young children it is produced for. The book has only a few words and relies on pictures to convey meaning.

The second book is a comprehensive technical journal (TJ). It is produced in monthly production runs, 12 times a year. The paper used is of relatively poor quality and is not subject to any governmental controls and consequently only a small number of inspections are carried out. The TJ uses far more machine hours than the CB in its production.

The directors are concerned about the performance of the two books and are wondering what the impact would be of a switch to an activity based costing (ABC) approach to accounting for overheads. They currently use absorption costing, based on machine hours for all overhead calculations. They have produced an analysis for the coming year as follows:

	CB $ per unit		TJ $ per unit
Paper (400g @ $2 per kg)	0.80	(100g @ $1 per kg)	0.10
Printing ink (50 ml @ $30 per litre)	1.50	(150 ml @ $30 per litre)	4.50
Machine costs (6 mins @ $12 per hour)	1.20	(10 mins @ $12 per hour)	2.00
Overheads (6 mins @ $24 per hour)	2.40	(10 mins @ $24 per hour)	4.00
Total cost	5.90		10.60
Selling price	9.30		14.00
Margin	3.40		3.40

The main overheads involved are:

Overhead	% of total overhead	Activity driver
Property costs	75.0%	Machine hours
Quality control	23.0%	Number of inspections
Production set up costs	2.0%	Number of set ups

If the overheads for the previous accounting year were re-allocated under ABC principles then the results would be that the overhead allocation to CB would be $0·05 higher at $2.35 per unit, and the overhead allocated to TJ would be $0·30 lower at $3.65 per unit.

Required

(a)   Explain why the overhead allocations have changed in the way indicated above.   **(8 marks)**

(b)   Briefly explain the implementation problems often experienced when ABC is first introduced.   **(4 marks)**

As mentioned above there are three main overheads, the data for these are:

Overhead	Annual cost for the coming year $
Property costs	2,160,000
Quality control	668,000
Production set up costs	52,000
Total	2,880,000

The CB will be inspected on 180 occasions next year, whereas the TJ will be inspected just 20 times.

Jola Publishing will produce its annual output of 1,000,000 CBs in four production runs and approximately 10,000 TJs per month in each of 12 production runs.

Required

(c)   Calculate the cost per unit and the margin for the CB and the TJ using activity based costing principles to absorb the overheads.   **(8 marks)**

(Total = 20 marks)

7 The Gadget Co (12/10)   **36 mins**

The Gadget Co produces three products, A, B and C, all made from the same material. Until now, it has used traditional absorption costing to allocate overheads to its products. The company is now considering an activity based costing system in the hope that it will improve profitability. Information for the three products for the last year is as follows:

	A	B	C
Production and sales volumes (units)	15,000	12,000	18,000
Selling price per unit	$7.50	$12	$13
Raw material usage (kg) per unit	2	3	4
Direct labour hours per unit	0.1	0.15	0.2
Machine hours per unit	0.5	0.7	0.9
Number of production runs per annum	16	12	8
Number of purchase orders per annum	24	28	42
Number of deliveries to retailers per annum	48	30	62

The price for raw materials remained constant throughout the year at $1.20 per kg. Similarly, the direct labour cost for the whole workforce was $14.80 per hour. The annual overhead costs were as follows:

	$
Machine set up costs	26,550
Machine running costs	66,400
Procurement costs	48,000
Delivery costs	54,320

Required

(a)   Calculate the full cost per unit for products A, B and C under traditional absorption costing, using direct labour hours as the basis for apportionment.   **(5 marks)**

(b)   Calculate the full cost per unit of each product using activity based costing.   **(9 marks)**

(c)   Using your calculation from (a) and (b) above, explain how activity based costing may help The Gadget Co improve the profitability of each product.   **(6 marks)**

(Total = 20 marks)

8 GEEWHIZZ   **36 mins**

GEEWHIZZ, a manufacturer of computer games, has developed a new game called the Action Accountant (AA). This is an interactive 3D game and is the first of its kind to be introduced to the market. GEEWHIZZ is due to launch the AA in time for the peak selling season.

GEEWIZZ has been using a traditional absorption costing system to calculate costs and price its products. The new management accountant believes that this is inappropriate for this company and is arguing for a new approach to be adopted.

Required

As management accountant of GEEWHIZZ, do the following.

(a)   Discuss the principles of the following techniques and explain how each could have been applied to the AA.

- Life cycle costing
- Target costing   **(13 marks)**

A few months later, GEEWHIZZ is in the process of introducing another new game, the Laughing Lawyer (LL) and has undertaken market research to find out about customers' views on the value of the product and also to obtain a comparison with competitors' products. The results of this research have been used to establish a target selling price of $55 and a projected lifetime volume of 200,000 games.

Cost estimates have also been prepared based on the proposed product specification.

Manufacturing cost	$
Direct material	3.21
Direct labour	4.23
Direct machinery costs	1.12
Ordering and receiving	0.23
Quality assurance	4.60
Design	19.80
Non-manufacturing costs	
Marketing	8.15
Distribution	3.25
After-sales service and warranty costs	1.30

The target profit margin for the LL is 30% of the proposed selling price.

Required

(b)   Calculate the target cost of the LL and discuss the implications of the result. Explain the limitations of target costing for GEEWIZZ.   **(7 marks)**

(Total = 20 marks)

9 Edward Limited (12/07, amended)   36 mins

Edward Limited assembles and sells many types of radio. It is considering extending its product range to include digital radios. These radios produce a better sound quality than traditional radios and have a large number of potential additional features not possible with the previous technologies (station scanning, more choice, one touch tuning, station identification text and song identification text etc).

A radio is produced by assembly workers assembling a variety of components. Production overheads are currently absorbed into product costs on an assembly labour hour basis.

Edward Limited is considering a target costing approach for its new digital radio product.

Required

(a)   Briefly describe the target costing process that Edward Limited should undertake.   **(3 marks)**

(b)   Explain the benefits to Edward Limited of adopting a target costing approach at such an early stage in the product development process.   **(4 marks)**

A selling price of $44 has been set in order to compete with a similar radio on the market that has comparable features to Edward Limited's intended product. The board have agreed that the acceptable margin (after allowing for all production costs) should be 20%. *Margine*

Cost information for the new radio is as follows:

Component 1 (Circuit board) – these are bought in and cost $4·10 each. They are bought in batches of 4,000 and additional delivery costs are $2,400 per batch.

0.25M. → 98%

Component 2 (Wiring) – in an ideal situation 25 cm of wiring is needed for each completed radio. However, there is some waste involved in the process as wire is occasionally cut to the wrong length or is damaged in the assembly process. Edward Limited estimates that 2% of the purchased wire is lost in the assembly process. Wire costs $0·50 per metre to buy.

Other material – other materials cost $8·10 per radio.

Assembly labour – these are skilled people who are difficult to recruit and retain. Edward Limited has more staff of this type than needed but is prepared to carry this extra cost in return for the security it gives the business. It takes 30 minutes to assemble a radio and the assembly workers are paid $12·60 per hour. It is estimated that 10% of hours paid to the assembly workers is for idle time.

0.5hr
1
90%

Production Overheads – recent historic cost analysis has revealed the following production overhead data:

↳ Variable & fixed?

	Total production overhead $	Total assembly labour hours
Month 1	620,000	19,000
Month 2	700,000	23,000

high low

per Month

Fixed production overheads are absorbed on an assembly hour basis based on normal annual activity levels. In a typical year 240,000 assembly hours will be worked by Edward Limited.

FC = overheads/the year.
240,000

Required

(c)   Calculate the expected cost per unit for the radio and identify any cost gap that might exist.   **(13 marks)**

(Total = 20 marks)

Target cost – estimated cost

10 Cambs Co   36 mins

Cambs Co is an innovative, high technology company which has recently completed the development and testing of a new product, the Fentiger. The development of the product has cost $500,000 and the company has also bought a machine to produce the new product costing $175,000. The production machine is capable of producing 1,500 units of Fentigers per month and is not expected to have a residual value due to its specialised nature.

The company has decided that the unit selling prices it will charge will change with the cumulative numbers of units sold as follows.

Cumulative sales units	Selling price $ per unit in this band
0 to 1,900	120
1,901 to 4,900	90
4,901 to 13,400	60
13,401 to 73,400	50
73,401 and above	40

Based on these selling prices, it is expected that sales demand will be as shown below.

Months	Sales demand per month (units)
1 – 10	190
11 – 20	300
21 – 30	850
31 – 70	1,500
71 – 80	900
81 – 90	700
91 – 100	450
101 – 110	300
Thereafter	NIL

Unit variable costs are expected to be as follows.

	$ per unit
First 1,900 units	50
Next 11,500 units	40
Next 30,000 units	30
Next 30,000 units	25
Thereafter	30

Cambs Co operates a Just in Time (JIT) purchasing and production system and operates its business on a cash basis.

Required

(a) Explain each stage in the life cycle of the Fentiger and the issues that the management team will need to consider at each stage. Your answer should include a diagram to illustrate the product life cycle of the Fentiger. **(12 marks)**

(b) Calculate the total cash flow expected from the production and sale of Fentigers and briefly comment on your calculations. **(8 marks)**

(Total = 20 marks)

11 Sapu   36 mins

Sapu make and sell a number of products. Products A and B are products for which market prices are available at which Sapu can obtain a share of the market as detailed below. Estimated data for the forthcoming period is as follows.

Product data

	Product A	Product B	Other products
Production/sales (units)	5,000	10,000	40,000
	$'000	$'000	$'000
Total direct material cost	80	300	2,020
Total direct labour cost	40	100	660

Variable overhead cost is $1,500,000 of which 40% is related to the acquisition, storage and use of direct materials and 60% is related to the control and use of direct labour.

It is current practice in Sapu to absorb variable overhead cost into product units using overall company wide percentages on direct material cost and direct labour cost as the absorption bases.

Market prices for Products A and B are $75 and $95 per unit respectively.

Required

(a) Prepare estimated unit product costs for Product A and Product B where variable overhead is charged to product units as follows.

   (i) Using the existing absorption basis as detailed above. **(4 marks)**

   (ii) Using an activity based costing approach where cost drivers have been estimated for material and labour related overhead costs as follows.

	Product A	Product B	Other products
Direct material related overheads – cost driver is material bulk. The bulk proportions per unit are:	4	1	1.5
Direct labour related overheads – cost driver is number of labour operations(not directly time related). Labour operations per product unit are:	6	1	2

(6 marks)

(b)   Explain how Sapu could make use of target costing in conjunction with activity based costing with respect to Products A and B.   **(4 marks)**

The Managing Director is considering implementing a system of throughput accounting.

Required

(c)   Explain the principles and limitations of throughput accounting.   **(6 marks)**

(Total = 20 marks)

12 Throughput accounting   36 mins

(a)   MN manufactures automated industrial trolleys, known as TRLs. Each TRL sells for $2,000 and the material cost per unit is $600. Labour and variable overhead are $5,500 and $8,000 per week respectively. Fixed production costs are $450,000 per annum and marketing and administrative costs are $265,000 per annum.

The trolleys are made on three different machines. Machine X makes the four frame panels required for each TRL. Its maximum output is 180 frame panels per week. Machine X is old and unreliable and it breaks down from time to time. It is estimated that, on average, between 15 and 20 hours of production are lost per month. Machine Y can manufacture parts for 52 TRLs per week and machine Z, which is old but reasonably reliable, can process and assemble 30 TRLs per week.

The company has recently introduced a just-in-time (JIT) system and it is company policy to hold little work-in-progress and no finished goods inventory from week to week. The company operates a 40-hour week, 48 weeks a year (12 months × 4 weeks).

Required

Calculate the throughput accounting ratio for the key resource for an average hour next year.   **(5 marks)**

(b)   Corrie produces three products, X, Y and Z. The capacity of Corrie's plant is restricted by process alpha. Process alpha is expected to be operational for eight hours per day and can produce 1,200 units of X per hour, 1,500 units of Y per hour, and 600 units of Z per hour.

Selling prices and material costs for each product are as follows.

Product	Selling price $ per unit	Material cost $ per unit	Throughput contribution $ per unit
X	150	70	80
Y	120	40	80
Z	300	100	200

Conversion costs are $720,000 per day.

Required

(i)   Calculate the profit per day if daily output achieved is 6,000 units of X, 4,500 units of Y and 1,200 units of Z.

(ii)   Determine the efficiency of the bottleneck process given the output in (a).

(iii)   Calculate the TA ratio for each product.

(iv)   In the absence of demand restrictions for the three products, advise Corrie's management on the optimal production plan.

(v)   State FOUR actions that management could consider to improve the TA ratio of a particular product.

(15 marks)

(Total = 20 marks)

13 A Co
36 mins

A Co makes two products, B1 and B2. Its machines can only work on one product at a time. The two products are worked on in two departments by differing grades of labour. The labour requirements for the two products are as follows:

	Minutes per unit of product	
	B1	B2
Department 1	12	16
Department 2	20	15

There is currently a shortage of labour and the maximum times available each day in Departments 1 and 2 are 480 minutes and 840 minutes, respectively. The current selling prices and costs for the two products are shown below:

	B1	B2
	$ per unit	$ per unit
Selling price	50·00	65·00
Direct materials	10·00	15·00
Direct labour	10·40	6·20
Variable overheads	6·40	9·20
Fixed overheads	12·80	18·40
Profit per unit	10·40	16·20

As part of the budget-setting process, A Co needs to know the optimum output levels. All output is sold.

(a)   Calculate the maximum number of each product that could be produced each day, and identify the limiting factor/bottleneck.   **(3 marks)**

(b)   Using traditional contribution analysis, calculate the 'profit-maximising' output each day, and the contribution at this level of output.   **(3 marks)**

(c)   Using a throughput approach, calculate the 'throughput-maximising' output each day, and the 'throughput contribution' at this level of output.   **(3 marks)**

The company is currently developing a system of environmental costing.

(d)   Describe the key features of an environmental management system.   **(5 marks)**

(e)   Explain the difference between internalised environmental costs and externalised environmental impacts and state **two** examples of each.   **(6 marks)**

(Total = 20 marks)

14 Yam Co (6/09)
36 mins

Yam Co is involved in the processing of sheet metal into products A, B and C using three processes, pressing, stretching and rolling. Like many businesses Yam faces tough price competition in what is a mature world market.

The factory has 50 production lines each of which contain the three processes: Raw material for the sheet metal is first pressed then stretched and finally rolled. The processing capacity varies for each process and the factory manager has provided the following data:

	Processing time per metre in hours		
	Product A	Product B	Product C
Pressing	0·50	0·50	0·40
Stretching	0·25	0·40	0·25
Rolling	0·40	0·25	0·25

The factory operates for 18 hours each day for five days per week. It is closed for only two weeks of the year for holidays when maintenance is carried out. On average one hour of labour is needed for each of the 225,000 hours of factory time. Labour is paid $10 per hour.

The raw materials cost per metre is $3·00 for product A, $2·50 for product B and $1·80 for product C. Other factory costs (excluding labour and raw materials) are $18,000,000 per year. Selling prices per metre are $70 for product A, $60 for product B and $27 for product C.

Yam carries very little inventory.

Required

(a) Identify the bottleneck process and briefly explain why this process is described as a 'bottleneck'. **(3 marks)**

(b) Calculate the throughput accounting ratio (TPAR) for each product assuming that the bottleneck process is fully utilised. **(8 marks)**

(c) Assuming that the TPAR of product C is less than 1:

(i)   Explain how Yam could improve the TPAR of product C. **(4 marks)**

(ii) Briefly discuss whether this supports the suggestion to cease the production of product C and briefly outline three other factors that Yam should consider before a cessation decision is taken. **(5 marks)**

(Total = 20 marks)

15 Thin Co (6/11)   36 mins

Thin Co is a private hospital offering three types of surgical procedures known as A, B and C. Each of them uses a pre-operative injection given by a nurse before the surgery. Thin Co currently rent an operating theatre from a neighbouring government hospital. Thin Co does have an operating theatre on its premises, but it has never been put into use since it would cost $750,000 to equip. The Managing Director of Thin Co is keen to maximise profits and has heard of something called 'throughput accounting', which may help him to do this. The following information is available:

1   All patients go through a five step process, irrespective of which procedure they are having:

Step 1: consultation with the advisor;

Step 2: pre-operative injection given by the nurse;

Step 3: anaesthetic given by anaesthetist;

Step 4: procedure performed in theatre by the surgeon;

Step 5: recovery with the recovery specialist.

2   The price of each of procedures A, B and C is $2,700, $3,500 and $4,250 respectively.

3   The only materials' costs relating to the procedures are for the pre-operative injections given by the nurse, the anaesthetic and the dressings. These are as follows:

	Procedure A $ per procedure	Procedure B $ per procedure	Procedure C $ per procedure
Pre-operative nurse's injections	700	800	1,000
Anaesthetic	35	40	45
Dressings	5·60	5·60	5·60

4   There are five members of staff employed by Thin Co. Each works a standard 40-hour week for 47 weeks of the year, a total of 1,880 hours each per annum. Their salaries are as follows:

–   Advisor: $45,000 per annum;

–   Nurse: $38,000 per annum;

–   Anaesthetist: $75,000 per annum;

–   Surgeon: $90,000 per annum;

–   Recovery specialist: $50,000 per annum.

The only other hospital costs (comparable to 'factory costs' in a traditional manufacturing environment) are general overheads, which include the theatre rental costs, and amount to $250,000 per annum.

5   Maximum annual demand for A, B and C is 600, 800 and 1,200 procedures respectively. Time spent by each of the five different staff members on each procedure is as follows:

	Procedure A Hours per procedure	Procedure B Hours per procedure	Procedure C Hours per procedure
Advisor	0·24	0·24	0·24
Nurse	0·27	0·28	0·30
Anaesthetist	0·25	0·28	0·33
Surgeon	0·75	1.00	1.25
Recovery specialist	0·60	0·70	0·74

Part hours are shown as decimals e.g. 0·24 hours = 14·4 minutes (0·24 × 60).

Surgeon's hours have been correctly identified as the bottleneck resource.

Required:

(a)   Calculate the throughput accounting ratio for procedure C.

Note: It is recommended that you work in hours as provided in the table rather than minutes.   **(6 marks)**

(b)   The return per factory hour for products A and B has been calculated and is $2,612·53 and $2,654·40 respectively. The throughput accounting ratio for A and B has also been calculated and is 8·96 and 9·11 respectively.

Calculate the optimum product mix and the maximum profit per annum.   **(7 marks)**

(c)   Assume that your calculations in part (b) showed that, if the optimum product mix is adhered to, there will be excess demand for procedure C of 696 procedures per annum. In order to satisfy this excess demand, the company is considering equipping and using its own theatre, as well as continuing to rent the existing theatre. The company cannot rent any more theatre time at either the existing theatre or any other theatres in the area, so equipping its own theatre is the only option. An additional surgeon would be employed to work in the newly equipped theatre.

Required:

Discuss whether the overall profit of the company could be improved by equipping and using the extra theatre.

Note: Some basic calculations may help your discussion.   **(7 marks)**

(Total = 20 marks)

DECISION-MAKING TECHNIQUES

Questions 16 to 40 cover Decision-making techniques, the subject of Part B of the BPP Study Text for Paper F5.

16 ABC plc

36 mins

ABC manufactures three products from different combinations of the same direct materials and direct labour. An extract from the flexible budgets for next quarter for each of these products is as follows.

Product	W		Y		Z	
Units	6,000	10,000	6,000	10,000	6,000	10,000
	$'000	$'000	$'000	$'000	$'000	$'000
Revenue	60	100	90	150	180	300
Direct Material A (note 1)	18	30	9	15	36	60
Direct Material B (note 2)	12	20	27	45	72	120
Direct Labour (note 3)	12	20	45	75	18	30
Overhead (note 4)	12	16	22	34	22	34

Notes

(1) Material A was purchased some time ago at a cost of $10 per kg. There are 10,000 kgs in inventory. The costs shown in the flexible budget are based on this historical cost. The material is in regular use and currently has a replacement cost of $14 per kg.

(2) Material B is purchased as required; its expected cost is $20 per kg. The costs shown in the flexible budget are based on this expected cost.

(3) Direct labour costs are based on an hourly rate of $20 per hour. Employees work the number of hours necessary to meet production requirements.

(4) Overhead costs of each product include a specific fixed cost of $2,000 per quarter which would be avoided if the product was to be discontinued. Other fixed overhead costs are apportioned between the products but are not affected by the mix of products manufactured.

ABC has been advised by the only supplier of Material B that the quantity of Material B that will be available during the next quarter will be limited to 10,000 kgs. Accordingly the company is being forced to reconsider its production plan for the next quarter. ABC has already entered into contracts to supply one of its major customers with the following:

1,000 units of product W
1,600 units of product Y
800 units of product Z

Apart from this, the demand expected from other customers is expected to be

7,200 units of product W
6,000 units of product Y
8,000 units of product Z

Required

(a) For each of the three products, calculate the relevant contribution per $ of material B for the next quarter.

(6 marks)

(b) Calculate the relevant contribution to sales ratios for each of the three products.   **(2 marks)**

(c) Assuming that the limiting factor restrictions no longer apply, prepare a sketch of a multi product profit volume chart by ranking the products according to your contribution to sales ratio calculations based on total market demand. Your sketch should plot the products using the highest contribution to sales ratio first.

(6 marks)

(d) Explain briefly, stating any relevant assumptions and limitations, how the multiproduct profit volume chart that you prepared in *(c)* above may be used by the manager of ABC to understand the relationships between costs, volume and profit within the business.   **(6 marks)**

(Total = 20 marks)

17 Devine Desserts   36 mins

You are the Assistant Accountant of Devine Desserts plc, a food manufacturer. The Board of Directors is concerned that its operational managers may not be fully aware of the importance of understanding the costs incurred by the business and the effect that this has on their operational decision making.

In addition, the operational managers need to be aware of the implications of their pricing policy when trying to increase the volume of sales.

You are scheduled to make a presentation to the operational managers to explain to them the different costs that are incurred by the business, the results of some research that has been conducted into the implications for pricing and the importance of understanding these issues for their decision making. **The below has already been prepared for the presentation.**

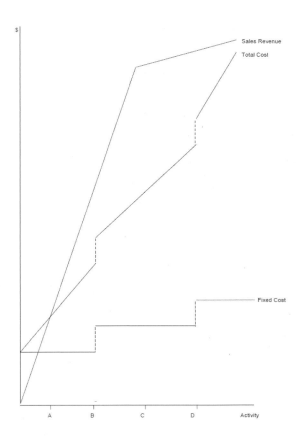

Required

(a) You are required to interpret the diagram and explain how it illustrates issues that the operational managers should consider when making decisions. (*Note*: your answer must include explanations of the Sales Revenue, Total Cost and Fixed Cost lines, and the significance of each of the activity levels labelled A, B, C, D). **(10 marks)**

The budgeted sales and profit for two of the company's latest products, the Strawberry Sundae and the Caramel Delight are as follows:

	Sales Units	Revenue $	Costs $	Profit $	Profit per unit $
Caramel Delight	800	16,000	12,000	4,000	5
Strawberry Sundae	600	24,000	22,200	1,800	3
				5,800	

Actual sales were 560 units of Caramel Delight and 1,260 units of Strawberry Sundae. Company management are able to control the relative sales of each product through the allocation of sales effort, advertising and sales promotion expenses.

Required

(b) Calculate the sales volume variance, the sales mix variance and the sales quantity variance. **(6 marks)**

(c) Comment on the likely reasons for the variances in part (b). **(4 marks)**

(Total = 20 marks)

18 Preparation question: Linear programming

A company uses linear programming to establish an optimal production plan in order to maximise profit.

The company finds that for the next year materials and labour are likely to be in short supply.

Details of the company's products are as follows:

	A $	B $
Materials (at $2 per kg)	6	8
Labour (at $6 per hour)	30	18
Variable overheads (at $1 per hour)	5	3
Variable cost	41	29
Selling price	50	52
Contribution	9	23

There are only 30,000 kg of material and 36,000 labour hours available. The company also has an agreement to supply 1,000 units of product A which must be met.

Required

(a) Formulate the objective function and constraint equations for this problem.
(b) Plot the constraints on a suitable graph and determine the optimal production plan.
(c) Explain what is meant by slack and surplus using your answers from parts (a) and (b).
(d) Explain how this company could use shadow prices.

19 LD Co

LD Co provides two cleaning services for staff uniforms to hotels and similar businesses. One of the services is a laundry service and the other is a dry cleaning service. Both of the services use the same resources, but in different quantities. Details of the expected resource requirements, revenues and costs of each service are shown below.

		Laundry $ per service	Dry cleaning $ per service
Selling price		5.60	13.20
Cleaning materials	($10.00 per litre)	2.00	3.00
Direct labour	($6.00 per hour)	1.20	2.00
Variable machine cost	($3.00 per hour)	0.50	1.50
Fixed costs *		1.15	2.25
Profit		0.75	4.45

* Total annual fixed costs are $32,825.

The maximum resources expected to be available in December 20X3 are

Cleaning materials	5,000 litres
Direct labour hours	6,000 hours
Machine hours	5,000 hours

LD Co has one particular contract which it entered into six months ago with a local hotel to guarantee 1,200 laundry services and 2,000 dry cleaning services every month. If LD Co does not honour this contract it has to pay substantial financial penalties to the local hotel.

The maximum demand for laundry is expected to be 14,000 services and for dry cleaning 9,975 services.

Required

(a)   Assuming that a graphical linear programming solution is to be used to maximise profit:

    (i)   State the constraints and objective function.   **(5 marks)**

    (ii)   Determine the maximum profit that can be made.   **(7 marks)**

(b)   Calculate the value of any slack and surplus and explain what they mean for LD Co.   **(5 marks)**

(c)   Calculate the shadow price of a machine hour and explain what this means for LD Co.   **(3 marks)**

                      (Total = 20 marks)

20 Higgins Co (6/08, amended)

Higgins Co (HC) manufactures and sells pool cues and snooker cues. The cues both use the same type of good quality wood (ash) which can be difficult to source in sufficient quantity. The supply of ash is restricted to 5,400 kg per period. Ash costs $40 per kg.

The cues are made by skilled craftsmen (highly skilled labour) who are well known for their workmanship. The skilled craftsmen take years to train and are difficult to recruit. HC's craftsmen are generally only able to work for 12,000 hours in a period. The craftsmen are paid $18 per hour.

HC sells the cues to a large market. Demand for the cues is strong, and in any period, up to 15,000 pool cues and 12,000 snooker cues could be sold. The selling price for pool cues is $41 and the selling price for snooker cues is $69.

Manufacturing details for the two products are as follows:

	Pool cues	Snooker cues
Craftsmen time per cue	0.5 hours	0.75 hours
Ash per cue	270 g	270 g
Other variable costs per cue	$1.20	$4.70

HC does not keep inventory.

Required

(a) Calculate the contribution earned from each cue. **(2 marks)**

(b) Determine the optimal production plan for a typical period assuming that HC is seeking to maximise the contribution earned. You should use a linear programming graph, identify the feasible region and the optimal point and accurately calculate the maximum contribution that could be earned using whichever equations you need. **(12 marks)**

(c) Explain the meaning of a shadow price (dual price) and calculate the shadow price of both the labour (craftsmen) and the materials (ash). **(6 marks)**

(Total = 20 marks)

21 Cut and Stitch (6/10)

36 mins

Cut and Stitch (CS) make two types of suits using skilled tailors (labour) and a delicate and unique fabric (material). Both the tailors and the fabric are in short supply and so the accountant at CS has correctly produced a linear programming model to help decide the optimal production mix.

The model is as follows:

Variables:

Let W = the number of work suits produced
Let L = the number of lounge suits produced

Constraints

Tailors' time: $7W + 5L \leq 3,500$ (hours) – this is line T on the diagram
Fabric: $2W + 2L \leq 1,200$ (metres) – this is line F on the diagram
Production of work suits: $W \leq 400$ – this is line P on the diagram

Objective is to maximise contribution subject to:

$C = 48W + 40L$

On the diagram provided the accountant has correctly identified OABCD as the feasible region and point B as the optimal point.

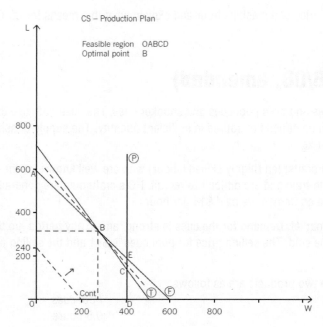

BPP
LEARNING MEDIA

Required

(a) Find by appropriate calculation the optimal production mix and related maximum contribution that could be earned by CS. **(4 marks)**

(b) Calculate the shadow prices of the fabric per metre and the tailor time per hour. **(6 marks)**

The tailors have offered to work an extra 500 hours provided that they are paid three times their normal rate of $1·50 per hour at $4·50 per hour.

Required

(c) Briefly discuss whether CS should accept the offer of overtime at three times the normal rate. **(6 marks)**

(d) Calculate the new optimum production plan if maximum demand for W falls to 200 units. **(4 marks)**

(Total = 20 marks)

22 The Cosmetic Co (12/10)   36 mins

The Cosmetic Co is a company producing a variety of cosmetic creams and lotions. The creams and lotions are sold to a variety of retailers at a price of $23.20 for each jar of face cream and $16.80 for each bottle of body lotion. Each of the products has a variety of ingredients, with the key ones being silk powder, silk amino acids and aloe vera. Six months ago, silk worms were attacked by disease causing a huge reduction in the availability of silk powder and silk amino acids. The Cosmetic Co had to dramatically reduce production and make part of its workforce, which it had trained over a number of years, redundant.

The company now wants to increase production again by ensuring that it uses the limited ingredients available to maximise profits by selling the optimum mix of creams and lotions. Due to the redundancies made earlier in the year, supply of skilled labour is now limited in the short-term to 160 hours (9,600 minutes) per week, although unskilled labour is unlimited. The purchasing manager is confident that they can obtain 5,000 grams of silk powder and 1,600 grams of silk amino acids per week. All other ingredients are unlimited. The following information is available for the two products:

	Cream	Lotion
Materials required: silk powder (at $2.20 per gram) S.P	3 grams	2 grams
– silk amino acids (at $0.80 per gram) S.A	1 gram	0.5 grams
– aloe vera (at $1.40 per gram)	4 grams	2 grams
Labour required: skilled ($12 per hour) L.A	4 minutes	5 minutes
– unskilled (at $8 per hour)	3 minutes	1.5 minutes

Each jar of cream sold generates a contribution of $9 per unit, whilst each bottle of lotion generates a contribution of $8 per unit. The maximum demand for lotions is 2,000 bottles per week, although demand for creams is unlimited. Fixed costs total $1,800 per week. The company does not keep inventory although if a product is partially complete at the end of one week, its production will be completed in the following week.

Required

(a) On the graph paper provided, use linear programming to calculate the optimum number of each product that the Cosmetic Co should make per week, assuming that it wishes to maximise contribution. Calculate the total contribution per week for the new production plan. All workings MUST be rounded to 2 decimal places. **(14 marks)**

(b) Calculate the shadow price for silk powder and the slack for silk amino acids. All workings MUST be rounded to 2 decimal places. **(6 marks)**

(Total = 20 marks)

23 RB Co

Just over two years ago, RB Co was the first company to produce a specific 'off-the-shelf' accounting software package. The pricing strategy, decided on by the managing director, for the packages was to add a 50% mark-up to the budgeted full cost of the packages. The company achieved and maintained a significant market share and high profits for the first two years.

Budgeted information for the current year (Year 3) was as follows.

Production and sales	15,000 packages
Full cost	$400 per package

At a recent board meeting, the finance director reported that although costs were in line with the budget for the current year, profits were declining. He explained that the full cost included $80 for fixed overheads. This figure had been calculated by using an overhead absorption rate based on labour hours and the budgeted level of production of 15,000 packages. He pointed out that this was much lower than the current capacity of 25,000 packages.

The marketing director stated that competitors were beginning to increase their market share. He also reported the results of a recent competitor analysis which showed that when RB Co announced its prices for the current year, the competitors responded by undercutting them by 15%. Consequently, he commissioned an investigation of the market. He informed the board that the market research showed that at a price of $750 there would be no demand for the packages but for every $10 reduction in price the demand would increase by 1,000 packages.

The managing director appeared to be unconcerned about the loss of market share and argued that profits could be restored to their former level by increasing the mark-up.

Required

(a) Discuss the managing director's pricing strategy in the circumstances described above. **(5 marks)**

(b) Suggest and explain two alternative strategies that could have been implemented at the launch of the packages. **(4 marks)**

(c) Based on the data supplied by the market research, derive a straight line demand equation for the packages. **(3 marks)**

(d) RB's total costs (TC) can be modelled by the equation $TC = 1,200,000 + 320Q$. Explain the meaning of this equation. **(3 marks)**

(e) Explain what is meant by price elasticity of demand and explain the implications of elasticity for RB's pricing strategy. **(5 marks)**

(Total = 20 marks)

24 New product

A company has developed a new product which it is about to launch on its local market.

The new product will be in competition with a large number of products from some 25 to 30 companies and particularly from one product selling at $65 per unit in quantities of 6,000 per month which represents some 30% of the potential market for this new product. The company manufactures and sells other products, none of whose local market share is less than 5% or more than 35%. Prices in this local market have been fairly steady for some years.

The new product involves an advanced technology and is demonstrably better in performance and quality than its major competitor. The company believes that it has at least 12 to 18 months before competitors could achieve a comparable quality of product.

The company estimates that its production costs for the new product will be as follows.

Direct materials	$12 per unit*
Direct labour	$28 per unit*

For each of its three production departments, the following data applies.

Production department	Unit of measurement	Full cost overhead rate (x)	Normal monthly volume on which (x) is based	Fixed and/or allocated overhead in (x)	Department time on new product*
X	Machine hours	$2.40	12,500	$5,000	2
Y	Direct labour hours	$1.80	15,000	$6,000	1.5
Z	Direct labour hours	$0.80	25,000	$7,500	3

* All these estimates are subject to an error of ± 10%.

Selling and administration expenses for the new product are expected to be $20,000 per month and will be virtually unaffected by the price or sales level achieved by the new product.

The company generally sets its selling prices by adding a mark-up on factory cost of between 30% and 45%, mostly towards the upper end.

Required

(a) Explain the factors the company should consider when setting a price for the new product. **(6 marks)**

(b) Assuming that a full cost-plus based approach is to be taken, recommend a selling price for the new product, with supporting figures, explaining briefly the reasons for your recommendation. **(14 marks)**

(Total = 20 marks)

25 IB
36 mins

IB manufactures and retails computer game consoles. The following details relate to one console:

	$/unit
Budgeted selling price	120
Budgeted variable cost	50
Budgeted fixed cost	10

Month	January	February	March
Budgeted production and sales (units)	1,040	1,180	1,320
Fixed overhead volume variance	$2,400 (A)	$3,800 (A)	$5,200 (A)

There was no change in the level of stock during any month.

Following strong results towards the end of last year, sales appear to have stabilised in recent months. This has led to the adverse fixed overhead volume variances.

It is now the start of April and the Board of Directors is concerned at the large variances that have occurred during the first three months of the year. Market research has confirmed that the past trend of sales is likely to continue unless changes are made to the selling price of the product. Further analysis of the market for computer consoles suggests that demand would be zero if the selling price was raised to $200 or more.

Required

(a) (i) Calculate the price that IB should charge for the console assuming that it wishes to maximise the contribution from this product.

Note. If price = a − bQ then marginal revenue = a − 2bQ **(7 marks)**

(ii) Calculate the difference between the contribution that would have been earned at the optimal price and the actual contribution earned during March, assuming the variable costs per unit were as budgeted. **(3 marks)**

(b) Identify and explain two reasons why it may be inappropriate for IB to use this theoretical pricing model in practice. **(4 marks)**

(c) IB has committed to reduce its environmental impact by 60% over the next five years to comply with legislation and ensure positive media coverage.

Outline two management accounting techniques that IB could use to account for environmental costs.

(6 marks)

(Total = 20 marks)

26 A1

A1 manufactures and sells 4th generation mobile phones. The mobile phone market is continually evolving and A1 regularly reviews its product portfolio to ensure it continues to develop new models that satisfy consumer demand.

The company is currently reviewing three products:

Product A is due to be launched in three months time. A1 management believe this to be an innovative, product that competitors are likely to attempt to copy. A market skimming approach to pricing will be used during the introduction stage.

Product B was introduced to the market four months ago on the back of an expensive marketing campaign. The product is now about to enter its growth stage which is expected to last between six and eight weeks. Each unit has a variable cost of $45 and takes 3.75 standard hours to produce. Market research has indicated that there is a linear relationship between its selling price and the number of units demanded, of the form $P = a - bQ$. At a selling price of $300 per unit demand is expected to be 3,000 units per week. For every $30 increase in selling price the weekly demand will reduce by 600 units and for every $30 decrease in selling price the weekly demand will increase by 600 units.

Product C was first introduced to the market twelve months ago and is now about to enter the maturity stage of its life cycle. The maturity stage is expected to last for three months. The Director of Sales and Marketing has suggested four possible prices that the company could charge during the next three months. The following table shows the results of some market research into the level of weekly demand at alternative prices:

Selling price per unit	$300	$255	$240	$225
Weekly demand (units)	1,800	2,400	3,600	4,200

Each unit of product C has a variable cost of $114 and takes 1 standard hour to produce.

The company currently has a production facility which has a capacity of 6,000 standard hours per week.

Required

(a) (i) Calculate which of the four selling prices should be charged for product C, in order to maximise its contribution during its maturity stage. **(4 marks)**

and as a result, in order to utilise all of the spare capacity from your answer to (i) above,

(ii) Calculate the selling price of product B during its growth stage. **(6 marks)**

(b) Explain with reasons, for the growth, maturity and decline stages of As product life cycle, the changes that would be expected in the

(i) average unit production cost
(ii) unit selling price **(10 marks)**

(Total = 20 marks)

27 Heat Co (6/11)

Heat Co specialises in the production of a range of air conditioning appliances for industrial premises. It is about to launch a new product, the 'Energy Buster', a unique air conditioning unit which is capable of providing unprecedented levels of air conditioning using a minimal amount of electricity. The technology used in the Energy Buster is unique so Heat Co has patented it so that no competitors can enter the market for two years. The company's development costs have been high and it is expected that the product will only have a five-year life cycle.

Heat Co is now trying to ascertain the best pricing policy that they should adopt for the Energy Buster's launch onto the market. Demand is very responsive to price changes and research has established that, for every $15 increase in price, demand would be expected to fall by 1,000 units. If the company set the price at $735, only 1,000 units would be demanded.

$b = \dfrac{15}{1000} = 0.015$ $P = 735$

$Q = 1000$

The costs of producing each air conditioning unit are as follows:

	$
Direct materials	42
Labour	12 (1·5 hours at $8 per hour. See note below)
Fixed overheads	6 (based on producing 50,000 units per annum)
Total cost	60

Note

The first air conditioning unit took 1·5 hours to make and labour cost $8 per hour. A 95% learning curve exists, in relation to production of the unit, although the learning curve is expected to finish after making 100 units. Heat Co's management have said that any pricing decisions about the Energy Buster should be based on the time it takes to make the 100th unit of the product. You have been told that the learning co-efficient, b = −0·0740005.

All other costs are expected to remain the same up to the maximum demand levels.

Required

$P = a - bQ$

(a) (i)   Establish the demand function (equation) for air conditioning units;   **(3 marks)**

(ii)   Calculate the marginal cost for each air conditioning unit after adjusting the labour cost as required by the note above;   **(6 marks)**

(iii)   Equate marginal cost and marginal revenue in order to calculate the optimum price and quantity.

Max profit = MR = MC

(3 marks)

$a - 2bQ$ VC (11)

(b)   Explain what is meant by a 'penetration pricing' strategy and a 'market skimming' strategy and discuss whether either strategy might be suitable for Heat Co when launching the Energy Buster.   **(8 marks)**

(Total = 20 marks)

28 Sunrise   36 mins

Sunrise is a holiday park specialising in family holidays. Sunrise management is planning for the next year. The park has 100 holiday homes. The price of a holiday home night includes breakfast for the guests. Other meals are available from the bar and restaurant but are not included in the price of a holiday home night. Meals are served to holiday park guests only (the bar and restaurant is not open to the general public).

For planning purposes Sunrise divides the year (based on 360 days) into three seasons: peak, mid and low.

Details of the holiday park and its services and forecasts for the next year are given below.

1   Seasons, home charges, home occupancy, guests per home and home revenue

Sunrise charges a price per holiday home per night (including breakfast) irrespective of the number of guests per home. The price charged is different in each of the seasons.

Season	Peak	Mid	Low
Number of days	90	120	150
Price charged per holiday home per night ($)	120.00	100.00	60.00
Holiday home occupancy %	90	65	35
Average number of guests per home	3.8	3.5	3.2
Total home revenue ($)	972,000	780,000	315,000

2   Home related costs

Sunrise incurs some costs that are directly related to the number of holiday homes occupied. These include cleaning costs of $3 per occupied holiday home per night regardless of season. There are also power and lighting costs of $4 in the peak season, $5 in the mid season and $7 in the low season per occupied room per night.

3   Guest related costs

The hotel incurs some costs, including providing breakfast, that are directly related to the number of guests in the hotel. These are $7 per guest per night in all seasons.

4   Restaurant & Bar

Past records show that the usage of the restaurant and bar is seasonal. The forecast usage is shown below.

Season	Daily demand
Peak	60% of hotel guests spend an average of $13 each
Mid	40% of hotel guests spend an average of $11 each
Low	20% of hotel guests spend an average of $8 each

Sunrise earns a 30% gross contribution from this income and employs three kitchen staff on a combined salary of $84,000 per year to provide this facility. All of the costs in the restaurant and bar, except for the salaries of the kitchen, are variable.

The three kitchen staff could be made redundant with no redundancy costs.

5   General costs

These include the costs of reception staff, the heating and lighting of the common areas and other facility related costs. The forecast costs for next year are:

Peak season	$310,000
Mid season	$410,000
Low season	$510,000

These costs could be reduced by 80% if Sunrise were to close temporarily for one or more seasons of the year.

Sunrise also incurs some costs that can only be avoided by its permanent closure. These are estimated to be $250,000 for next year.

Required

(a)   Prepare, in an appropriate format, a statement that will help the managers of Sunrise plan for the next year.

Note: Your statement should show the holiday park's activities by season and in total. **(15 marks)**

(b)   Using the statement from part (a):

    (i)   Identify the actions that the managers could take to maximise the profit of the holiday park for the next year. **(2 marks)**

    (ii) Explain TWO factors that the managers should consider before implementing the actions you have described above. **(3 marks)**

(Total = 20 marks)

29 Ennerdale   36 mins

Ennerdale has been asked to quote a price for a one-off contract. The company's management accountant has asked for your advice on the relevant costs for the contract. The following information is available:

Materials

The contract requires 3,000 kg of material K, which is a material used regularly by the company in other production. The company has 2,000 kg of material K currently in inventory which had been purchased last month for a total cost of $19,600. Since then the price per kilogram for material K has increased by 5%.

The contract also requires 200 kg of material L. There are 250 kg of material L in inventory which are not required for normal production. This material originally cost a total of $3,125. If not used on this contract, the inventory of material L would be sold for $11 per kg.

Labour

The contract requires 800 hours of skilled labour. Skilled labour is paid $9.50 per hour. There is a shortage of skilled labour and all the available skilled labour is fully employed in the company in the manufacture of product P. The following information relates to product P:

	$ per unit	$ per unit
Selling price		100
Less:		
Skilled labour	38	
Other variable costs	22	
		(60)
		40

Required

(a) Prepare calculations showing the total relevant costs for making a decision about the contract in respect of the following cost elements:

    (i)   Materials K and L

    (ii)   Skilled labour   **(8 marks)**

The company also manufactures three joint products (M, N and P) from the same common process. The following process account relates to the common process last month and is typical of the monthly results of operating this process:

COMMON PROCESS ACCOUNT

	Litres	$		Litres	$
Opening work in process	1,000	5,320	Normal loss	10,000	20,000
Materials	100,000	250,000	Output M	25,000	141,875
Conversion costs:			Output N	15,000	85,125
Variable		100,000	Output P	45,000	255,375
Fixed		180,000	Closing work in process	800	3,533
			Abnormal loss	5,200	29,412
	101,000	535,320		101,000	535,320

Each one of the products can be sold immediately after the common process, but each one of them can be further processed individually before being sold. The following further processing costs and selling prices per litre are expected:

Product	Selling price after common process $/litre	Selling price after further processing $/litre	Further variable processing cost $/litre
M	6.25	8.40	1.75
N	5.20	6.45	0.95
P	6.80	7.45	0.85

Required

(b) State the method used to apportion the common costs between the products M, N and P and comment on its acceptability. Explain why it is necessary to apportion the common costs between each of the products.

                                                                           (6 marks)

(c) Evaluate the viability of the common process, and determine the optimal processing plan for each of the three products, showing appropriate calculations.   **(6 marks)**

                                                                          (Total = 20 marks)

30 John Robertson

John Robertson, a self employed builder, has been asked to provide a fixed price quotation for some building work required by a customer. Robertson's accountant has compiled the following figures, together with some notes as a basis for a quotation.

	$	
Direct materials		
Bricks 200,000 at $100 per thousand	20,000	note 1
200,000 at $120 per thousand	24,000	
Other materials	5,000	note 2
Skilled 3,200 hours at $12 per hour	38,400	note 3
Unskilled 2,000 hours at $6 per hour	12,000	note 4
Other costs		
Scaffolding hire	3,500	note 5
Depreciation of general purpose machinery	2,000	note 6
General overheads 5,200 hours at $1 per hour	5,200	note 7
Plans	2,000	note 8
Total cost	112,100	
Profit	22,420	note 9
Suggested price	134,520	

Notes

(1)   The contract requires 400,000 bricks, 200,000 are already in inventory and 200,000 will have to be bought in. This is a standard type of brick regularly used by Robertson. The 200,000 in inventory were purchased earlier in the year at $100 per 1,000. The current replacement cost of this type of brick is $120 per 1,000. If the bricks in inventory are not used on this job John is confident that he will be able to use them later in the year.

(2)   Other materials will be bought in as required; this figure represents the purchase price.

(3)   Robertson will need to be on site whilst the building work is performed. He therefore intends to do 800 hours of the skilled work himself. The remainder will be hired on an hourly basis. The current cost of skilled workers is $12 per hour. If John Robertson does not undertake the building work for this customer he can either work as a skilled worker for other builders at a rate of $12 per hour or spend the 800 hours completing urgently needed repairs to his own house. He has recently had a quotation of $12,000 for labour to repair his home.

(4)   John employs four unskilled workers on contract guaranteeing them a 40 hours week at $6 per hour. These unskilled labourers are currently idle and would have sufficient spare time to complete the proposal under consideration.

(5)   This is the estimated cost of hiring scaffolding.

(6)   John estimates that the project will take 20 weeks to complete. This represents 20 weeks' straight line depreciation on the equipment used. If the equipment is not used on this job it will stand idle for the 20 week period. In either case its value at the end of the 20 week period will be identical.

(7)   This represents the rental cost of John's storage yard. If he does not undertake the above job he can rent his yard out to a competitor who will pay him rent of $500 per week for the 20 week period.

(8)   This is the cost of the plans that John has already had drawn for the project.

(9)   John attempts to earn a mark up of 20% on cost on all work undertaken.

John is surprised at the suggested price and considers it rather high. He knows that there will be a lot of competition for the work.

Required

(a)   Explain how each item in the accountant's estimate should be treated **(6 marks)**

(b)   Using relevant costing principles, calculate the lowest price that John could quote for the customer's building work. Explain why in practice the minimum price is never actually used. **(10 marks)**

(c)   Discuss the advantages and disadvantages of full cost-plus pricing. **(4 marks)**

(Total = 20 marks)

31 Pixie Pharmaceuticals

36 mins

Pixie Pharmaceuticals is a research-based company which manufactures a wide variety of drugs for use in hospitals. The purchasing manager has recently been approached by a new manufacturer based in a newly industrialised country who have offered to produce three of the drugs at their factory. The following cost and price information has been provided.

Drug	Fairyoxide	Spriteolite	Goblinex
Production (units)	20,000	40,000	80,000
	$	$	$
Direct material cost, per unit	0.80	1.00	0.40
Direct labour cost, per unit	1.60	1.80	0.80
Direct expense cost, per unit	0.40	0.60	0.20
Fixed cost per unit	0.80	1.00	0.40
Selling price each	4.00	5.00	2.00
Imported price	2.75	4.20	2.00

Required

(a) Calculate the profit figure the company will make by producing all the drugs itself. **(4 marks)**

(b) Recommend to the management whether any drugs should be purchased on the basis of cost only.

(4 marks)

(c) How will your recommendation in (a) above affect the profit and by how much? **(2 marks)**

(d) Explain the other factors that the management should consider before making a final decision. **(5 marks)**

(e) Discuss the factors that have led to a growth in the use of outsourcing. **(5 marks)**

(Total = 20 marks)

32 Sniff Limited (12/07, amended)

36 mins

Sniff Limited manufactures and sells its standard perfume by blending a secret formula of aromatic oils with diluted alcohol. The oils are produced by another company following a lengthy process and are very expensive. The standard perfume is highly branded and successfully sold at a price of $39·98 per 100 millilitres (ml).

Sniff Limited is considering processing some of the perfume further by adding a hormone to appeal to members of the opposite sex. The hormone to be added will be different for the male and female perfumes. Adding hormones to perfumes is not universally accepted as a good idea as some people have health concerns. On the other hand, market research carried out suggests that a premium could be charged for perfume that can 'promise' the attraction of a suitor. The market research has cost $3,000.

Data has been prepared for the costs and revenues expected for the following month (a test month) assuming that a part of the company's output will be further processed by adding the hormones.

The output selected for further processing is 1,000 litres, about a tenth of the company's normal monthly output. Of this, 99% is made up of diluted alcohol which costs $20 per litre. The rest is a blend of aromatic oils costing $18,000 per litre. The labour required to produce 1,000 litres of the basic perfume before any further processing is 2,000 hours at a cost of $15 per hour.

Of the output selected for further processing, 200 litres (20%) will be for male customers and 2 litres of hormone costing $7,750 per litre will then be added. The remaining 800 litres (80%) will be for female customers and 8 litres of hormone will be added, costing $12,000 per litre. In both cases the adding of the hormone adds to the overall volume of the product as there is no resulting processing loss.

Sniff Limited has sufficient existing machinery to carry out the test processing.

The new processes will be supervised by one of the more experienced supervisors currently employed by Sniff Limited. His current annual salary is $35,000 and it is expected that he will spend 10% of his time working on the hormone adding process during the test month. This will be split evenly between the male and female versions of the product.

Extra labour will be required to further process the perfume, with an extra 500 hours for the male version and 700 extra hours for the female version of the hormone-added product. Labour is currently fully employed, making the standard product. New labour with the required skills will not be available at short notice.

Sniff Limited allocates fixed overhead at the rate of $25 per labour hour to all products for the purposes of reporting profits.

The sales prices that could be achieved as a one-off monthly promotion are:

- Male version: $75·00 per 100 ml
- Female version: $59·50 per 100 ml

Required:

(a) Outline the financial and other factors that Sniff Limited should consider when making a further processing decision.

Note: no calculations are required.

(3 marks)

(b) Evaluate whether Sniff Limited should experiment with the hormone adding process using the data provided. Provide a separate assessment and conclusion for the male and the female versions of the product.

(14 marks)

(c) Sniff Limited is considering outsourcing the production of the standard perfume. Outline the main factors it should consider before making such a decision.

(3 marks)

(Total = 20 marks)

33 Stay Clean (12/09)   36 mins

Stay Clean manufactures and sells a small range of kitchen equipment. Specifically the product range contains a dishwasher (DW), a washing machine (WM) and a tumble dryer (TD). The TD is of a rather old design and has for some time generated negative contribution. It is widely expected that in one year's time the market for this design of TD will cease, as people switch to a washing machine that can also dry clothes after the washing cycle has Completed.

Stay Clean is trying to decide whether or not to cease the production of TD now *or* in 12 months' time when the new combined washing machine/drier will be ready. To help with this decision the following information has been provided:

(1) The normal selling prices, annual sales volumes and total variable costs for the three products are as follows:

	DW	WM	TD
	$	$	$
Selling price per unit	200	350	80
Material cost per unit	70	100	50
Labour cost per unit	50	80	40
Contribution per unit	80	170	-10
Annual sales	5,000 units	6,000 units	1,200 units

(2) It is thought that some of the customers that buy a TD also buy a DW and a WM. It is estimated that 5% of the sales of WM and DW will be lost if the TD ceases to be produced.

(3) All the direct labour force currently working on the TD will be made redundant immediately if TD is ceased now. This would cost $6,000 in redundancy payments. If Stay Clean waited for 12 months the existing labour force would be retained and retrained at a cost of $3,500 to enable them to produce the new washing/drying product. Recruitment and training costs of labour in 12 months' time would be $1,200 in the event that redundancy takes place now.

(4) Stay Clean operates a just in time (JIT) policy and so all material cost would be saved on the TD for 12 months if TD production ceased now. Equally, the material costs relating to the lost sales on the WM and the DW would also be saved. However, the material supplier has a volume based discount scheme in place as follows:

Total annual expenditure	Discount
$	%
0-600,000	0
600,001-800,000	1
800,001-900,000	2
900,001-960,000	3
960,001 and above	5

Stay Clean uses this supplier for all its materials for all the products it manufactures. The figures given above in the cost per unit table for material cost per unit are net of any discount Stay Clean already qualifies for.

(5) The space in the factory currently used for the TD will be sublet for 12 months on a short-term lease contract if production of TD stops now. The income from that contract will be $12,000.

(6) The supervisor (currently classed as an overhead) supervises the production of all three products spending approximately 20% of his time on the TD production. He would continue to be fully employed if the TD ceases to be produced now.

Required

(a) Calculate whether or not it is worthwhile ceasing to produce the TD now rather than waiting 12 months (ignore any adjustment to allow for the time value of money). **(13 marks)**

(b) Explain two pricing strategies that could be used to improve the financial position of the business in the next 12 months assuming that the TD continues to be made in that period. **(4 marks)**

(c) Briefly describe three issues that Stay Clean should consider if it decides to outsource the manufacture of one of its future products. **(3 marks)**

(Total = 20 marks)

34 Bits and Pieces (6/09)   36 mins

Bits and Pieces (B&P) operates a retail store selling spares and accessories for the car market. The store has previously only opened for six days per week for the 50 working weeks in the year, but B&P is now considering also opening on Sundays.

The sales of the business on Monday through to Saturday averages at $10,000 per day with average gross profit of 70% earned.

B&P expects that the gross profit % earned on a Sunday will be 20 percentage points lower than the average earned on the other days in the week. This is because they plan to offer substantial discounts and promotions on a Sunday to attract customers. Given the price reduction, Sunday sales revenues are expected to be 60% **more than** the average daily sales revenues for the other days. These Sunday sales estimates are for new customers only, with no allowance being made for those customers that may transfer from other days.

B&P buys all its goods from one supplier. This supplier gives a 5% discount on **all** purchases if annual spend exceeds $1,000,000.

It has been agreed to pay time and a half to sales assistants that work on Sundays. The normal hourly rate is $20 per hour. In total five sales assistants will be needed for the six hours that the store will be open on a Sunday. They will also be able to take a half-day off (four hours) during the week. Staffing levels will be allowed to reduce slightly during the week to avoid extra costs being incurred.

The staff will have to be supervised by a manager, currently employed by the company and paid an annual salary of $80,000. If he works on a Sunday he will take the equivalent time off during the week when the assistant manager is available to cover for him at no extra cost to B&P. He will also be paid a bonus of 1% of the extra sales generated on the Sunday project.

The store will have to be lit at a cost of $30 per hour and heated at a cost of $45 per hour. The heating will come on two hours before the store opens in the 25 'winter' weeks to make sure it is warm enough for customers to come in at opening time. The store is not heated in the other weeks.

The rent of the store amounts to $420,000 per annum.

Required

(a)   Calculate whether the Sunday opening incremental revenue exceeds the incremental costs over a year (ignore inventory movements) and on this basis reach a conclusion as to whether Sunday opening is financially justifiable.   **(12 marks)**

(b)   Discuss whether the manager's pay deal (time off and bonus) is likely to motivate him.   **(4 marks)**

(c)   Briefly discuss whether offering substantial price discounts and promotions on Sunday is a good suggestion.   **(4 marks)**

(Total = 20 marks)

35 BDU Co   **36 mins**

BDU Co is a manufacturer of baby equipment and is planning to launch a revolutionary new style of sporty pushchair. The company has commissioned market research to establish possible demand for the pushchair and the following information has been obtained.

If the price is set at $425, demand is expected to be 1,000 pushchairs, at $500 it will be 730 pushchairs and at $600 it will be 420 pushchairs. Variable costs are estimated at either $170, $210 or $260.

A decision needs to be made on what price to charge.

Required

(a)   Produce a table showing the expected contribution for each of the nine possible outcomes.   **(4 marks)**

(b)   Explain what is meant by maximax, maximin and minimax regret decision rules, using the information in the scenario to illustrate your explanations.   **(10 marks)**

(c)   Explain the use of expected values and sensitivity analysis and suggest how BDU could make use of such techniques.   **(6 marks)**

(Total = 20 marks)

36 Envico (PM, 12/05, amended)   **36 mins**

Envico is a business services company which provides seminars on various aspects of current and recently announced changes in employment legislation. Envico has decided to enter into a one-year renewable contract with Mieras Business Associates, which owns large premises that are suitable for holding educational seminars in each of eight cities.

Mieras Business Associates has offered a choice of four different contracts, each of which relates to seminar rooms of differing sizes. These are known as room types A, B, C and D, which are capable of accommodating 100, 200, 300 and 400 delegates respectively.

Envico will charge an all-inclusive fee of $80 per delegate at every seminar throughout the year.

Envico must decide in advance of the forthcoming year which size of conference room to contract for. It is not possible to contract for a different size conference room in different cities, ie only one size of room can be the subject of the contract with Mieras Business Associates.

Due to the rapid growth in interest regarding environmental issues and corporate social responsibility, and the large amount of forthcoming legislative changes, Envico has decided to hold one seminar in every week of the year in each city. Sometimes a regional government representative will attend and speak at such seminars. On other occasions a national government representative will attend and speak at such seminars. The rest of the time the speakers at seminars are representatives from within Envico.

Envico has estimated the following frequency regarding seminars to be held during the forthcoming year:

Category of speaker:	%
Envico representative	20
Regional government representative	50
National government representative	30

Market research has indicated that where a national government representative is in attendance, Envico can be reasonably assured of selling 400 seminar places and where a regional government representative is in attendance 200 seminar places can be sold. Envico expects to sell only 100 seminar places when there is no attendance by a government representative.

The following contribution table has been devised to calculate the expected annual contribution from each decision option.

Places sold	Contribution if 100 places available $	Contribution if 200 places available $	Contribution if 300 places available $	Contribution if 400 places available $
100	832,000	(1,164,800)	(2,662,400)	(3,328,000)
200	832,000	2,163,200	665,600	0
400	832,000	2,163,200	3,993,600	6,656,000

Required

(a)   Calculate the cost incurred by Envico for each type of room per seminar.   **(4 marks)**

(b)   (i)   Advise Envico on the size of seminar room that should be contracted from Mieras Business Associates, using the criterion of expected value. Your answer should use the expected annual contribution from each decision option.

       (ii)   Explain the limitations of the expected value approach.   **(7 marks)**

(c)   Determine whether your decision in (a) would change if you were to use the maximin and minimax regret decision criteria. Your answer should be supported by relevant workings.   **(5 marks)**

(d)   Suggest research techniques that could be used to reduce uncertainty.   **(4 marks)**

(Total = 20 marks)

37 Rotanola Co   36 mins

Rotanola Co manufactures mobile phones. It has been extremely successful in the past but the market has become extremely competitive. The company is considering a number of different strategies to improve its profitability.

The most successful product is the RTN99 which is sold for $110. Weekly demand is currently 20,000 phones. Market research has revealed that if Rotanola Co reduced the price of the RTN99 by $10, demand would increase by 2,000 phones.

Each time the phone is produced, Rotanola Co incurs extra costs of $30 for materials, $18 for labour, $14 for variable overheads and $23 for fixed costs, based on expected weekly output of 20,000 phones. The most expensive component in the phone is the battery which costs $15. Rotanola has been offered a discounted price of $12 by the supplier if it buys 22,000 batteries per week.

The company needs to come up with innovative new products as the technology moves very fast and what is useful today becomes obsolete tomorrow. The latest idea is to produce a phone incorporating virtual touch technology which makes the phone vibrate in a number of ways.

The following estimates for this phone (the RTNBZ) have been produced.

		$	$
Sales	(25,000 units @ $150)		3,750,000
Materials	(@ $50)	1,250,000	
Labour	(@ $18)	450,000	
Variable overheads	(@ $16)	400,000	
			2,100,000
Attributable fixed overheads			575,000
Profit			1,075,000

There is some doubt as to the likely cost of materials. The probability of it being $50 as expected is 0.6, the probability of it rising it to $60 is 0.3 and the probability of it falling to $40 is 0.1.

Forecast sales units are also subject to economic conditions. There is a 50% chance that sales will be as expected, a 40% chance that sales will be 10% lower than expected and a 10% chance that sales will be 5% higher than expected.

Required

(a) Explain the role of market research in reducing uncertainty. **(2 marks)**

(b) Derive the straight line demand equation for the RTN99. **(3 marks)**

(c) Derive and explain the total cost function for the RTN99 before and after the volume discount. **(4 marks)**

(d) Explain how Rotanola Co could use sensitivity analysis to help with the decision whether to produce the RTNBZ. **(7 marks)**

(e) Calculate the expected profit on the RTNBZ. **(4 marks)**

(Total = 20 marks)

38 Cement Co (6/11) 36 mins

Cement Co is a company specialising in the manufacture of cement, a product used in the building industry. The company has found that when weather conditions are good, the demand for cement increases since more building work is able to take place. Last year, the weather was so good, and the demand for cement was so great, that Cement Co was unable to meet demand. Cement Co is now trying to work out the level of cement production for the coming year in order to maximise profits. The company doesn't want to miss out on the opportunity to earn large profits by running out of cement again. However, it doesn't want to be left with large quantities of the product unsold at the end of the year, since it deteriorates quickly and then has to be disposed of. The company has received the following estimates about the probable weather conditions and corresponding demand levels for the coming year:

Weather	Probability	Demand
Good	25%	350,000 bags
Average	45%	280,000 bags
Poor	30%	200,000 bags

Each bag of cement sells for $9 and costs $4 to make. If cement is unsold at the end of the year, it has to be disposed of at a cost of $0·50 per bag.

Cement Co has decided to produce at one of the three levels of production to match forecast demand. It now has to decide which level of cement production to select.

Required

(a) Construct a pay off table to show all the possible profit outcomes. **(8 marks)**

(b) Decide the level of cement production the company should choose, based on the following decision rules:

   (i) Maximin **(1 mark)**
   (ii) Maximax **(1 mark)**
   (iii) Expected value **(4 marks)**

You must justify your decision under each rule, showing all necessary calculations.

(c)   Describe the 'maximin' and 'expected value' decision rules, explaining when they might be used and the attitudes of the decision makers who might use them.

(6 marks)

(Total = 20 marks)

39 Elsewhere   36 mins

Rubbish Records Co are considering the launch of a new pop group, Elsewhere.

If the group is launched without further market research being carried out it is thought that demand for their records and the present value of profit earned from record sales will be as follows.

Demand	Probability	Present value of profit $'000
High	0.5	800
Medium	0.2	100
Low	0.3	(300)

It is possible, however, to commission a market research survey which will forecast either a successful or unsuccessful career for Elsewhere. The probability of an unsuccessful career is 0.3.

Probabilities of high, medium or low demand for Elsewhere's records under each of the two market research results are as follows.

	Demand		
	High	Medium	Low
Successful chart career	0.7	0.1	0.2
Unsuccessful chart career	0.1	0.3	0.6

So, for example, if the research indicated an unsuccessful chart career, then the probability of medium demand for the group's records would be 0.3.

The survey would cost $50,000.

Required

(a)   Calculate the expected value of profit if Rubbish Records do not commission a market research survey.

(3 marks)

(b)   Draw a decision tree to show the choices facing Rubbish Records and briefly explain whether or not the record company should commission the survey.

(12 marks)

(c)   (i)   Determine the maximum the company should pay for the survey.

(2 marks)

(ii)   Briefly explain the disadvantages of using expected values and decision trees as decision-making tools.

(3 marks)

(Total = 20 marks)

40 SH (12/08, amended)

36 mins

Shifters Haulage (SH) is considering changing some of the vans it uses to transport crates for customers. The new vans come in three sizes; small, medium and large. SH is unsure about which type to buy. The capacity is 100 crates for the small van, 150 for the medium van and 200 for the large van.

Demand for crates varies and can be either 120 or 190 crates per period, with the probability of the higher demand figure being 0·6.

The sale price per crate is $10 and the variable cost $4 per crate for all van sizes subject to the fact that if the capacity of the van is greater than the demand for crates in a period then the variable cost will be lower by 10% to allow for the fact that the vans will be partly empty when transporting crates.

SH is concerned that if the demand for crates exceeds the capacity of the vans then customers will have to be turned away. SH estimates that in this case goodwill of $100 would be charged against profits per period to allow for lost future sales regardless of the number of customers that are turned away.

Depreciation charged would be $200 per period for the small, $300 for the medium and $400 for the large van.

SH has in the past been very aggressive in its decision-making, pressing ahead with rapid growth strategies. However, its managers have recently grown more cautious as the business has become more competitive.

Required

(a) Prepare a profits table showing the SIX possible profit figures per period. **(8 marks)**

(b) Using your profit table from (b) above discuss which type of van SH should buy taking into consideration the possible risk attitudes of the managers. **(6 marks)**

(c) Describe THREE methods other than those mentioned in (a) above, which businesses can use to analyse and assess the risk that exists in its decision-making. **(6 marks)**

(Total = 20 marks)

BUDGETING

Questions 41 to 52 cover Budgeting, the subject of Part C of the BPP Study Text for Paper F5.

41 Preparation question: Budgeting

(a) Critically discuss the relative merits of periodic budgeting and continuous budgeting.

(b) Discuss the consequences of budget bias for cost control.

(c) Discuss the ways in which budgets and the budgeting process can be used to motivate managers to endeavour to meet the objectives of the company. Your answer should refer to:

    (i) Setting targets for financial performance
    (ii) Participation in the budget-setting process

42 Preparation question: Happy Hotels

Happy Hotels operates a chain of upmarket hotels across Europe. Each hotel manager is responsible for producing an annual budget, based on targets set by Head Office.

According to last year's budget, the company had hoped to turn an expected 8% rise in total revenue into a 16% increase in hotel profits.

At the year end it was found that hotel profits had increased by 10% with the primary reason for the shortfall appearing to be excessive spending.

(a) Explain why zero based budgeting might be a useful tool for Happy Hotels.
(b) Describe the steps needed to be undertaken in order to implement a zero based budgeting system.
(c) Explain how the use of zero based budgeting can motivate employees.
(d) Discuss the problems that Happy Hotels may encounter if ZBB was introduced.
(e) Explain the advantages of encouraging employee participation in budget setting.

43 Brunti   36 mins

Brunti is a manufacturing company which manufactures and assembles car components. The following budgeted information relates to Brunti for the forthcoming period.

	Products		
	XYI	YZT	ABW
	'000	'000	'000
Sales and production (units)	50	40	30
	$	$	$
Selling price (per unit)	45	95	73
Prime cost (per unit)	32	84	65
	Hours	Hours	Hours
Machine department (machine hours per unit)	2	5	4
Assembly department (direct labour hours per unit)	7	3	2

Overheads can be re-analysed into 'cost pools' as follows.

Cost pool	$'000	Cost driver	Quantity for the period
Machining services	357	Machine hours	420,000
Assembly services	318	Direct labour hours	530,000
Set up costs	26	Set ups	520
Order processing	156	Customer orders	32,000
Purchasing	84	Suppliers' orders	11,200
	941		

You have also been provided with the following estimates for the period.

	Products		
	XYI	YZT	ABW
Number of set-ups	120	200	200
Customer orders	8,000	8,000	16,000
Suppliers' orders	3,000	4,000	4,200

Required

(a) Prepare and present a profit statement using activity based costing. **(11 marks)**

(b) Explain the weaknesses of an incremental budgeting system for a company such as Brunti. **(4 marks)**

(c) Describe the main features of an activity based budgeting system and comment on the advantages its use could have for Brunti. **(5 marks)**

(Total = 20 marks)

44 Cushair Designs   36 mins

In June 20X3 the managing director of a large furniture store, Cushair Designs, engaged a management consultant to devise a simple and practical method of forecasting the store's quarterly sales levels for a period of six months ahead. On taking up the task the consultant felt that a forecasting method appropriate for the purpose would first require him to deseasonalise the store's gross quarterly sales over the last 30 months. The time series obtained could then be plotted, and a line of best fit determined and extrapolated over the next two quarters. By applying an appropriate seasonal index to these figures, sales for the two periods ahead could be estimated.

Gross sales data for Cushair Designs

Sales period	Value of retail sales
	$'000
Q1	285
Q2	310
Q3	315
Q4	385
Q5	340
Q6	370
Q7	375
Q8	460
Q9	395
Q10	425

The management consultant also gave some thought to how he could avoid getting the store to compute its own seasonal indices, an operation he felt inappropriate considering the small amount of past data he had available. He decided to use a national quarterly seasonal index as published in a national journal. He thought that his client's furniture store had a product mix not too different from the aggregate mix on which the index was based.

National quarterly seasonal index (multiplicative) for furniture

Q1	94
Q2	98
Q3	96
Q4	112

Required

(a) Plot the actual quarterly sales figures on graph paper and explain why the multiplicative model may be more appropriate for these data than the additive model. **(5 marks)**

(b) Calculate the values of the deseasonalised data and plot these data on your graph. **(5 marks)**

(c) Use the method of least squares to determine the equation of the straight line through the deseasonalised data. **(5 marks)**

(d) Estimate the gross sales figures for Quarters 11 and 12. **(2 marks)**

(e) Comment on the likely accuracy of your estimates and outline factors that could change and make it difficult to forecast future sales. **(3 marks)**

(Total = 20 marks)

45 Wargrin (12/08, amended)   36 mins

Wargrin designs, develops and sells many PC games. Games have a short lifecycle lasting around three years only. Performance of the games is measured by reference to the profits made in each of the expected three years of popularity. Wargrin accepts a net profit of 35% of turnover as reasonable. A rate of contribution (sales price less variable cost) of 75% is also considered acceptable.

Wargrin has a large centralised development department which carries out all the design work before it passes the completed game to the sales and distribution department to market and distribute the product.

Wargrin has developed a brand new game called Stealth and this has the following budgeted performance figures.

The selling price of Stealth will be a constant $30 per game. Analysis of the costs show that at a volume of 10,000 units a total cost of $130,000 is expected. However at a volume of 14,000 units a total cost of $150,000 is expected. If volumes exceed 15,000 units the fixed costs will increase by 50%.

Stealth's budgeted volumes are as follows:

	Year 1	Year 2	Year 3
Sales volume	8,000 units	16,000 units	4,000 units

In addition, marketing costs for Stealth will be $60,000 in year one and $40,000 in year two. Design and development costs are all incurred before the game is launched and has cost $300,000 for Stealth. These costs are written off to the income statement as incurred (ie before year 1 above).

Required

(a) Explain the principles behind lifecycle costing and briefly state why Wargrin in particular should consider these lifecycle principles. **(3 marks)**

(b) Produce the budgeted results for the game 'Stealth' and briefly assess the game's expected performance, taking into account the whole lifecycle of the game. **(7 marks)**

(c) Explain why incremental budgeting is a common method of budgeting and outline the main problems with such an approach. **(6 marks)**

(d) Discuss the extent to which a *meaningful* standard cost can be set for games produced by Wargrin. You should consider each of the cost classifications mentioned above. **(4 marks)**

(Total = 20 marks)

46 ZBB (12/10)

Some commentators argue that: 'With continuing pressure to control costs and maintain efficiency, the time has come for all public sector organisations to embrace zero-based budgeting. There is no longer a place for incremental budgeting in any organisation, particularly public sector ones, where zero-based budgeting is far more suitable anyway.'

Required

(a) Discuss the particular difficulties encountered when budgeting in public sector organisations compared with budgeting in private sector organisations, drawing comparisons between the two types of organisations.

(5 marks)

(b) Explain the terms 'incremental budgeting' and 'zero-based budgeting'. **(4 marks)**

(c) State the main stages involved in preparing zero-based budgets. **(3 marks)**

(d) Discuss the view that 'there is no longer a place for incremental budgeting in any organisation, particularly public sector ones,' highlighting any drawbacks of zero-based budgeting that need to be considered.

(8 marks)

(Total = 20 marks)

47 Northland (6/09)

36 mins

Northland's major towns and cities are maintained by local government organisations (LGO), which are funded by central government. The LGOs submit a budget each year which forms the basis of the funds received.

You are provided with the following information as part of the 20X2 budget preparation.

Overheads

Overhead costs are budgeted on an incremental basis, taking the previous year's actual expenditure and adding a set % to allow for inflation. Adjustments are also made for known changes. The details for these are:

Overhead cost category	20X1 cost $	Known changes	Inflation adjustment between 20X1 and 20X2
Property cost	120,000	None	+5%
Central wages	150,000	Note 1 below	+3%
Stationery	25,000	Note 2 below	0%

Note 1: One new staff member will be added to the overhead team; this will cost $12,000 in 20X2

Note 2: A move towards the paperless office is expected to reduce stationery costs by 40% on the 20X1 spend

Road repairs

In 20X2 it is expected that 2,000 metres of road will need repairing but a contingency of an extra 10% has been agreed.

In 20X1 the average cost of a road repair was $15,000 per metre repaired, but this excluded any cost effects of extreme weather conditions. The following probability estimates have been made in respect of 20X2:

Weather type predicted	Probability	Increase in repair cost
Good	0·7	0
Poor	0·1	+10%
Bad	0·2	+25%

Inflation on road repairing costs is expected to be 5% between 20X1 and 20X2.

New roads

New roads are budgeted on a zero base basis and will have to compete for funds along with other capital projects such as hospitals and schools.

Required

(a)   Calculate the overheads budget for 20X2.   **(3 marks)**

(b)   Calculate the budgets for road repairs for 20X2.   **(6 marks)**

(c)   Explain the problems associated with using expected values in budgeting by an LGO and explain why a contingency for road repairs might be needed.   **(8 marks)**

(d)   Explain the process involved for zero based budgeting.   **(3 marks)**

(Total = 20 marks)

48 Velo Racers (PM, 6/03, amended)   36 mins

Velo Racers has designed a radical new concept in racing bikes with the intention of selling them to professional racing teams. The estimated cost and selling price of the first bike to be manufactured and assembled is as follows.

	$
Materials	1,000
Assembly labour (50 hours at $10 per hour)	500
Fixed overheads (200% of assembly labour)	1,000
Profit (20% of total cost)	500
Selling price	3,000

Velo Racers plans to sell all bikes at a total cost plus 20% and the material cost per bike will remain constant irrespective of the number sold.

Velo Racers' management expects the assembly time to gradually improve with experience and has estimated an 80% learning curve for the first 16 bikes, after which a steady state production time will apply with the labour time per bike after the first 16 bikes being equal to the time for the 16th bike.

A racing club has approached the company and asked for the following quotations.

(1)   If we were to purchase the first bike assembled, and immediately put in an order for the second, what would be the price of the second bike?

(2)   If we waited until you had sold two bikes to another team, and then ordered the third and fourth bikes to be assembled, what would be the average price of the third and fourth bikes?

(3)   If we decided to immediately equip our racing team with the new bike, what would be the price per bike if we placed an order for the first eight to be assembled?

(4)   If we decided to buy 20 bikes in total, what would be the price of the entire order?

Required

(a)   Explain Learning Curve Theory, circumstances where its use is appropriate, and in particular the concept of cumulative average time.   **(5 marks)**

(b)   Provide detailed price quotations for each of the four enquires outlined above.   **(7 marks)**

(c)   Identify the major areas within management accounting where learning curve theory is likely to affect Velo Racers and suggest potential limitations of this theory.   **(8 marks)**

(Total = 20 marks)

Top tip. Cumulative average time is the average time per unit for **all** units produced (including the first unit made).

In part (b), do not forget to divide the total selling price by the number of bikes being sold to arrive at a figure per bike. Be careful to be clear about the **incremental** hours needed for each additional ordered bike when making your calculations.

Learning curve effects have particular relevance when setting budgets or making forecasts.

---

49 Q Organisation

36 mins

(a) The Q organisation is a large, worldwide respected manufacturer of consumer electrical and electronic goods. Q constantly develops new products that are in high demand as they represent the latest technology and are 'must haves' for those consumers that want to own the latest consumer gadgets. Recently Q has developed a new handheld digital DVD recorder and seeks your advice as to the price it should charge for such a technologically advanced product.

Required

Suggest pricing policies that would be suitable for each stage of the product life cycle of the DVD recorder.

(5 marks)

(b) Market research has discovered that the price demand relationship for the item during the initial launch phase will be as follows.

Price	Demand
$	Units
100	10,000
80	20,000
69	30,000
62	40,000

Production of the DVD recorder would occur in batches of 10,000 units and the production director believes that 50% of the variable manufacturing cost would be affected by a learning and experience curve. This would apply to each batch produced and continue at a constant rate of learning up to a production volume of 40,000 units when the learning would be complete. Thereafter, the unit variable manufacturing cost of the product would be equal to the unit cost of the fourth batch. The production director estimates that the unit variable manufacturing cost of the first batch would be $60 ($30 of which is subject to the effect of the learning and experience curve, and $30 of which is unaffected), whereas the average unit variable manufacturing cost of all four batches would be $52.71.

There are no non-manufacturing variable costs associated with the DVD recorder.

Required

(i) Calculate the rate of learning that is expected by the production director. **(4 marks)**

(ii) Calculate the optimum price at which Q should sell the DVD recorder in order to maximise its profits during the initial launch phase of the product. **(3 marks)**

(iii) Q expects that after the initial launch phase the market price will be $57 per unit. Estimated product specific fixed costs during this phase of the product's life are expected to be $15,000 per month. During this phase of the product life cycle Q wishes to achieve a target monthly profit from the product of $30,000.

Using an average cost approach, calculate the number of units that need to be sold each month during this phase in order that Q achieves this target monthly profit. **(8 marks)**

(Total = 20 marks)

50 BFG (Pilot paper, amended)

36 mins

BFG Limited is investigating the financial viability of a new product the S-pro. The S-pro is a short-life product for which a market has been identified at an agreed design specification. The product will only have a life of 12 months.

The following estimated information is available in respect of S-pro:

(1) Sales should be 1,200 units in the year. An average selling price of $1,050 per unit is expected. All sales are for cash.

(2) An 80% learning curve will apply for the first 700 units after which a steady state production time will apply, with the labour time per unit after the first 700 units being equal to the time for the 700th unit. The cost of the first unit was measured at $2,500. This was for 500 hours at $5 per hour.

(3) Variable overhead is estimated at $2 per labour hour.

(4) Direct material costs will be $514,000 for the year. All purchases are made for cash.

A target net cash flow of $350,000 is required in order for this project to be acceptable.

Note: The learning curve formula is given on the formulae sheet. At the learning rate of 0.8 (80%), the learning factor (b) is equal to –0.3219.

Required

(a) Prepare detailed calculations to show whether product S-pro will provide the target net cash flow.

(9 marks)

(b) Calculate what length of time the second unit will take if the actual rate of learning is:

   (i)   80%;
   (ii) 90%.

   Explain which rate shows the faster learning. **(5 marks)**

(c) Suggest specific actions that BFG could take to improve the net cash flow calculated above. **(6 marks)**

(Total = 20 marks)

51 HC (12/08, amended) 36 mins

Henry Company (HC) provides skilled labour to the building trade. They have recently been asked by a builder to bid for a kitchen fitting contract for a new development of 600 identical apartments. HC has not worked for this builder before. Cost information for the new contract is as follows:

Labour for the contract is available. HC expects that the first kitchen will take 24 man-hours to fit but thereafter the time taken will be subject to a 95% learning rate. After 200 kitchens are fitted the learning rate will stop and the time taken for the 200th kitchen will be the time taken for all the remaining kitchens. Labour costs $15 per hour.

Overheads are absorbed on a labour hour basis. HC has collected overhead information for the last four months and this is shown below:

	Hours worked	Overhead cost $
Month 1	9,300	115,000
Month 2	9,200	113,600
Month 3	9,400	116,000
Month 4	9,600	116,800

HC normally works around 120,000 labour hours in a year.

HC uses the high low method to analyse overheads.

The learning curve equation is $y = ax^b$, where $b = \dfrac{\text{Log LR}}{\text{Log 2}} = -0.074$

Required

(a) Describe THREE factors, other than the cost of labour and overheads mentioned above, that HC should take into consideration in calculating its bid. **(6 marks)**

(b) Calculate the total cost including all overheads for HC that it can use as a basis of the bid for the new apartment contract. **(12 marks)**

(c) If the second kitchen alone is expected to take 21·6 man-hours to fit demonstrate how the learning rate of 95% has been calculated. **(2 marks)**

(Total = 20 marks)

52 Big Cheese Chairs (12/09)

36 mins

Big Cheese Chairs (BCC) manufactures and sells executive leather chairs. They are considering a new design of massaging chair to launch into the competitive market in which they operate.

They have carried out an investigation in the market and using a target costing system have targeted a competitive selling price of $120 for the chair. BCC wants a margin on selling price of 20% (ignoring any overheads).

The frame and massage mechanism will be bought in for $51 per chair and BCC will upholster it in leather and assemble it ready for despatch.

Leather costs $10 per metre and two metres are needed for a complete chair although 20% of all leather is wasted in the upholstery process.

The upholstery and assembly process will be subject to a learning effect as the workers get used to the new design. BCC estimates that the first chair will take two hours to prepare but this will be subject to a learning rate (LR) of 95%. The learning improvement will stop once 128 chairs have been made and the time for the 128th chair will be the time for all subsequent chairs. The cost of labour is $15 per hour.

The learning formula is shown on the formula sheet and at the 95% learning rate the value of b is –0·074000581.

Required

(a) Calculate the average cost for the first 128 chairs made and identify any cost gap that may be present at that stage.

(8 marks)

(b) Assuming that a cost gap for the chair exists suggest four ways in which it could be closed.

(6 marks)

The production manager denies any claims that a cost gap exists and has stated that the cost of the 128th chair will be low enough to yield the required margin.

(c) Calculate the cost of the 128th chair made and state whether the target cost is being achieved on the 128th chair.

(6 marks)

(Total = 20 marks)

Questions 53 to 67 cover Standard Costing and Variances Analysis, the subject of Part D of the BPP Study Text for Paper F5.

53 Mermus (FMC, 12/04, amended)   36 mins

Mermus is comparing budget and actual data for the last three months.

	Budget		Actual	
	$	$	$	$
Sales		950,000		922,500
Cost of sales				
Raw materials	133,000		130,500	
Direct labour	152,000		153,000	
Variable production overheads	100,700		96,300	
Fixed production overheads	125,400		115,300	
		511,100		495,100
		438,900		427,400

The budget was prepared on the basis of 95,000 units produced and sold, but actual production and sales for the three-month period were 90,000 units.

Mermus uses standard costing and absorbs fixed production overheads on a machine hour basis. A total of 28,500 standard machine hours were budgeted. A total of 27,200 machine hours were actually used in the three-month period.

Required

(a) Prepare a revised budget at the new level of activity using a flexible budgeting approach and briefly explain why such a revised budget should be prepared.   **(6 marks)**

(b) Calculate the following.

     (i) Raw material total cost variance;
     (ii) Direct labour total cost variance;
     (iii) Fixed overhead efficiency variance;
     (iv) Fixed overhead capacity variance;
     (v) Fixed overhead expenditure variance.   **(8 marks)**

(c) Suggest possible explanations for the following variances.

     (i) Raw materials total cost variance;
     (ii) Fixed overhead efficiency variance;
     (iii) Fixed overhead expenditure variance.   **(6 marks)**

     (Total = 20 marks)

54 Ash (FMC, 6/06, amended)   36 mins

Ash recorded the following actual results for Product RS8 for the last month:

Product RS8	2,100 units produced and sold for $14.50 per unit
Direct material M3	1,050 kg costing $1,680
Direct material M7	1,470 kg costing $2,793
Direct labour	525 hours costing $3,675
Variable production overhead	$1,260
Fixed production overhead	$4,725

Standard selling price and cost data for one unit of Product RS8 is as follows.

Selling price	$15.00
Direct material M3	0.6 kg at $1.55 per kg
Direct material M7	0.68 kg at $1.75 per kg
Direct labour	14 minutes at $7.20 per direct labour hour
Variable production overhead	$2.10 per direct labour hour
Fixed production overhead	$9.00 per direct labour hour

At the start of the last month, 497 standard labour hours were budgeted for production of Product RS8. No inventories of raw materials are held. All production of Product RS8 is sold immediately to a single customer under a just-in-time agreement.

Required

(a) Prepare an operating statement that reconciles budgeted profit with actual profit for Product RS8 for the last month. You should calculate variances in as much detail as allowed by the information provided.

(15 marks)

(b) Discuss how the operating statement you have produced can assist managers in:

(i) Controlling variable costs
(ii) Controlling fixed production overhead costs.

(5 marks)

(Total = 20 marks)

55 Product RYX

36 mins

A manufacturing company, Hexicon, has provided you with the following data which relates to product RYX, for the period which has just ended.

	Budget	Actual
Number of labour hours	8,400	7,980
Production units	1,200	1,100
Overhead cost (all fixed)	$22,260	$25,536

Overheads are absorbed at a rate per standard labour hour.

Required

(a) (i) Calculate the fixed production overhead cost variance and the following subsidiary variances.

- Expenditure
- Efficiency
- Capacity

(ii) Provide a summary statement of these four variances.

(8 marks)

(b) Discuss the possible reasons why adverse fixed production overhead expenditure, efficiency and capacity variances occur.

(9 marks)

(c) Briefly discuss two examples of inter-relationships between the fixed production overhead efficiency variances and the material and labour variances.

(3 marks)

(Total = 20 marks)

56 Woodeezer (FMC, 12/02, amended)

36 mins

Woodeezer makes quality wooden benches for both indoor and outdoor use. Results have been disappointing in recent years and a new managing director, Peter Beech, was appointed to raise production volumes. After an initial assessment Peter Beech considered that budgets had been set at levels which made it easy for employees to achieve. He argued that employees would be better motivated by setting budgets which challenged them more in terms of higher expected output.

Other than changing the overall budgeted output, Mr Beech has not yet altered any part of the standard cost card. Thus, the budgeted output and sales for November 20X2 was 4,000 benches and the standard cost card below was calculated on this basis:

	$
Wood 25 kg at $3.20 per kg	80.00
Labour 4 hours at $8 per hour	32.00
Variable overheads 4 hours at $4 per hour	16.00
Fixed overhead 4 hours at $16 per hour	64.00
	192.00
Selling price	220.00
Standard profit	28.00

Overheads are absorbed on the basis of labour hours and the company uses an absorption costing system. There were no inventories at the beginning of November 20X2. Inventories are valued at standard cost.

Actual results for November 20X2 were as follows:

		$
Wood	80,000 kg at $3.50	280,000
Labour	16,000 hours at $7	112,000
Variable overhead		60,000
Fixed overhead		196,000
Total production cost (3,600 benches)		648,000
Closing inventory (400 benches at $192)		76,800
Cost of sales		571,200
Sales (3,200 benches)		720,000
Actual profit		148,800

The average monthly production and sales for some years prior to November 20X2 had been 3,400 units and budgets had previously been set at this level. Very few operating variances had historically been generated by the standard costs used.

Mr Beech has made some significant changes to the operations of the company. However, the other directors are now concerned that Mr Beech has been too ambitious in raising production targets. Mr Beech had also changed suppliers of raw materials to improve quality, increased selling prices, begun to introduce less skilled labour, and significantly reduced fixed overheads.

The finance director suggested that an absorption costing system is misleading and that a marginal costing system should be considered at some stage in the future to guide decision-making.

Required

(a) Prepare an operating statement for November 20X2. This should show all operating variances and should reconcile budgeted and actual profit for the month for Woodeezer Co. **(14 marks)**

(b) In so far as the information permits, examine the impact of the operational changes made by Mr Beech on the profitability of the company. In your answer, consider each of the following.

    (i) Motivation and budget setting; and

    (ii) Possible causes of variances. **(6 marks)**

(Total = 20 marks)

57 Carat (FMC, 12/03, amended)   36 mins

Carat, a premium food manufacturer, is reviewing operations for a three-month period of 20X3. The company operates a standard marginal costing system and manufactures one product, ZP, for which the following standard revenue and cost data per unit of product is available:

Selling price	$12.00
Direct material A	2.5 kg at $1.70 per kg
Direct material B	1.5 kg at $1.20 per kg
Direct labour	0.45 hrs at $6.00 per hour

Fixed production overheads for the three-month period were expected to be $62,500.

Actual data for the three-month period was as follows:

Sales and production	48,000 units of ZP were produced and sold for $580,800
Direct material A	121,951 kg were used at a cost of $200,000
Direct material B	67,200 kg were used at a cost of $84,000
Direct labour	Employees worked for 18,900 hours, but 19,200 hours were paid at a cost of $117,120
Fixed production overheads	$64,000

Budgeted sales for the three-month period were 50,000 units of Product ZP.

Required

(a)   Calculate the following variances.

   (i)   Sales volume contribution and sales price variances;
   (ii)   Price, mix and yield variances for each material;
   (iii)   Labour rate, labour efficiency and idle time variances.   **(7 marks)**

(b)   Prepare an operating statement that reconciles budgeted gross profit to actual gross profit with each variance clearly shown.   **(4 marks)**

(c)   Suggest possible explanations for the following variances.

   (i)   Material price, mix and yield variances for material A;
   (ii)   Labour rate, labour efficiency and idle time variances.   **(5 marks)**

(d)   Explain what is meant by basic standards and ideal standards and their effect on employee motivation.
                                                                                                       (4 marks)

                                                                                              (Total = 20 marks)

58 Chaff Co (6/08, amended)   **36 mins**

Chaff Co processes and sells brown rice. It buys unprocessed rice seeds and then, using a relatively simple process, removes the outer husk of the rice to produce the brown rice. This means that there is substantial loss of weight in the process. The market for the purchase of seeds and the sales of brown rice has been, and is expected to be, stable. Chaff Co uses a variance analysis system to monitor its performance.

There has been some concern about the interpretation of the variances that have been calculated in month 1.

*   The purchasing manager is adamant, despite criticism from the production director, that he has purchased wisely and saved the company thousands of dollars in purchase costs by buying the required quantity of cheaper seeds from a new supplier.

*   The production director is upset at being criticised for increasing the wage rates for month 1; he feels the decision was the right one, considering all the implications of the increase. Morale was poor and he felt he had to do something about it.

The variances for month 1 are as follows:

	$
Material price	48,000 (Fav)
Material usage	52,000 (Adv)
Labour rate	15,000 (Adv)
Labour efficiency	18,000 (Fav)
Labour idle time	12,000 (Fav)
Variable overhead expenditure	18,000 (Adv)
Variable overhead efficiency	30,000 (Fav)
Fixed overhead expenditure	8,000 (Fav)
Sales price	85,000 (Adv)
Sales volume	21,000 (Adv)

Fav = Favourable, Adv = Adverse

Chaff Co uses labour hours to absorb the variable overhead.

Required

(a)   Comment on the performance of the purchasing manager and the production director using the variances and other information above and reach a conclusion as to whether or not they have each performed well.

(6 marks)

In month 2 the following data applies:

Standard costs for 1 tonne of brown rice

- 1·4 tonnes of rice seeds are needed at a cost of $60 per tonne
- It takes 2 labour hours of work to produce 1 tonne of brown rice and labour is normally paid $18 per hour. Idle time is expected to be 10% of hours paid; this is not reflected in the rate of $18 above
- 2 hours of variable overhead at a cost of $30 per hour
- The standard selling price is $240 per tonne
- The standard contribution per tonne is $56 per tonne

Budget information for month 2

- Fixed costs were budgeted at $210,000 for the month
- Budgeted production and sales were 8,400 tonnes

The actual results for month 2

Actual production and sales were 8,000 tonnes

- 12,000 tonnes of rice seeds were bought and used, costing $660,000
- 15,800 labour hours were paid for, costing $303,360
- 15,000 labour hours were worked
- Variable production overhead cost $480,000
- Fixed costs were $200,000
- Sales revenue achieved was $1,800,000

Required

(b)   Calculate the variances for month 2 in as much detail as the information allows and reconcile the budget profit to the actual profit using marginal costing principles. You are not required to comment on the performance of the business or its managers for their performance in month 2.   (14 marks)

(Total = 20 marks)

59 AHW Co   36 mins

AHW Co is a food processing company that produces high-quality, part-cooked meals for the retail market. The five different types of meal that the company produces (products A to E) are made by subjecting ingredients to a series of processing activities. The meals are different, and therefore need differing amounts of processing activities.

Budget and actual information for October 20X2 is shown below:

Budgeted data

	Product A	Product B	Product C	Product D	Product E
Number of batches	20	30	15	40	25
Processing activities per batch					
Processing activity W	4	5	2	3	1
Processing activity X	3	2	5	1	4
Processing activity Y	3	3	2	4	2
Processing activity Z	4	6	8	2	3

Budgeted costs of processing activities

	$'000
Processing activity W	160
Processing activity X	130
Processing activity Y	80
Processing activity Z	200

All costs are expected to be variable in relation to the number of processing activities.

Actual data

Actual output during October 20X2 was as follows:

	Product A	Product B	Product C	Product D	Product E
Number of batches	18	33	16	35	28

Actual processing costs incurred during October 20X2 were:

	$'000
Processing activity W	158
Processing activity X	139
Processing activity Y	73
Processing activity Z	206

Required

(a) Prepare a budgetary control statement (to the nearest $'000) that shows the original budget costs, flexed budget costs, the actual costs, and the total variances of each processing activity for October 20X2.

(11 marks)

(b) Explain how budgetary control might act as (i) an incentive and (ii) a disincentive in achieving maximum performance. Describe the action that might be taken to overcome the disincentive effects.   **(9 marks)**

(Total = 20 marks)

60 Linsil (FMC, 6/04, amended)   36 mins

Linsil has produced the following operating statement reconciling budgeted and actual gross profit for the last three months, based on actual sales of 122,000 units of its single product:

Operating statement	$	$	$
Budgeted gross profit			800,000
Budgeted fixed production overhead			352,000
Budgeted contribution			1,152,000
Sales volume contribution variance		19,200	
Sales price variance		(61,000)	
			(41,800)
Actual sales less standard variable cost of sales			1,110,200
Planning variances	Favourable	Adverse	
Material	18,099		
Labour		286,358	
			(268,259)
Operational variances			
Material		16,635	
Labour	117,998		
			101,363
Actual contribution			943,304
Budgeted fixed production overhead		(352,000)	
Fixed production overhead expenditure variance		27,000	
Actual fixed production overhead			(325,000)
Actual gross profit			618,304

The standard direct costs and selling price applied during the three-month period and the actual direct costs and selling price for the period were as follows:

	Standard	Actual
Selling price ($/unit)	31.50	31.00
Direct material usage (kg/unit)	3.00	2.80
Direct material price ($/kg)	2.30	2.46
Direct labour efficiency (hrs/unit)	1.25	1.30
Direct labour rate ($/hr)	12.00	12.60

After the end of the three-month period and prior to the preparation of the above operating statement, it was decided to revise the standard costs retrospectively to take account of the following.

1   A 3% increase in the direct material price per kilogram;

2   A labour rate increase of 4%;

3   The standard for labour efficiency had anticipated buying a new machine leading to a 10% decrease in labour hours; instead of buying a new machine, existing machines had been improved, giving an expected 5% saving in material usage.

Required

(a)   Calculate the revised standard costs.   **(4 marks)**

(b)   Using the information provided demonstrate how the planning and operational variances in the operating statement have been calculated.   **(8 marks)**

(c)   Explain the significance of separating variances into planning and operational elements and the problems which could arise.   **(8 marks)**

                                                                                                    (Total = 20 marks)

61 Simply Soup (Pilot paper, amended)   36 mins

Simply Soup Limited manufactures and sells soups in a JIT environment. Soup is made in a manufacturing process by mixing liquidised vegetables, melted butter and stock (stock in this context is a liquid used in making soups). They operate a standard costing and variances system to control its manufacturing processes. At the beginning of the current financial year they employed a new production manager to oversee the manufacturing process and to work alongside the purchasing manager. The production manager will be rewarded by a salary and a bonus based on the directly attributable variances involved in the manufacturing process.

After three months of work there is doubt about the performance of the new production manager. On the one hand, the cost variances look on the whole favourable, but the sales director has indicated that sales are significantly down and the overall profitability is decreasing.

The table below shows the variance analysis results for the first three months of the manager's work.

Table 1

F = Favourable   A = Adverse

	Month 1	Month 2	Month 3
Material Price Variance	$300 (F)	$900 (A)	$2,200 (A)
Material Mix Variance	$1,800 (F)	$2,253 (F)	$2,800 (F)
Material Yield Variance	$2,126 (F)	$5,844 (F)	$9,752 (F)
Total Variance	$4,226 (F)	$7,197 (F)	$10,352 (F)

The actual level of activity was broadly the same in each month and the standard monthly material total cost was approximately $145,000.

The standard cost card is as follows for the period under review

	$
0.90 litres of liquidised vegetables @ $0.80/ltr	0.72
0.05 litres of melted butter @$4/ltr	0.20
1.10 litres of stock @ $0.50/ltr	0.55
Total cost to produce 1 litre of soup	1.47

Required

(a)   Using the information in Table 1:

(i)   Explain the meaning of each type of variances above (price, mix and yield but excluding the total variance) and briefly discuss to what extent each type of variance is controllable by the production manager.   **(6 marks)**

(ii)   Evaluate the performance of the production manager considering both the cost variance results above and the sales director's comments.   **(5 marks)**

(b)   The board has asked that the variances be calculated for Month 4. In Month 4 the production department data is as follows:

Actual results for Month 4

Liquidised vegetables:	Bought	82,000 litres	costing $69,700
Melted butter:	Bought	4,900 litres	costing $21,070
Stock:	Bought	122,000 litres	costing $58,560

Actual production was 112,000 litres of soup.

Required

Calculate the material price, mix and yield variances for Month 4. You are not required to comment on the performance that the calculations imply. Round variances to the nearest $.   **(9 marks)**

(Total = 20 marks)

62 Spike Limited (12/07, amended)   36 mins

Spike Limited manufactures and sells good quality leather bound diaries. Each year it budgets for its profits, including detailed budgets for sales, materials and labour. If appropriate, the departmental managers are allowed to revise their budgets for planning errors.

In recent months, the managing director has become concerned about the frequency of budget revisions. At a recent board meeting he said 'There seems little point budgeting any more. Every time we have a problem the budgets are revised to leave me looking at a favourable operational variance report and at the same time a lot less profit than promised.'

Two specific situations have recently arisen, for which budget revisions were sought:

Materials

A local material supplier was forced into liquidation. Spike Limited's buyer managed to find another supplier, 150 miles away at short notice. This second supplier charged more for the material and a supplementary delivery charge on top. The buyer agreed to both the price and the delivery charge without negotiation. 'I had no choice', the buyer said, 'the production manager was pushing me very hard to find any solution possible!' Two months later, another, more competitive, local supplier was found.

A budget revision is being sought for the two months where higher prices had to be paid.

Labour

During the early part of the year, problems had been experienced with the quality of work being produced by the support staff in the labour force. The departmental manager had complained in his board report that his team were 'unreliable, inflexible and just not up to the job'.

It was therefore decided, after discussion of the board report, that something had to be done. The company changed its policy so as to recruit only top graduates from good quality universities. This has had the effect of pushing up the costs involved but increasing productivity in relation to that element of the labour force.

The support staff departmental manager has requested a budget revision to cover the extra costs involved following the change of policy.

(a)   Discuss each request for a budget revision, putting what you see as both sides of the argument and reach a
       conclusion as to whether a budget revision should be allowed.   **(8 marks)**

The market for leather bound diaries has been shrinking as the electronic versions become more widely available
and easier to use. Spike Limited has produced the following data relating to leather bound diary sales for the year to
date:

Budget

Sales volume	180,000 units
Sales price	$17·00 per unit
Standard contribution	$7·00 per unit

The total market for diaries in this period was estimated in the budget to be 1·8m units. In fact, the actual total
market shrank to 1·6m units for the period under review.

Actual results for the same period

Sales volume	176,000 units
Sales price	$16·40 per unit

Required

(b)   Calculate the total sales price and total sales volume variance.   **(4 marks)**
(c)   Analyse the total sales volume variance into components for market size and market share.   **(4 marks)**
(d)   Comment on the sales performance of the business.   **(4 marks)**

                                                                                                  (Total = 20 marks)

63 Crumbly Cakes (6/09)   **36 mins**

Crumbly Cakes make cakes, which are sold directly to the public. The new production manager (a celebrity chef)
has argued that the business should use only organic ingredients in its cake production. Organic ingredients are
more expensive but should produce a product with an improved flavour and give health benefits for the customers.
It was hoped that this would stimulate demand and enable an immediate price increase for the cakes.

Crumbly Cakes operates a responsibility based standard costing system which allocates variances to specific
individuals. The individual managers are paid a bonus only when net favourable variances are allocated to them.

The new organic cake production approach was adopted at the start of March 20X9, following a decision by the new
production manager. No change was made at that time to the standard costs card. The variance reports for
February and March are shown below (Fav = Favourable and Adv = Adverse).

Manager responsible	Allocated variances	February Variance $	March Variance $
Production manager	Material price (total for all ingredients)	25 Fav	2,100 Adv
	Material mix	0	600 Adv
	Material yield	20 Fav	400 Fav
Sales manager	Sales price	40 Adv	7,000 Fav
	Sales contribution volume	35 Adv	3,000 Fav

The production manager is upset that he seems to have lost all hope of a bonus under the new system. The sales
manager thinks the new organic cakes are excellent and is very pleased with the progress made.

Crumbly Cakes operate a JIT stock system and holds virtually no inventory.

Required

(a)   Assess the performance of the production manager and the sales manager and indicate whether the current
       bonus scheme is fair to those concerned.   **(7 marks)**

In April 20X9 the following data applied:

Standard cost card for one cake (not adjusted for the organic ingredient change)

Ingredients	Kg	$
Flour	0·10	0·12 per kg
Eggs	0·10	0·70 per kg
Butter	0·10	1·70 per kg
Sugar	0·10	0·50 per kg
Total input	0·40	
Normal loss (10%)	(0·04)	
Standard weight of a cake	0·36	
Standard sales price of a cake		0·85
Standard contribution per cake after all variable costs		0·35

The budget for production and sales in April was 50,000 cakes. Actual production and sales was 60,000 cakes in the month, during which the following occurred:

Actual
Input → Output
23,478kg → 60K

Ingredients used	Kg	$
Flour	5,700	$741
Eggs	6,600	$5,610
Butter	6,600	$11,880
Sugar	4,578	$2,747
Total input	23,478	$20,978
Actual loss	(1,878)	
Actual output of cake mixture	21,600	
Actual sales price of a cake		$0·99

All cakes produced must weigh 0·36 kg as this is what is advertised.

Required

(b) Calculate the material price, mix and yield variances and the sales price and sales contribution/volume variances for April. You are not required to make any comment on the performance of the managers.

(13 marks)

(Total = 20 marks)

64 Secure Net (12/09)

36 mins

Secure Net (SN) manufacture security cards that restrict access to government owned buildings around the world.

The standard cost for the plastic that goes into making a card is $4 per kg and each card uses 40g of plastic after an allowance for waste. In November 100,000 cards were produced and sold by SN and this was well above the budgeted sales of 60,000 cards.

The actual cost of the plastic was $5·25 per kg and the production manager (who is responsible for all buying and production issues) was asked to explain the increase. He said 'World oil price increases pushed up plastic prices by 20% compared to our budget and I also decided to use a different supplier who promised better quality and increased reliability for a slightly higher price. I know we have overspent but not all the increase in plastic prices is my fault. The actual usage of plastic per card was 35g per card and again the production manager had an explanation. He said 'The world-wide standard size for security cards increased by 5% due to a change in the card reader technology, however, our new supplier provided much better quality of plastic and this helped to cut down on the waste.'

SN operates a just in time (JIT) system and hence carries very little inventory.

Required

(a) Calculate the total material price and total material usage variances ignoring any possible planning error in the figures.

(4 marks)

(b) Analyse the above total variances into component parts for planning and operational variances in as much detail as the information allows.

(8 marks)

(c)   Assess the performance of the production manager.   **(8 marks)**

                                                                            (Total = 20 marks)

65 Sticky Wicket (6/10)   **36 mins**

Sticky Wicket (SW) manufactures cricket bats using high quality wood and skilled labour using mainly traditional manual techniques. The manufacturing department is a cost centre within the business and operates a standard costing system based on marginal costs.

At the beginning of April 20X0 the production director attempted to reduce the cost of the bats by sourcing wood from a new supplier and de-skilling the process a little by using lower grade staff on parts of the production process. The standards were not adjusted to reflect these changes.

The variance report for April 20X0 is shown below (extract).

	Adverse ($)	Favourable ($)
Variances		
Material price		5,100
Material usage	7,500	
Labour rate		43,600
Labour efficiency	48,800	
Labour idle time	5,400	

The production director pointed out in his April 20X0 board report that the new grade of labour required significant training in April and this meant that productive time was lower than usual. He accepted that the workers were a little slow at the moment but expected that an improvement would be seen in May 20X0. He also mentioned that the new wood being used was proving difficult to cut cleanly resulting in increased waste levels.

Sales for April 20X0 were down 10% on budget and returns of faulty bats were up 20% on the previous month. The sales director resigned after the board meeting stating that SW had always produced quality products but the new strategy was bound to upset customers and damage the brand of the business.

Required

(a)   Assess the performance of the production director using all the information above taking into account both the decision to use a new supplier and the decision to de-skill the process.   **(7 marks)**

(b)   In May 20X0 the budgeted sales were 19,000 bats and the standard cost card is as follows:

	Std cost ($)	Std cost ($)
Materials (2kg at $5/kg)	10	
Labour (3hrs at $12/hr)	36	
Marginal cost		46
Selling price		68
Contribution		22

In May 20X0 the following results were achieved:

40,000kg of wood were bought at a cost of $196,000, this produced 19,200 cricket bats. No inventory of raw materials is held. The labour was paid for 62,000 hours and the total cost was $694,000. Labour worked for 61,500 hours.

The sales price was reduced to protect the sales levels. However, only 18,000 cricket bats were sold at an average price of $65.

Required

Calculate the materials, labour and sales variances for May 20X0 in as much detail as the information allows.

You are not required to comment on the performance of the business.   **(13 marks)**

                                                                            (Total = 20 marks)

66 Carad Co (12/10)

36 mins

Carad Co is an electronics company which makes two types of televisions – plasma screen TVs and LCD TVs. It operates within a highly competitive market and is constantly under pressure to reduce prices. Carad Co operates a standard costing system and performs a detailed variance analysis of both products on a monthly basis. Extracts from the management information for the month of November are shown below:

		Note
Total number of units made and sold	1,400	1
Material price variance	$28,000 A	2
Total labour variance	$6,050 A	3

Notes

(1) The budgeted total sales volume for TVs was 1,180 units, consisting of an equal mix of plasma screen TVs and LCD screen TVs. Actual sales volume was 750 plasma TVs and 650 LCD TVs. Standard sales prices are $350 per unit for the plasma TVs and $300 per unit for the LCD TVs. The actual sales prices achieved during November were $330 per unit for plasma TVs and $290 per unit for LCD TVs. The standard contributions for plasma TVs and LCD TVs are $190 and $180 per unit respectively.

(2) The sole reason for this variance was an increase in the purchase price of one of its key components, X. Each plasma TV made and each LCD TV made requires one unit of component X, for which Carad Co's standard cost is $60 per unit. Due to a shortage of components in the market place, the market price for November went up to $85 per unit for X. Carad Co actually paid $80 per unit for it.

(3) Each plasma TV uses 2 standard hours of labour and each LCD TV uses 1.5 standard hours of labour. The standard cost for labour is $14 per hour and this also reflects the actual cost per labour hour for the company's permanent staff in November. However, because of the increase in sales and production volumes in November, the company also had to use additional temporary labour at the higher cost of $18 per hour. The total capacity of Carad's permanent workforce is 2,200 hours production per month, assuming full efficiency. In the month of November, the permanent workforce were wholly efficient, taking exactly 2 hours to complete each plasma TV and exactly 1.5 hours to produce each LCD TV. The total labour variance therefore relates solely to the temporary workers, who took twice as long as the permanent workers to complete their production.

Required

(a) Calculate the following for the month of November, showing all workings clearly:

    (i)   The sales price variance and sales volume contribution variance;   **(6 marks)**
    (ii)   The material price planning variance and material price operational variance;   **(2 marks)**
    (iii)   The labour rate variance and the labour efficiency variance.   **(7 marks)**

(b) Explain the reasons why Carad Co would be interested in the material price planning variance and the material price operational variance.   **(5 marks)**

(Total = 20 marks)

67 Noble (6/11)

36 mins

Noble is a restaurant that is only open in the evenings, on SIX days of the week. It has eight restaurant and kitchen staff, each paid a wage of $8 per hour on the basis of hours actually worked. It also has a restaurant manager and a head chef, each of whom is paid a monthly salary of $4,300. Noble's budget and actual figures for the month of May was as follows:

↳ FC×2 = 8600

	Budget	$	Actual	$
Number of meals	1,200		1,560	
	$		$	
Revenue: Food	48,000		60,840	
Drinks	12,000		11,700	
		60,000		72,540
Variable costs:				
Staff wages	(9,216)		(13,248)	
Food costs	(6,000)		(7,180)	
Drink costs	(2,400)		(5,280)	
Energy costs	(3,387)		(3,500)	
		(21,003)		(29,208)
Contribution		38,997		43,332
Fixed costs:				
Manager's and chef's pay	(8,600)		(8,600)	
Rent, rates and depreciation	(4,500)	(13,100)	(4,500)	(13,100)
Operating profit		25,897		30,232

The budget above is based on the following assumptions:

6×4×50, = 1200 meals.

(1)   The restaurant is only open six days a week and there are four weeks in a month. The average number of orders each day is 50 and demand is evenly spread across all the days in the month.

$10 per → customer Drinks

(2)   The restaurant offers two meals: Meal A, which costs $35 per meal and Meal B, which costs $45 per meal. In addition to this, irrespective of which meal the customer orders, the average customer consumes four drinks each at $2·50 per drink. Therefore, the average spend per customer is either $45 or $55 including drinks, depending on the type of meal selected. The May budget is based on 50% of customers ordering Meal A and 50% of customers ordering Meal B.

(3)   Food costs represent 12·5% of revenue from food sales.

(4)   Drink costs represent 20% of revenue from drinks sales.

(5)   When the number of orders per day does not exceed 50, each member of hourly paid staff is required to work exactly six hours per day. For every incremental increase of five in the average number of orders per day, each member of staff has to work 0·5 hours of overtime for which they are paid at the increased rate of $12 per hour. You should assume that all costs for hourly paid staff are treated wholly as variable costs.

(6)   Energy costs are deemed to be related to the total number of hours worked by each of the hourly paid staff, and are absorbed at the rate of $2·94 per hour worked by each of the eight staff.

Required

Act Volume:

(a)   Prepare a flexed budget for the month of May, assuming that the standard mix of customers remains the same as budgeted.   **(12 marks)**

(b)   After preparation of the flexed budget, you are informed that the following variances have arisen in relation to total food and drink sales:

Sales mix contribution variance	$1,014 Adverse
Sales quantity contribution variance	$11,700 Favourable

BRIEFLY describe the sales mix contribution variance and the sales quantity contribution variance. Identify why each of them has arisen in Noble's case.   **(4 marks)**

(c)   Noble's owner told the restaurant manager to run a half-price drinks promotion at Noble for the month of May on all drinks. Actual results showed that customers ordered an average of six drinks each instead of the usual four but, because of the promotion, they only paid half of the usual cost for each drink. You have calculated the sales margin price variance for drink sales alone and found it to be a worrying $11,700 adverse. The restaurant manager is worried and concerned that this makes his performance for drink sales look very bad.

Required

Briefly discuss TWO other variances that could be calculated for drinks sales or food sales in order to ensure that the assessment of the restaurant manager's performance is fair. These should be variances that COULD be calculated from the information provided above although no further calculations are required here.

(4 marks)

(Total = 20 marks)

68 Heighway

36 mins

Heighway Co is a railway company. Heighway Co operates a passenger railway service and is responsible for the operation of services and the maintenance of track signalling equipment and other facilities such as stations. In recent years it has been criticised for providing a poor service to the travelling public in terms of punctuality, safety and the standard of facilities offered to passengers. In the last year Heighway Co has invested over $20 million in new carriages, station facilities and track maintenance programmes in an attempt to counter these criticisms. Summarised financial results for Heighway Co for the last two years are given below.

Summarised income statement for the year ended 31 December

	20X3	20X4
	$ million	$ million
Sales revenue	180.0	185.0
Earnings before interest and tax	18.0	16.5
Interest	(3.2)	(4.7)
Tax	(4.4)	(3.5)
Earnings available to ordinary shareholders	10.4	8.3

Summarised statement of financial position (balance sheet) as at 31 December

	20X3		20X4	
	$m	$m	$m	$m
Non-current assets (net)		100.4		120.5
Current assets				
Inventory	5.3		5.9	
Receivables	2.1		2.4	
Cash	6.2		3.6	
		13.6		11.9
		114.0		132.4
Ordinary share capital ($1 shares)		25.0		25.0
Reserves		45.6		48.2
Amounts payable after more than one year				
8% Debenture 20X9		15.0		15.0
Bank loan		20.0		35.0
Payables due within one year		8.4		9.2
		114.0		132.4

Required

(a) Calculate the following ratios for Heighway Co for 20X3 and 20X4, clearly showing your workings.

    (i)   Return on capital employed (also known as return on investment) based upon closing capital employed

    (ii)   Net profit margin

    (iii) Asset turnover

    (iv) Current ratio   **(4 marks)**

(b) Briefly comment on the financial performance of Heighway Co in 20X3 and 20X4 as revealed by the above ratios and suggest causes for any changes.   **(6 marks)**

(c) Suggest THREE non-financial indicators that could be useful in measuring the performance of a passenger railway company and explain why your chosen indicators are important.   **(3 marks)**

(d) Explain what is meant by short-termism and suggest ways in which a long-term view can be encouraged.   **(7 marks)**

(Total = 20 marks)

69 Preparation question: Accounting for business

Accounting for Business (AFB) is a national organisation which provides private tuition courses in accounting. The courses are generally attended by individuals who work as bookkeepers for other companies and who want to develop their practical skills. None of the attendees is aiming towards any professional qualification or examination.

Courses are run on basic bookkeeping, value added tax, payroll, credit control, company administration and basic business management. Other bespoke courses, run on demand, are charged out at higher than normal rates.

AFB has six branches nationwide with individual branch managers. Head office is situated at Nottingham and has responsibility for company accounting, payroll and inventory ordering activities. Individual branch mangers have responsibility for all other areas of the business, such as pricing, product mix and staffing.

Each branch rents its premises (a national company policy) and staff numbers range from 4 in Newcastle to 18 in Cardiff. Staff are generally former accountants, bankers and tax inspectors who concentrate on keeping courses practical and applicable to their customers.

To date managers have always been appraised by return on investment (ROI) with a target return of 40%. Branches have regularly exceeded this target and branch mangers seem happy to be appraised in this manner.

Jim Buxton, the company's main shareholder and managing director recently visited all branches in order to promote corporate identity and inspect performance at a local level. He returned dismayed at the condition of some branch premises and feels overall that, although recent financial performance has been consistent with previous years, the company does not seem to have changed or developed since he last visited branches five years ago.

Jim believes that he needs to change the appraisal method for branches so that they fit more closely with what he expects from the company. He wants the business to develop and grow and become the leading provider of business training in the UK.

Required

Answer the following questions, considering each independently from the others, and supporting your answers with appropriate calculations.

(a)   Outline the problems the business is likely to have from its use of ROI as its sole performance indicator.

(b)   Describe the balanced scorecard approach to performance measurement and how it might rectify these problems.

(c)   Outline possible performance measures which might be used in each area of the balanced scorecard by AFB.

70 Brace Co (6/11)   36 mins

(a)   Brace Co is an electronics company specialising in the manufacture of home audio equipment. Historically, the company has used solely financial performance measures to assess the performance of the company as a whole. The company's Managing Director has recently heard of the 'balanced scorecard approach' and is keen to learn more.

   Required

   Describe the balanced scorecard approach to performance measurement.   **(10 marks)**

(b)   Brace Co is split into two divisions, A and B, each with their own cost and revenue streams. Each of the divisions is managed by a divisional manager who has the power to make all investment decisions within the division. The cost of capital for both divisions is 12%. Historically, investment decisions have been made by calculating the return on investment (ROI) of any opportunities and at present, the return on investment of each division is 16%.

   A new manager who has recently been appointed in division A has argued that using residual income (RI) to make investment decisions would result in 'better goal congruence' throughout the company.

Each division is currently considering the following separate investments:

	Project for Division A	Project for Division B
Capital required for investment	$82·8 million	$40·6 million
Sales generated by investment	$44·6 million	$21·8 million
Net profit margin	28%	33%

The company is seeking to maximise shareholder wealth.

Required

Calculate both the return on investment and residual income of the new investment for each of the two divisions. Comment on these results, taking into consideration the manager's views about residual income.

(10 marks)

(Total = 20 marks)

71 Investment group
36 mins

H is an investment group which owns a number of subsidiary companies. Each subsidiary produces a particular product, product range or service.

For the purposes of management control, the subsidiary companies are organised into three sectors.

Consulting and Services (CS): comprising a consultancy practice which provides advice on product design, manufacturing technique and material usage both to H group companies and to businesses outside the group. Salaries comprise about 95% of costs in the CS sector.

Heavy Engineering (HE): comprising two subsidiary companies producing machinery, equipment and tools used in a variety of industrial applications. These companies require a major investment in the form of factory premises, plant and transport facilities.

Light Engineering (LE): comprising four subsidiaries which produce a range of small mechanical and electrical components, many of which are designed into the products of HE sector companies. The production of these components is generally considered to be labour-intensive.

At the start of 20X2 the management of H decides to prepare a five-year strategic plan for the group. A team of H executives is assembled to prepare this plan.

At its first meeting, the team is provided with the following summary of the group's performance in 20X1.

	CS $'000	HE $'000	LE $'000
Book value at 31 December 20X1			
Non-current assets	80	4,970	810
Current assets	90	820	180
Current liabilities	(20)	(140)	(65)
Capital employed	150	5,650	925
Year to 31 December 20X1			
Sales	860	6,320	1,918
Trading profit	220	1,073	240

All the above figures are taken from the H group's main accounting system and are prepared on a historical cost basis.

The group finance charge is 12% of the capital employed in each sector at the end of the year. This figure is H Co's cost of money and is also used as the discount rate for project evaluation.

(a)   Calculate the return on investment (ROI) and residual income for each sector and comment on your
        calculations.   **(6 marks)**

(b)   Discuss the relative merits of ROI and RI as performance indicators.   **(4 marks)**

(c)   Discuss the relevance of the information given in the question, and state what additional information you
        would find helpful in advising H on which of its three sectors should be expanded.   **(6 marks)**

(d)   Briefly explain Fitzgerald & Moon's Building Block model and discuss whether it would be useful in
        measuring the performance of H investment group.   **(4 marks)**

                                                                                         (Total = 20 marks)

72 Boats and cladding   **36 mins**

The following figures for the years ending 31 December 20X4 and 20X3 relate to the Boats and Cladding divisions
of Cordeline.

The return on capital employed (ROCE) figure is the basis for awarding a 20% bonus to the manager of the Boats
division (actual ROCE/target ROCE). The below target ROCE for the Cladding division has resulted in a zero bonus
award to its manager.

	Division			
	Boats		Cladding	
	20X4	20X4	20X4	20X3
	$'000	$'000	$'000	$'000
Sales	9,850	7,243	4,543	2,065
Profit before interest and taxes (PBIT)	1,336	1,674	924	363
Included in profit calculation:				
Depreciation for year	960	919	1,300	251
Net book value (NBV) of non-current assets*	5,540	6,000	7,700	2,600
Original cost of non-current assets	12,600	12,100	9,500	3,100
Replacement cost of non-current assets	25,000	24,500	9,750	3,350
New investment in non-current assets	500	750	6,400	2,400
Cost of capital	8%	8%	8%	8%
Return on capital employed**	24%	28%	12%	14%
Target return on capital	20%	20%	20%	20%

* Net book value is original cost less accumulated depreciation to date.
** Cordeline consider ROCE for bonus purposes to be PBIT as a % of NBV.

Required

(a)   Explain what type of possible counter-productive behaviour could result from using the current ROCE
        calculation for performance appraisal.   **(10 marks)**

(b)   Suggest a revised ROCE measure together with justification for your suggestion.   **(5 marks)**

(c)   Suggest an alternative financial performance measure for consideration by the board – without any
        recommendation for bonus calculation as this can be regarded as a board prerogative.   **(5 marks)**

                                                                                         (Total = 20 marks)

73 Pasta division

A well-established food manufacturing and distribution company, specialising in Italian food products, currently has an annual turnover in excess of $15 million. At present, the company has three production and distribution divisions, each responsible for specific product groups.

The summary information of the pasta division relating to divisional assets and profitability is as follows.

Pasta division

This division produces a wide range of both dried and fresh pasta products which it sells to both the supermarket sector and the restaurant trade.

Last year the divisional figures were as follows.

	$m
Investment in non-current assets	1.5
Investment in working capital	1.0
Operating profit	0.5

The company is keen to ensure that each division operates as an autonomous profit-making unit to ensure efficiency prevails and motivation and competitiveness are maximised. Managers are given as much freedom as possible to manage their divisions. Divisional budgets are set at the beginning of each year and these are then monitored on a month by month basis. Divisional managers are rewarded in terms of divisional return on investment.

The company is currently considering expansion into a new but allied product range. This range consists of sauces and canned foods. Projected figures for the expansion into sauces and canned foods are as follows.

	$m
Additional non-current assets required	0.75
Additional investment in working capital	0.35
Budgeted additional profit	0.198

The company has a cost of capital of 15%.

The manager of the pasta division has produced successful results over the past few years for her division. She and her staff have enjoyed handsome bonuses on the basis of return on investment. The company has traditionally calculated return on investment as operating profit as a percentage of return on all net divisional assets, and bonuses are paid as a percentage on this basis. The board proposes that the pasta division will be responsible for the expansion into sauces and canned foods.

Required

(a) Calculate the return on investment for the division both before and after the proposed divisional expansion.

(4 marks)

(b) Calculate the residual income for the division both before and after the proposed divisional expansion.

(4 marks)

(c) Using return on investment as a performance measure, determine whether the divisional manager will be happy to accept the proposed expansion. Explain how your answer would differ if residual income was used as a performance measure instead of return on investment. **(5 marks)**

(d) Briefly outline the advantages and disadvantages of return on investment and residual income as divisional performance measures. **(7 marks)**

(Total = 20 marks)

74 Preparation question: Transfer pricing

(a)   Explain the advantages of divisionalisation

(b)   SK is divided into five divisions that provide consultancy services to each other and to outside customers. Discuss the implications for SK, and the consequences for the managers of the supplying and receiving divisions, of each of the following possible cost-based approaches to setting a transfer price.

      (i)   Marginal cost
      (ii)   Total cost
      (iii)   Cost plus
      (iv)   Opportunity cost

(c)   (i)   Discuss briefly whether standard costs or actual costs should be used as the basis for cost-based transfer prices.

      (ii)   State one context in which a transfer price based on marginal cost would be appropriate and briefly describe any issues that may arise from such a transfer pricing policy.

75 FP Photocopiers and SW Ltd
36 mins

FP sells and repairs photocopiers. The company has operated for many years with two departments, the Sales Department and the Service Department, but the departments had no autonomy. The company is now thinking of restructuring so that the two departments will become profit centres.

The Sales Department

This department sells new photocopiers. The department sells 2,000 copiers per year. Included in the selling price is $60 for a one year guarantee. All customers pay this fee. This means that during the first year of ownership if the photocopier needs to be repaired then the repair costs are not charged to the customer. On average 500 photocopiers per year need to be repaired under the guarantee. The repair work is carried out by the Service Department who, under the proposed changes, would charge the Sales Department for doing the repairs. It is estimated that on average the repairs will take 3 hours each and that the charge by the Service Department will be $136,500 for the 500 repairs.

The Service Department

This department has two sources of work: the work needed to satisfy the guarantees for the Sales Department and repair work for external customers. Customers are charged at full cost plus 40%. The details of the budget for the next year for the Service Department revealed standard costs of:

Parts	at cost $54
Labour	$15 per hour
Variable overheads	$10 per labour hour
Fixed overheads	$22 per labour hour

The calculation of these standards is based on the estimated maximum market demand and includes the expected 500 repairs for the Sales Department. The average cost of the parts needed for a repair is $54. This means that the charge to the Sales Department for the repair work, including the 40% mark-up, will be $136,500.

Proposed Change

It has now been suggested that FP should be structured so that the two departments become profit centres and that the managers of the Departments are given autonomy. The individual salaries of the managers would be linked to the profits of their respective departments.

Budgets have been produced for each department on the assumption that the Service Department will repair 500 photocopiers for the Sales Department and that the transfer price for this work will be calculated in the same way as the price charged to external customers.

However the manager of the Sales Department has now stated that he intends to have the repairs done by another company, RS, because they have offered to carry out the work for a fixed fee of $180 per repair and this is less than the price that the Sales Department would charge.

Required

(a)   Calculate the individual profits of the Sales Department and the Service Department, and of FP as a whole from the guarantee scheme if:

   (i)   The repairs are carried out by the Service Department and are charged at full cost plus 40%;
   (ii)   The repairs are carried out by the Service department and are charged at marginal cost;
   (iii) The repairs are carried out by RS.   **(8 marks)**

(b)   (i)   Explain, with reasons, why a 'full cost plus' transfer pricing model may not be appropriate for FP.
                                                                                                                         (2 marks)

        (ii)   Comment on other issues that the managers of FP should consider if they decide to allow RS to carry out the repairs.   **(3 marks)**

(c)   SW Limited and AL Limited are members of the same group. SW Limited supplies its output to AL Limited, as well as selling to its external market.

      SW Limited has capacity to produce up to 500,000 litres a week. The external market demand is 350,000 litres per week, and previously AL Limited demanded 100,000 litres per week. AL Limited has now advised SW Limited that it will require 250,000 litres per week from January 20X2.

      SWAL group policy

      •   Evaluate the performance of group companies on the basis of their individual profits
      •   Set transfer prices that will encourage the maximisation of group profits

      Required

      Explain how an appropriate transfer pricing policy would provide a satisfactory basis for appraising the performance of individual companies. Comment on the implications of this policy for the maximisation of group profits.   **(7 marks)**

                                                                                                          (Total = 20 marks)

76 Hammer (6/10)   36 mins

Hammer is a large garden equipment supplier with retail stores throughout Toolland. Many of the products it sells are bought in from outside suppliers but some are currently manufactured by Hammer's own manufacturing division 'Nail'.

The prices (a transfer price) that Nail charges to the retail stores are set by head office and have been the subject of some discussion. The current policy is for Nail to calculate the total variable cost of production and delivery and add 30% for profit. Nail argues that all costs should be taken into consideration, offering to reduce the mark-up on costs to 10% in this case. The retail stores are unhappy with the current pricing policy arguing that it results in prices that are often higher than comparable products available on the market.

Nail has provided the following information to enable a price comparison to be made of the two possible pricing policies for one of its products.

Garden shears

Steel: the shears have 0·4kg of high quality steel in the final product. The manufacturing process loses 5% of all steel put in. Steel costs $4,000 per tonne (1 tonne = 1,000kg)

Other materials: Other materials are bought in and have a list price of $3 per kg although Hammer secures a 10% volume discount on all purchases. The shears require 0·1kg of these materials.

The labour time to produce shears is 0·25 hours per unit and labour costs $10 per hour.

Variable overheads are absorbed at the rate of 150% of labour rates and fixed overheads are 80% of the variable overheads.

Delivery is made by an outsourced distributor that charges Nail $0·50 per garden shear for delivery.

Required

(a)   Calculate the price that Nail would charge for the garden shears under the existing policy of variable cost plus 30%.   **(6 marks)**

(b)   Calculate the increase or decrease in price if the pricing policy switched to total cost plus 10%.   **(4 marks)**

(c)   Discuss whether or not including fixed costs in a transfer price is a sensible policy.   **(4 marks)**

(d)   Discuss whether the retail stores should be allowed to buy in from outside suppliers if the prices are cheaper than those charged by Nail.   **(6 marks)**

(Total = 20 marks)

77 All Premier Services (FMC, 12/01, amended)   36 mins

All Premier Services is a fee charging hospital that has two specialist wards, X and Y. A third ward, Z, is used for patients who are well enough to leave wards X and Y but who require a short period of hospital rest before being discharged. It is intended that ward Z will be only occupied by patients transferred from the other wards. Budgeted details relating to the wards are as follows (fixed and variable costs are for a complete week):

Ward:	X	Y	Z
Number of beds	60	40	45
Budgeted fee per bed per night ($)	225	200	170
Budgeted occupancy %	65	80	100
Budgeted costs:	$		
Fixed overheads	127,300		
Variable overheads	42,412		

Fixed overheads are allocated to the wards on the basis of the number of beds available in each ward. Variable overheads are allocated to beds in proportion to the fees earned per ward.

Required

(a)   (i)   Prepare a budgeted income statement (based on one week) for each of the wards and for the three wards combined. Calculate the total cost incurred per bed occupied per week (seven nights).

                                                                                                                          (5 marks)

        (ii)   A proposal has been put forward to increase the number of beds in ward Z to 75. This proposal would be expected to increase occupancy in wards X and Y to 80% and 95%, respectively. Budgeted occupancy in ward Z will remain at 100%. It is expected that total variable overheads would increase to $57,881 as a result.

                Evaluate this proposal on the same basis as your answer to part (a) (i).   **(5 marks)**

(b)   (i)   Describe the characteristics of a responsibility accounting system and discuss what factors exist in non-profit organisations that make responsibility accounting difficult to implement.   **(6 marks)**

        (ii)   Suggest alternative measures for ward performance at All Premier Services.   **(4 marks)**

                                                                                                                  (Total = 20 marks)

78 Woodside (FMC, 6/07, amended)

Woodside is a local charity dedicated to helping homeless people in a large city. The charity owns and manages a shelter that provides free overnight accommodation for up to 30 people, offers free meals each and every night of the year to homeless people who are unable to buy food, and runs a free advice centre to help homeless people find suitable housing and gain financial aid. Woodside depends entirely on public donations to finance its activities and had a fundraising target for the last year of $700,000. The budget for the last year was based on the following forecast activity levels and expected costs:

Free meals provision: 18,250 meals at $5 per meal
Overnight shelter: 10,000 bed-nights at $30 per night
Advice centre: 3,000 sessions at $20 per session
Campaigning and advertising: $150,000

The budgeted surplus (budgeted fundraising target less budgeted costs) was expected to be used to meet any unexpected costs. Included in the above figures are fixed costs of $5 per night for providing shelter and $5 per advice session representing fixed costs expected to be incurred by administration and maintaining the shelter. The number of free meals provided and the number of beds occupied each night depends on both the weather and the season of the year. The Woodside charity has three full-time staff and a large number of voluntary helpers.

The actual costs for the last year were as follows:

Free meals provision: 20,000 meals at a variable cost of $104,000
Overnight shelter: 8,760 bed-nights at a variable cost of $223,380
Advice centre: 3,500 sessions at a variable cost of $61,600
Campaigning and advertising: $165,000

The actual costs of the overnight shelter and the advice centre exclude the fixed costs of administration and maintenance, which were $83,000.

The actual amount of funds raised in the last year was $620,000.

Required

(a) Prepare an operating statement, reconciling budgeted surplus and actual shortfall and discuss the charity's performance over the last year. **(12 marks)**

(b) Discuss problems that may arise in the financial management and control of a not-for-profit organisation such as the Woodside charity. **(8 marks)**

(Total = 20 marks)

79 Trenset Co

Trenset Co has a semi-automated machine process in which a number of tasks are performed. The process is controlled by machine minders who are paid a fixed rate per hour of process time.

The nature of the process is such that the machines incur variable costs even during non-productive (idle time) hours. Non-productive hours include time spent on the rework of products. *Note that gross machine hours = productive hours + non-productive (idle time) hours.*

The standard data for the machine process are as follows.

(i) Standard non-productive (idle time) hours as a percentage of gross machine hours is 10%.

(ii) Standard variable machine cost per gross hour is $270.

(iii) Standard output productivity is 100% ie one standard hour of work is expected in each productive machine hour.

(iv) Machine costs are charged to production output at a rate per standard hour sufficient to absorb the cost of the standard level of non-productive time.

Trenset uses activity based costing to charge overheads to its products. One of the biggest overheads is the cost of order handling which is allocated according to the number of customer orders. Budgeted order costs are $28,000 per month and Trenset has the capacity to handle 500 orders per month.

Actual data for the past month has been summarised as follows:

Standard hours of output achieved	3,437
Machine hours (gross)	3,800
Non-productive machine hours	430
Variable machine costs ($'000)	1,070
Number of customer orders	380
Costs of order handling ($)	27,360

Required

(a) Explain what is meant by idle time and how it can be accounted for. **(3 marks)**

(b) Calculate the machine variances for excess idle time and expenditure for the past month. **(3 marks)**

(c) Explain the problems involved in using standard times for output where a learning effect is taking place. **(4 marks)**

(d) Calculate the overhead expenditure variance relating to the order handling activity and explain how fixed overhead variance analysis differs between an activity based costing system and a traditional approach. **(5 marks)**

(e) Explain what is meant by the controllability principle and its implications for a company such as Trenset Co. **(5 marks)**

(Total = 20 marks)

80 The Western (12/09) 36 mins

The Western is a local government organisation responsible for waste collection from domestic households. The new management accountant of The Western has decided to introduce some new forecasting techniques to improve the accuracy of the budgeting. The next budget to be produced is for the year ended 31 December 20X2.

Waste is collected by the tonne (T). The number of tonnes collected each year has been rising and by using time series analysis the new management accountant has produced the following relationship between the tonnes collected (T) and the time period in question Q (where Q is a quarter number. So Q = 1 represents quarter 1 in 20X1 and Q = 2 represents quarter 2 in 20X1 and so on)

$T = 2,000 + 25Q$

Each quarter is subject to some seasonal variation with more waste being collected in the middle quarters of each year. The adjustments required to the underlying trend prediction are:

Quarter	Tonnes
1	-200
2	+250
3	+150
4	-100

Once T is predicted the new management accountant hopes to use the values to predict the variable operating costs and fixed operating costs that The Western will be subjected to in 20X2. To this end he has provided the following operating cost data for 20X1.

Volume of waste	Total operating cost in 20X1 (fixed +variable)
Tonnes	$'000s
2,100	950
2,500	1,010
2,400	1,010
2,300	990

Inflation on the operating cost is expected to be 5% between 20X1 and 20X2.

The regression formula is shown on the formula sheet.

Required

(a)   Calculate the tonnes of waste to be expected in the calendar year 20X2.   **(4 marks)**

(b)   Calculate the variable operating cost and fixed operating cost to be expected in 20X2 using regression
       analysis on the 20X1 data and allowing for inflation as appropriate.   **(10 marks)**

Many local government organisations operate incremental budgeting as one of their main budgeting techniques.

They take a previous period's actual spend, adjust for any known changes to operations and then add a % for
expected inflation in order to set the next period's budget.

(c)   Describe two advantages and two disadvantages of a local government organisation funded by taxpayer's
       money using incremental budgeting as its main budgeting technique.   **(6 marks)**

(Total = 20 marks)

81 Preston Financial Services (Pilot paper, amended)   36 mins

The following information relates to Preston Financial Services, an accounting practice. The business specialises in
providing accounting and taxation work for dentists and doctors. In the main the clients are wealthy, self-employed
and have an average age of 52.

The business was founded by and is wholly owned by Richard Preston, a dominant and aggressive sole
practitioner. He feels that promotion of new products to his clients would be likely to upset the conservative nature
of his dentists and doctors and, as a result, the business has been managed with similar products year on year.

You have been provided with financial information relating to the practice in appendix 1. In appendix 2, you have
been provided with non-financial information which is based on the balanced scorecard format.

Appendix 1: Financial information

	Current year	Previous year
Turnover ($'000)	945	900
Net profit ($'000)	187	180
Average cash balances ($'000)	21	20
Average debtor/trade receivables days (industry average 30 days)	18 days	22 days
Inflation rate (%)	3	3

Appendix 2: Balanced Scorecard (extract)
Internal Business Processes

	Current year	Previous year
Error rates in jobs done	16%	10%
Average job completion time	7 weeks	10 weeks

Customer Knowledge

	Current year	Previous year
Number of customers	1,220	1,500
Average fee levels ($)	775	600
Market Share	14%	20%

Learning and Growth

	Current year	Previous year
Percentage of revenue from non-core work	4%	5%
Industry average of the proportion of revenue from non-core work in accounting practices	30%	25%
Employee retention rate	60%	80%

(1) Error rates measure the number of jobs with mistakes made by staff as a proportion of the number of clients serviced

(2) Core work is defined as being accountancy and taxation. Non-core work is defined primarily as pension advice and business consultancy. Non core work is traditionally high margin work

Required

(a) Using the information in appendix 1 only, comment on the financial performance of the business (briefly consider growth, profitability, liquidity and credit management). **(5 marks)**

(b) Explain why non financial information, such as the type shown in appendix 2, is likely to give a better indication of the likely future success of the business than the financial information given in appendix 1. **(5 marks)**

(c) Using the data given in appendix 2 comment on the performance of the business. Include comments on internal business processes, customer knowledge and learning/growth, separately, and provide a concluding comment on the overall performance of the business. **(10 marks)**

(Total = 20 marks)

82 Ties Only Limited (12/07) 36 mins

Ties Only Limited is a new business, selling high quality imported men's ties via the internet. The managers, who also own the company, are young and inexperienced but they are prepared to take risks. They are confident that importing quality ties and selling via a website will be successful and that the business will grow quickly. This is despite the well recognised fact that selling clothing is a very competitive business.

They were prepared for a loss-making start and decided to pay themselves modest salaries (included in administration expenses in Table 1 below) and pay no dividends for the foreseeable future.

The owners are so convinced that growth will quickly follow that they have invested enough money in website server development to ensure that the server can handle the very high levels of predicted growth. All website development costs were written off as incurred in the internal management accounts that are shown below in Table 1.

Significant expenditure on marketing was incurred in the first two quarters to launch both the website and new products. It is not expected that marketing expenditure will continue to be as high in the future.

Customers can buy a variety of styles, patterns and colours of ties at different prices.

The business's trading results for the first two quarters of trade are shown below in Table 1.

Table 1

	Quarter 1		Quarter 2	
	$	$	$	$
Sales		420,000		680,000
less Cost of Sales		(201,600)		(340,680)
Gross Profit		218,400		339,320
less expenses				
Website development	120,000		90,000	
Administration	100,500		150,640	
Distribution	20,763		33,320	
Launch marketing	60,000		40,800	
Other variable expenses	50,000		80,000	
Total expenses		(351,263)		(394,760)
Loss for quarter		(132,863)		(55,440)

(a) Assess the financial performance of the business during its first two quarters using only the data in Table 1 above. **(10 marks)**

(b) Briefly consider whether the losses made by the business in the first two quarters are a true reflection of the current and likely future performance of the business. **(3 marks)**

The owners are well aware of the importance of non-financial indicators of success and therefore have identified a small number of measures to focus on. These are measured monthly and then combined to produce a quarterly management report.

The data for the first two quarters management reports is shown below:

Table 2

	Quarter 1	Quarter 2
Number of ties sold	27,631	38,857
On time delivery	95%	89%
Sales returns	12%	18%
System downtime	2%	4%

The industry average for sales returns was 13%.

Required

(c) Comment on each of the non-financial data in Table 2 above taking into account, where appropriate, the industry averages provided, providing your assessment of the performance of the business. **(7 marks)**

(Total = 20 marks)

83 Jump (6/10)   36 mins

Jump has a network of sports clubs which is managed by local managers reporting to the main board. The local managers have a lot of autonomy and are able to vary employment contracts with staff and offer discounts for membership fees and personal training sessions. They also control their own maintenance budget but do not have control over large amounts of capital expenditure.

A local manager's performance and bonus is assessed relative to three targets. For every one of these three targets that is reached in an individual quarter, $400 is added to the manager's bonus, which is paid at the end of the year. The maximum bonus per year is therefore based on 12 targets (three targets in each of the four quarters of the year). Accordingly the maximum bonus that could be earned is 12 x $400 = $4,800, which represents 40% of the basic salary of a local manager. Jump has a 31 March year end.

The performance data for one of the sports clubs for the last four quarters is as follows.

	Qtr to 30 June 20X9	Qtr to 30 September 20X9	Qtr to 31 December 20X9	Qtr to 31 March 20Y0
Number of members	3,000	3,200	3,300	3,400
Member visits	20,000	24,000	26,000	24,000
Personal training sessions booked	310	325	310	339
Staff days	450	480	470	480
Staff lateness days	20	28	28	20
Days in quarter	90	90	90	90

Agreed targets are:

(1) Staff must be on time over 95% of the time (no penalty is made when staff are absent from work)
(2) On average 60% of members must use the clubs' facilities regularly by visiting at least 12 times per quarter
(3) On average 10% of members must book a personal training session each quarter

Required

(a) Calculate the amount of bonus that the manager should expect to be paid for the latest financial year.

(6 marks)

(b) Discuss to what extent the targets set are controllable by the local manager (you are required to make a case for both sides of the argument).

(9 marks)

(c) Describe two methods as to how a manager with access to the accounting and other records could unethically manipulate the situation so as to gain a greater bonus.

(5 marks)

(Total = 20 marks)

84 The Accountancy Teaching Co (12/10)   36 mins

The Accountancy Teaching Co (AT Co) is a company specialising in the provision of accountancy tuition courses in the private sector. It makes up its accounts to 30 November each year. In the year ending 30 November 20X9, it held 60% of market share. However, over the last twelve months, the accountancy tuition market in general has faced a 20% decline in demand for accountancy training leading to smaller class sizes on courses. In 20X9 and before, AT Co suffered from an ongoing problem with staff retention, which had a knock-on effect on the quality of service provided to students. Following the completion of developments that have been ongoing for some time, in 20Y0 the company was able to offer a far-improved service to students. The developments included:

- A new dedicated 24 hour student helpline
- An interactive website providing instant support to students
- A new training programme for staff
- An electronic student enrolment system
- An electronic marking system for the marking of students' progress tests. The costs of marking electronically were expected to be $4 million less in 20Y0 than marking on paper. Marking expenditure is always included in cost of sales

Extracts from the management accounts for 20X9 and 20Y0 are shown below:

	20X9		20Y0	
	$'000	$'000	$'000	$'000
Turnover		72,025		66,028
Cost of sales		(52,078)		(42,056)
Gross profit		19,947		23,972
Indirect expenses:				
Marketing	3,291		4,678	
Property	6,702		6,690	
Staff training	1,287		3,396	
Interactive website running costs	–		3,270	
Student helpline running costs	–		2,872	
Enrolment costs	5,032		960	
Total indirect expenses		(16,312)		(21,866)
Net operating profit		3,635		2,106

On 1 December 20X9, management asked all 'freelance lecturers' to reduce their fees by at least 10% with immediate effect ('freelance lecturers' are not employees of the company but are used to teach students when there are not enough of AT Co's own lecturers to meet tuition needs). All employees were also told that they would not receive a pay rise for at least one year. Total lecture staff costs (including freelance lecturers) were $41.663 million in 20X9 and were included in cost of sales, as is always the case. Freelance lecturer costs represented 35% of these total lecture staff costs. In 20Y0 freelance lecture costs were $12.394 million. No reduction was made to course prices in the year and the mix of trainees studying for the different qualifications remained the same. The same type and number of courses were run in both 20X9 and 20Y0 and the percentage of these courses that was run by freelance lecturers as opposed to employed staff also remained the same.

Due to the nature of the business, non-financial performance indicators are also used to assess performance, as detailed below.

	20X9	20Y0
Percentage of students transferring to AT Co from another training provider	8%	20%
Number of late enrolments due to staff error	297	106
Percentage of students passing exams first time	48%	66%
Labour turnover	32%	10%
Number of student complaints	315	84
Average no. of employees	1,080	1,081

Required

Assess the performance of the business in 20Y0 using both financial performance indicators calculated from the above information AND the non-financial performance indicators provided.

Note: Clearly state any assumptions and show all workings clearly. Your answer should be structured around the following main headings: turnover; cost of sales; gross profit; indirect expenses; net operating profit. However, in discussing each of these areas you should also refer to the non-financial performance indicators, where relevant.

(20 marks)

85 Bridgewater Co (6/08, amended)　　　　　　　**36 mins**

Bridgewater Co provides training courses for many of the mainstream software packages on the market.

The business has many divisions within Waterland, the one country in which it operates. The senior managers of Bridgewater Co have very clear objectives for the divisions and these are communicated to divisional managers on appointment and subsequently in quarterly and annual reviews. These are:

- Each quarter, sales should grow and annual sales should exceed budget
- Trainer (lecture staff) costs should not exceed $180 per teaching day
- Room hire costs should not exceed $90 per teaching day
- Each division should meet its budget for profit per quarter and annually

It is known that managers will be promoted based on their ability to meet these targets. A member of the senior management is to retire after quarter 2 of the current financial year, which has just begun. The divisional managers anticipate that one of them may be promoted at the beginning of quarter 3 if their performance is good enough.

The manager of the Northwest division is concerned that his chances of promotion could be damaged by the expected performance of his division. He is a firm believer in quality and he thinks that if a business gets this right, growth and success will eventually follow.

The current quarterly forecasts, along with the original budgeted profit for the Northwest division, are as follows:

	Q1 $'000	Q2 $'000	Q3 $'000	Q4 $'000	Total $'000
Sales	40.0	36.0	50.0	60.0	186.0
less:					
Trainers	8.0	7.2	10.0	12.0	37.2
Room hire	4.0	3.6	5.0	6.0	18.6
Staff training	1.0	1.0	1.0	1.0	4.0
Other costs	3.0	1.7	6.0	7.0	17.7
Forecast net profit	24.0	22.5	28.0	34.0	108.5
Original budgeted profit	25.0	26.0	27.0	28.0	106.0
Annual sales budget					180.0
Teaching days	40	36	50	60	

Required

(a)   Assess the financial performance of the Northwest division against its targets and reach a conclusion as to the promotion prospects of the divisional manager.   **(8 marks)**

The manager of the Northwest division has been considering a few steps to improve the performance of his division.

Voucher scheme

As a sales promotion, vouchers will be sold for $125 each, a substantial discount on normal prices. These vouchers will entitle the holder to attend four training sessions on software of their choice. They can attend when they want to but are advised that one training session per quarter is sensible. The manager is confident that if the promotion took place immediately, he could sell 80 vouchers and that customers would follow the advice given to attend one session per quarter. All voucher holders would attend planned existing courses and all will be new customers.

Software upgrade

A new important software programme has recently been launched for which there could be a market for training courses. Demonstration programs can be bought for $1,800 in quarter 1. Staff training would be needed, costing $500 in each of quarters 1 and 2 but in quarters 3 and 4 extra courses could be offered selling this training. Assuming similar class sizes and the usual sales prices, extra sales revenue amounting to 20% of normal sales are expected (measured before the voucher promotion above). The manager is keen to run these courses at the same tutorial and room standards as he normally provides. Software expenditure is written off in the income statement as incurred.

Delaying payments to trainers

The manager is considering delaying payment to the trainers. He thinks that, since his commitment to quality could cause him to miss out on a well deserved promotion, the trainers owe him a favour. He intends to delay payment on 50% of all invoices received from the trainers in the first two quarters, paying them one month later than is usual.

Required

(b)   Revise the forecasts to take account of all three of the proposed changes.   **(6 marks)**

(c)   Comment on each of the proposed steps and reach a conclusion as to whether, if all the proposals were taken together, the manager will improve his chances of promotion.   **(6 marks)**

(Total = 20 marks)

86 PC (12/08, amended)   36 mins

Pace Company (PC) runs a large number of wholesale stores and is increasing the number of these stores all the time. It measures the performance of each store on the basis of a target return on investment (ROI) of 15%. Store managers get a bonus of 10% of their salary if their store's annual ROI exceeds the target each year. Once a store is built there is very little further capital expenditure until a full four years have passed.

PC has a store (store W) in the west of the country. Store W has historic financial data as follows over the past four years.

	20X5	20X6	20X7	20X8
Sales ($'000)	200	200	180	170
Gross profit ($'000)	80	70	63	51
Net profit ($'000)	13	14	10	8
Net assets at start of year ($'000)	100	80	60	40

The market in which PC operates has been growing steadily. Typically, PC's stores generate a 40% gross profit margin.

Required

(a)   Discuss the past financial performance of store W using ROI and any other measure you feel appropriate and, using your findings, discuss whether the ROI correctly reflects Store W's actual performance.

(8 marks)

(b)   Explain how a manager in store W might have been able to manipulate the results so as to gain bonuses
       more frequently.   **(4 marks)**

PC has another store (store S) about to open in the south of the country. It has asked you for help in calculating the gross profit, net profit and ROI it can expect over each of the next four years. The following information is provided:

Sales volume in the first year will be 18,000 units. Sales volume will grow at the rate of 10% for years two and three but no further growth is expected in year 4. Sales price will start at $12 per unit for the first two years but then reduce by 5% per annum for each of the next two years.

Gross profit will start at 40% but will reduce as the sales price reduces. All purchase prices on goods for resale will remain constant for the four years.

Overheads, including depreciation, will be $70,000 for the first two years rising to $80,000 in years three and four.

Store S requires an investment of $100,000 at the start of its first year of trading.

PC depreciates non-current assets at the rate of 25% of cost. No residual value is expected on these assets.

Required

(c)   Calculate (in columnar form) the revenue, gross profit, net profit and ROI of store S over each of its first four
       years.   **(8 marks)**

(Total = 20 marks)

87 Oliver's Salon (6/09)   **36 mins**

Oliver is the owner and manager of Oliver's Salon which is a quality hairdresser that experiences high levels of competition. The salon traditionally provided a range of hair services to female clients only, including cuts, colouring and straightening.

A year ago, at the start of his 20X9 financial year, Oliver decided to expand his operations to include the hairdressing needs of male clients. Male hairdressing prices are lower, the work simpler (mainly hair cuts only) and so the time taken per male client is much less.

The prices for the female clients were not increased during the whole of 20X8 and 20X9 and the mix of services provided for female clients in the two years was the same.

The latest financial results are as follows:

	20X8		20X9	
	$	$	$	$
Sales		200,000		238,500
Less cost of sales:				
Hairdressing staff costs	65,000		91,000	
Hair products– female	29,000		27,000	
Hair products – male			8,000	
		94,000		126,000
Gross profit		106,000		112,500
Less expenses:				
Rent	10,000		10,000	
Administration salaries	9,000		9,500	
Electricity	7,000		8,000	
Advertising	2,000		5,000	
Total expenses		28,000		32,500
Profit		78,000		80,000

Oliver is disappointed with his financial results. He thinks the salon is much busier than a year ago and was expecting more profit. He has noted the following extra information:

Some female clients complained about the change in atmosphere following the introduction of male services, which created tension in the salon.

Two new staff were recruited at the start of 20X9. The first was a junior hairdresser to support the specialist hairdressers for the female clients. She was appointed on a salary of $9,000 per annum. The second new staff member was a specialist hairdresser for the male clients. There were no increases in pay for existing staff at the start of 20X9 after a big rise at the start of 20X8 which was designed to cover two years' worth of increases.

Oliver introduced some non-financial measures of success two years ago.

	20X8	20X9
Number of complaints	12	46
Number of male client visits	0	3,425
Number of female client visits	8,000	6,800
Number of specialist hairdressers for female clients	4	5
Number of specialist hairdressers for male clients	0	1

Required

(a) Calculate the average price for hair services per male and female client for each of the years 20X8 and 20X9.
(3 marks)

(b) Assess the financial performance of the Salon using the data above. **(11 marks)**

(c) Analyse and comment on the non-financial performance of Oliver's business, under the headings of quality and resource utilisation. **(6 marks)**

(Total = 20 marks)

88 Thatcher International Park (12/09) 36 mins

Thatcher International Park (TIP) is a theme park and has for many years been a successful business, which has traded profitably. About three years ago the directors decided to capitalise on their success and reduced the expenditure made on new thrill rides, reduced routine maintenance where possible (deciding instead to repair equipment when it broke down) and made a commitment to regularly increase admission prices. Once an admission price is paid customers can use any of the facilities and rides for free.

These steps increased profits considerably, enabling good dividends to be paid to the owners and bonuses to the directors. The last two years of financial results are shown below.

	20X1	20X2
	$	$
Sales	5,250,000	5,320,000
Less Expenses		
Wages	2,500,000	2,200,000
Maintenance – routine	80,000	70,000
Repairs	260,000	320,000
Directors salaries	150,000	160,000
Directors bonuses	15,000	18,000
Other costs (including depreciation)	1,200,000	1,180,000
Net profit	1,045,000	1,372,000
Book value of assets at start of year	13,000,000	12,000,000
Dividend paid	500,000	650,000
Number of visitors	150,000	140,000

Required

(a) Assess the financial performance of TIP using the information given above. **(14 marks)**

During the early part of 20X1 TIP employed a newly qualified management accountant. He quickly became concerned about the potential performance of TIP and to investigate his concerns he started to gather data to measure some non-financial measures of success. The data he has gathered is shown below:

	20X1	*20X2*
Hours lost due to breakdown of rides (see note 1)	9,000 hours	32,000 hours
Average waiting time per ride	20 minutes	30 minutes

Note 1: TIP has 50 rides of different types. It is open 360 days of the year for 10 hours each day

(b) Assess the *quality* of the service that TIP provides to its customers using Table 1 and any other relevant data and indicate the *risks* it is likely to face if it continues with its current policies. **(6 marks)**

(Total = 20 marks)

Answers

1 Preparation question: Cassiop

(a) **Fixed overhead absorption rate**

The first step is to **calculate the fixed overhead absorption rates for each period on the basis of budgeted figures.**

	Period 1	Period 2	Period 3
Budgeted fixed overhead	$10,400	$19,170	$17,360
Budgeted production in units	8,000	14,200	12,400
Fixed overhead absorption rate per unit	$1.30	$1.35	$1.40

These can now be used to determine the amount of fixed overhead absorbed each period (fixed overhead absorption rate × actual number of units produced). By **comparing the fixed overhead absorbed with the actual overhead, the under or over recovery of overhead can be calculated.**

	Period 1	Period 2	Period 3
Fixed overhead absorbed	$(8,400 \times \$1.30)$ 10,920	$(13,600 \times \$1.35)$ 18,360	$(9,200 \times \$1.40)$ 12,880
Actual fixed overhead	11,200	18,320	16,740
(Under-)/over-recovered overhead	(280)	40	(3,860)
Effect on profit	Reduce	Increase	Reduce

(b) **Use of marginal costing**

In marginal costing, inventories are valued at variable production cost whereas in absorption costing they are valued at their full production cost (in other words, including fixed production overhead). Consequently **if the amount of fixed overhead included in opening and closing inventory values differ, the reported profits under the two systems will also differ. If the fixed overhead included in closing inventory is less than that in opening inventory** then more overhead than that actually incurred will be included in the profit calculation and hence **profit under absorption costing will be lower than that under marginal costing** (in marginal costing only overheads incurred being included in the profit calculation). If the fixed overhead included in closing inventory is higher than that in opening inventory then absorption costing will report the higher profit.

Effect on profit

An assessment of the effect on profit of using absorption or marginal costing by Cassiop Co can be made as follows.

	Period 0 Units	Period 1 Units	Period 2 Units	Period 3 Units
Opening inventory		2,600	1,400	2,600
Production		8,400	13,600	9,200
Sales		(9,600)	(12,400)	(10,200)
Closing inventory	2,600	1,400	2,600	1,600

	$	$	$	$
Fixed o/hd absorbed per unit		1.30	1.35	1.40
Fixed o/hd absorbed in closing inventory	3,315	1,820	3,510	2,240
Fixed o/hd absorbed in opening inventory		3,315	1,820	3,510
Fixed o/hd absorbed taken to P&L a/c		1,495	1,690	1,270

The fixed overhead absorbed in opening inventory is higher than that absorbed in closing inventory in periods 1 and 3. Absorption costing will therefore show a lower profit than marginal costing in periods 1 and 3 but a higher profit in period 2.

(c) **Aim of absorption costing**

The **aim of absorption costing is to produce a product cost which ensures that overheads incurred during a period are recovered** via the inclusion of a share of overhead in each unit of output. Its principal aim is not, therefore, to produce accurate product costs.

Subjective judgements

The determination of absorption costing product costs **depends on a great deal of subjective judgement and hence, due to the requirement of accurate product costs for decision making, it is totally unsuitable for decision making. Areas of absorption costing requiring subjective judgement** include the following.

(i) **Estimates**
Costs directly allocated to cost centres are only estimates made during the budgeting process and the overhead absorbed into products will depend on these estimates.

(ii) **Methods of apportionment**
There is often **more than one method for apportioning an overhead** to a cost centre, the choice of method being at the discretion of, for example, the management accountant. The cost of the stores function could be apportioned to production departments on the basis of the number of issues made to departments or on the level of inventory held for each department.

(iii) **Recovery rate**
The **choice of recovery rate** (labour hours, percentage of prime cost and so on) will affect the amount of overhead absorbed per product and hence the product cost.

(iv) **Denominator of absorption rate**
The denominator of the absorption rate (direct labour hours, machine hours and so on) is a budgeted figure.

(v) **Research and development**
In some absorption costing systems the full cost of areas such as research and development and administration may be absorbed into product costs. In other systems the costs may be written off directly to the profit and loss account.

(vi) **Use of estimates**
All of the costs (and activity levels) included in the calculation of the amount of overhead to be included in each product **are based on estimates**. Such estimates are based on assumptions about the environment in which the organisation operates.

Example

It is not just the inaccuracy of the resulting product cost which makes absorption costing information unsuitable for decision making, however. Consider the following example.

Suppose that a sales manager has **an item of product** which he is having difficulty in selling. Its **historical full cost is $80**, made up of **variable costs of $50 and fixed costs of $30. A customer offers $60** for it.

(i) **If there is no other customer** for the product, $60 would be better than nothing and the **product should be sold to improve income and profit** by this amount.

(ii) If the company has **spare production capacity** which would otherwise not be used, it would be **profitable to continue making more** of the same product, if customers are willing to pay $60 for each extra unit made. This is because the additional costs are only $50 so that the profit would be increased marginally by $10 per unit produced.

(iii)   **In absorption costing terms, the product makes a loss of $20, which would discourage the sales manager from accepting a price of $60 from the customer. His decision would be a bad one.**

    (1)   If the product is not sold for $60, it will presumably be scrapped eventually, so the **choice is really between making a loss in absorption costing terms of $20**, or a loss of **$80 when the inventory is written off**, whenever this happens.

    (2)   If there is demand for some extra units at $60 each, the absorption costing loss would be $20 per unit, but at the end of the year there would be an additional **contribution to overheads and profit of $10 per unit**. In terms of absorption costing the **under-absorbed overhead would be reduced by $30 for each extra unit made and sold**.

Thus, for **once-only decisions or decisions affecting the use of marginal spare capacity, absorption costing information about unit profits is** *irrelevant*. On the other hand, since total contribution must be sufficient to cover the fixed costs of the business, **marginal costing would be unsuitable as a basis for establishing** *long-term* **prices for all output**.

(d)   **Full cost absorption costing**

The advantages and disadvantages, including the motivational aspects, of the 'full cost' absorption costing method for dealing with the costs of internal services are as follows.

Advantages

(i)   **Recovery of service costs**
It attempts to ensure that the **costs of service departments will be recovered** by including a fair share of such costs in the various product costs.

(ii)   **Awareness of all costs**
It **makes managers aware of the less obvious costs** incurred in supporting their particular area of the organisation's operations and provides them with the incentive to encourage the managers of service departments to control their costs.

Disadvantages

(i)   **Demotivation of management**
Managers responsible for production may become demotivated if they feel they are being held accountable for costs that are outside their area of control.

(ii)   **Inter-departmental conflict**
The system may give rise to **inter-departmental conflict** if departmental managers feel that the way in which costs have been shared out is unfair.

(iii)   **Distortion of profits**
Where production departments are profit centres, their **profits may be distorted** by a subjective method of cost apportionment.

(iv)   **Outsourcing**
Managers of production departments may feel that it is in their interests to **source services from outside the organisation** to reduce their departmental costs, although it may be in the interests of the organisation as a whole to source services internally.

2 Linacre Co

Marking scheme

			Marks
(a)	ABC recovery rates		4
(b)	Cost drivers for Product ZT3	2	
	ABC overheads for Product ZT3	2	
	General overheads for Product ZT3	1	
	Total overhead per unit	1	
	Direct labour cost	1	
	Standard total unit cost	1	
	Standard selling price	1	9
(c)	Discussion of relevant issues		7
			20

(a) **ABC recovery rates for each cost pool**

Cost Pool	Cost ($)	Cost driver	Number of drivers	ABC recovery rate ($)
Production set ups	105,000	Set-ups	300	350 per set –up
Product testing	300,000	Tests	1,500	200 per test
Component supply and storage	25,000	Component orders	500	50 per order
Customer orders and delivery	112,500	Customer orders	1,000	112.50 per order

(b) **Total unit cost and selling price for Product ZT3**

Cost	Working	$/unit	
Component cost		1.00	Unit cost as stated
Direct labour	2	1.30	
General O/H	3	0.50	
Overheads	4	3.33	
Total unit cost		6.13	
Mark-up		2.45	At 40% of total unit cost
Selling price		8.58	

Workings

(1) **Orders.** 100 orders × 60 units + 60 orders × 50 units = 9,000 units

(2) 10 minutes per unit at $7.80 per hour = 10/60 × 7.80 = $1.30 per unit

(3) $900,000/300,000 = $3/direct labour hour

9,000/6 or 1,500 direct labour hours spent on manufacture (10 minutes per unit)

1,500 hours/9,000 units × $3/unit = $0.50/unit

(4) **Set ups.** 10 runs × 900 units each. So $350 × 10 annual cost = $3,500. Divide by 9,000 units gives $0.39/unit.

Product test. 4 tests per run × 10 runs = 40 tests. At $200/test = $8,000 annual cost. Divide by 9,000 units gives $0.89/unit.

Component supply. 1 order per run × 10 runs = 10 orders. At $50/order = $500 annual cost. Divide by 9,000 units gives $0.056/unit.

Customer supply. 160 orders × $112.50/order = $18,000 annual cost. Divide by 9,000 units gives $2/unit.

Total overhead costs from cost pools.

This is $(0.39 + 0.89 + 0.056 + 2) = $3.33/unit.

(c) **Reasons why ABC costing may be preferred to traditional absorption costing in a modern manufacturing environment**

ABC involves the identification of factors known as **cost drivers**, which drive the costs of an organisation's major activities. Support overheads are then charged to products on the basis of their usage of an activity. ABC has evolved as a response to the increase in **support activities** in modern organisations as well as the falling cost of processing information used in making management decisions. Modern organisations typically use **shorter production runs** and so the proportion of overhead costs to total costs has risen.

Absorption costing is a traditional system of costing which arose in organisations when most organisations made a smaller range of products and overheads represented a smaller proportion of costs. Although overheads are allocated to production, the basis is by **volume only** rather than looking at the underlying true cost activity. Volume bases might include labour hours or machine hours.

Therefore it appears that ABC might be a more suitable basis for apportioning costs in a modern manufacturing system. There are several reasons why this might be and these are as follows:

(i) Absorption costing uses **volume** as a basis for cost allocation. Therefore it tends to allocate too great a proportion of overheads to high volume products and too small to low volume products.

(ii) ABC uses several **bases** or **cost drivers** to apportion overheads and as such will more closely link overhead apportionment to the causes of overhead costs.

(iii) Therefore ABC recognises the **complexity** of manufacturing in its use of multiple cost drivers and so more detailed cost information is available.

(iv) ABC also enables a good understanding of what **drives** overhead costs as it accumulates a good deal of data for analysis. Therefore ABC can be used as an information source for budget planning based on activity rather than incremental budgeting.

(v) ABC also establishes a **long run product cost**.

3 Z Co

(a) (i) Budgeted annual total list price/total budgeted overheads $\dfrac{\$880,000}{\$8\,\text{million}} = \$0.11$

> **Top tips.** Under the current system customers are charged the list price of the drugs plus a charge for selling a distribution overheads based on the annual selling and distribution costs and the annual total list price of the drugs ordered. Every order will have a surcharge of $0.11 per $1 of list price of drugs supplied, for selling and distribution overheads.

Charge for selling and distribution overheads

Order A $1,200 × $0.11 = $132
Order B $900 × $0.11 = $99

(ii) **Activity based costing approach**

> **Top tips.** There are four components to the total selling and distribution overheads.
>
> Applying the correct cost driver to each of the overheads is the trickiest part of the question and the one that presented most problems to candidates.
>
> In allocating delivery overhead costs you need to take into account the number of packages each vehicle can take when filled to capacity.

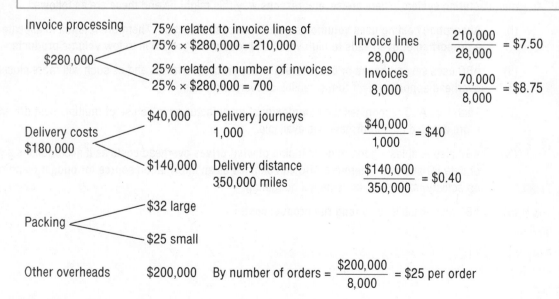

Invoice processing
$280,000
  75% related to invoice lines of
  75% × $280,000 = 210,000
  Invoice lines 28,000 $\dfrac{210,000}{28,000} = \$7.50$
  25% related to number of invoices
  25% × $280,000 = 700
  Invoices 8,000 $\dfrac{70,000}{8,000} = \$8.75$

Delivery costs $180,000
  $40,000 Delivery journeys 1,000 $\dfrac{\$40,000}{1,000} = \$40$
  $140,000 Delivery distance 350,000 miles $\dfrac{\$140,000}{350,000} = \$0.40$

Packing
  $32 large
  $25 small

Other overheads $200,000 By number of orders = $\dfrac{\$200,000}{8,000} = \$25$ per order

Overhead costs – Order A

	$
Invoice costs	
One invoice per order 1 × $8.75 = 8.75	8.75
Two invoice lines 2 × $7.50 = $7.50	15.00
Packing costs – small package	25.00
Delivery costs per journey 8 miles × $0.40 per mile	3.20
per package $40/12	3.33
Other overhead costs per order	25.00
	80.28

Overhead costs – Order B

	$
Invoice costs	
For one invoice 1 × $8.75	8.75
Eight invoice lines 8 × $7.50	60.00
Packaging costs – large package	32.00
Delivery costs per journey 40 miles × $0.40	16.00
per package 1 × $40/6	6.67
Other overhead costs per order	25.00
	148.42

(b) The current approach is **simple** and relatively **inexpensive** to operate. The charge for overheads though, does not reflect the actual costs incurred by each order.

A pricing policy that recovers overheads based on this simple approach is satisfactory where **all output can be sold**. However, it does not reflect the fact that some orders such as those with many different products and those delivered over a long distance are more expensive than orders with few products delivered over shorter distances.

ABC gives **a better understanding** of what drives overhead costs. By adopting ABC, Z Co will be able to set prices that **relate more closely** to actual overheads consumed.

However, ABC is a **costly** approach and the expense of identifying cost pools and appropriate cost drivers may exceed the expected benefits. It is also probably **too complex** to be practicable as a pricing system.

A new pricing strategy

It is recommended that Z develops a **pricing structure** that would enable the key cost drivers to be reflected in the charge over and above the list price.

The company may consider several options in respect of the high costs of long distance deliveries. For example, deliveries may be undertaken only within a certain radius. Long distance ones may be outsourced, or an extra high charge imposed. The extra cost of multiple invoice lines needs further investigation. Customers could be informed of an additional charge relating to multiple orders.

Care must be taken to avoid losing customers if competitors are able to offer cheaper terms.

4 Triple

Text references. Absorption costing is revised in Chapter 1 and activity based costing is covered in Chapter 2a.

Top tips. Parts (a) and (b) require methodical, clear calculations with all of your workings shown so that you can gain as many marks as possible. Make sure you refer to the specific circumstances of Triple Limited in part (c).

Easy marks. Part (a) is a very easy 3 marks and a clear layout for the calculations in part (b) will gain you marks for workings even if you cannot complete all of it.

		Marks
(a)	For each product	1
	Total	3
(b)	Total machine hours	2
	Cost per driver calculation	3
	Overheads split by product table	4
	Cost per unit calculation	3
		12
(c)	Explanation	5
		20

(a) Traditional cost per unit

	Product D	Product C	Product P
	$	$	$
Material	20	12	25
Labour @$6 per hour	3	9	6
Direct costs	23	21	31
Production overhead @ $28 per machine hour	42	28	84
Total production cost per unit	65	49	115

(b) Total machine hours (needed as the driver for machining overhead)

Product	Hours/unit	Production units	Total hours
D	1½	750	1,125
C	1	1,250	1,250
P	3	7,000	21,000
Total machine hours			23,375

Analysis of total overheads and cost per unit of activity

Type of overhead	Driver	%	Total overhead $	Level of driver activity	Cost/driver
Set-ups	Number of set-ups	35	229,075	670	341.90
Machining	Machine hours	20	130,900	23,375	5.60
Materials handling	Material movements	15	98,175	120	818.13
Inspection	Number of inspections	30	196,350	1,000	196.35
		100	654,000		

Total overheads by product and per unit

Overhead	Product D Activity	Cost $	Product C Activity	Cost $	Product P Activity	Cost $	Total Activity	Cost $
Set-ups	75	25,643	115	39,319	480	164,113	670	229,075
Machining	1,125	6,300	1,250	7,000	21,000	117,600	23,375	130,900
Material handling	12	9,817	21	17,181	87	71,177	120	98,175
Inspection	150	29,453	180	35,343	670	131,554	1,000	196,350
Total overhead cost		71,213		98,843		484,444		654,500
Units produced		750		1,250		7,000		
Costs per unit		$94.95		$79.07		$69.21		

Cost per unit

	D	C	P
	$	$	$
Direct costs (from (a))	23.00	21.00	31.00
Overheads	94.95	79.07	69.21
	117.95	100.07	100.21

(c)   **Summary**

	Product D	Product C	Product P
Production units	750	1,250	7,000
Conventional overhead cost	$42	$28	$84
ABC overhead cost	$95	$79	$69

This table shows that overheads for products D and C are **higher** using activity based costing and those of product P are **lower.** This reflects the different **volume** of activities involved in making each product. Using conventional costing, product P absorbs a high proportion of overheads as it takes more machine hours to produce and it is a high volume product. However, machinery costs are only 20% of total overheads so this does not fairly reflect the costs involved in making this product.

Products D and C are much lower volume products so, in order to compare the activities involved for each product, it would be useful to calculate the activity per unit for each product. In order to make the numbers easier to read, the following table calculates the activity per 1,000 units.

	Set-ups	Material movements	Inspections
Product D	100	16	200
Product C	92	17	144
Product P	69	12	96

Product P has less set-ups, material movements and inspections per 1,000 units than D or C. Therefore overheads for P calculated using ABC are **lower** than those calculated using conventional costing. The machining overhead, although still high for Product P, is a smaller proportion of total overhead using ABC.

In contrast, overheads for products C and D are **higher** using ABC as it more accurately reflects their higher volume of set-ups, material movements and inspections.

5 Brick by Brick

Text references. Absorption and marginal costing are covered in Chapter 1 and activity based costing is covered in Chapter 2A. Pricing decisions are covered in Chapter 5.

Top tips. Read the question carefully. Parts (a) and (b) require the cost <u>and</u> the quoted price. Make sure that you relate your answers to part (c) and (d) to the scenario.

Easy marks. There are 10 marks available for calculating the cost and quoted price of the GC and EC using absorption costing and ABC.

Examiner's comments. Many candidates scored highly in parts (a) and (b), demonstrating a good understanding of the area. Answers to part (c) tended to be repetition of paragraphs learnt from textbooks rather than actually giving thought to the question and thinking about what pricing strategies would really be suitable. For example, to suggest 'market skimming' was hardly appropriate for a company that is struggling with sales. Good answers to part (c) were hard to find.

Part (d) was similarly not well answered. The main points it was looking for were that marginal cost plus pricing is simpler than full cost plus pricing and takes away some of the uncertainty that unknown sales volumes cause when using full cost plus pricing. If marginal cost plus pricing is used, however, the mark up must be sufficiently high to cover both the company's fixed cost and also its required profit. This latter point should have been obvious but was mentioned by a minority of candidates.

			Marks
(a)	Materials	1	
	Labour	1	
	OAR	1	
	Overhead costs per unit	1	
	Price	1	
			5
(b)	Materials	½	
	Labour	½	
	Overheads per unit per category (3 categories)	3	
	Price	1	
			5
(c)	GC reduce price by 7%	1	
	GC reduce by < 7%	1	
	Quality, reputation, reliability, sales documentation quality	2	
	EX increase price by 2%	1	
	EX hold price	1	
			6
(d)	MC and TAC definitions	1	
		2	
		1	
			4
			20

(a) **Costs and quoted prices for the GC and the EX using labour hours to absorb overheads**

		GC	EX
		$	$
Materials		3,500	8,000
Labour	300hrs× $15/hr	4,500	
	500hrs × $15/hr		7,500
Overheads	300hrs× $10/hr (W1)	3,000	
	500hrs × $10/hr		5,000
Total cost		11,000	20,500
Quoted price (× 150%)		16,500	30,750

Workings

(1) **Overhead absorption rate** is calculated as $400,000/40,000hrs = $10/hr

(b) **Costs and quoted prices for the GC and the EX using ABC to absorb overheads**

		GC	EX
		$	$
Materials		3,500	8,000
Labour	300hrs × $15/hr	4,500	
	500hrs × $15/hr		7,500
Overheads			
– Supervisors	(W2)/(W3)	180	1,080
– Planners	(W2)/(W3)	280	1,400
– Property	(W2)/(W3)	1,800	3,000
Total cost		10,260	20,980
Quoted price		15,390	31,470

Workings

2 **Cost drivers**

	Costs $	Number of drivers	Cost per driver
Supervisor	90,000	500	180
Planners	70,000	250	280
Property	240,000	40,000	6

3 **Cost per product**

	Supervisor	Planner	Property
Cost per driver (W2)	$180	$280	$6
GC	180 × 1 = 180	280 × 1 = 280	6 × 300 = 1,800
EX	180 × 6 = 1,080	280 × 5 = 1,400	6 × 500 = 3,000

(c) The poor sales of GC may be due to **ineffective marketing** and advertising by BBB. Consumers may not be aware that the company offer garage conversions (GC). Alternatively, the methods used by the sales team to generate interest in GC may be limited and even discourage customers from placing work with the company.

BBB's **reputation** could also **contribute** to the **poor sales** of GC. BBB may be renowned for being unreliable and providing poor customer service, particularly in relation to GC.

Addressing each of the above factors will require careful planning and investment and will not be solved by simply reducing prices.

BBB could **lower the price** of a GC by 7%, in proportion with the reduction in costs. This could make the company more **competitive**.

Alternatively BBB could choose to only pass on 3% of the cost reduction to the customer. This will **increase the margin** on the GC.

The company may attempt to gain a foothold in the market by employing a policy of **penetration pricing** and offering cheap prices for the GC and the EX in the hope of attracting new customers.

There is no indication that sales of the EX are struggling. As such, it is likely that the 2% increase in the cost of the EX can be passed onto the customer without causing a significant reduction in revenue.

(d) Advocates of marginal costing believe that only the **variable costs** of making and selling a product or service should be identified. In the case of BBB this would only include material and labour costs. Absorption costing allocates and apportions overheads to individual products.

It could be argued that the marginal cost is more easily understood by the managers of BBB. However, even if **overheads** are not allocated to specific products they **still need to be paid for** and covered by sales in order for the company to show a profit. This means adding a **larger margin** onto the cost of each product. Marginal cost plus pricing is **easier** than absorption cost plus pricing because absorption costing requires **OAR calculations** and **estimates of unknown sales volumes**.

A modern alternative to absorption costing is **activity based costing**. Under this method, activities that cause costs (cost drivers) are identified and overheads are charged to products on the basis of their usage of each activity. For example, the number of site visits drives the cost of the supervisor.

In summary, businesses have to **cover all costs** including fixed overheads in order to make a profit, regardless of the pricing strategy that is adopted.

6 Jola Publishing Co

Marking scheme

			Marks
(a)	Comment on property costs	2	
	Comment on quality control	2	
	Comment on production set up cost	2	
	Comment on overall effect	2	
			8
(b)	For each explanation	2	
			4
(c)	Split of property costs	2	
	Split of quality control	2	
	Split of production set up cost	2	
	Overhead cost per unit CB	1	
	Overhead cost per unit TJ	1	
	Direct cost	1	
	Maximum		8
			20

(a) **Overall effect**

The change in overheads following re-allocation is not particularly significant overall. CB has only absorbed $0.05 more overhead which is 2% (0.05/2.30 × 100) and the overheads for TJ have fallen by 8% (0.3/3.95 × 100).

Property costs

The **largest overhead** is property costs which comprise 75% of total overhead. The activity driver for property costs is **machine hours** and this is also the basis used for absorption costing. This explains why the overall overhead change is not significant.

Quality control

Quality control comprises 23% of total overhead so is important. The activity driver for quality control is **number of inspections** and this will have a significant effect on the way overheads are allocated using ABC.

CB takes **fewer machine hours** to produce than TJ as it is a shorter book. It does however go through **frequent quality checks** so under ABC, will incur **much more** of the quality control overhead than TJ which has only a small number of inspections.

Production set-up costs

Production set-up costs comprise only 2% of total overhead so a change in overhead allocation will **not have a significant effect**.

However, the treatment of the overheads will be **very different** under ABC. CB is produced in four long production runs, whereas TJ is produced monthly in 12 production runs. Each production run incurs a set-up cost so TJ will incur a much higher proportion of these costs than if traditional absorption costing is used.

(b) **Implementation problems**

Lack of data

ABC requires **detailed accounting records** which may not be available in the business. Information is required on cost pools and cost drivers. This information is usually time consuming to derive and there may be resistance from employees.

Identifying cost drivers

It can be very difficult to identify a **single cost driver** which explains the behaviour of all items in its associated pool. For example, the property costs for this company could be driven by a number of different activities.

Lack of understanding

ABC is a **complex, time consuming technique** which will not necessarily be sufficiently understood and accepted by managers to enable them to provide **meaningful product costs** or extra information.

There can be an incorrect belief that ABC can solve all an organisation's problems but **costs of implementation** may **exceed the benefits**.

(c) **Number of machine hours**

CB
1,000,000 units × 6 mins/60 = 100,000 hours

TJ
(10,000 × 12) units × 10 mins/60 = 20,000 hours

Cost per driver

Cost pool	Cost $'000	Quantity of cost drivers	Rate per cost driver $	
Property costs	2,160	120,000	18	per machine hour
Quality control	668	200	3,340	per number of inspections
Production set-up	52	16	3,250	per set-up

ABC overheads

	CB $	TJ $
Property costs	1,800,000	360,000
Quality control	601,200	66,800
Production set-up	13,000	39,000
Total	2,414,200	465,800
Production level	1,000,000	120,000
Cost per unit	2.41	3.88

Cost per unit and margin using ABC

	CB $	TJ $
Direct cost	3.50	6.60
Overheads	2.41	3.88
Total cost	5.91	10.48
Sales price	9.30	14.00
Margin	3.39	3.52

7 The Gadget Co

Marking scheme

			Marks
(a)	Contribution per unit:		
	Overhead absorption rate	2	
	Cost for A	1	
	Cost for B	1	
	Cost for C	1	
			5
(b)	Cost under ABC:		
	Correct cost driver rates	5	
	Correct overhead unit cost for A	1	
	Correct overhead unit cost for B	1	
	Correct overhead unit cost for C	1	
	Correct cost per unit under ABC	1	
			9
(c)	Using ABC to improve profitability:		
	One mark per point about Gadget Co		Max 6
			20

(a) **Cost per unit under traditional absorption costing**

Annual overhead costs

	$
Machine set up costs	26,550
Machine running costs	66,400
Procurement costs	48,000
Delivery costs	54,320
	195,270

Overhead absorption rate

	Product A	Product B	Product C	Total
Production volumes	15,000	12,000	18,000	
Labour hours per unit	0.1	0.15	0.2	
Total labour hours	1,500	1,800	3,600	6,900

Overhead absorption rate = $195,270 (total overhead costs) / 6,900 (total hours) = $28.30 per hour

Cost per unit

		Product A $	Product B $	Product C $
Raw materials	($1.20 × 2/3/4 kg)	2.40	3.60	4.80
Direct labour	($14.80 × 0.1/0.15/0.2 hours)	1.48	2.22	2.96
Overhead	($28.30 × 0.1/0.15/0.2 hours)	2.83	4.25	5.66
Full cost per unit		6.71	10.07	13.42

(b) **Cost per unit using activity based costing**

ABC recovery rates for each cost pool

Cost pool	Cost ($)	Cost driver	Number of drivers	ABC recovery rate
Machine set up costs	26,550	Production runs	36 (16 + 12 + 8)	$737.50 per set up
Machine running costs	66,400	Machine hours	32,100 (7,500 + 8,400 +16,200)	$2.0685 per hour
Procurement costs	48,000	Purchase orders	94 (24 + 28 + 42)	$510.6383 per order
Delivery costs	54,320	Deliveries	140 (48 + 30 + 62)	$388 per delivery
	195,270			

Total overheads by product and per unit

	Product A Activity	Product A Cost $	Product B Activity	Product B Cost $	Product C Activity	Product C Cost $	Total Activity	Total Cost $
Overhead								
Machine set-ups	16	11,800	12	8,850	8	5,900	36	26,550
Machine running costs	7,500	15,514	8,400	17,375	16,200	33,510	32,100	66,400
Procurement costs	24	12,255	28	14,298	42	21,447	94	48,000
Delivery costs	48	18,624	30	11,640	62	24,056	140	54,320
Total overhead cost		58,193		52,163		84,913		195,270
Units produced		15,000		12,000		18,000		
Overhead cost per unit		3.88		4.35		4.72		

Total cost per unit

	A $	B $	C $
Materials	2.40	3.60	4.80
Labour	1.48	2.22	2.96
Overheads	3.88	4.35	4.72
	7.76	10.17	12.48

(c) **How activity based costing can improve product profitability**

Product A

The cost of product A under an ABC system is $7.76. This is 16% higher than the costs under traditional absorption costing ($6.71) and is significant given that The Gadget Co sells product A for $7.50.

Product A therefore makes a loss under ABC. Management may consider increasing the selling price of product A as well as investigating ways to reduce the costs associated with the product. Machine product costs for product A are higher than the other products due to the number of production runs. Management should investigate whether it is possible to reduce the number of production runs associated with the product.

Product B

The cost of product B is $0.10 higher under ABC. This difference is minimal and the product makes a healthy profit under both methods, given its selling price of $12.

Product C

Product C appears to be loss making under the traditional costing system with costs totalling $13.42 in comparison to the selling price of $13.00, yielding a loss of $0.42 per unit. In contrast, the product is profitable under ABC with costs totalling $12.48 per unit.

The difference in product profitability between the two systems can be explained by the number of production runs required to produce C. Production runs are low compared to the volumes produced, leading to a lower apportionment of machine costs to C under an ABC system. Also, the number of product tests carried out on C is also low in relation to product volumes.

Activity based costing is effective in showing The Gadget Co that product C is actually more profitable than product A. The company should investigate whether the efficiencies identified in product C such as the relatively low number of product tests and production runs can be transferred to product A. If the efficiency of processes relating to product A can not be improved, management may consider discontinuing the product.

8 GEEWHIZZ

Text references. Target costing is covered in Chapter 2b and life-cycle costing in Chapter 2c.

Top tips. In part (a) you obviously needed to apply the techniques to GEEWHIZZ. Part (b) requires a simple calculation but you then need to discuss what it means which, as we say in the Passing F5 section of the front pages of this kit, is a key aspect of the F5 exam.

Easy marks. This question requires standard explanations which, provided you have learned the material in sufficient detail, should be straightforward.

(a)   **Life-cycle costing**

Life-cycle costing is an **alternative** approach to that traditionally used to determine product profitability.

Traditional approach to determining product profitability

Traditional management accounting practice at GEEWHIZZ would be to report costs at the **production stage** of the AA, with **profitability** assessed on a **periodic** basis. Costs would tend to be reported according to **function**; research, design, development and customer service costs incurred on all of GEEWHIZZ's products during a period would be **totalled** and recorded as a **period expense**.

The inappropriateness of the traditional approach for the AA

Given that the AA is the **first of its kind** to be introduced to the market, GEEWHIZZ no doubt expended a great deal on research, development and design. A large proportion of the AA's **life cycle costs** will have been **determined** and **committed** by decisions made at these **early stages of its life cycle**. This necessitates the need for a management accounting **system** that monitors spending and commitments to spend at these **early stages**, and which recognises the **reduced life cycle** and the subsequent challenge to profitability of **high-tech** products such as AA.

The life-cycle approach

Life-cycle costing would have offered an alternative approach more suited to the requirements of AA.

(i) **Costs** would have been **traced** to the AA over its **complete life cycle**, from design stage right through to when the product is removed from the market, thereby increasing their **visibility**. AA's **accumulated costs** would have been **compared** with the **revenues** it had earned, so that its **total profitability** could be determined.

(ii) Traditional comparisons between AA's budgeted and actual costs on a month by month basis would have been replaced by comparing the actual plus projected costs and revenues with original (or revised) budgeted life cycle costs and revenues.

(iii) Life cycle costing would have ensured that the **initial proposals** for AA were very **carefully costed** and that there were **tight cost controls** at its **design stage**, the point at which the majority of its costs were committed.

(iv) Overall the system would have assisted in the planning and control of AA's life cycle costs and would have monitored spending and commitments to spend during the early stages of its life cycle.

(v) Life-cycle costing would have **increased the visibility of costs** such as those associated with research, design, development and customer service, costs which are traditionally simply totalled and recorded as a period expense. AA's research and development costs would have been particularly high and would have to be recovered quickly.

Because individual product profitability is therefore more fully understood, more accurate **feedback** information is available on GEEWHIZZ's **success or failure in developing new products.** In the market in which GEEWHIZZ operates, where the ability to produce new and updated versions of products is of paramount importance to organisational survival, this information is vital.

Target costing

Traditional costing versus target costing for AA

GEEWHIZZ's approach to pricing the AA has been to develop the product, work out its total cost (manufacturing plus selling and administration costs) and add a profit margin, thereby setting what it believes is an appropriate selling price.

The target costing approach is radically different. If it had been applied to the AA, the product would have been developed, a selling **price based on capturing a target market share set** and a **profit based on GEEWHIZZ's required level of return established**. The **balancing figure** in the price/cost/profit relationship would have been the cost of the AA, a **target** that GEEWHIZZ would have had to aim to achieve.

Applying target costing

(i) In an effort to attain the target cost, all ideas for **cost reduction** would have been examined during AA's **planning, research and development processes**, the stage in AA's life cycle when the largest proportion of its costs would have been committed.

(ii) As a system of control, target costing would have proved **less inflexible** than a traditional method such as **standard costing**. For example, initial production costs, determined by GEEWHIZZ's current technology and processes, would probably have been greater than the target cost. But given the rapidly-moving nature of the technology used in the manufacture of computer games, this would probably have changed. Management would therefore have had to set **benchmarks for improvement towards the target cost**. Any **learning effect** in the manufacture of AA could have been incorporated.

(iii) These benchmarks would have become increasingly more stringent as the target cost was reduced over AA's life. **Cost savings** would have had to have been actively sought and **made continuously**.

(b)

	$
Target selling price	55.00
Target profit margin (30% of selling price)	16.50
Target cost (55.00 – 16.50)	38.50
Projected cost	45.89

The projected cost **exceeds** the target cost by $7.39. This is the **target cost gap**. GEEWHIZZ will therefore have to investigate ways to drive the actual cost down to the target cost.

The highest cost is the **design** of the product. This will have been calculated by dividing the total design costs by the projected lifetime sales volume. Reducing the designing costs will have the most effect on the target cost but the ability to do this will obviously depend on the current stage of development of the game.

Each part of the cost estimate needs to be carefully analysed to determine if savings can be made. For example, **cheaper materials** could be used, staff can be **trained** in more efficient techniques or new, more efficient **technology** could be used.

Limitations of target costing

If **unrealistic and hence unachievable targets** were set, however, the workforce would **not be committed to them** or else would be **demotivated** if unable to achieve them. If, on the other hand, GEEWHIZZ management set them too low, the workforce would not be motivated to improve.

GEEWHIZZ **current costing systems** may **be unable to provide the data needed** to operate target costing effectively, but in time the company would be able to build up enough relevant data to create cost tables. **Cost tables** are a very sophisticated version of standard cost setting data and can be used to predict the costs of even new products with an acceptable degree of accuracy.

9 Edward Limited

Text reference. Target costing is covered in Chapter 2b.

Top tips. Parts (a) and (b) require straightforward explanations. The number of marks suggests the number of points you should be aiming to make. Show your workings clearly in part (c) and, if you get stuck, make an assumption and move on.

Easy marks. There are easy marks available throughout this question if you use your common sense and read the question carefully.

Examiner's comments. A substantial number of candidates had very little idea of what target costing is. The benefits of target costing was not well done. The examiner wants to know why something is done as well as how it is done.

High-low was poorly done by large numbers of candidates. This must be revised as it is likely to be examined again. Allowances for waste and idle time were often incorrectly done and this is an area that will be revisited so students must learn the correct method.

Marking scheme

			Marks
(a)	Product specification	1	
	Selling price	1	
	Cost calculation	1	
			3
(b)	1 mark per benefit		4
(c)	Component 1	2	
	Component 2	2	
	Material other	1	
	Assembly labour	2	
	Variable production overhead	1	
	High low calculation	2	
	Fixed production OAR calculation	1	
	Fixed production overhead	1	
	Cost gap identified	1	
			13
			20

(a) **Target costing process**

Target costing involves setting a **target cost** by subtracting a desired **profit margin** from a **competitive market price**.

The process starts by determining a **product specification** using analysis of what customers want. This will determine the **product features** that should be incorporated.

The next stage is to **set a selling price** taking into account competitors' products and expected market conditions. The **desired profit margin** is deducted from the selling price to arrive at the **target cost**.

If the costs are higher than target, there is a **cost gap** and efforts will be made to close the gap.

(b) **Benefits of adopting a target costing approach**

External focus

Traditionally the approach is to use an **internal focus** when developing a new product by calculating the costs and then adding a margin to decide on the selling price. Target costing makes the business look at what competitors are offering at a much earlier stage in the development process.

Customer focus

Customer requirements for quality, cost and time are **incorporated** into product and process decisions. The value of product features to the customers must be greater than the cost of providing them and only those features that are of **value to customers** are included.

Cost control

Cost control is emphasised at the **design stage** so any engineering changes must happen before production starts. This is much more effective than the traditional method of trying to control costs **too late** to make a significant impact.

Faster time to market

The **early external focus** enables the business to get the process **right first time** and avoids the need to go back and change aspects of the design and/or production process. This then reduces the time taken to get a product to the market.

(c) **Production overheads**

Using the high-low method:

$$\text{Variable cost per hour} = \frac{700,000 - 620,000}{23,000 - 19,000} = \frac{80,000}{4,000} = \$20$$

Fixed costs = 620,000 − (19,000 × $20) = $240,000

Annual fixed production overhead = $240,000 × 12 = $2,880,000

Absorption rate = $2,880,000/240,000 = $12 per hour

Expected cost per unit

		$ per unit
Component 1	$4.10 + $\dfrac{\$2,400}{4,000}$	4.70
Component 2	25/100 × $0.50 × 100/98	0.13
Other material		8.10
Assembly labour	30/60 × $12.60 × 100/90	7.00
Variable production overhead	30/60 × $20	10.00
Fixed production overhead	30/60 × $12	6.00
Total cost		35.93
Target cost	$44 × 80%	(35.20)
Cost gap		0.73

10 Cambs Co

(a)   Every product goes through a **life cycle**, the **curve** of which resembles the generic curve in the following diagram.

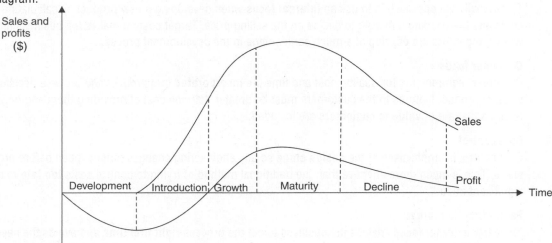

The life cycle is divided into a number of distinct stages, although the time span of each stage can vary significantly for different products.

The **current tendency** is towards **shorter product life cycles** and this is particularly the case for products in the high-technology sector. Products becomes rapidly outdated by new technological developments and competitors are quick to launch their own, better versions of products.

Stages in the product life-cycle of the Fentiger

(i)   **Development**

Issues

During this stage the product is not earning revenue but high levels of costs are being incurred on research and product development and possibly on assets for production. For Cambs Co, these costs amounted to $675,000.

A very high proportion of the product's costs will have been determined by decisions made early in the life cycle, at the development stage. **Life-cycle costing and target costing** are particularly useful at this stage to ensure that costs will be kept to a minimum over the product's life cycle.

(ii)   **Introduction**

This stage represents a period of high business risk and Cambs Co should expect negative net cash flow.

Customer interest in the product should be high given the **novelty** of the product. The level of initial sales achieved will very much depend on the amount of **advertising and promotion.**

Issues

For Cambs Co, costs are high at $50/unit and the selling price is also (compared with those over the entire lifecycle) high at $120/unit. A unit contribution of $70/unit sold is the highest contribution over

the product life cycle. Cambs Co therefore appears to be seeking to recoup as much R&D expenditure and non-current asset expenditure as possible at this stage.

The sooner the Fentiger is launched, the quicker its research and development costs will be repaid, providing Cambs Co with funds to develop further products. At this stage in its life cycle, **growth in sales** is the key performance measure.

(iii) **Growth**

The growth stage typically shows a **rapid increase in sales.** From month 11 to 30, growth in sales of Fentigers is expected to increase rapidly so this is probably the growth stage for this product. The product should by now be making a profit, although much of the cash it generates may be being used for expansion.

Issues

The aim during this stage is to **build market share. Costs will still be high** as more promotion is needed to advertise the product more widely. Distribution channels may be expanded to take up more market share. **The price will be high** but may need to fall if demand is seen as falling. Cambs Co charges between $60 and $90/unit sold and the price drops over the period in response to market conditions. However, the unit variable cost is also falling. Margins are falling but volume has risen so the product is contributing more at this stage than the last one.

By now **competitors** may be in the process of developing or even launching competing products, and so management should be analysing their marketing strategies.

(iv) **Maturity**

The rate of sales growth slows down during this period and the Fentiger will reach a period of maturity. Cash flow should be positive and profits should be good. This is the **most profitable stage** of the product's life cycle. **Costs will continue falling** as economies of production are achieved. Advertising costs should fall as product awareness is stronger. Marketing is concentrated in reaching new customers. **The price will fall** in response to competition and to retain market share. From the demand figures, it looks as though this is expected in months 31 to 70.

Issues

Using the cash flows generated by the Fentiger, Cambs Co should have developed and be ready to launch an **updated version** of, or the successor to, the Fentiger. (Unless driven by competitors' actions, Cambs Co should **guard against product proliferation** (launching an updated version or a successor too quickly), however, as the Fentigers' life cycle would be cut short and it may only just cover its development costs).

(v) **Decline**

This is the stage at which the product is **losing popularity and market share is falling**.

Issues

Cambs Co can adopt a **choice of strategies** including running the product down or discontinuing it. Costs fall as marketing support is withdrawn but economies of scale begin to decline so the **unit variable cost actually rises** again to $30/unit. **Prices are reduced** to mop up market share.

(b)

Months	1-10	11-20	21-30	31-70	71-80	81-90	91-100	101-110
Number of units produced and sold	1,900	3,000	8,500	60,000	9,000	7,000	4,500	3,000
	$	$	$	$	$	$	$	$
Selling price per unit	120	90	60	50	40	40	40	40
Unit variable cost (W1)	50	40	40	30 & 25	30	30	30	30
Unit contribution (W1)	70	50	20	20 & 25	10	10	10	10
Total contribution	133,000	150,000	170,000	1,350,000	90,000	70,000	45,000	30,000
Cumulative cash flow (W2)	(542,000)	(392,000)	(222,000)	1,128,000	1,218,000	1,288,000	1,333,000	1,363,000

Workings

(1) $(30,000 \times \$20) + (30,000 \times \$25) = \$1,350,000$

(2) The initial cash outflow of $500,000 + $175,000 is deducted from the cash inflows.

Fentigers are expected to generate a **positive cash inflow of $1,363,000** over the product's life cycle. As expected from the life cycle analysis outlined in part (a), Cambs Co does not make a profit from Fentigers in the **introductory** stage. It should be expected to start making a profit in the **growth** stage but this does not actually happen until the product reaches **maturity** in months 31 to 70. Cambs Co may want to look at reducing costs or raising prices further in the early stages of the life cycle.

11 Sapu

Text references. Activity based costing is covered in Chapter 2a, target costing in Chapter 2b and throughput accounting in Chapter 2d.

Top tips. The calculations required in this question were very straightforward. Note how many of the marks available were actually for written answers. This is to be expected in your exam so make sure you can answer the written parts as well as do the calculations.

(a) (i) **Absorption costing approach**

	Product A	Product B
	$	$
Direct material cost per unit	16	30.00
Direct labour cost per unit	8	10.00
Variable overhead per unit (W)	13	18.75
	37	58.75

Workings

Materials-related overhead

Overhead = $1,500,000 \times 40\% = \$600,000$

Absorption base = total direct materials cost of all three products = $2,400,000

$\therefore$ Absorption rate $= \$(600,000 \div 2,400,000) \times 100\%$
$= 25\%$ on direct material cost

Labour-related overhead

Overhead = $1,500,000 \times 60\% = \$900,000$

Absorption base = total direct labour cost for all three products = $800,000

$\therefore$ Absorption rate $= \$(900,000 \div 800,000) \times 100\%$
$= 112.5\%$ on direct labour cost

Variable overhead per unit

	A	B
	$	$
Material related		
$25\% \times \$16/\$30$	4	7.50
Labour related		
$112.5\% \times \$8/\$10$	9	11.25
	13	18.75

(ii) ABC approach

	A $	B $
Direct material cost per unit	16.00	30.00
Direct labour cost per unit	8.00	10.00
Variable overhead cost per unit (W)	71.68	14.17
	95.68	54.17

Workings

Material-related overheads

		Bulk $$'000
Number of cost drivers		
(product A)	$4 \times 5,000$	20
(product B)	$1 \times 10,000$	10
(product C)	$1.5 \times 40,000$	60
		90

∴ Overhead per cost driver = $600,000 ÷ 90,000
                                         = $6.67

Labour-related overheads

		Labour operations $'000
Number of cost drivers		
Product A	$6 \times 5,000$	30
Product B	$1 \times 10,000$	10
Product C	$2 \times 40,000$	80
		120

∴ Overhead per cost driver = $900,000 ÷ 120,000 = $7.50

Variable overhead per unit

	A $	B $
Material related		
$6.67 × 4/1	26.68	6.67
Labour related		
$7.50 × 6/1	45.00	7.50
	71.68	14.17

(b) **Target costing** is a term that has been defined in a number of ways. The essence of the concept is that a **product should cost less than the price that can be obtained for it in the market**.

Targets for reductions in the high rate of both material bulk and labour operations cost drivers for product A would, if achieved, produce a considerable reduction in the unit cost of product A. This may mean redesigning the product entirely or simply reorganising production methods. Such changes may, of course, also reduce the level of direct material and direct labour costs.

ABC can be combined usefully with target costing if it is felt that overheads are the main area in which costs can be reduced. Activity analysis identifies the factors that cause overheads to be incurred and so draws attention to the factors that need to be more closely controlled.

(c) **Basis of throughput accounting**

Throughput accounting (TA) is a system of cost and management accounting which is primarily designed for use in a **JIT manufacturing environment. Throughput** is defined as **sales revenue less direct material cost** and the **aim** of throughput accounting is to **maximise this measure**.

The system is based on **three concepts**.

(i)   In the short run, most factory costs, other than materials, are fixed.

(ii)   In a JIT environment, inventory holding is discouraged and zero inventory is a business target. Accordingly, there should be no incentive for production managers to manufacture for inventory simply to keep idle plant or labour occupied.

(iii) Profitability is determined by the rate at which revenue is generated which, because there are no significant inventories, depends on how quickly goods can be produced to meet customer orders.

Throughput is therefore maximised by minimising material costs, maximising prices and maximising saleable output.

Bottlenecks

The aim of modern manufacturing approaches is to match production resources with the demand for them. This implies that there are no constraints, termed **bottleneck resources** in throughput accounting, within an organisation. The throughput philosophy entails the **identification and elimination** of these bottleneck resources. Where it cannot be eliminated, the bottleneck resource should be used to 100% of its availability.

Limitations of throughput

The **factors which limit throughput** may include constraints other than a lack of production resources (bottlenecks).

(i)   The existence of an uncompetitive selling price
(ii)   The need to deliver on time to particular customers
(iii) Poor product quality and reliability
(iv)   The lack of reliable material suppliers

One other criticism of TA is that it pays too little attention to overhead costs. This problem can be alleviated, however, by simultaneously operating an **activity based costing system**. In fact, the two systems are complementary.

12 Throughput accounting

Text references. Throughput accounting is covered in Chapter 2d.

Top tips. This is a straightforward question including both a numerical and a discursive part as can be expected in your exam. You need to learn how to calculate the throughput accounting ratio and be prepared to discuss its implications.

(a)   **Machine X output**

Up to 5 hours production time lost per week = one eighth of maximum production time per week.

Output = $7/8 \times (180/4)$ TRLs = 39 TRLs

Machine Y output = parts for 52 TRLs

Machine Z output = process/assemble 30 TRLs

The **key resource** is therefore **machine Z time**.

Throughput contribution = sales price – material cost = $(2,000 – 600) = \$1,400$

Time on key resource = 40 hours per week/30 TRLs = 1.3333 hrs per TRL

Throughput contribution per factory hour = \$1,400/1.3333 hours = \$1,050

Conversion cost per factory hour = labour + variable overhead + fixed production costs = $(5,500 + 8,000 + (450,000/48 weeks))/40$ hours per week = \$571.88

Throughput accounting ratio = \$1,050/\$571.88 = 1.84

(b) (i) **Profit per day** = throughput contribution − conversion cost

= [($80 × 6,000) + ($80 × 4,500) + ($200 × 1,200)] − $720,000 = $360,000

(ii)

Product	Minutes in alpha per unit	Minutes in alpha per day
X	60/1,200 = 0.05	6,000 × 0.05 = 300
Y	60/1,500 = 0.04	4,500 × 0.04 = 180
Z	60/600 = 0.10	1,200 × 0.10 = 120
		600

Total hours = 600 minutes ÷ 60 = 10 hours

Hours available = 8, hours produced = 10, ∴**Efficiency** = 125%

(iii) **TA ratio** = throughput contribution per factory hour/conversion cost per factory hour

Conversion cost per factory hour = $720,000/8 = $90,000

Product	Throughput contribution per factory hour	Cost per factory hour	TA ratio
X	$80 × (60 ÷ 0.05 mins) = $96,000	$90,000	1.07
Y	$80 × (60 ÷ 0.04 mins) = $120,000	$90,000	1.33
Z	$200 × (60 ÷ 0.10 mins) = $120,000	$90,000	1.33

(iv) An attempt should be made to **remove the restriction on output** caused by process alpha's capacity. This will probably result in another bottleneck emerging elsewhere.

The extra capacity required to remove the restriction could be obtained by **working overtime**, making **process improvements** or **product specification** changes.

Until the volume of throughput can be increased, output should be concentrated upon products Y and Z (greatest TA ratios), unless there are good marketing reasons for continuing the current production mix.

(v) Actions that could be considered to improve the TA ratio are as follows.

(1) **Increase the selling price** of the product. This will increase the throughput per time period.

(2) **Reduce the material cost** per unit of the product. This will also increase the throughput per time period.

(3) Reduce the total expenditure on **conversion costs**. This would reduce the conversion cost per time period.

(4) Change the **working practices** on the bottleneck resource (eg machine hours) to increase the number of hours of capacity available. This should be achieved without extra conversion cost being incurred, perhaps by altering the method of setting up the machine, to improve productivity. This action would reduce the conversion cost per time period.

13 A Co

Text references. Throughput accounting is covered in Chapter 2d and environmental accounting in Chapter 2e.

Top tips. Parts (a) to (c) involve straightforward calculations partly using knowledge brought forward from your earlier studies. Part (d) and (e) are relatively straight forward and test your knowledge on environmental systems and environmental costs.

(a)

	Maximum number of B1 units	Maximum number of B2 units
Department 1	480/12 = 40	480/16 = 30
Department 2	840/20 = 42	840/15 = 56

The bottleneck or limiting factor is labour in Department 1 as Department 2 has capacity to produce more of both B1 and B2.

(b) The question requires us to use **traditional contribution analysis**:

We need to calculate the contribution (sales less direct materials, labour and variable overheads) per unit of the bottleneck resource, which is time in Department 1. The contribution maximising output is found by dividing contribution per unit of product B1 and B2 by the time in minutes required by each product in department 1.

		B1		B2
	$	$	$	$
Sales price		50.00		65.00
Less variable costs				
Direct materials	10.00		15.00	
Direct labour	10.40		6.20	
Variable overheads	6.40		9.20	
		(26.80)		(30.40)
Contribution		23.20		34.60

	$		$	
Contribution per unit of limiting factor	$\dfrac{23.20}{12}$ = $1.933		$\dfrac{34.60}{16}$ = $2.1625	

Contribution is maximised by making as many B2 as possible as it makes a more profitable use of the scarce resource and all units made can be sold.

The maximum number of B2 units that can be sold, given the limitations on labour, is 30:

Total contribution is $34.60 × 30 units = $1,038

(c) The **throughput approach** is based on throughput maximisation. Throughput is defined as **sales less direct materials**.

	B1	B2
	$	$
Sales price	50	65
Less: direct materials	(10)	(15)
	40	50

Throughput per minute of bottleneck resource is:

	B1	B2
	$	$
	40/12 = 3.333	50/16 = 3.125

Contribution is maximised by producing 40 units of B1, the maximum number of B1 that can be produced, given the bottleneck resource of labour in Department 1.

The **maximum throughput contribution** is 40 × $40 = $1,600.

(d) There are a number of key features to any environmental management system.

Each environmental management system should contain an **environmental policy statement**. This can be developed through review of environmental impacts of materials, issues and products and of business issues arising.

Effective systems should take steps to ensure **regulatory compliance**. Environmental **audits** will help to confirm current legal requirements are being fulfilled as well as ensuring that the business is up-to-date with practical implications of likely **changes in legislation**.

Realistic and measurable **targets** should be set. Targets should be **quantified** within a specified time period. For example, reducing carbon dioxide emissions by X% within a 12 month period.

An effective system should be established to **account for environmental costs**. Key features include budgeting, forecasting, a clear structure of responsibilities as well as the establishment of an environmentally-friendly **culture** and performance appraisal process.

The business should make a **public declaration** of environmental standards that are met such as the ISO standards. This could lead to the business establishing a competitive advantage over competitors.

(e) **Internalised environmental costs**

Internalised environmental costs are **incurred within the organisation.** They can be identified from the accounting records, can be **quantified and valued in monetary terms** and can often be traced to individual products and services, perhaps using an activity based costing system.

Two examples of internalised environmental costs are the cost of environmental certification and waste disposal costs.

Externalised environmental impacts

Externalised environmental impacts are the **effects that the organisation's activities have on the external environment.** Not all externalised environmental impacts result in the organisation itself incurring a cost that can be quantified and recorded in the costing system. However, environmental costing is concerned with monitoring an organisation's external environmental impact, even if not all impacts can be quantified in financial terms. Such impacts might also be **traced to individual products and services** to assess the effect on the external environment of the manufacturing of specific products and the provision of individual services.

As part of its environmental costing, the organisation might **develop measures** to ensure that external standards concerning the impact of the organisation on the external environment are adhered to.

Two examples of externalised environmental impacts are carbon emissions and resource consumption.

14 Yam Co

Text references. Throughput accounting is covered in Chapter 2d.

Top tips. In part (a), to save time, you don't need to calculate the output capacity of each process. You can see that the processing time for the pressing process is the slowest, so then just need to explain why this creates a bottleneck.

Read the question carefully and make sure you answer the specific question. In Part (c), don't be tempted to explain what a TPAR is in part (i) as this explanation will only gain you marks in part (ii).

Easy marks. The calculations in part (b) should provide easy marks, provided you have learnt how to calculate a throughput accounting ratio. Four good, common sense points should earn you easy marks in Part (c) (i).

Examiner's comments. It was clear that many candidates had poor knowledge of throughput accounting. Few could properly identify the bottleneck process and many used total hours per product as their guide to a wrong answer.

In the throughput calculations many included labour in the calculation of contribution, whereas its exclusion is more normal. Labour is properly treated as a fixed cost and yet many did not include it in the overheads part of the calculations.

Most candidates could give some reasonable suggestions on how to improve a TPAR, however not enough scored the four easy marks on offer.

The final part of the question was least well done, as expected. It is an easy mistake to feel that an unprofitable product should cease to be made but the world is a more complicated place. Current profitability is a factor but the future is more relevant.

Marks

(a) Identification of bottleneck   1
    Explanation   2
                                                                    3

(b) Sales prices   1
    Raw material cost   1
    Throughput per bottleneck hour   2
    Fixed costs   1
    Fixed cost per hour   2
    TPAR   1
                                                                    8

(c) Increase speed of bottleneck   1
    Increase selling prices – difficult to do   1
    Reduce material prices   1
    Reduce level of fixed costs   1
                                                                    4

    Explain a TPAR   1
    Long-term cash flows   1
    Lost related sales   1
    Use of spare capacity   1
    Fixed costs   1
    Any other reasonable factor eg lost contribution   1
    Maximum   5
                                                                   20

(a) **Output capacity for each process**

Total processing hours for the factory = 225,000

	Product A Metres	Product B Metres	Product C Metres
Pressing	225,000/0.50 = 450,000	225,000/0.50 = 450,000	225,000/0.40 = 562,500
Stretching	225,000/0.25 = 900,000	225,000/0.40 = 562,500	225,000/0.25 = 900,000
Rolling	225,000/0.40 = 562,500	225,000/0.25 = 900,000	225,000/0.25 = 900,000

The **bottleneck process** is **pressing** which has a lower output capacity for all three processes. Pressing has a **longer processing time** for each product than the other products. This means that pressing acts as a **limiting factor** and will **constrain throughput**.

(b) **Throughput accounting ratios**

TPAR = Return per factory hour/total conversion cost per factory hour

Conversion cost = Labour costs + factory costs
                = (225,000 hours × $10) + $18,000,000
                = $20,250,000

Conversion cost per factory hour = $20,250,000/225,000 hours
                                     = $90

Return per factory hour = Sales − direct costs/usage of bottleneck resource in hours

	Product A	Product B	Product C
	$	$	$
Selling price per metre	70.00	60.00	27.00
Raw material cost per metre	3.00	2.50	1.80
Return	67.00	57.50	25.20
Usage of bottleneck resource in hours	0.50	0.50	0.40
Return per factory hour	134.00	115.00	63.00
Conversion cost per factory hour	90.00	90.00	90.00
TPAR	1.49	1.28	0.70

(c) (i) **How to improve the TPAR of Product C**

Increase the selling price

Product C has the **lowest selling price** of the three products and Yam carries **very little inventory** so is presumably selling all that it produces. This could mean that there is potential to increase the selling price and therefore the TPAR.

However, Yam faces **tough price competition** in a mature world market so a price increase could simply result in lower sales.

Increase the speed of the pressing process

The pressing process has been identified as a bottleneck so if this process is **speeded up**, throughput would increase. This could be achieved by increasing the productivity of the workforce, perhaps through **workflow optimisation** or more **training**. Alternatively, greater **automation** of the process may increase the speed but this could require investment in new machinery. This will only work if the extra output of all three products can be sold.

Reduce factory costs

The factory costs should be investigated to determine if there is any way to make cost savings. A **detailed budget** and **variance analysis** would help with this process. Some aspects could be **outsourced** or **alternative cheaper suppliers** identified.

Reduce material costs

There may be opportunities to buy the metal raw material from **cheaper, alternative suppliers**. The danger with this is a fall in **quality** which would impact on the quality of the final products and/or increase the risk of breakdown in production. **Bulk buying** could result in discounted raw material prices but the cost of **holding inventory** may outweigh the cost benefit.

(ii) **Cessation of production of Product C**

Product C has the lowest TPAR and it is **below one**. This means that it incurs factory costs quicker than it generates throughput and is **losing money** every time it is being produced. In simple terms, Yam should therefore consider ceasing production of Product C.

Other issues to consider

Firstly, customers who buy Products A and B may also need Product C and would **turn to another supplier** if it was not available. Cessation of a product line does not project a positive image of a business.

Secondly, cessation of Product C production will **create excess capacity** and Yam needs to consider what would then happen. For example, redundancy and machine scrapping costs may be incurred if alternative uses for the excess capacity cannot be found.

Thirdly, the costs and benefits from the production of Product C may be expected to **change** in the future. Fixed factory costs may become variable and could be reduced, or the selling price could be increased. The **contribution** from Product C needs to be analysed in more detail before a cessation decision could be taken.

15 Thin Co

Marking scheme

			Marks
(a)	Throughput accounting ratio:		
	Cost per hour	3	
	Return per hour (procedure C)	2	
	Ratio (procedure C)	1	
			6
(b)	Optimum production plan:		
	Ranking	1	
	Optimum number of A	1½	
	Optimum number of B	1½	
	Optimum number of C	1½	
	Total throughput	½	
	Less cost	½	
	Profit	½	
			7
(c)	Discussion:		
	Demand satisfied for A and B	1	
	Unsatisfied demand for C	1	
	Calculation re recovery specialist	2	
	Would need another surgeon	1	
	Other staff have lots of idle time	1	
	Need extra theatre time	1	
	Profit calculation	1	
	Financially feasible	1	
	Each other valid point	1	
	Conclusion	1	
		Max	7
			20

BPP
LEARNING MEDIA

(a) **Throughput accounting ratio (TAR)**

The throughput accounting ratio is usually defined as return per factory hour / total conversion cost per factory hour.

In the context of a hospital, the TAR will be return per hospital hour / cost per hospital hour.

Performance measures in throughput accounting are based around the concept that only **direct materials** are regarded as **variable costs**. All other costs are treated as fixed costs.

Cost per hospital hour

Total hospital costs are therefore all **salaries** plus **general overheads**.
$45,000 + $38,000 + $75,000 + $90,000 + $50,000 + $250,000 = $548,000

The question states that surgeon's hours have been correctly identified as the bottleneck resource. 40 hours × 47 weeks = 1,880 hours.

Total cost per hospital hour = $548,000 / 1,880 hours = $291.49

Return per hospital hour

Return per hospital hour = (Sales – direct material costs) / usage of bottleneck resource in hours

	$ per procedure C
Selling price	4,250.00
Materials cost:	
Injection	(1,000.00)
Anaesthetic	(45.00)
Dressings	(5.60)
Throughput per procedure (unit)	3,199.40
Time on bottleneck resource (surgeon's hours)	1.25 hrs
Return per hour ($)	2,559.52

TAR = $2,559.52 / $291.49 = 8.78.

(b) **Optimum production plan**

In a throughput environment, **production priority** must be given to the products best able to generate throughput. That is those products (in this case procedures) that **maximise throughput per unit of bottleneck resource**.

Step 1   **Rank products**

	A	B	C
TAR	8.96	9.11	8.78
Ranking	2nd	1st	3rd

Step 2   **Allocate resources to arrive at optimum production plan**

The optimum product mix per annum is as follows.

Procedure	Number	Hours per procedure	Total hours	Throughput per hour $	Total throughput $
B	800	1	800	2,654.40	2,123,520.00
A	600	0.75	450	2,612.53	1,175,638.50
C	504*	1.25	630	2,559.52	1,612,497.60
			1,880		4,911,656.10

* Balancing number of procedure C (630 hours remaining / 1.25 hours per procedure).

Total profit per annum is as follows.

	$
Throughput	4,911,656.10
Less: Total costs	(548,000.00)
Profit	4,363,656.10

(c) **Profitability increase**

To assess whether the overall profitability of the company could be improved by equipping and using the extra theatre, Thin Co should compare the extra revenue it would earn from catering for an additional 696 of procedure C against the extra costs that would be incurred.

The costs involved in equipping and using the extra theatre to satisfy customer demand are as follows.

Staff costs

Each member of staff works 1,880 hours per annum.

The total number of hours for each member of staff to fulfill demand for each procedure is shown below.
Note: The number of hours per procedure is displayed in brackets.

	Procedure						
	A	*B*	*C*	*Additional C*	*Total hours required*	*Total hours available*	*Shortfall*
	(600 procedures)	*(800)*	*(504)*	*(696)*			
	Number of hours required to meet demand for each procedure						
Advisor	144	192	120.96	167.04	624	1,880	–
	(0.24)	(0.24)	(0.24)	(0.24)			
Nurse	162	224	151.20	208.80	746	1,880	–
	(0.27)	(0.28)	(0.30)	(0.30)			
Anaesthetist	150	224	166.32	229.68	770	1,880	–
	(0.25)	(0.28)	(0.33)	(0.33)			
Surgeon	450	800	630.00	870.00	2,750	1,880	870
	(0.75)	(1.00)	(1.25)	(1.25)			
Recovery specialist	360	560	372.96	515.04	1,808	1,880	–
	(0.60)	(0.70)	(0.74)	(0.74)			

From the calculation above, it is clear that the majority of hospital staff have capacity to cater for the additional 696 procedures of C.

There is a shortfall of 870 surgeon hours. Employing an additional surgeon would solve this problem. A surgeon salary is $90,000 per annum.

Theatre costs

The other theatre would need to be equipped with the necessary equipment so the additional surgeon could operate in it. This would cost $750,000.

Extra throughput

Throughput from the additional 696 procedures would be as follows.
696 × 1.25 hours = 870 hours
870 × $2,559.52 (throughput per hour) = $2,226,782

Summary

It is clear that the costs we be more than covered in the first year alone.
$2,226,782 – $750,000 – $90,000 = $1,386,782

Without taking into account future years and on the basis of one year's throughput, Thin Co should employ an additional surgeon and equip the other theatre in order to increase profit and exploit the extra demand for procedure C.

16 ABC plc

(a)

Product	W	Y	Z
	$	$	$
Selling price (W1)	10.00	15.00	30.00
Material A (W2)	4.20	2.10	8.40
Material B (W3)	2.00	4.50	12.00
Direct labour (W4)	2.00	7.50	3.00
Overhead (W5)	1.00	3.00	3.00
	9.20	17.10	26.40
Relevant contribution per unit	0.80	(2.10)	3.60
Relevant contribution per $ of material B (W6)	0.40	(0.47)	0.30

Workings

(1) Take the revenue in $ as stated in the question and divide by the number of units. So for product W, take $60,000 and divide by 6,000 units to get $10 per unit selling price.

(2) Costs shown in the budget are based on $10 per kg but the relevant cost will be the $14 replacement cost of material A. So taking Product W as an example:

Cost of material A per unit of W was $18,000/6,000 units = $3
Kgs of material A per unit of W = $3/$10
Revised cost of material A per unit of W = ($3/$10) × $14 = $4.20

(3) The relevant cost here is based on the $20 per kg replacement cost so there is no need to substitute a replacement cost as in working 2 above and you can use the figures straight from the budget.

(4) Likewise, the relevant cost here is the $20 hourly rate and you can take the cost from the budget.

(5) You need to use the high-low method to calculate the variable element of the overheads, after deducting the specific fixed cost of $2,000.

Product	W		Y		Z	
	$	Units	$	Units	$	Units
Low volume	10,000	6,000	20,000	6,000	20,000	6,000
High volume	14,000	10,000	32,000	10,000	32,000	10,000
Difference	4,000(1)	4,000(2)	12,000	4,000	12,000	4,000
Variable costs per unit ((1)/(2))	4,000/4,000 = $1		$3		$3	

(6)   Let's consider product W again. The cost of material B per the table above is $2 per unit. Apply this to the relevant contribution per unit you have already worked out and you will get the relevant contribution per $ of material B.

(b)   **Relevant contribution to sales ratios for all four products**

Take the information calculated in part (a) above and use to calculate C/S ratios for each product.

Product	W	Y	Z
	$	$	$
Selling price	10.00	15.00	30.00
Relevant contribution	0.80	(2.10)	3.60
Contribution to sales ratios (%)	8%	(14%)	12%

(c)   **Sketch a graph showing multi product profit volume (PV) chart**

Step 1

A P/V chart has revenue on the x axis and profit on the y axis, and so for each product you need to know the revenue that can be earned from total market demand (contract + other customers) and the profit from this level of revenue. Remember that the limiting factor restriction on material B no longer applies as demand will be the sum of that for the minimum contract plus the demand expected from other customers.

Product	W	Y	Z	Total
Total demand (units) (W1)	8,200	7,600	8,800	
	$	$	$	$
Sales revenue (W2)	82,000	114,000	264,000	460,000
Contribution to sales ratios (%) (W3)	8%	(14%)	12%	
Contribution	6,560	(15,960)	31,680	22,280

Workings

(1)   You need to add the demand from the minimum contract to the other demand stated, for each product. All information is in the question.

(2)   Use the selling price you calculated in part (a) total demand for units

(3)   From part (b)

Step 2

You need a 'starting point' for the graph (ie at the point of nil revenue on the x axis) and so you need to determine the profit when revenue is nil (the point on the y axis). Profit – or loss - when revenue is nil = fixed costs.

Product	W	Y	Z	Total
	$	$	$	$
Overhead costs per the question	12,000	22,000	22,000	
Units	6,000	6,000	6,000	
Variable overhead cost per unit (from (a))	$1	$3	$3	
Total variable costs (units x variable cost per unit)	6,000	18,000	18,000	
Fixed cost (total overhead costs – total variable costs)	6,000	4,000	4,000	14,000
Less avoidable fixed cost (from note 4 of question)				(6,000)
Fixed cost at which sales are nil				8,000

Step 3

The question states that the products are to be plotted in order of their C/S ratios so (from (b)) they need to be plotted in the order ZWY.

You now need to work out cumulative revenues and profits.

As each product is produced, a directly attributable fixed cost is incurred. We assume that the fixed cost occurs immediately and the revenue and contribution occur when we finish selling each product.

Products	Revenue	Cumulative revenue (x axis coordinate)	Profit	Cumulative profit (y axis coordinate)
	$	$	$	$
None	None	None	(8,000)	(8,000)
Start selling Z	None	None	(2,000)*	(10,000)
Finish selling Z	264,000	264,000	31,680**	21,680
Start selling W	None	264,000	(2,000)	19,680
Finish selling W	82,000	346,000	6,560	26,240
Start selling Y	None	346,000	(2,000)	24,240
Finish selling Y	114,000	460,000	(15,960)	8,280

*   Fixed cost
** Contribution

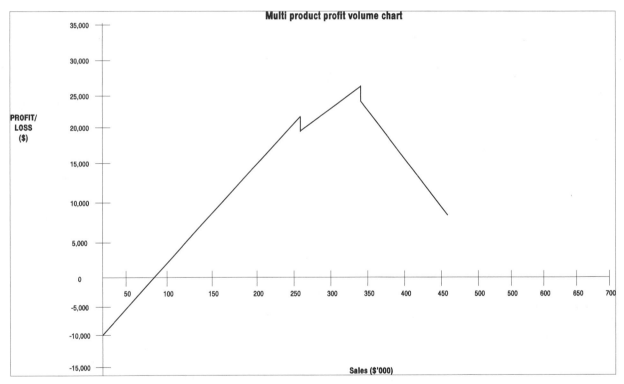

(d)   The chart would **show further information about the contribution earned by each product individually**, so that their performance and profitability can be compared. By convention, the **products are shown individually** on a P/V chart from **left to right**, in **order of the size of their C/S ratio**. In the question, product Z will be plotted first, then product W and finally product Y.

The **jagged line** is used to show the **cumulative profit/loss and the cumulative sales** as each product's sales and contribution in turn are added to the sales mix.

It is also possible to plot a single line from the two end points on the **line** to indicate **the average profit, which** will be earned from sales of the products in this mix.

The diagram **highlights** the following points.

(i) Since Z is the most profitable in terms of C/S ratio, it might be worth considering an increase in the sales of Z, at the expense of less profitable products such as Y.

(ii) Alternatively, the pricing structure of the products should be reviewed and a decision made as to whether the price of product Y should be raised so as to increase its C/S ratio (although an increase is likely to result in some fall in sales volume).

The **multi-product P/V chart** therefore helps to **identify** the following.

(i) The overall company breakeven point.

(ii) Which products should be expanded in output and which, if any, should be discontinued.

(iii) What effect changes in selling price and sales volume will have on the company's breakeven point and profit.

Assumptions

(1) The technique assumes that all variable costs are the same per unit at all levels of output and that fixed costs are the same in total.

(2) It also assumes that sales price will be the same across all levels of activity.

(3) There are no changes in levels of inventory so the consequences of increases and decreases in inventory levels are ignored.

17 Devine Desserts

> **Text references.** CVP analysis is covered in Chapter 3. Sales mix and quantity variances are covered in Chapter 12.
>
> **Top tips.** Make sure that you are able to comment on the variances you have calculated in part (b) and offer suggestions as to why they have arisen.

(a) The diagram shows the monetary values of costs and revenues over a range of activity levels.

The diagram shows that significant fixed costs are incurred at an activity level of zero. Examples of such costs are rent and rates on business premises that need to be paid regardless of the level of sales.

Fixed costs increase significantly at certain activity levels (at points B and D in the diagram). This is an example of **a stepped fixed cost**. Managers should be made aware of these activity levels, otherwise there is a risk that an order may be accepted which significantly increases costs for a small additional amount of revenue.

Variable costs are proportional to the level of activity and may include the costs such as raw ingredients and the packaging for the desserts. The diagram shows that the variable costs are constant per unit of activity up to activity level B as the gradient of the line is constant throughout this activity range. Between activity levels B and D the variable costs are constant per unit, but the unit cost is lower than that up to point B possibly due to **economies of scale** and **learning effects**. However, above activity level D it can be seen that the gradient of the line increases. This represents a higher unit cost for these units.

Total costs are the sum of the fixed costs and variable costs.

Sales revenue up to point C on the diagram is constant, implying that the selling price per unit is constant. Above point C, sales revenue continues to increase but at a slower rate. This shows that in order to sell a volume higher than activity level C the price per unit must be reduced.

Profits are maximized where the vertical distance between the sales revenue and total cost lines is greatest.

Activity level A is the breakeven point where **total revenue is equal to total costs** yielding a profit of zero. At activity levels beyond point A, the company makes a profit but activity levels below point A yield a loss.

Activity level B has already been explained as the point at which the fixed costs and total costs increase due to the step effect. It can be seen that this has a significant effect on the profit being earned.

Activity level C shows the point at which reductions in selling price are required in order to increase the volume of sales being achieved. Beyond this point the slopes of the total cost and sales revenue lines show that total costs are rising faster than total revenues and thus **profits are falling**.

Activity level D shows the impact of the next step in the fixed costs which has a similar effect on profit as that indicated in relation to activity point B above.

(b) **Volume profit variance**

	Caramel Delight	Strawberry Sundae
Budgeted sales	800 units	600 units
Actual sales	560 units	1,260 units
Sales volume variance in units	240 units (A)	660 units (F)
× standard margin per unit	× $5	× $3
Sales volume variance in $	$1,200 (A)	$1,980 (F)
Total **sales volume variance**		$780 (F)

Mix variance

> **Top tips.** The method for calculating the variance is as follows.
>
> (i) Take the actual total of sales and convert this total into a standard or budgeted mix, on the assumption that sales should have been in the budgeted proportions or mix.
>
> (ii) The difference between actual sales and 'standard mix' sales for each product is then converted into a variance by multiplying by the standard margin.

		Units
Total quantity sold (560 + 1,260)		1,820
Budgeted mix for actual sales:	4/7 Caramel Delight	1,040
	3/7 Strawberry Sundae	780
		1,820

	'Should' mix Actual quantity Standard mix	'Did' mix Actual quantity Actual mix	Difference	× Standard margin	Variance
Caramel Delight	1,040 units	560 units	480 (A)	× $5	$2,400 (A)
Strawberry Sundae	780 units	1,260 units	480 (F)	× $3	$1,440 (F)
	1,820 units	1,820 units	–		$960 (A)

Quantity variance

The sales quantity variance is calculated as follows.

	Actual sales Standard mix	Standard sales Standard mix	Difference in units	× Standard profit	Variance
Caramel Delight	1,040 units	800 units	240 units (F)	× $5	$1,200 (F)
Strawberry Sundae	780 units	600 units	180 units (F)	× $3	$540 (F)
	1,820 units	1,400 units	420 units		$1,740 (F)

Summary

	$
Sales mix variance	960 (A)
Sales quantity variance	1,740 (F)
Sales volume variance	780 (F)

If an organisation uses standard marginal costing instead of standard absorption costing then standard contribution rather than standard profit margin is used in the calculations.

(c)   The favourable **sales volume variance** indicates that a potential increase in profit was achieved as a result of the change in sales volume compared with the budgeted volume.

The **sales mix variance** is adverse due to the fact that more of the less profitable Strawberry Sundae was sold than budgeted.

Profit would have been $960 higher if the 1,820 units had been sold in the budgeted mix of Caramel Delight 4: Strawberry Sundae 3.

The favourable **sales quantity variance** of $1,740 is the difference in profit because sales volumes of both products were higher than budgeted, possibly due to effective marketing campaigns.

18 Preparation question: Linear Programming

Text reference. Linear programming is covered in Chapter 3.

Top tips. When dealing with linear programming questions, you need to define the variables, state the objective function and state the constraints. You will lose marks if you forget any of these. The most common failing (because it is not specifically stated in the question) is to forget to define the variables. The marker will become confused if he or she does not know what you mean by x or y.

(a)   **Define variables**

Let   **a** = number of units of Product A to be produced
      b = number of units of Product B to be produced

Establish objective function

Profits will be maximised when contribution (C) is maximised. Contributions earned from Products A and B are $9 and $23 per unit respectively.

The objective function is therefore:

Maximise C = 9a + 23b, subject to the constraints below.

Establish constraints

The constraint equations for this problem are as follows.

Non-negativity constraint	$b \geq 0$
Minimum supply – Product A	$a \geq 1,000$
Materials constraint	$3a + 4b \leq 30,000$ (see W1)
Labour constraints	$5a + 3b \leq 36,000$ (see W2)

Workings

(1)   Product A requires 3kg material ($6 ÷ $2 per kg)
       Product B requires 4kg material ($8 ÷ $2 per kg)

(2)   Product A requires 5 labour hours ($30 ÷ $6 per hour)
       Product B requires 3 labour hours ($18 ÷ $6 per hour)

(b)   **Establish coordinates to plot lines representing the inequalities**

Materials: If a = 0, b = 7,500
              If b = 0, a = 10,000

Labour: If a = 0, b = 12,000
              If b = 0, a = 7,200

Also plot the line a = 1,000 (minimum supply of product A).

Construct an iso-contribution line
C = 9a + 23b
Say 9a + 23b = 103,500 (where 103,500 = 9 × 23 × 500*), then:
If a = 0, b = 4,500
If b = 0, a = 11,500

* Multiplied by 500 to enable line to be plotted on graph.

Draw the graph

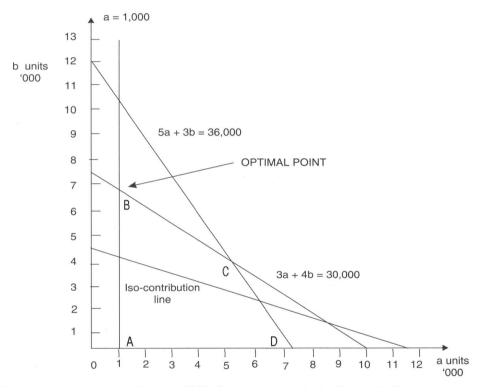

The **feasible region** is the area inside area ABCD. Make sure you shade this area in the exam.

Find the optimal solution

The optimal production plan occurs at the OPTIMAL POINT (B) shown on the graph ie where (a = 1,000) crosses (3a + 4b = 30,000).

Solving at point B

If a = 1,000
(3 × 1,000) + 4b = 30,000
4b = 30,000 − 3,000
4b = 27,000
$$b = \frac{27,000}{4}$$
= 6,750

Therefore the optimal production plan is to make 1,000 units of Product A (a = 1,000) and 6,750 units of Product B (b = 6,750).

Contribution at this point = (1,000 × \$9) + (6,750 × \$23) = \$164,250

(c)   **Slack** occurs when maximum availability of a resource is not used. If, at the optimal solution, the resource used equals the resource available, the constraint is **binding** and there is no slack.

For this company:

Material: $3a + 4b \leq 30,000$

If a = 1,000 and b = 6,750

$(3 \times 1,000) + (4 \times 6,750) = 30,000 =$ availability

Constraint is **binding**

Labour: $5a + 3b \leq 36,000$

$(5 \times 1,000) + (3 \times 6,750) = 25,250 < 36,000$

There is **slack** of 10,750 hours

If a minimum quantity of a resource must be used and, at the optimal solution, **more** than that quantity is used, there is a **surplus** on the minimum requirement. Here there is a minimum supply of Product A of 1,000 units and this is what will be produced under the optimal production plan. There is therefore no surplus.

(d)   The **shadow price** or dual price of a limiting factor is the increase in value which would be created by having one additional unit of the limiting factor at the original cost. For this company under these conditions, material is a binding constraint and a limiting factor so we can calculate how much extra contribution will be obtained if one extra kilogram of the material becomes available.

The materials constraint will now be $3a + 4b \leq 30,001$ and the optimal point will be where this line crosses the line representing $a \geq 1,000$.

If a = 1,000
$(3 \times 1,000) + 4b = 30,001$
$4b = 30,001 - 3,000$
$4b = 27,001$
$b = \dfrac{27,001}{4} = 6,750.25$

Contribution at this point = (1,000 × \$9) + (6,750.25 × \$23) = \$164,255.75

Therefore the shadow price of material is \$(164,255.75 − 164,250) = \$5.75

19 LD Co

Text references. Linear programming is covered in Chapter 4.

Top tips. Follow the step-by step process in this question, clearly labelling your workings and it should be straightforward. Make sure you read all parts of the question very carefully as it is easy to miss an essential element.

Easy marks. Being able to explain the meaning of slack, surplus and shadow process should provide easy marks even you make a mistake in the calculations.

(a) (i) **Define variables**

Let L = number of laundry services provided
Let D = number of dry cleaning services provided

Establish objective function

Fixed costs will be the same irrespective of the optimal mix and so the objective is to maximise contribution (C).

Laundry contribution	= \$5.60 − \$(2 + 1.2 + 0.5)
	= \$1.90
Dry cleaning contribution	= \$13.20 − \$(3 + 2 + 1.5)
	= \$6.70

Maximise C = 1.9L + 6.7D, subject to the constraints below.

Establish constraints

Cleaning materials:
$$\frac{2}{10}L + \frac{3}{10}D \leq 5{,}000$$
$$0.2L + 0.3D \leq 5{,}000$$

Direct labour:
$$\frac{1.2}{6}L + \frac{2}{6}D \leq 6{,}000$$
$$0.2L + 0.333D \leq 6{,}000$$

Variable machine cost:
$$\frac{0.5}{3}L + \frac{1.5}{3}D \leq 5{,}000$$
$$0.167L + 0.5D \leq 5{,}000$$

Maximum and minimum services (for contract): $L \leq 14{,}000$
$L \geq 1{,}200$
$D \geq 2{,}000$
$D \leq 9{,}975$

(ii) Establish coordinates to plot lines representing the inequalities.

Cleaning materials: If L = 0, D = 16,667
If D = 0, L = 25,000

Direct labour: If L = 0, D = 18,000
If D = 0, L = 30,000

Variable machine cost: If L = 0, D = 10,000
If D = 0, L = 30,000

Also plot the lines L = 1,200, D = 2,000, L = 14,000 and D = 9,975

Construct an iso-contribution line

C = 1.9L + 6.7D

If C = (1.9 × 6.7 × 1,000) = 12,730, then:

if L = 6,700, D = 0
if D = 1,900, L = 0

Draw the graph

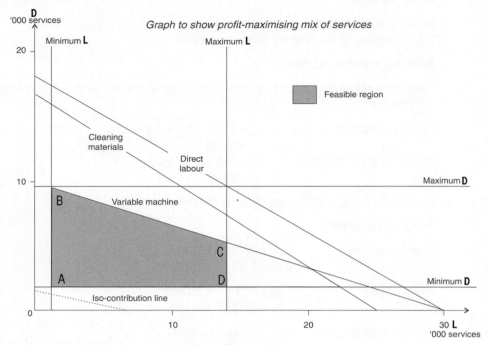

The **feasible region** is the area inside area ABCD.

Find the optimal solution

By moving the iso-contribution line out across the graph, it is clear that the optimal solution lies at the intersection of lines representing the constraints for minimum number of laundry services and machine hours.

∴ Optimal solution occurs when:

L = 1,200 and 0.167L + 0.5D = 5,000

If L = 1,200, then D = (5,000 – 200) × 2 = 9,600

The **optimal solution** is to carry out 1,200 laundry services and 9,600 dry cleaning services.

Maximum profit

		$
Contribution		
Laundry:	1,200 × unit contribution of $1.90	2,280
Dry cleaning:	9,600 × unit contribution of $6.70	64,320
		66,600
Less: fixed costs (32,825/12)		2,735
		63,865

(b) **Slack** occurs when maximum availability of a resource is not used. If, at the optimal solution, the resource used equals the resource available, the constraint is **binding** and there is no slack .

For LD Co:

Cleaning materials: 0.2L + 0.3D ≤ 5,000

If L = 1,200 and D = 9,600
(0.2 × 1,200) + (0.3 × 9,600) = 3,120 < 5,000

There is **slack** of 1,880 litres

Labour hours: 0.2L + 0.333D ≤ 6,000
(0.2 × 1,200) + (0.333 × 9,600) = 3,437 < 6,000

There is **slack** of 2,563 hours

Machine hours: $0.167L + 0.5D \leq 5{,}000$
$(0.167 \times 1{,}200) + (0.5 \times 9{,}600) = 5{,}000$ = availability
Constraint is **binding**

If a minimum quantity of a resource must be used and, at the optimal solution, **more** than that quantity is used, there is a **surplus** on the minimum requirement. This will only apply to dry cleaning services.

(c) The **shadow price** or dual price of a limiting factor is the increase in value which would be created by having one additional unit of the limiting factor at the original cost. For this company under these conditions, machine hours are a binding constraint and a limiting factor so we can calculate how much extra contribution will be obtained if one extra hour of machine time becomes available.

The machine hours constraint will now be $0.167L + 0.5D \leq 5{,}001$ and the optimal point will be where this line crosses the line representing $L \geq 1{,}200$.

If $L = 1{,}200$
$(0.167 \times 1{,}200) + 0.5D = 5{,}001$
$0.5D = 5{,}001 - 200$
$0.5D = 4{,}801$
$D = 4{,}801 \times 2 = 9{,}602$

Contribution at this point = $(1{,}200 \times \$1.90) + (9{,}602 \times \$6.70) = \$66{,}613.40$

The shadow price is the price over and above the usual price that LD Co would pay for a machine hour. This is calculated as $\$(66{,}613.40 - 66{,}600) = \$13.40$. This means that the price they would be prepared to pay is $\$13.40 + \$3 = \$16.40$.

This means that extra machine time could be rented, for example, provided the *extra cost* is less than $\$13.40$ per hour.

20 Higgins Co

Text references. Linear programming is covered in Chapter 4.

Top tips. The biggest problem with this question is time management. There is a lot to do in the time allowed.

Make sure all calculations and the graph are neatly laid out and easy for the marker to read.

Easy marks. Parts (a) and (b) should be very straightforward.

Examiner's comments. This question was in the main reasonably well done, certainly in parts a) and b). Some common errors were made though in the construction of the basic model including ignoring the demand (external) constraints completely and missing out the non-negativity constraints. Some candidates did not fully understand what a shadow prices was and fewer still how to calculate it.

Marks

(a)   Selling prices   ½
      Ash costs   ½
      Craftsmen costs   ½
      Contribution identified   ½

                                                                           2

(b)   Assigning letters for variables   ½
      Defining ash constraint   1
      Defining craftsmen constraint   1
      Demand constraint – pool   ½
      Demand constraint - snooker   ½
      Non-negativity constraint   ½
      Correctly drawn diagram
      Labels   ½
      Title   ½
      Ash constraint line   ½
      Craftsmen constraint line   ½
      Pool demand line   ½
      Snooker demand line   ½
      Identified feasible region   ½
      Contribution line   1
      Identified optimal point   ½
      Solve at optimal   2
      Calculation of contribution   1

                                                                           12

(c)   Explanation of a shadow price   2
      Ash shadow price   2
      Craftsmen shadow price   2

                                                                           6
                                                                          ―――
                                                                           20

(a)   **Contribution per cue**

	Pool cue	Snooker cue
	$	$
Selling price	41.00	69.00
Material cost @ $40 per kg	(10.80)	(10.80)
Craftsmen cost @ $18 per hour	(9.00)	(13.50)
Other variable costs	(1.20)	(4.70)
Contribution	20.00	40.00

(b)   **Define variables**

Let   **P** = number of pool cues sold per period
      S = number of snooker cues sold per period

Establish constraints

Craftsmen	$0.5P + 0.75S \leq 12,000$
Ash	$0.27P + 0.27S \leq 5,400$
Demand for pool cues	$P \leq 15,000$
Demand for snooker cues	$S \leq 12,000$
Non-negativity	$P \geq 0, S \geq 0$

BPP LEARNING MEDIA

Construct objective function

The objective is to maximise contribution (C):

C = 20P + 40S

Construct an iso-contribution line

C = 20P + 40S

Say 20P + 40S = 80 (where 80 = 20 × 40 / 10*), then:

If P = 0, S = 2

If S = 0, P = 4

* Divided by 10 to enable line to be plotted on graph.

Linear programming graph

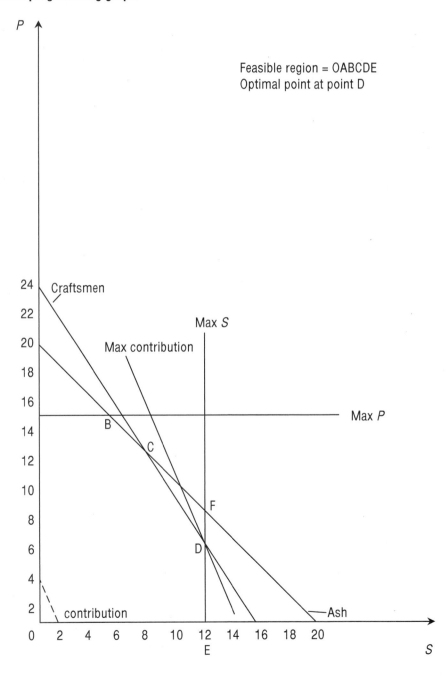

Feasible region = OABCDE
Optimal point at point D

The **feasible region** is the area inside OABCDE.

The iso-contribution line is the dotted line which can be pushed outwards to increase the contribution gained. This gives a maximum contribution at **point D** where the craftsmen constraint line meets the maximum demand for S constraint line.

Solving at point D

Maximum demand S = 12,000 (1)
Craftsmen 0·5P + 0·75S = 12,000 (2)
Substituting S = 12,000 in equation (2)
0·5P + (0·75 × 12,000) = 12,000
0·5P + 9,000 = 12,000
0·5P = 12,000 − 9,000
0·5P = 3,000
P = 6,000

Therefore the maximum contribution is earned when 6,000 pool cues and 12,000 snooker cues are made and sold in a three month period.

The **contribution** earned	= (20 × 6,000) + (40 × 12,000)
	= 120,000 + 480,000
	= $600,000

Alternative solution

Instead of using an iso-contribution line, the contribution at each inter-section of the feasible region can be calculated and the point with the largest contribution chosen.

Point B

Maximum demand	P = 15,000 (1)
Ash	0.27P + 0.27S = 5,400 (2)
Substituting	P = 15,000 in equation (2)
	(0·27 × 15,000) + 0.27S = 5,400
	4,050 + 0.27S = 5,400
	0·27S = 1,350
	S = 5,000
Contribution earned	= (20 × 15,000) + (40 × 5,000)
	= 300,000 + 200,000
	= $500,000

Point C

Ash	0.27P + 0.27S = 5,400 (1)
Craftsmen	0·5P + 0·75S = 12,000 (2)
	(1) × 0.5
	0.135P + 0.135S = 2,700 (3)
	(2) × 0.27
	0.135P + 0.2025S = 3,240 (4)
	(4) − (3)
	0.0675S = 540
	S = 8,000

Substituting in (1)

$$0.27P + (0.27 \times 8{,}000) = 5{,}400$$
$$0.27P = 5{,}400 - 2{,}160$$
$$P = 12{,}000$$

Contribution earned
$$= (20 \times 12{,}000) + (40 \times 8{,}000)$$
$$= 240{,}000 + 320{,}000$$
$$= \$560{,}000$$

Point D

Contribution = $600,000 (already calculated above)

(c) **Shadow price**

The shadow price is the **extra contribution** or profit that may be earned if one more unit of a **binding resource** or **limiting factor** becomes available.

It can be used to inform managers of the **maximum price** that should be paid for more of a scarce resource over and above the basic rate. The shadow price of a constraint that is not binding at the optimal solution is zero.

Calculation of shadow prices

At the optimal solution, P = 6,000 and S = 12,000

Contribution = $600,000

Ash

$$0.27P + 0.27S = 5{,}400$$

$$(0.27 \times 6{,}000) + (0.27 \times 12{,}000) = 4{,}860 < 5{,}400$$

There is **slack** of ash so it is not a binding constraint and there is no shadow price.

Craftsmen

$$0{\cdot}5P + 0{\cdot}75S = 12{,}000$$

$$(0.5 \times 6{,}000) + (0.75 \times 12{,}000) = 12{,}000 = \text{availability}$$

The constraint is **binding.** If one more hour of labour was available, the new optimal product mix would be at the intersection of the lines:

Maximum demand	$S = 12{,}000$ (1)
Craftsmen	$0{\cdot}5P + 0{\cdot}75S = 12{,}001$ (2)
Substituting	$S = 12{,}000$ in equation (2)
	$0{\cdot}5P + (0{\cdot}75 \times 12{,}000) = 12{,}001$
	$0{\cdot}5P + 9{,}000 = 12{,}001$
	$0{\cdot}5P = 12{,}001 - 9{,}000$
	$0{\cdot}5P = 3{,}001$
	$P = 6{,}002$
The contribution earned	$= (20 \times 6{,}002) + (40 \times 12{,}000)$
	$= 120{,}040 + 480{,}000$
	$= \$600{,}040$

The **shadow price** of one hour of craftsman's time is the extra contribution generated which is **$40.**

21 Cut and Stitch

Marking scheme

		Marks
(a)	Optimal point calculation	3
	Contribution	1
		4
(b)	For each shadow price	3
		6
(c)	Rate discussion	3
	Other factors e.g. tiredness, negotiation	3
		6
(d)	Find optimum point	1
	Solve 2 equations	2
	Conclusion	1
		4
		20

(a)   **The optimal production mix can be found by solving the constraint equations for F and T**

$$7W + 5L = 3,500 \quad (1)$$
$$2W + 2L = 1,200 \quad (2)$$

Multiply the second equation by 2.5 to yield a common value for L in each equation

7W + 5L = 3,500   (1)
5W + 5L = 3,000   (3)
2W = 500   (1) – (3)
W = 250

Substitute W = 250 into the fabric equation to calculate L

2 x 250 + 2L = 1,200
2L = 700
L = 350

Calculate the related contribution to the optimal production mix

C = 48W + 40L
C = (48 × 250) + (40 × 350)
C = 26,000

The contribution gained is $26,000

(b)   **The shadow prices can be found by adding one unit to each constraint in turn.**

Shadow price of T

7W + 5L = 3,501   (1)
2W + 2L = 1,200   (2)

Multiply the second equation by 2.5 to yield a common value for L in each equation

7W + 5L = 3,501   (1)
5W + 5L = 3,000   (3)
2W = 501   (1) – (3)
W = 250.5

Substitute W = 250.5 into the fabric equation to calculate L

(2 × 250.5) + 2L = 1,200
2L = 1,200 – 501
L = 349.5

Contribution earned at this point would be = (48 x 250.5) + (40 x 349.5) = 26,004 (increase of $4).

The shadow price of T is $4 per hour.

Shadow price of F

7W + 5L = 3,500
2W + 2L = 1,201

Multiply the second equation by 2.5 to yield a common value for L in each equation

7W + 5L = 3,500.0
5W + 5L = 3,002.5
2W = 497.5
W = 248.75

Substitute W = 248.75 into the fabric equation to calculate L

(2 × 248.75) + 2L = 1,201
2L = 1,201 – 497.5
L = 351.75

Contribution earned at this point would be = (48 x 248.75) + (40 x 351.75) = 26,010 (increase of $10).

The shadow price of F is $10 per metre.

(c)   The **shadow price** is the increase in contribution created by the availability of an extra unit of a limited resource at its original cost.

In this instance, it represents the maximum **premium** above the normal rate that a business should be willing to pay for one more unit of a scarce resource.

The shadow price of labour is $4 per hour (as calculated in part (b)). The tailors are usually paid $1.50 per hour and have offered to work the extra time providing they are paid three times their normal rate ($4.50). This represents a premium of $3.00 per hour.

This is $1.00 per hour below the maximum premium and so the offer appears to be acceptable.

The company should consider negotiating with the tailors in order to reduce the premium further. Furthermore, there is a potential risk that the tailors may be tired from working the extra hours which could detract from the quality of the suits and have an adverse impact on the reputation of the Cut and Stitch brand.

(d)   If the maximum demand for W falls to 200 units, the constraint for W will move left to 200 on the X axis on the graph. The new optimum point will then be at the intersection of:

W = 200 and
2W + 2L = 1,200

Solving the equation simultaneously:

(2 × 200) + 2L = 1,200
L = 400

Therefore, the new production plan will be to make 400L and 200W.

22 The Cosmetic Co

Text reference. Graphical linear programming is covered in Chapter 4.

Top tips. Perhaps the biggest challenge in this question is time management. There is a lot to do in the time allowed.

Use the step by step approach in part (a), clearly labelling your workings to make it easy for the marker to follow. Make sure your read the question scenario very carefully as it is easy to miss an element.

Easy marks. There are plenty of easy marks available throughout for establishing the constraints and clearly drawing and labelling each line on the graph.

Examiner's comments. Much of this question could have been examined at F2. Why then, was it in the F5 paper? It is becoming more and more apparent that the assumed F2 knowledge for F5 simply isn't there and it is therefore necessary to make candidates realise that it is examinable under F5 and that, if they don't know the subject matter, they need to go away and study it!

Candidates who had revised this area made a decent attempt at this question, with many of them scoring full marks in part (a) at least. It is important, when answering a linear programming question like this, to set out your workings clearly, with a logical progression in steps from defining the variables and constraints, through to drawing the graph and finding the solution. This makes it easier to mark. The recommended approach is to use the iso-contribution line to find the optimum solution; it is the quickest way to do it. Candidates weren't penalised if they used the simultaneous equations method, because they were not told which method to use, but they penalised themselves because it took them longer to do it.

It is essential to show all of your workings. So, for example, the iso-contribution line needs to be worked out and then drawn onto the graph. If you didn't show how you worked it out, you stood to lose some marks.

Where you are asked to work to 2 decimal places, you should do it. In this question, it was necessary in order to keep a level of accuracy required to answer part (b) as well. Whilst we gave follow on marks for part (b) wherever possible, if fundamental mistakes had been made in part (a) so that, for example, there was no slack for amino acids, it was hard to award marks.

Marking scheme

		Marks
(a)	Optimum production plan:	
	Assigning letters for variables	½
	Defining constraint for silk powder	½
	Defining constraint for amino acids	½
	Defining constraint for labour	½
	Non-negativity constraint	½
	Sales constraint: x	½
	Sales constraint: y	½
	Iso-contribution line worked out	1
	The graph:	
	Labels	½
	Silk powder	½
	Amino acids	½
	Labour line	½
	Demand for x line	½
	Demand for y line	½
	Iso-contribution line	½
	Vertices a–e identified	½
	Feasible region shaded	½
	Optimum point identified	1
	Equations solved at optimum point	3
	Total contribution	1
		14
(b)	Shadow prices and slack:	
	Shadow price	4
	Slack	2
		6
		20

(a) Define variables

Let x = number of jars of face cream to be produced
Let y = number of bottles of body lotion to be produced
Let C = contribution

Establish objective function

The objective is to maximise contribution (C).

Face cream contribution (x) = $9.00 per unit

Body lotion contribution (y) = $8.00 per unit

Maximise $C = 9x + 8y$, subject to the constraints below.

Establish constraints

Silk powder:	$3x + 2y \leq 5,000$
Silk amino acids:	$1x + 0.5y \leq 1,600$
Skilled labour:	$4x + 5y \leq 9,600$
Non-negativity constraints:	$x, y \geq 0$
Maximum demand for body lotion:	$y \leq 2,000$

Establish coordinates to plot lines representing the inequalities

Silk powder:	$3x + 2y \leq 5,000$
	If $x = 0$, $y = 2,500$
	If $y = 0$, $x = 1,666.7$
Silk amino acids:	$1x + 0.5y \leq 1,600$
	If $x = 0$, $y = 3,200$
	If $y = 0$, $x = 1,600$
Skilled labour:	$4x + 5y \leq 9,600$
	If $x = 0$, $y = 1,920$
	If $y = 0$, $x = 2,400$

Also plot the line $y = 2,000$ (maximum weekly demand for body lotion).

Draw the graph

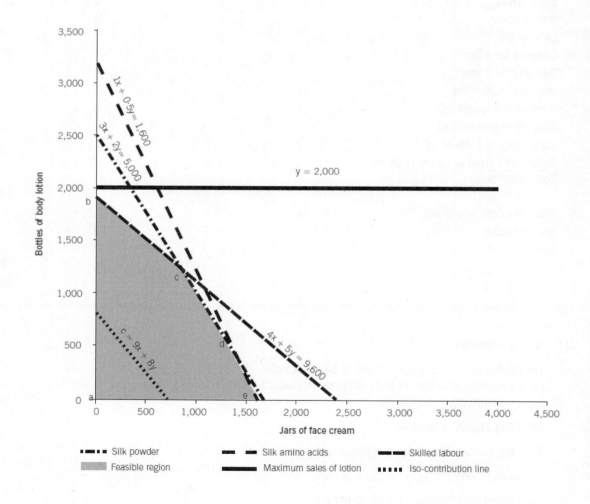

BPP
LEARNING MEDIA

Find the optimal solution using an iso-contribution line

$C = 9x + 8y$

If $C = (8 \times 800) = 6{,}400$, then:

If $y = 0$, $9x = 6{,}400$
Therefore $x = 711.11$

By moving the iso-contribution line out across the graph, it is clear that the optimal solution lies as point C, the intersection of the constraints for skilled labour and silk powder.

Solving the simultaneous equations for these constraints:
$4x + 5y = 9{,}600 \qquad \times 3$
$3x + 2y = 5{,}000 \qquad \times 4$

$12x + 15y = 28{,}800 \quad (1)$
$12x + 8y = 20{,}000 \quad (2)$
Subtract (2) from (1):
$7y = 8{,}800$
$y = 1{,}257.14$

If $y = 1{,}257.14$ and;
$4x + 5y = 9{,}600$

The $5 \times 1{,}257.14 + 4x = 9{,}600$
Therefore $x = 828.58$

The **optimal solution** is therefore to make 828.58 jars of face cream and 1,257.14 bottles of body lotion.

Maximum profit

		$
Contribution		
Face cream:	828.58 units × unit contribution of $9.00	7,457.22
Body lotion:	1,257.14 units × unit contribution of $8.00	10,057.12
		17,514.34

(b) **Shadow price for silk powder**

The shadow price for silk powder can be found by solving the two simultaneous equations that intersect at point C on the graph in part (a). The **shadow price** is the **increase in value which would be created by having one additional unit** of limiting factor. For this reason, we must add one more hour to the equation for silk powder.

$4x + 5y = 9{,}600 \qquad \times 3$
$3x + 2y = 5{,}001 \qquad \times 4$

$12x + 15y = 28{,}800 \quad (1)$
$12x + 8y = 20{,}004 \quad (2)$

Subtract (2) from (1):
$7y = 8{,}796$
$y = 1{,}256.57$

$3x + (2 \times 1{,}256.57) = 5{,}001$
$x = 829.29$

$C = (9 \times 829.29) + (8 \times 1{,}256.57) = \$17{,}516.17$

Original contribution = $17,514.34

The **shadow price for silk powder** is therefore $1.83 per gram.

Slack for amino acids

Each unit of face cream requires 1 gram of silk amino acids and each unit of body lotion requires 0.5 grams of amino acids.

$(828.58 \times 1) + (0.5 \times 1,257.14) = 1,457.15$ grams used.

Grams available = 1,600 grams.

Therefore slack = 142.85 grams.

23 RB Co

Text reference. Pricing is covered in Chapter 5.

Top tips. In part (a) make sure you relate your discussion to the specific circumstances of RB Co rather than just regurgitating a text book explanation of cost-plus pricing.

In part (b) the problem is deciding on the alternative pricing strategies to suggest. You may have included target pricing, for example.

Part (c) is a straightforward use of the demand curve formula which you will be given in the exam and part (d) requires a simple explanation of the total cost function.

Part (e) requires a good understanding of price elasticity of demand again applied to the specific company circumstances.

(a) **Managing director's pricing strategy**

The managing director has adopted what is known as a **full cost plus** pricing strategy, which means that a profit margin (in this case, of 50%) is added to the budgeted full cost of the product.

Given the information in the question, the **selling price used by RB Co** is calculated as follows.

	$
Full cost	400
50% mark up	200
Selling price	600

Disadvantages of this pricing strategy

Its **focus** is **internal** – internal costs and internal targets. It therefore takes **no account of the market conditions** faced by RB Co, which is why the company's selling price bears little resemblance to those of competitors. By adopting a fixed mark-up, **it does not allow the company to react to competitors'** pricing decisions.

Absorption bases used when calculating the full cost are **decided arbitrarily**. The current basis of absorption is based on the budgeted level of production, which is lower than the current capacity. **Depending on the absorption basis** used in the calculation of total cost, the strategy can **produce different selling prices**.

Advantages of this pricing strategy

It is **quick, cheap** and relatively **easy** to apply. Pricing can therefore be delegated to more junior management if necessary.

It ensures that **all costs are covered** and that the organisation **makes a profit**, provided budget figures used in the pricing calculation are reasonably accurate. This was the case in the first two years for RB Co.

The **costs of collecting market information** on demand and competitor activity are **avoided**.

(b) **Alternative pricing strategies**

    (1)   **Market penetration pricing**

        Market penetration pricing is a policy of **low prices** when a product is first launched in order to achieve **high sales volumes** and hence gain a **significant market share**. If RB Co had adopted this strategy it might have discouraged competitors from entering the market.

    (2)   **Market skimming**

        This pricing strategy involves charging **high prices** when a product is first launched and **spending heavily on advertising and promotion** to obtain sales so as to exploit any price insensitivity in the market. Such an approach would have been particularly suitable for RB's circumstances: demand for the software would have been relatively inelastic, customers being prepared to pay high prices for the software given its novelty appeal. As the product moves into later stages of its life cycle, prices can be reduced in order to remain competitive.

(c) When demand is linear the equation for the demand curve is:

$$P = a - bQ$$

where P = the price

           Q = the quantity demanded

           a = the price at which demand would be nil

           b $= \dfrac{\text{change in price}}{\text{change in quantity}}$

$a = \$750$

$b = \dfrac{\$10}{1{,}000}$

$ = 0.01$

$\therefore P = 750 - 0.01Q$

(d) **Cost behaviour** can be modelled using a **simple linear equation** of the form $y = a + bx$ where 'a' represents the fixed costs, which for RB are $1,200,000 (15,000 × \$80$), and 'b' represents the variable costs per unit ie $320 (400 − 80)$ per unit for RB. This cost model assumes fixed costs remain unchanged over all ranges of output and a constant unit variable cost.

(e) **Price elasticity of demand**

Price elasticity of demand is a measure of the extent of change in market demand for a good in response to a change in its price. It is measured as:

$$\frac{\text{The change in quantity demanded, as a \% of demand}}{\text{The change in price, as a \% of the price}}$$

Since the demand goes up when the price falls, and goes down when the price rises, the elasticity has a negative value, but it is usual to ignore the minus sign.

The value of demand elasticity may be anything from zero to infinity.

Elastic and inelastic demand

Demand is referred to as **inelastic** if the absolute value is less than 1. Where demand is **inelastic**, the **quantity demanded falls by a smaller percentage than the percentage increase in price**.

Where demand is **elastic, demand falls** by a **larger percentage than the percentage rise in price** the absolute value is greater than 1.

Pricing decisions

An awareness of the concept of elasticity can assist management with **pricing decisions**.

In circumstances of **inelastic demand**, **prices should be increased** because revenues will increase and total costs will reduce (because quantities sold will reduce).

In circumstances of **elastic demand**, increases in prices will bring decreases in revenue and decreases in price will bring increases in revenue. Management therefore have to **decide** whether the **increase/decrease in costs will be less than/greater than the increases/decreases in revenue**.

In situations of **very elastic demand**, overpricing can lead to a massive drop in quantity sold and hence a massive drop in profits whereas underpricing can lead to costly stock outs and, again, a significant drop in profits. **Elasticity must therefore be reduced by creating a customer preference which is unrelated to price** (through advertising and promotional activities).

In situations of **very inelastic demand**, customers are **not sensitive to price**. **Quality, service, product mix and location** are therefore **more important** to a firm's pricing strategy.

Cost-plus pricing

Cost-plus pricing is based on the **assumption** that demand for the company's software is **inelastic** and prices should be increased in order to increase total revenue and hence profit. The market research information for RB Co does not support this view, however. It suggests that increasing prices will lead to a drop in demand and hence a reduction in profit.

24 New product

Text references. Pricing is covered in Chapter 5.

Top tips. In part (a) look for the key points within the scenario. Your answer to part (b) may be different to ours but provided you stated assumptions, set out your arguments and worked through your reasoning in a logical fashion you would have received marks.

Always check the reasonableness of your answer. Given a competitor's product sells for $65, prices of $1.50 and $3,000 are unlikely to be in the range of possible acceptable prices.

Easy marks. You should be able to put down some basic points in part (a) covering pricing strategy. You will get better marks by relating these to the scenario.

(a)   Pricing strategy is **concerned with the level of price** (high, average or low) charged and should have regard to a number of factors.

Profitability

The product must be profitable, and so its price must cover costs. A mark-up on factory cost in the range 30%-45% is indicated as typical for the company, but the mark-up must also be sufficient to cover selling and administration expenses.

Product life cycle

The new product involves an advanced technology. This indicates a relatively short life cycle, in which case a high price strategy should be preferred.

Quality

The product has an unrivalled quality, which again suggests that the price can be higher than the competition (ie well above $65). Since it is unlikely that competitors will be able to match this quality for 12-18 months, the company will have the benefit of being in a **monopoly situation** during this time. This has the following implications.

(i)   It is in a strong position to decide its own price rather than accept the ruling market price.
(ii)   Its price will probably be higher than if the company had faced more direct competition.

Market share

The company would probably be dissatisfied with a market share below 5%, and since the major competitor has 30% of the market with an inferior product, it should be possible to capture 5% or more of the market with a higher-priced but better-quality product.

Competition

The monopoly position might only last for 12-18 months, however, and a price review will be necessary in due course. In order to build up customer loyalty, the company should not charge extremely high prices, otherwise its market share might dwindle rapidly when competitors do eventually begin to offer products of rival quality.

Conclusion

A fairly high price strategy is advised for the first 12-18 months, subject to the limitation that the longer-term market share should be safeguarded by trying to build up a reasonably large market share in this 12-18 month period. Eventually, prices are likely to have to come down in response to competition.

(b)   **Initial reasoning**

(i)   A **full-cost-plus based approach** is to be taken so the company is pursuing a high price strategy.

(ii) The cost estimates should **provide in full for the possible costing errors** (given a high price strategy).

(iii) The profit mark-up should be at least 45% on factory cost and probably more. Given the monopolistic position of the company as regards product quality, a **mark-up of 50%** is not considered unreasonable and is used here as a **starting point** for making the pricing decision. It is assumed that 'factory cost' means **full factory cost** and not variable factory cost.

(iv) **Selling and administration expenses** must be covered too, but these will be **excluded** from the cost-plus-based price, since this is the approach normally taken by the company. These costs ($20,000) cannot be ignored, however, and will be considered later in the context of sales volume and market share.

Calculation of full factory cost

	$ per unit		$ per unit
Direct materials			12.00
Direct labour			28.00
			40.00
Production overhead			
Dept X (2 hrs × $2.40)	4.8	(note 1)	
Dept Y (1.5 hrs × $1.80)	2.7	(note 1)	
Dept Z (3 hrs × $0.80)	2.4	(note 1)	
			9.90
			49.90
Add potential costing error of up to 10%			4.99
			54.89
Profit mark-up (50%)			27.45
Suggested sales price, initial estimate (note 2)			82.34

Notes

(1)   The figures in the table in the question allow us to calculate the variable and fixed overhead rates in each department.

		Dept X	Dept Y	Dept Z
(A)	Full cost overhead rate per hour	$2.40	$1.80	$0.80
(B)	Normal volume (hrs)	12,500	15,000	25,000
		$	$	$
	Total monthly overheads ((A) × (B))	30,000	27,000	20,000
	Fixed and/or allocated overhead	5,000	6,000	7,500
	Variable overhead	25,000	21,000	12,500
	Variable overhead per hour	$2.00	$1.40	$0.50
	Fixed/allocated overhead per hour	$0.40	$0.40	$0.30

If it were assumed that the profit mark-up should be based on variable factory cost, not full factory cost, these **variable overhead rates** should be **used** in the computation of the selling price instead of the full cost overhead rate.

(2)   The variable cost per unit of product is determined as follows.

	$
Direct materials	12.00
Direct labour	28.00
Variable overhead	
Department X (2 hrs × $2)	4.00
Department Y (1.5 hrs × $1.40)	2.10
Department Z (3 hrs × $0.50)	1.50
	47.60
Plus potential error in estimate (10%)	4.76
	52.36

At a **price of $82.34, the unit contribution** would be about **$30**. Since **selling and administration expenses** would be $20,000 per month, monthly sales would have to be at least $20,000/$30 = 667 units just to **cover these costs. In addition** a **share of fixed production overheads** should be covered, and the product should also make a sizeable **profit**, not least to recover development costs already incurred.

We know that 30% of the potential market is 6,000 units per month. If the company could obtain a **10% market share**, monthly sales would be **2,000 units.** At a **price of $82.50**, say, (rounded up from $82.34) **monthly contribution** would be about $30 per unit × 2,000 = **$60,000.**

This contribution figure might seem acceptable to the company.

Recommendation

(i)   A **sales price of $82.50** per unit is recommended.

(ii)   This would give a **profit mark-up of about 50%** on full factory cost, even allowing for possible costing errors. It would also provide a unit contribution of $30.

(iii)   If the market share is 10%, **monthly contribution would be $60,000**, leaving a net contribution of $40,000 after deducting directly attributable selling and administration expenses of $20,000.

(iv)   The allocated fixed factory overhead per unit is $(54.89 – 52.36) = $2.53, and so **even if the market share is only 5%**, or 1,000 units per month, the **product would still be profitable at this price**.

(v)   In view of the unrivalled quality of the product, however, a price of $82.50, compared with the $65 charged by the competition, might be **expected to win a market share in excess of 5%**.

(vi)   The price is **based on a high price strategy**. If demand is disappointingly low, the price should be reviewed with a view to reducing it.

(vii)   When competitors begin to match the product for quality, **some reduction in price** will be **inevitable** given the fairly steady prices in the market in recent years.

25 IB

Text references. Chapter 5 covers profit-maximising price calculations. Environmental accounting is covered in Chapter 2e.

Top tips. You may have floundered around for a few minutes at the beginning of this question, not knowing quite how to start. You can use the information about the volume variance and the budgeted production and sales volumes to find out actual volumes (given that the volume variance is the difference between budgeted and actual volumes). As the link between the demand curve and marginal revenue is provided, hopefully you realised that you had to derive the demand curve, which you couldn't do without the actual volumes. Part (i) certainly needed a fair amount of mathematical ability, but once you grasp the key steps in these questions you should find they become easier with practice.

(a)   (i) $P = a - bQ$

Where P   =   the selling price

        Q   =   the quantity demanded at that price

        a   =   theoretical maximum price. If price is set at "a" or above, demand will be zero

        b   =   the change in price required to change demand by one unit.

a and b are constants and are calculated as follows:

$$a = \$ \text{ (current price)} + \left(\frac{\text{Current quantity at current price}}{\text{Current quantity when price changed by \$b}} \times \$b \right)$$

$$b = \frac{\text{Change in price}}{\text{Change in quantity}}$$

Step 1   Establish the demand function (values for 'a' and 'b')

Find a:

When P = 200, Q = 0

Therefore, a = 200

Using fixed overhead volume variance to find actual sales units:

Fixed overhead volume variance = (Budgeted units − actual units) × standard fixed overhead rate

Rearranging:

$$\text{Actual units} = \text{budgeted units} - \frac{\text{Fixed overhead volume variance}}{\text{Standard fixed overhead rate}}$$

Month	Budgeted units	−	Fixed overhead volume variance / Standard fixed overhead rate	−	Actual units
Jan	1,040	−	$\frac{2,400}{10}$	−	800
Feb	1,180	−	$\frac{3,800}{10}$	−	800
Mar	1,320	−	$\frac{5,200}{10}$	−	800

Using high-low method to calculate b:

$$b = \frac{\text{Change in P}}{\text{Change in Q}}$$

When

P = 120, Q = 800

    = 200, Q = 0

$$b = \frac{(200 - 120)}{800}$$

    = 0.10

Step 2   Establish MC (the marginal cost)

We assume that MC = variable cost per unit of $50

Step 3 **State MR, assuming MR = a – 2bQ**

We can now write equations as:

P = 200 – 0.1Q

Therefore, MR = 200 – 0.2Q

Step 4 **Equate MC and MR to find Q**

To maximise contribution: MR = MC

200 – 0.2Q = 50

Q = 750

Step 5 **Substitute Q into the demand function and solve to find P**

To sell 750 units:

P = 200 – (0.1 × 750)

= $125.00 (this is the price at which contribution will be maximised).

(ii)	Optimal price	Actual price
	$	$
Selling price	125.00	120.00
Variable costs	50.00	50.00
Contribution per unit	75.00	70.00
Units sold	750 units	800 units
Total contribution	$56,250.00	$56,000.00

Difference in contribution = $250.00.

(b) **Why the theoretical pricing model may be inappropriate**

It is extremely difficult to determine a demand factor with any degree of accuracy, therefore IB may end up making the wrong pricing decision. In a highly competitive environment, this could prove to be disastrous, as customers will simply switch to a different supplier.

Rather than aiming for maximum profit, most organisations will try to achieve a target profit. As IB operates in a highly competitive environment, profit maximisation is unrealistic – it would be more appropriate (and motivational) to have a target profit in mind and price accordingly.

(c) **Lifecycle costing**

IB could implement a system of lifecycle costing in order to track and manage environmental costs. Such a system would **recognise environmental costs at each stage in the product lifecycle**, from the design stage up to and including end-of-life costs such as the disposal of computer consoles that have become obsolete.

Consideration of environmental costs at the design stage **may influence the design** of consoles and could save the company money in the future.

Environmental activity-based costing

For a system of environmental ABC to be successful, IB would need to clearly distinguish between **environment-related costs** and **environment-driven costs**. Environment-driven costs such as higher staff costs would be allocated to general overheads as they do not relate directly to a joint environmental cost centre.

Environment-related costs such as those relating to an environmentally friendly waste disposal facility would be allocated to a joint environmental cost centre. IB would also need to decide upon **environmental cost drivers**, for example the volume of emissions or waste at each stage of the production process and the relative costs of treating the different kinds of emissions.

26 A1

(a) (i) **Selling price for product C to maximise contribution during the maturity stage**

Selling price / unit ($)	300	255	240	225
Contribution / unit ($)	186	141	126	111
Demand (units)	1,800	2,400	3,600	4,200
	$334,800	$338,400	$453,600	$466,200

From the above table it is clear that a selling price of $225 / unit maximises contribution for Product C.

The company production facility has a capacity of 6,000 hours per week. 4,200 units of Product C will take 4,200 hours to produce (standard production time of 1 hour per unit). This leaves 1,800 hours remaining to produce Product B.

Production of Product B takes 3.75 hours per unit. Therefore the maximum number of units of Product B that can be produced in a week is 480 units.

(ii) **The selling price of product B during the growth stage**

When demand is linear the equation for the demand curve is $P = a - bQ$

Where P	=	the selling price
Q	=	the quantity demanded at that price
a	=	theoretical maximum price. If price is set at "a" or above, demand will be zero
b	=	the change in price required to change demand by one unit.

a and b are constants and are calculated as follows:

$$a = \$ \text{ (current price)} + \left(\frac{\text{Current quantity at current price}}{\text{Current quantity when price changed by } \$b} \times \$b \right)$$

$$b = \frac{\text{Change in price}}{\text{Change in quantity}}$$

Step 1 Find the price at which demand would be nil

The question states that there is a linear relationship between the selling price of the product and the number of units demanded. Therefore, each increase of $30 in the price would result in a fall in demand of 600 units. For demand to be nil, the price needs to rise from its current level by as many times as there are 600 units in 3,000 units (expected demand per week for the product).

(3,000/600 = 5) ie to $300 + (5 × $30) = $450.

Using the formula above, this can be shown as a = $300 + ((3,000/600) × $30) = $450.

Step 2 Calculate b

$$b = \frac{\text{change in price}}{\text{change in quantity}} = \frac{\$30}{600} = 0.05$$

Step 3 Complete the equation

Where Q represents the quantity demanded. We know from part (a)(i) that the maximum level of production for Product L is 480 units a week.
P = 450 − (0.05Q)
P = 450 − (0.05 x 480units)
P = 450 - 24
P = 426

Product B should be sold for $426 per unit at the growth stage.

(b) Unit production costs

Unit production costs of Product A are likely to change throughout the product's life cycle.

Production costs at the growth stage

The impact of **learning and experience curves** is likely to result in a reduction in production costs per unit at the growth stage. Costs may also decrease due to **economies of scale**.

The extent to which costs fall will depend upon the **skill level** and **experience** of the workforce and the complexity of the manufacturing process.

Production costs at the maturity stage

The workforce is likely to have become used to the manufacturing process by the maturity stage. The **learning period** will have ended and production costs per unit are likely to remain fairly constant.

Production costs at the decline stage

Sales volumes at the decline stage are likely to be low as the product is **surpassed by new exciting products** that have been introduced to the market. Furthermore, the workforce may be less interested in manufacturing a declining product and may be looking to learn new skills. For both of these reasons, **unit production costs are likely to increase** at the decline stage.

Unit selling price

The selling price will initially be high if a policy of **market skimming** is employed. The uniqueness of the product should **justify the high selling price** and will enable the company to quickly **recoup product development costs**.

Selling price at the growth stage

The high selling price will encourage competitors to attempt to produce the same product at a lower cost. Competitors may attempt to do this through **reverse engineering**.

The company should **reduce the selling price** at the growth stage to maximise unit sales as the product is more affordable to lower social economic groups.

Selling price at the maturity stage

It is likely that the price of the product will be lowered further at the maturity stage in a bid to **preserve sales volumes**. The company may attempt to preserve sales volumes by employing an **extension strategy** rather than reducing the selling price. For example, they may introduce product add-ons to the market that are compatible with Product A.

Selling price at the decline stage

At the decline stage, Product A is likely to have been **surpassed by more advanced products** in the market and consequently will **become obsolete**. The company will not want to incur **inventory holding costs** for an obsolete product and is likely to sell Product A at **marginal cost or perhaps lower.**

27 Heat Co

Text references. The demand equation, the profit-maximising price/output level and pricing strategies are covered in Chapter 5. The learning curve is covered in Chapter 10.

Top tips. Set out your workings in part (a) in stages to maximise your score. Do not forget to exclude the fixed overheads relating to the air conditioning unit in part (a)(ii) – the question asks you to calculate the marginal cost for each unit.

Easy marks. There are 8 marks available for explaining penetration pricing and market skimming and discussing their suitability for Heat Co in part (b).

Examiner's comments. The requirement to calculate the optimum price and quantity in part (a) was new to the syllabus in June 2011 and about half of candidates seemed not to have revised it and could not attempt it. It was really pleasing to see some good attempts at part (a) (ii) which tested the ability to adjust the labour cost for the learning effect.

Part (b) was really well-answered, with most candidates being able to describe both pricing strategies and suggest a suitable one.

ACCA examiner's answers. The ACCA examiner's answer to this question can be found at the back of this kit.

Marking scheme

			Marks
(a)	(i) Establish demand function:		
	Find 'b'	1	
	Find 'a'	1	
	Write out demand function	1	
			3
	(ii) Find MC:		
	Average cost of 100	1	
	Total cost of 100	1	
	Average cost of 99	1	
	Total cost of 99	1	
	Difference	1	
	Correct total MC excluding fixed cost	1	
			6
	(iii) Establish MR function	1	
	Equate MC and MR to find Q	1	
	Find optimum price	1	
			3

(b)   Penetration pricing – 1 mark per valid point   Max 4
        Market skimming – 1 mark per valid point   Max 4

(a)   **Profit**

Apply the demand equation to calculate the optimum price:

P = a – bQ

Where   P = the price

            Q = the quantity demanded

            a = the price at which demand would be nil

            b = $\dfrac{\text{change in price}}{\text{change in quantity}}$

(i)   **Establish the demand function (equation)**

Step 1   Calculate 'b'

b = $\dfrac{\text{change in price}}{\text{change in quantity}}$ = $15/1,000 = 0.015

Step 2   Substitute the known value for 'b' into the demand function to find 'a'

We know that if the company set the price at $735, demand would be 1,000 units.

735 = a – 0.015Q

735 = a – (0.015 × 1,000)

735 = a – 15

735 + 15 = a

a = 750

The demand function is therefore P = 750 – 0.015Q

(ii)   **Establish marginal cost**

Labour time is calculated using the learning curve formula and then converted to cost.

$Y = ax^b$

Where   Y = the cumulative average time per unit to produce x units

            x = the cumulative number of units

            a = the time taken for the first unit of output

            b = the index of learning (logLR/log2)

The labour cost for 100 units:

We are told that b = –0.0740005. We are also told that a = 1.5 (the first air conditioning unit took 1.5 hours to make).

x = 100.

$Y = 1.5 \times 100^{-0.0740005}$

Y = 1.0668178

Therefore cost per unit = 1.0668178 × $8 = $8.5345

Total cost for 100 units = $8.5345 × 100 = $853.45

Similarly, the labour cost for 99 units (x = 99):

$Y = 1.5 \times 99^{-0.0740005}$

Y = 1.0676115

Therefore cost per unit = 1.0676115 × $8 = $8.5409

Total cost for 99 units = $8.5409 × 99 = $845.55

Therefore cost of 100th unit = $853.45 − $845.55 = $7.90

Total marginal cost = $42 (direct materials) + $7.90 = $49.90.

Fixed overheads are ignored as they are not part of the marginal cost.

(iii)   **Find profit**

Step 1   **Establish the marginal revenue function (equation)**

MR = a − 2bQ

Using the values of 'a' and 'b' from part (i):

MR = 750 − 0.03Q

Step 2   **Equate MC and MR to find Q (quantity demanded)**

MC = MR

49.90 = 750 − 0.03Q

0.03Q = 750 − 49.90

0.03Q = 700.10

Q = 700.10/0.03

Q = 23,337

Step 3   **Find optimum price**

P = a − bQ

P = 750 − (0.015 × 23,337)

P = $399.95

(b)   **Penetration pricing**

Penetration pricing is a policy of low prices when a product is first launched in order to obtain **sufficient penetration into the market**.

A company such as Heat Co might deliberately build excess production capacity and set its prices very low. As demand increases (due to the low price) the spare capacity will be used up gradually and unit costs will fall. In this way, any early losses will be compensated for when the company eventually dominates the market and has the lowest costs.

A policy of penetration pricing may be appropriate in the cases below.

Penetration pricing is likely to **discourage new entrants** from entering the market. However, Heat Co already has a patent which prevents competitors from entering the market for two years.

If Heat Co wishes **to shorten the initial period** of the Energy Buster's **life cycle** to enter the growth and maturity stages quickly, a policy penetration pricing may prove effective. There is no evidence to suggest Heat Co wishes to do this.

Penetration pricing is particularly effective in scenarios where there are significant **economies of scale** to be achieved from a high volume of output. This is not the case for Heat Co as we are told that the learning curve is expected to finish after making 100 units.

Products with **highly elastic demand** (the lower the price, the higher the demand) lend themselves to a policy of penetration pricing. However, there is no evidence to suggest that demand for the Energy Buster is highly elastic.

From the above, it is evident that a policy of penetration pricing is suitable for Heat Co in some respects, but is not necessarily the best option.

Market skimming

Market skimming involves **charging high prices** when a product is first launched in order to **maximise short-term profitability**. Initially, there is heavy spending on advertising and sales promotion to obtain sales.

Progressively lower prices are charged as the product moves into the later stages of its life cycle (growth, maturity, decline).

A policy of market skimming is most appropriate in the cases below.

Customers are often prepared to pay high prices for a product that is **new and different**. This is indeed the case with the Energy Buster.

Market skimming is appropriate when the strength of **demand and the sensitivity of demand to price are unknown**. This is not the case for Heat Co and the Energy Buster.

Barriers to entry need to exist as high unit prices make it more likely that competitors will enter the market. Heat Co has an effective barrier to prevent competitors from entering the market (the patent for the Energy Buster).

Market skimming is also appropriate when a product has a **short life cycle** and there is a need to recover the development costs and make a profit very quickly. The life cycle of the Energy Buster is relatively short (five years) and high development costs have been incurred.

Again, the Energy Buster only meets some of the conditions to suggest that a policy of market skimming is appropriate. Given the high development costs incurred to date and relatively short life cycle, it could be argued that market skimming is the safer policy for Heat Co.

28 Sunrise

> **Text references.** Relevant costing and short-term decisions are covered in Chapter 6.
>
> **Top tips.** Carefully read through the scenario, noting the relevant costs and their causes as you do so. There is a lot of information to prepare for part (a) so presentation is key. Remember to show all of your workings!

(a) **Sunrise holiday park plan**

	Peak $	Mid $	Low $	Total $
Holiday home revenue	972,000.00	780,000.00	315,000.00	2,067,000.00
Guest related cost (guests (W1) × $7)	(215,460.00)	(191,100.00)	(117,600.00)	(524,160.00)
Holiday home costs (Days × homes (W1) × $7, $8, $10)	(56,700.00)	(62,400.00)	(52,500.00)	(171,600.00)
Avoidable general costs (W3)	(248,000.00)	(328,000.00)	(408,000.00)	(984,000.00)
Holiday home / Guest contribution	451,840.00	198,500.00	(263,100.00)	387,240.00
Restaurant contribution (W2)	72,025.20	36,036.00	8,064.00	116,125.20
Staff costs (W4)	(21,000.00)	(28,000.00)	(35,000.00)	(84,000.00)
Total contribution	502,865.20	206,536.00	(290,036.00)	419,365.20
No-avoidable costs (W5)	(62,000.00)	(82,000.00)	(102,000.00)	(246,000.00)

	Peak $	Mid $	Low $	Total $
Net contribution	440,865.20	124,536.00	(392,036.00)	173,365.20
Annual fixed costs				(250,000.00)
Annual profit / (loss)				(76,634.80)

Workings

1 **Number of hotel guests**

Season	Days	Rooms	Homes	Occupants	Guests
Peak	90	× 90	= 8,100	× 3.8	30,780.00
Mid	120	× 65	= 7,800	× 3.5	27,300.00
Low	150	× 35	= 5,250	× 3.2	16,800.00

2 **Restaurant contribution**

Season	Guests	Daily demand	Contribution	Gross contribution ($)
Peak	30,780	× 0.6 × $13	× 0.3	72.025.20
Mid	27,300	× 0.4 × $11	× 0.3	36,036.00
Low	16,800	× 0.2 × $8	× 0.3	8,064.00

3 **Avoidable general costs**

Forecast general costs for the next year are as follows. Costs could be reduced by 80% if Sunrise were to close temporarily for one or more seasons of the year.

Peak	$310,000 × 0.80	= $248,000.00
Mid	$410,000 × 0.80	= $328,000.00
Low	$510,000 × 0.80	= $408,000.00

4 **Staff costs**

The hotel employs three kitchen staff on a combined salary of $84,000 per year.

Peak (90 days)	$84,000 × (90/360)	= $21,000.00
Mid (120 days)	$84,000 × (120/360)	= $28,000.00
Low (150 days)	$84,000 × (150/360)	= $35,000.00

5 **Non-avoidable costs**

Forecast general costs for next year are as follows. Costs could be reduced by 85% (W3). Therefore, 20% are non-avoidable.

Peak	$310,000 × 0.20	= $62,000.00
Mid	$410,000 × 0.20	= $82,000.00
Low	$510,000 × 0.20	= $102,000.00

(b) (i)   The above statement shows that Sunrise makes an overall **annual loss**.

Further analysis shows that Sunrise could be profitable if the holiday park was **closed during the low season** when it makes a significant loss.

(ii) **Regular guests**

One factor that should be considered is the regular guests who stay at the holiday park a number of times a year.

If the holiday park closes for the low season these guests may find another holiday park for the whole year which may **reduce profitability** in the other seasons. There may also be a **loss of reputation** as guests feel the holiday park isn't customer focused.

Employees

In addition, closing the holiday park for the low season means that the park will only be open for 210 days (7 months). Staff at the holiday park may not be willing to accept this arrangement and may leave the park in search of full-time work, yielding a high staff turnover. Sunrise will have to take steps to replace any staff that leave.

29 Ennerdale

Text references. Short-term decisions are covered in Chapter 6.

Top tips. Part (a) deals with a price for a one–off contract. Therefore it is important to look at the quantities needed for that contract, when calculating the relevant costs. When looking at labour costs, remember that there is a shortage of skilled labour which must be built into the cost.

In part (b) think about the possible methods for apportioning joint costs and see if there is any relationship between the cost per litre for the three products. This should tell you that litres is the basis of apportionment.

In part (c) remember to only look at the incremental revenues and costs after the common process.

(a) (i) **Relevant cost – Material K**

Since the material is regularly used by the company, the relevant cost of material K is the current price of the material.

$$\text{Cost last month} = \frac{\$19,600}{2,000\,\text{kg}}$$
$$= \$9.80$$

Revised cost (+5%) $= \$9.80 \times 1.05$
$= \$10.29$

∴ Relevant cost of Material K $= 3,000\,\text{kg} \times \$10.29\text{ per kg}$
$= \$30,870$

Relevant cost – Material L

Since the material is **not** required for normal production, the relevant cost of this material is its net realisable value if it were sold.

∴ Relevant cost of Material L $= 200\,\text{kg} \times \$11\text{ per kg}$
$= \$2,200$

(ii) **Relevant cost – skilled labour**

Skilled labour is in short supply and therefore the relevant cost of this labour will include both the actual cost and the opportunity cost of the labour employed.

	$
Cost of skilled labour (800 hours × $9.50)	7,600
Opportunity cost of skilled labour (see working)	8,000
Relevant cost – skilled labour	15,600

Working

Skilled labour cost per unit of Product P = $38

Cost per skilled labour hour = $9.50

∴ Number of hours required per unit of Product P $= \dfrac{\$38}{\$9.50}$
$= 4\text{ hours}$

	Contribution per unit of Product P	= $40

∴ Contribution per skilled labour hour $= \dfrac{\$40}{4\,hours}$

= $10 per hour

∴ Opportunity cost of skilled labour = 800 hours × $10 per hour

= $8,000

(b)

Product	Value at end of process (i) $	Litres (ii)	Value per litre from process ((i)/(ii)) $
M	141,875	25,000	5.675
N	85,125	15,000	5.675
P	255,375	45,000	5.675
	482,375	85,000	

As $482,375/85,000 = $5.675, the method used to apportion common costs between the joint products is litres produced.

This method is only suitable when products remain in the same state, that is they don't separate into liquid and gas products. It also doesn't take into account the relative income earning potential of each product.

However, it does allow values to be put on the products for inventory financial reporting purposes.

It is necessary to apportion the common costs between each product to put a value on inventory for financial reporting and so sales can be matched with the cost of sales.

(c) **Viability of the common process**

Product	Selling price after common process $/litre	Litres	Total revenue $
M	6.25	25,000	156,250
N	5.20	15,000	78,000
P	6.80	45,000	306,000
			540,250

Less costs at end of common process (per (c) above)   (482,375)

Net revenue at the end of the common process   57,875

Therefore the common process is viable as net revenue is positive.

Optimal processing plan for each product

Product	Further revenues $	Further costs $	Net revenue $
M	$2.15 × 25,000 = 53,750	$1.75 × 25,000 = 43,750	10,000
N	$1.25 × 15,000 = 18,750	$0.95 × 15,000 = 14,250	4,500
P	$0.65 × 45,000 = 29,250	$0.85 × 45,000 = 38,250	(9,000)

Therefore products M and N make additional profit and so should be processed further.

Product P should not be processed beyond the common stage as net revenue is negative.

30 John Robertson

Text reference. Short-term decisions are covered in Chapter 6.

Top tips. The question focuses on relevant costs. It is important to set out adequate narrative analysis for each item on the pricing schedule. Part (c) is a straightforward use of textbook knowledge.

(a) The relevant costs which should be used for arriving at the minimum contract price are those *future* cash flows that will arise as a direct consequence of the decision to undertake the contract.

(1)   As bricks are used in the course of business, any used in this contract will need to be replaced. The relevant cost is therefore the replacement cost of $120 per 1,000.

(2)   Other materials are costed at their purchase price.

(3)   John Robertson's labour is charged at the opportunity cost, ie the benefit foregone as a result of working on the contract (or best alternative use). The best alternative use would be a saving of $12,000 by repairing his own house. The remainder of the skilled labour, after deducting John's hours, is charged at the incremental cost of $12 per hour.

(4)   Unskilled labour would have been incurred irrespective of the decision to undertake the project. The relevant cost is therefore nil.

(5)   The relevant cost is the cost of hiring the scaffolding.

(6)   Depreciation is not a cash flow. The general purpose machinery is already owned by John Robertson and is not purchased specifically for this contract. Its value is unaffected by the contract.

(7)   The relevant cost is the best alternative use of the yard.

(8)   The cost of the plans is a sunk cost and therefore not relevant to the pricing decision.

(9)   No profit is included as the price calculated is the minimum price which John can quote in a competitive environment.

(b)   **Minimum price to be quoted for building work**

	$
Direct materials:	
Bricks (400,000 @ $120 per thousand)	48,000
Other materials (at purchase price)	5,000
Direct labour:	
John Robertson's time	12,000
Skilled labour 2,400 @ $12 per hour	28,800
Unskilled	–
Other costs:	
Scaffolding hire (at the incremental cost)	3,500
Depreciation of general purpose machinery	–
General overheads	–
Opportunity cost of using yard	10,000
Plans	–
Total cost	107,300
Profit	–
Minimum price	107,300

A minimum price would leave the business **no better or worse off** than if John did not do the job. It is unlikely that a minimum price would actually be charged because if it were, it would not provide the business with any **incremental profit**. It does show the **absolute minimum** below which the price should not be set and the incremental profit that would be obtained from any price that is actually charged in **excess of the minimum**. The minimum price also fails to incorporate any **changes to long-term costs**.

(c)   **Advantages of full cost-plus pricing**

(i)   It is a **quick, simple and cheap** method of pricing which can be delegated to junior managers. This may be particularly important with jobbing work where many prices must be decided and quoted each day.

(ii) A price in excess of full cost should ensure that a company working at normal capacity will **cover all of its costs and make a profit**.

(iii) There may be **no readily identifiable market** for the product, for example, a jobbing engineering company makes products to customers' specific specifications. In such cases it will be difficult to determine a suitable starting point for pricing other than full cost.

Disadvantages of full cost-plus pricing

(i)   It fails to recognise that since demand may be determining price, there will be a profit-maximising combination of price and demand.

(ii) There may be a need to adjust prices to market and demand conditions.

(iii)   Budgeted output volume needs to be established. Output volume is a key factor in the overhead absorption rate.

(iv)   A suitable basis for overhead absorption must be selected, especially where a business produces more than one product.

31 Pixie Pharmaceuticals

Text reference. Short-term decisions are covered in Chapter 6.

Top tips. The calculations in this question are very straightforward, set them out clearly. Answer the written parts of the question in full, you can expect questions on this topic to include both calculations and discussion.

(a)

	Fairyoxide	Spriteolite	Goblinex	Total
	$'000	$'000	$'000	$'000
Sales value	80	200	160	440
Variable costs	56	136	112	304
Contribution	24	64	48	136
Fixed costs	16	40	32	88
Profit	8	24	16	48

If we produce our three drugs in-house our total profits are $48,000.

(b)

	Fairyoxide	Spriteolite	Goblinex
	$	$	$
Unit variable costs:			
direct material	0.80	1.00	0.40
direct labour	1.60	1.80	0.80
direct expense	0.40	0.60	0.20
Total variable cost	2.80	3.40	1.40
Imported price	2.75	4.20	2.00
Saving/(increased cost) of purchasing	0.05	(0.80)	(0.60)

On the basis of cost only, we should continue to produce Spriteolite and Goblinex but Fairyoxide should be purchased from the overseas producer.

(c)   The recommendation in (b) will increase profit because of the saving of $0.05 per unit of Fairyoxide.

∴ Increased profit = $0.05 × 20,000 = $1,000
∴ Total profit will be $49,000

If we buy Fairyoxide from the overseas producer total profit will increase by $1,000 to $49,000

(d)   **Other matters to be considered before importing drugs**

(i)   **Quality** is of vital importance in the manufacture of pharmaceuticals and the management would have to be convinced that the quality of production by the overseas producer would be acceptable. It will be harder to check quality if a supplier is overseas.

(ii)   The management will also need to be sure that **continuity of supply** can be guaranteed

(iii)   The quoted price may not be fixed and could be affected by changes in **exchange rates**.

(iv)   If Fairyoxide is no longer produced by the company, management should investigate whether the available capacity freed up can be used to generate additional profits from a different product.

(v)   Management should consider whether **labour morale** will be adversely affected by a decision to locate production overseas.

(e)   Companies and government bodies have increasingly tended to **concentrate on their core competences** – what they are really good at (or set up to achieve) – and turn other functions over to **specialist contractors**. A company that earns its profits from, say, manufacturing bicycles, does not also need to have expertise in, say, mass catering or office cleaning.

Outsourcing is the use of external suppliers for finished products, components or services. This is also known as **contract manufacturing** or **sub-contracting.**

Reasons for this trend include:

(i) Frequently the decision is made on the grounds that **specialist contractors** can offer **superior quality** and **efficiency**. If a contractor's main business is making a specific component it can invest in the specialist machinery and labour and knowledge skills needed to make that component. However, this component may be only one of many needed by the contractor's customer, and the complexity of components is now such that attempting to keep internal facilities up to the standard of specialists detracts from the main business of the customer.

(ii) Contracting out manufacturing **frees capital** that can then be invested in core activities such as market research, product definition, product planning, marketing and sales.

(iii) **Contractors** have the **capacity** and **flexibility** to start production very quickly to meet sudden **variations in demand**. In-house facilities may not be able to respond as quickly, because of the need to redirect resources from elsewhere.

In administrative and support functions, too, companies are increasingly likely to use specialist companies. Decisions such as the following are now common.

(i) Whether the **design and development of a new computer system** should be entrusted to in-house data processing staff or whether an external software house should be hired to do the work.

(ii) Whether **maintenance and repairs** of certain items of equipment should be dealt with by in-house engineers, or whether a maintenance contract should be made with a specialist organisation.

32 Sniff Limited

Text reference. The further processing decision and outsourcing are covered in Chapter 6.

Top tips. Part (a) simply requires you to outline the incremental costs and revenues which will change if the perfume is processed further. These costs and revenues are then calculated in part (b). Use a clear layout and workings for your calculations to gain as many marks as possible.

Part (c) has three marks so you will need to make three good points.

Easy marks. The discussion parts of this question provide opportunities for easy marks even if you struggle with the calculations.

Examiner's comments. Part (a) was fairly well done except for candidates who did not mention incremental revenue. Part (b) was very mixed with poor layout undermining many efforts. Sunk costs that are correctly omitted from calculations should be mentioned as sunk rather than simply ignored.

Marking scheme

			Marks
(a)	1 mark per factor outlined		3
(b)	Hormone costs	2	
	Supervisor excluded	1	
	Direct labour	3	
	Fixed cost allocation excluded	1	
	Market research	1	
	Incremental revenue	3	
	Net benefit	2	
	Concluding comment	1	
			14
(c)	1 mark per factor outlined		3
			20

(a) **The further processing decision**

A product should be processed further if the sales value minus further processing costs is greater than the sales value before further processing takes place.

Incremental revenue

The new perfume should sell at a **higher price** than the standard perfume.

Incremental costs

Sniff Limited needs to determine **which costs change** as a result of the further processing. For example, the extra materials and labour involved are relevant to the decision and, as there is a **shortage of labour**, the opportunity cost of labour is relevant. Any **sunk costs** such as fixed overheads already incurred, the cost of the market research, or the cost of the supervisor would **not** be relevant.

Impact on sales

The standard perfume is **highly branded** and customers may not be impressed with a change to a winning formula. This may have a negative impact on sales.

Impact on reputation

Adding hormones to perfumes is controversial and there are health concerns. Sniff Limited could therefore suffer from **adverse publicity**, which could damage its reputation and brand image. There is also the risk of litigation from customers who suffer health problems as a result of using the perfume.

(b) **Production cost of 1,000 litres of standard perfume**

		$
Diluted alcohol	$20 × 990 litres	
Aromatic oils	$18,000 × 10 litres	180,000
Materials cost		199,800
Labour	$15 × 2,000 hrs	30,000
Total cost		229,800
Cost per litre	$229,800/1,000 litres	229.80
Sales price per litre	$39.98 × 1,000/100	399.80

Opportunity cost of labour

Revenue from 1,000 litres of standard perfume = 1,000 litres × $399.80 = $399,800

Material cost = $199,800

Lost contribution of labour used on new products

= 399,800 – 199,800 = $200,000

Lost contribution per hour = $200,000/2,000 hrs = $100 per hour

Incremental costs

	Male version	$	Female version	$
Hormone	2 ltr × $7,750	15,500	8 ltr × $12,000	96,000
Labour	500 hrs × $100	50,000	700 hrs × $100	70,000
		65,500		166,000

Supervisor, fixed cost and market research are all **sunk costs** so have been ignored.

Incremental revenues

	Male version	$	Female version	$
Standard	200 ltr × $399.80	79,960	800 ltr × $399.80	319,840
With hormone added	202 ltr × $750	151,500	808 ltr × $595	480,760
		71,540		160,920

Net benefit/cost

Male version

Net benefit = 71,540 – 65,500 = **$6,040**

The male version of the perfume is therefore worth further processing.

Female version

Net cost = 160,920 − 166,000 = **($5,080)**

The female version of the perfume is therefore not worth further processing.

Conclusion

Based on the calculations, Sniff should further process the male perfume. However, the extra benefit is not particularly large and may not be sufficient to compensate for the risk of damage to the brand.

In the **longer term**, if Sniff can resolve the **labour shortages**, the figures could look much more promising as there would not be an additional opportunity cost of labour to consider. Sniff would also need to look in more detail at the **pricing strategy**.

(c) **Outsourcing**

Outsourcing is the use of **external suppliers** for finished products, components or services. It is not usually the **primary function** that is outsourced so it would be difficult to justify why Sniff would want to do so.

Cost

The main reason for outsourcing is often to reduce costs. For example, manufacturing may be cheaper in a country with lower labour costs.

Quality

Outsourcing may be used on the grounds that specialist contractors can offer **superior quality** and **efficiency**. The supplier may have **specialist skills** which will improve Sniff's products.

There is a danger however that quality will be **sacrificed** in favour of cost reduction. Sniff would need to be very careful that its brand image and reputation is not damaged by a change in the quality of its perfume.

Supplier reliability

Sniff would have to be sure that the supplier will deliver the products **on time** to avoid stock-outs in shops at crucial sales periods.

33 Stay Clean

Text reference. Short-term decisions are covered in Chapter 6 and pricing strategies in Chapter 5.

Top tips. This is a long scenario and may initially look daunting. However a step-by-step logical approach will gain marks throughout part (a), even if you get stuck on some of the trickier parts such as material discounts.

Make sure you leave enough time for parts (b) and (c) which are straightforward explanations.

Easy marks. There are easy marks available in part (a) for some of the calculations and there are three very easy marks for a brief outsourcing discussion in part (c).

Examiner's comments. In part (a) most candidates adopted the approach of doing two calculations: one considered the financial position if the production of TDs ceased immediately; the other considered the position if production stopped in twelve months. This approach was absolutely fine as long as candidates didn't include figures as costs in one calculation and then as savings in the other.

As regards the pricing strategies in part (b) the only really suitable strategies were to introduce complementary/product line pricing or to simply increase the price to cover costs. Many candidates suggested 'penetration pricing' or market skimming', which is inappropriate given that TD was not a new product. Part (c) was generally well answered.

BPP
LEARNING MEDIA

		Marks
(a)	Lost revenue	2
	Saved labour cost	2
	Lost contribution from other products	2
	Redundancy and recruitment cost	2
	Supplier payments	3
	Sublet income	1
	Supervisor	1
		13
(b)	Complementary pricing	2
	Product line pricing	2
	Other valid suggestions	2
	Maximum	4
(c)	Per issue	1
		3
		20

(a)   **Ceasing production now**

TD saved contribution

All sales of the TD will be lost for the next 12 months, this will result in contribution saved of 1,200 units x ($10) = $12,000

DW and WM lost contribution

Lost contribution = 5% x ((5,000 units x $80) + (6,000 units x $170)) = $71,000

Labour

If TD is ceased now:

	$
Redundancy cost	(6,000)
Retraining saved	3,500
Recruitment cost	(1,200)
Total cost	(3,700)

Lost discount

	DW	WM	TD	Net cost	Discount	Gross cost
	$	$	$	$		$
Current buying cost	350,000	600,000	60,000	1,010,000	5%	1,063,158
Saved cost	(17,500)	(30,000)	(60,000)			
New buying cost	332,500	570,000	0	902,500	5%	950,000
				921,500	3%	950,000
Lost discount				19,000		

Supervisor

There will be no saving or cost here as the supervisor will continue to be fully employed.

Short-term lease contract

The space currently issued for the TD will generate sublet income of $12,000.

Summary of relevant costs and benefits

Cash Flow	$
Saved contribution – TD	12,000
Lost contribution – other products	(71,000)
Labour	(3,700)
Lost discount	(19,000)
Sublet income	12,000
Net cash flow	69,700

It is **not worthwhile** to cease production of the TD now rather than waiting 12 months.

(b) Pricing strategies

Complementary pricing

Since the washing machine and the tumble dryer are products that tend to be used together, Stay Clean could **link their sales** with a complementary price. For example they could offer customers a discount on the second product bought, so if they buy a TD for $80 then they can get a WM for at a discounted price.

Product line pricing

All the products tend to be **related** to each other and used in the utility room or kitchen. If customers are upgrading their utility room or kitchen, a sale may involve all three products. A package price could be offered and as long as Stay Clean make a **contribution** on the overall deal then they will be better off.

(c) Outsourcing

Costs

The cost of manufacture should be compared to cost of buying in from the outsourcer. If the outsourcer can provide the same products at a **cheaper** cost then it is perhaps preferable to outsource.

Reliability

The reliability of the outsourcer should be assessed. If products are delivered late then the customer could be disappointed. This could damage the **reputation** of the business and future sales.

Quality

The quality of work that the outsourcer produces needs to be considered. Lower costs may be achieved **at the expense** of poor quality of materials or assembly. This again could ultimately damage the reputation of Stay Clean and future sales.

34 Bits and Pieces

Text references. Incremental costs and revenues are covered in Chapters 5 and 6.

Top tips. In part (a), use a clear layout, read the information carefully and make sure you state which costs should be excluded rather than not mentioning them at all.

In part (b) use your common sense to make sensible suggestions and don't be afraid to state the obvious.

Easy marks. There are plenty of easy marks available for the calculations in part (a).

Examiner's comments. Marks gained for part (a) were reasonable but the incremental heating cost was often incorrectly calculated for the whole year, rather than just the winter months as stated in the question.

This question required some common business sense which was lacking in many candidates with a lack of understanding or experience demonstrated in parts (b) and (c).

		Marks
(a)	Existing total sales	1
	Existing total gross profit	1
	New sales	1
	New gross profit	1
	Incremental gross profit	1
	Existing purchasing	1
	Discount allowed for	1
	Incremental Sunday purchasing costs	1
	Staff cost	1
	Lighting cost	1
	Heating cost	1
	Manager's bonus	1
		12
(b)	Time off at normal rate not time and a half	1
	Lack of flexibility	1
	Bonus per day worked calculation and comment	1
	Risk	1
		4
(c)	Changing customer buying pattern	2
	Complaints risk	2
	Quality link	2
	Maximum	4
		20

(a) Incremental revenue

	Sales $	Gross profit %	Gross profit $
Average	10,000	70	
Sunday (60% more than average)	16,000	50	8,000
Annual Sunday sales (50 weeks)	800,000	50	400,000

Purchasing costs

Current annual spending = 50 weeks × 6 days × 10,000 × 30%
                        = $900,000

New annual spending with discount = (900,000 + 400,000) × 95%
                        = $1,235,000

Incremental purchasing cost = $(1,235,000 − 900,000)
                        = $335,000

Staff costs

Additional staff costs on a Sunday = 5 sales assistants × 6 hours × 50 weeks × 1.5 × $20
                        = $45,000

Manager's costs

The salary of the manager is a sunk cost and there will be no additional costs for his time.
He will be entitled to an extra bonus of 1% × $800,000 = $8,000

Lighting costs

50 weeks × 6 hours × $30 = $9,000

Heating costs

25 weeks × 8 hours × $45 = $9,000

Rent

The rent of the store is a sunk cost so is not relevant to this decision.

Net incremental revenue

Net incremental revenue = 800,000 − (335,000 + 45,000 + 9,000 + 9,000 + 8,000)
= **$394,000**

Conclusion

Incremental revenue exceeds incremental costs by $394,000 so Sunday opening is **financially justifiable**.

(b) **Manager's pay deal**

Time off

If the manager works on a Sunday he will take the equivalent **time off** during the week. He is not entitled to extra pay in the same way as the sales assistants and this does not seem fair. Weekend working is disruptive to most people's family and social life and it is reasonable to expect **extra reward** for giving up time at weekends. It is unlikely that time off in lieu during the week will motivate the manager.

Bonus

The bonus has been calculated as $8,000 which equates to an extra $160 per day of extra work. The sales assistants will be paid $180 per day (6 × $20 × 1.5) so again the manager is **not getting a fair offer**.

The bonus is based on **estimated sales** so could be higher if sales are higher than predicted. However, there is a **risk** that sales and therefore the bonus could be lower. It is therefore again unlikely that this bonus will motivate the manager.

(c) **Price discounts and promotions**

B & P plans to offer substantial discounts and promotions on a Sunday to attract customers. This may indeed be a good **marketing strategy** to attract people to shop on a Sunday, but it is not necessarily good for the business.

Customer buying pattern

B & P wants to attract **new** customers on a Sunday but customers may simply **change the day** they do their shopping in order to take advantage of the discounts and promotions. The effect of this would be to **reduce the margin** earned from customer purchases and not increase revenue.

Customer dissatisfaction

Customers who buy goods at full price and then see their purchases for sale at lower prices on a Sunday may be disgruntled. They could then complain or switch their custom to another shop.

The **reputation** of B & P could be damaged by this marketing policy, especially if customers associate lower prices with **lower quality**.

35 BDU Co

Text reference. Risk and uncertainty techniques are covered in Chapter 7.

Top tips. Part (a) involves a very straightforward compilation of a contribution table which should not cause too many problems.

The trickiest part of part (b) is dealing with the minimax regret decision rule. You do need to have a good understanding not only of how to do the calculations but also what they mean.

Part (c) is straightforward application of knowledge but do make sure you apply it to this specific company.

(a)

Variable cost		Price		
		$425	$500	$600
	$170	255,000 (W1)	240,900 (W3)	180,600
	$210	215,000 (W2)	211,700	163,800
	$260	165,000	175,200	142,800

Workings

(1) (425 − 170) × 1,000 = $255,000
(2) (425 − 210) × 1,000 = $215,000
(3) (500 − 170) × 730 = $240,900

(b) **Maximax**

The **maximax criterion** looks at the **best possible results**. Maximax means 'maximise the maximum profit'. In this case, we need to **maximise the maximum contribution**.

Demand/price	Maximum contribution
1,000/$425	$255,000
730/$500	$240,900
420/$600	$180,600

BDU would therefore set a price of **$425**.

Maximin

The **maximin** decision rule involves choosing the outcome that offers the **least unattractive worst outcome,** in this instance choosing the outcome which **maximises the minimum contribution**.

Demand/price	Minimum contribution
1,000/$425	$165,000
730/$500	$175,200
420/$600	$142,800

BDU would therefore set a price of **$500**.

Minimax regret

The **minimax regret** decision rule involves choosing the **outcome that minimises the maximum regret** from making the wrong decision, in this instance choosing the outcome which **minimises the opportunity loss** from making the wrong decision.

We can use the calculations performed in (a) to draw up an **opportunity loss table.**

Variable cost	Price		
	$425	$500	$600
$170	–	$14,100	$74,400 (W1)
$210	–	$3,300	$51,200 (W2)
$260	$10,200	–	$32,400 (W3)
Minimax regret	$10,200	$14,100	$74,400

Minimax regret strategy (price of $425) is that which minimises the maximum regret ($10,200).

Workings

(1) At a variable cost of $170 per day, the best strategy would be a price of $425. The opportunity loss from setting a price of $600 would be $(255,000 − 180,600) = $74,400.

(2) At a variable cost of $210 per day, the best strategy would be a price of $425. The opportunity loss from setting a price of $600 would be $(215,000 − 163,800) = $51,200.

(3) At a variable cost of $260 per day, the best strategy would be a price of $500. The opportunity loss from setting a price of $600 would be $(175,200 − 142,800) = $32,400.

(c) **Expected values**

Where probabilities are assigned to different outcomes we can evaluate the worth of a decision as the **expected value**, or weighted average, of these outcomes. The principle is that when there are a number of alternative decisions, each with a range of possible outcomes, the optimum decision will be the one which gives the highest expected value. The expected value will **never actually occur.**

Expected values are more valuable as a guide to decision making where they refer to outcomes which will occur **many times over**. Examples would include the probability that so many customers per day will buy a can of baked beans, the probability that a customer services assistant will receive so many phone calls per hour, and so on.

We have not been given information on probabilities of each demand occurring for BDU's pushchairs and it is unlikely that demand will be sufficiently predictable to use this technique successfully.

Sensitivity analysis

Sensitivity analysis can be used in any situation so long as the relationships between the key variables can be established. Typically this involves changing the value of a variable and seeing how the results are affected.

For example, BDU could use sensitivity analysis to estimate by **how much costs and revenues would need to differ** from their estimated values before the decision would change or to estimate whether a decision would change if estimated costs were **x% higher** than estimated, or estimated revenues **y% lower** than estimated.

Sensitivity analysis can help to **concentrate management attention** on the most important factors and can be particularly useful when launching a new product.

36 Envico

Text references. Risk and uncertainty is covered in Chapter 7.

Top tips. Part (a) requires you to use the information in the contribution table and is a test of your basic maths skills.

Part (c) may have thrown you. The important point to note is that the contract can cover a room for 100, 200, 300 or 400 delegates, but we are only given information about attendance by 100, 200 or 400 delegates. You then need to look at contribution for each particular room size when the number of delegates is (where relevant) less than, the same as and greater than the room capacity.

Part (d) is a straightforward textbook explanation and you can expect the examiner to want you to be able to deal with practical uncertainties.

(a)   **Room A**

Contribution per seminar $= \dfrac{\$832,000}{8 \text{ cities} \times 52 \text{ weeks}}$ $= \$2,000$

Room cost $= \text{delegate fees} - \text{contribution}$
$= (100 \text{ delegates} \times \$80) - \$2,000$ $= \$6,000$

Room B

Contribution per seminar $= \dfrac{2,163,200}{8 \times 52}$ $= \$5,200$

Room cost $= (200 \text{ delegates} \times \$80) - \$5,200$ $= \$10,800$

Room C

Contribution per seminar $= \dfrac{\$3,993,600}{8 \times 52}$ $= \$9,600$

Room cost $= (300 \text{ delegates} \times \$80) - \$9,600$ $= \$14,400$

Room D

Contribution per seminar $= \dfrac{\$6,656,000}{8 \times 52}$ $= \$16,000$

Room cost $= (400 \text{ delegates} \times \$80) - \$16,000$ $= \$16,000$

(b)   (i)

Places sold	Probability	Contribution if 100 places available $	Expected value $	Contribution if 200 places available $	Expected value $
100	0.2	832,000	166,400	(1,164,800)	(232,960)
200	0.5	832,000	416,000	2,163,200	1,081,600
400	0.3	832,000	249,600	2,163,200	648,960
			832,000		1,497,600

Places sold	Probability	Contribution if 300 places available $	Expected value $	Contribution if 400 places available $	Expected value $
100	0.2	(2,662,400)	(532,480)	(3,328,000)	(665,600)
200	0.5	665,600	332,800	0	0
400	0.3	3,993,600	1,198,080	6,656,000	1,996,800
			998,400		1,331,200

This analysis shows that Envico should **contract for Room B with 200 capacity** as it has the **highest expected value** at $1,497,600.

(ii)   **Limitations of the expected value approach**

Expected values indicate what an outcome is likely to be in the long tem with repetition. The main limitation is that the expected value may **never actually occur**. Expected values are used to support a **risk-neutral** attitude and ignore any variability in the range of possible outcomes. The variables involved can only be estimated so great care should be taken to avoid relying too heavily on educated guesses.

(c)   The **minimum contribution for each decision** is as follows.

Room A	$832,000
Room B	($1,164,000)
Room C	($2,662,400)
Room D	($3,328,000)

Applying a **maximin approach (maximising the minimum contribution)**, Envico should **choose Room A**.

The **minimax regret rule** aims to **minimise the regret from making the wrong decision**. The regret matrix is shown below. The **regret** is calculated by taking the **maximum expected contribution from each demand level** (as shown in the table for (a) and **deducting the contribution that would result from the room size that was contracted for**. For example, if 200 places were demanded but only 100 places were contracted for, that would mean that the regret is $2,163,200 − $832,000 = $1,331,200.

	Room size			
Demand	100	200	300	400
100	0	1,996,800	3,494,400	4,160,000
200	1,331,200	0	1,497,600	2,163,200
400	5,824,000	4,492,800	2,662,400	0
Maximum regret	5,824,000	4,492,800	3,494,400	4,160,000

To **minimise the maximum regret, Room C** with 300 places needs to be contracted for.

(d)   Management accounting directs its attention towards the **future** and the future is **uncertain**. For this reason a number of methods of taking **uncertainty** into consideration have evolved.

Market research can be used to reduce uncertainty. **Market research** is the systematic process of gathering, analysing and reporting data about markets to investigate, describe, measure, understand or explain a situation or problem facing a company or organisation.

Market research involves **tackling problems**. The assumption is that these problems can be solved, no matter how complex the issues are, if the researcher follows a line of enquiry in a **systematic** way, without losing sight of the main objectives. Gathering and analysing all the facts will ultimately lead to **better decision making**.

Market research enables organisations to understand the needs and opinions of their customers and other stakeholders. Armed with this knowledge they are able to make better quality decisions and provide better products and better services.

Quantitative data usually deals with numbers and typically provides the decision maker with information about **how many** customers, competitors etc act in a certain way. Quantitative data can, for example, tell the researcher **what** people need or consume, or **where**, **when** and **how** people buy goods or consumer services.

Qualitative data tells us **why** consumers think/buy or act the way they do. Qualitative data is used in **consumer insight** (eg understanding what makes consumers prefer one brand to another), **media awareness** (eg how much of an advertisement is noticed by the public), **new product development** studies and for many other reasons.

Qualitative research has as its specific purpose the uncovering and understanding of thought and opinion. It is carried out on relatively small samples and unstructured or semi-structured techniques, such as individual in depth interviews and group discussions (also known as **focus groups**), are used.

37 Rotanola Co

Text reference. Demand and cost functions are covered in Chapter 5 and risk and uncertainty techniques are covered in Chapter 7.

Top tips. Read all of the information in the question carefully so you use the relevant information in the correct parts of the answer. Apply your answer to the specific circumstances of the company.

(a) **Market research** is the systematic process of gathering, analysing and reporting data about markets to investigate, describe, measure, understand or explain a situation or problem facing a company or organisation.

Market research involves **tackling problems**. The assumption is that these problems can be solved, no matter how complex the issues are, if the researcher follows a line of enquiry in a **systematic** way, without losing sight of the main objectives. Gathering and analysing all the facts will ultimately lead to **better decision making.**

Thus, research influences what is provided and the way it is provided. It **reduces uncertainty and monitors performance.** A management team which possesses accurate information relating to the marketplace will be in a strong position to make the best decisions in an increasingly competitive world.

Decision-makers need data to reduce **uncertainty** and **risk** when planning for the future and to monitor business performance. Market researchers provide the data that helps them to do this.

(b) Find the price at which demand would be nil: Each price increase of $10 results in a fall in demand of 2,000 phones. For demand to be nil, the price needs to rise by as many times as there are 2,000 units in 20,000 units (20,000/2,000 = 10) ie to $110 + (10 × $10) = $210. So a = 210

b = change in price/change in quantity = 10/2,000 = 0.005

The demand equation is therefore P = 210 − 0.005Q

Alternatively
P = a - bQ
110 = a − (0.005 × 20,000)
a = 110 + 100 = 210
P = 210 − 0.005Q

(c) **Cost behaviour** can be modelled using equations. These equations can be highly complex but in this case are quite simple.

b = variable cost = 30 + 18 + 14 = $62
a = fixed cost = $23 × 20,000 = 460,000
TC = 460,000 + 62Q where Q = number of units

With the **volume based discount**:

b = 27 + 18 + 14 = 59
TC = 460,000 + 59Q

This could be drawn on a graph as follows.

The **slope** of the line becomes **less steep** as more units are made and the variable cost per unit falls.

This assumes that **fixed costs** remain unchanged over all ranges of output and a **constant unit variable cost**.

(d) **Sensitivity analysis** is a term used to describe any technique whereby decision options are tested for their vulnerability to changes in any 'variable' such as expected sales volume, sales price per unit, material costs, or labour costs.

Here are three ways in which sensitivity analysis can be used.

(i)   To estimate by **how much costs and revenues would need to differ** from their estimated values before the decision would change.

(ii) To estimate whether a decision would change if estimated costs were **x% higher** than estimated, or estimated revenues **y% lower** than estimated.

(iii) To estimate by how much costs and/or revenues would need to differ from their estimated values before the decision maker would be **indifferent** between two options.

The essence of the approach, therefore, is to carry out the calculations with one set of values for the variables and then substitute other possible values for the variables to see how this affects the overall outcome.

For Rotanola and the proposed new phone:

(i)   If incremental **fixed costs** are more than 187% (1,075,000/575,000 × 100) above estimate, the project would make a loss.

(ii) If **unit costs of materials** are more than 86% (1,075,000/1,250,000 × 100) above estimate, the project would make a loss.

(iii) If **labour costs** are more than 239% (1,075,000/450,000 × 100) above estimate, the project would make a loss.

(iv) If **sales revenue** fell by 29% (1,075,000/3,750,000 × 100), the project would make a loss.

Management would then be able to judge more clearly whether the product is likely to be profitable. The items to which profitability is most sensitive in this example are the sales revenue (28%) and material costs (84%). Sensitivity analysis can help to **concentrate management attention** on the most important factors.

(e) **Materials**

Probability	Forecast material cost $	Expected value $
0.6	50	30
0.3	60	18
0.1	40	4
		52

Sales units

Probability	Forecast sales units	Expected value
0.5	25,000	12,500
0.4	22,500	9,000
0.1	26,250	2,625
		24,125

Expected profit

		$	$
Sales	(24,125 × $150)		3,618,750
Materials	(24,125 × $52)	1,254,500	
Labour	(24,125 × $18)	434,250	
Variable overheads	(24,125 × $16)	386,000	
			2,074,750
Attributable fixed overheads			575,000
Expected profit			969,000

38 Cement Co

Text references. Pay-off tables and decision rules are covered in Chapter 7.

Top tips. Ensure that your pay-off table in part (a) is neatly set out and clearly labelled to maximise your score. Remember to justify your decision under each rule in part (b) and show all supporting workings.

Easy marks. There are 6 marks available for describing the 'maximin' and 'expected value' decision rules, when they might be used and the attitudes of decision makers who use them.

Examiner's comments. Part (a) should have been easy but only about 5% of candidates got this completely correct. A vast number of candidates applied the probabilities to the profit figures before including the amounts in the table. Many tables were not clearly labelled and few candidates grasped the fact that any unsold bag of cement produces a loss of $4.50 in total ($4 buy in cost and $0.50 disposal cost).

Part (b) (i) and (ii) were fairly well attempted but even then, most correct answers were not justified as requested and only therefore scored half marks. It didn't matter whether justification had been given by either words or numbers but usually, there was neither. The requirement to calculate the expected value in part (b) (iii) was worth the most marks and it was really surprising to see that 90% of candidates could not do this. Candidates are clearly confused in this area and need to study it further.

The discursive part of this question was answered well in relation to maximin and poorly in relation to expected value.

ACCA examiner's answers. The ACCA examiner's answer to this question can be found at the back of this kit.

Marks

(a)   Pay off table:
        Calculation of profit   1
        Calculation of loss   1
        'Demand' label   ½
        'Supply' label   ½
        Weather column   ½
        Supply column – 350,000   1½
        Supply column – 280,000   1½
        Supply column – 200,000   1½

                                                                    8

(b)   (i) Maximin:
            Selecting highest of the low   1
        (ii) Maximax:
            Selecting highest of the high   1
        (iii) Expected value:
            Calculating EV when good   1
            Calculating EV average   1
            Calculating EV when poor   1
            Selecting highest   1

                                                                    6

(c)   Describe maximin   1
        Used when outcome cannot be assessed with any certainty   1
        Risk averse/pessimistic   1
        One-off/repeated decisions   1
        Describe EV   2
        Risk neutral   1
        Repeated decisions   1

                                                       Max   6
                                                            20

(a)   **Pay-off table**

		Probability *	SUPPLY (number of bags)		
			350,000	280,000	200,000
	Weather		$'000	$'000	$'000
	Good $'000	0.25	1,750 (W1)	1,400	1,000
DEMAND	Average $'000	0.45	1,085 (W2)	1,400	1,000
	Poor $'000	0.30	325	640	1,000

* Probability column is shown to assist in calculations to part (b) (iii).

Profit per bag sold in coming year = $9 – $4 = $5

Loss per bag disposed of = $4 + $0.50 = $4.50

Workings

(1)   350,000 × $5 = $1,750,000

(2)   (280,000 × $5) – (70,000 × $4.50) = $1,085,000 etc

(b)   (i)   **Maximin**

Select the least unattractive worst outcome (the option that maximises the minimum profits).

SUPPLY (number of bags)

	350,000 $'000	280,000 $'000	200,000 $'000
Worst	325	640	1,000

The highest of these is $1,000,000 therefore choose to supply only 200,000 bags to meet poor conditions.

(ii)   **Maximax**

Select the best possible outcome (the option that maximises the maximum profit).

SUPPLY (number of bags)

	350,000 $'000	280,000 $'000	200,000 $'000
Best	1,750	1,400	1,000

The highest of these is $1,750,000 therefore choose to supply 350,000 bags to meet good conditions.

(iii)   **Expected value**

Use the probabilities shown in part (a) to calculate the expected value of each of the supply levels.

Good $(0.25 \times \$1,750,000) + (0.45 \times \$1,085,000) + (0.30 \times \$325,000) = \$1,023,250$

Average $(0.7 \times \$1,400,000) + (0.3 \times \$640,000) = \$1,172,000$

Poor $1 \times \$1,000,000 = \$1,000,000$

The expected value of producing 280,000 bags when conditions are average is the highest at $1,172,000, therefore this supply level should be chosen.

(c)   **The 'maximin' decision rule**

Under the 'maximin' decision rule, the decision maker should select the alternative that offers the least unattractive worst outcome. This means choosing the alternative that maximises the minimum profits. It is used when the outcome cannot be assessed with any level of certainty.

The 'maximin' decision rule ignores the probability of each different outcome taking place and is seen as defensive and conservative – by using it the decision maker is intent on avoiding the worst outcomes without taking into account opportunities for maximising profits.

The 'expected value' decision rule

The 'expected value' rule calculates what an outcome is likely to be in the long term with repetition (if a decision is repeated again and again). Where probabilities are assigned to different outcomes, it is possible to evaluate the worth of a decision as the expected value or weighted average of these outcomes.

When there are a number of alternative decisions, each with a range of possible outcomes, the optimum decision will be the one which gives the highest expected value.

Expected values are likely to be used by risk-neutral decision makers (neither seeks risk nor avoids it), who will ignore any variability in the range of possible outcomes and be concerned only with the expected value of outcomes.

Expected values are most valuable as a guide to decision making when they refer to outcomes which will occur many times over.

39 Elsewhere

(a) The expected value of profit is calculated as follows.

Profit	Probability	Expected profit
$'000		$'000
800	0.5	400
100	0.2	20
(300)	0.3	(90)
		330

(b) **Expected value of profit ***

Profit	Probabilities outcome point			EV of profit outcome point		
	2	3	4	2	3	4
$'000				$'000	$'000	$'000
800	0.5	0.7	0.1	400	560	80
100	0.2	0.1	0.3	20	10	30
(300)	0.3	0.2	0.6	(90)	(60)	(180)
				330	510	(70)

* See decision tree on next page.

The record company should not commission the survey because the expected value of profit without the survey is $330,000. This is greater than the expected value of profit of $307,000 ($357,000 - $50,000) with the survey.

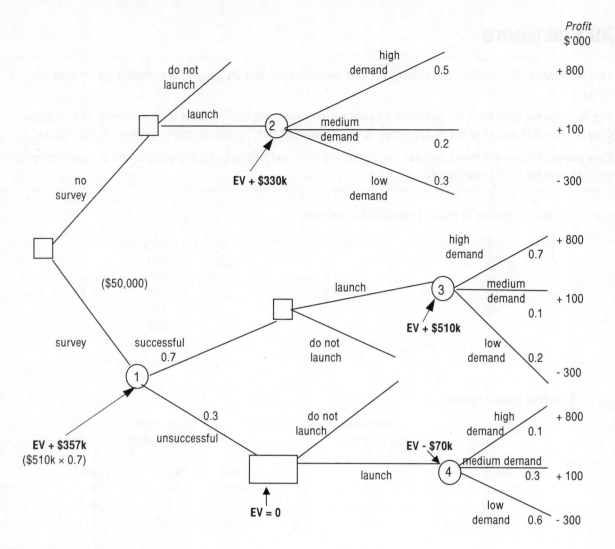

Profit
$'000

high demand   0.5   + 800

medium demand   0.2   + 100

low demand   0.3   - 300

EV + $330k

do not launch

launch

no survey

($50,000)

survey

successful 0.7

EV + $357k
($510k × 0.7)

unsuccessful 0.3

EV = 0

do not launch

do not launch

launch

EV + $510k

high demand   0.7   + 800

medium demand   0.1   + 100

low demand   0.2   - 300

EV - $70k

high demand   0.1   + 800

medium demand   0.3   + 100

low demand   0.6   - 300

Key: ☐ - decision point   ◯ - outcome point

(c)   (i)

	$'000
EV of profit without perfect information (no survey)	330
EV of profit with perfect information (survey)	357
Value of perfect information	27

The maximum that the company should pay for this survey is **$27,000**.

(ii)   Whenever a decision is made when the outcome of the decision is uncertain, there will always be some doubt that the correct decision has been taken. If a decision is based on selecting the option with the highest EV of profit, it can be assumed that in the long run, that is, with enough repetition, the decision so selected will give the **highest average profit**. But if the decision involves a once-only outcome, there will be a risk that in retrospect, it will be seen that the wrong decision was taken.

A decision tree is a **simplified representation of reality**, and it may omit some possible decision options, or it may simplify the possible outcomes. For example, in this question, 'success' and 'failure' are two extreme outcomes, whereas a variety of outcomes between success and failure may be possible. The decision tree is therefore likely to be a simplification of reality.

40 SH

Marking scheme

			Marks
(a)	Profit calculations:		
	Small van sales	½	
	Small van VC	½	
	Small van goodwill or VC adjustment	½	
	Small van depreciation	½	
	Medium van – as above for small van	3	
	Large van – as above for small van	3	
			8
(b)	Risk attitude issue	1	
	Optimist view	1	
	Pessimist view	1	
	Expected value calculation	1	
	Expected value discussion	1	
	Conclusion	1	
			6
(c)	Market research	2	
	Simulation	2	
	Sensitivity	2	
			6
			20

(a) Profits table

	Small van	Medium van	Large van
Capacity	100	150	200
Low demand (120 crates)	300(W1)	468(W3)	368(W5)
High demand (190 crates)	300(W2)	500(W4)	816(W6)

Working	1	2	3	4	5	6
Sales	1,000	1,000	1,200	1,500	1,200	1,900
Variable costs	(400)	(400)	(480)	(600)	(480)	(760)
Goodwill	(100)	(100)		(100)		
Variable cost adjustment @ 10%			48		48	76
Depreciation	(200)	(200)	(300)	(300)	(400)	(400)
Profit	300	300	468	500	368	816

(b)   The decision as to which van to buy depends on the managers' attitudes to risk.

Risk averse

If the managers are pessimistic and becoming **more cautious**, they will choose the van with the least unattractive worst outcome (the maximin criterion). This is the medium van with a profit of $468.

Risk taker

If the managers are **optimistic** about the future, they would choose the van with the best possible outcome (the maximax criteria). This is the large van as this has the highest profit of $816.

Expected values

Expected values support a **risk neutral attitude** and are used when a decision is being made more than once.

The expected values for this situation are:

Small van: $300
Medium van: ($468 × 0.4) + ($500 × 0.6) = $487
Large van: ($368 × 0.4) + (816 × 0.6) = $637

The large van therefore has the highest expected value.

Conclusion

The managers have become more cautious as the business has become more competitive so the medium van is probably the most likely to be chosen.

(c)   **Market research**

Decision-makers need data to reduce **uncertainty** and **risk** when planning for the future and to monitor business performance. Market researchers provide the data that helps them to do this. Data can be either **primary** (collected at first hand from a sample of respondents), or **secondary** (collected from previous surveys, other published facts and opinions, or from experts). Secondary research is also known as **desk research**, because it can be carried out from one's desk.

Sensitivity analysis

Sensitivity analysis is a term used to describe any technique whereby decision options are tested for their **vulnerability to changes** in any 'variable' such as expected sales volume, sales price per unit, material costs, or labour costs. It can be used in any situation so long as the **relationships** between the key variables can be established.

It enables the risks involved in a decision to be better understood.

Simulation

Simulation models can be used to deal with decision problems involving a number of uncertain variables. Where only a few factors are involved, probability analysis and expected value calculations can be used to find the most likely outcome of a decision. Often, however, in real life, there are so **many uncertain variables** that this approach does not give a true impression of possible variations in outcome.

To get an idea of what will happen in real life one possibility is to use a **simulation model** in which the values and the variables are selected at random. **Random numbers** are used to assign values to the variables. Obviously this is a situation **ideally suited to a computer** (large volume of data, random number generation).

41 Preparation question: Budgeting

Text references. The objectives of budgetary control are covered in Chapter 8.

Top tips. This question contains a variety of discussion topics which are each more likely to form part of a budgeting question. Make sure you answer the specific requirements of each part so, for example in part (a), do not simply provide a general discussion of the merits of budgeting. Use headings to structure your written answers.

(a)   A **continuous** or rolling budget is a budget which is continuously updated by adding a further accounting period (a month or quarter) when the earlier accounting period has expired. They are an attempt to prepare targets and plans which are more **realistic** and certain, particularly with a regard to price levels, by shortening the period between preparing budgets.

Instead of preparing a **periodic budget** annually for the full budget period, there might be budgets every one, two, three or four months (three to six, or even twelve budgets each year). Each of these budgets would plan for the next twelve months so that the current budget is extended by an extra period as the current period ends: hence the name rolling budgets.

The **advantage of a periodic budget** is that there is less time spent on budget revisions, as it is only prepared once for the full budget period and a new one is not introduced until the next budget period has begun.

The **advantages of continuous budgeting** are as follows.

(i)   They reduce the element of uncertainty in budgeting because they concentrate detailed planning and control on short-term prospects where the degree of uncertainty is much smaller.

(ii)   They force managers to reassess the budget regularly, and to produce budgets which are up to date in the light of current events and expectations.

(iii)   Planning and control will be based on a recent plan which is likely to be far more realistic than a fixed annual budget made many months ago.

(iv)   Realistic budgets are likely to have a better motivational influence on managers.

(v)   There is always a budget which extends for several months ahead. For example, if rolling budgets are prepared quarterly there will always be a budget extending for the next 9 to 12 months. This is not the case when periodic budgets are used.

(b)   **Budgetary bias** is where budgets are manipulated in order to make managers' performance look better. **Budgetary slack** is the difference between the minimum necessary costs and the costs built into the budget or actually incurred. In the process of preparing budgets, managers might deliberately overestimate costs and underestimate sales, so that they will not be blamed in the future for overspending and poor results. Indeed, they are more likely to achieve favourable results when actual and budgeted results are compared.

In controlling actual operations, managers must then ensure that their spending rises to meet their budget, otherwise they will be 'blamed' for careless budgeting.

A typical situation is for a manager to waste money on non-essential expenses so that all the budget allowance is used. He or she will be **less motivated** to look for ways to reduce costs. The reason behind such action is the fear that unless the allowance is fully spent it will be reduced in future periods, thus making the job more difficult as the future reduced budgets will not be so easy to attain. Because inefficiency and slack are allowed for in budgets, achieving a budget target means only that costs have remained within the accepted levels of inefficient spending. Inefficiency will be **perpetuated**.

Conversely, it has been noted that, after a run of mediocre results, some managers deliberately **overstate revenues** and **understate cost estimates**, no doubt feeling the need to make an **immediate favourable impact** by promising better performance in the future. They may merely delay problems, however, as the managers may well be censured when they fail to hit these optimistic targets.

(c)   One of the purposes of budgeting is to motivate managers to ensure the achievement of the organisation's objectives and to improve performance.

(i)   **Setting targets for financial performance**

Quantified expressions of the organisation's objectives are drawn up as **targets** to be achieved within the timescale of the budget plan. Managers will usually be more motivated to achieve required performance if there is a clearly defined, quantitative plan, but such targets must be **accepted** by managers responsible for them.

The individual personality of the manager, the quality of communication in the budgeting process and the level of difficulty of the budget target will affect motivation and performance.

There is likely to be a **demotivating** effect where an **ideal standard of performance** is set, because adverse efficiency variances will always be reported. It is important that adverse variances are not used to lay blame if targets have been set with the aim of motivation.

A **low standard of efficiency** is also demotivating, because there is no sense of achievement in attaining the required standards. Managers are likely to outperform the budget, but could have achieved a better level of performance without the low targets.

The best results will be achieved from the most difficult targets that individual managers are prepared to accept.

(ii) **Participation in the budget-setting process**

It has been argued that participation in the budgeting process will improve motivation and so will improve the quality of budget decisions and the efforts of individuals to achieve their budget targets (although obviously this will depend on the personality of the individual, the nature of the task (narrowly defined or flexible) and the organisational culture).

There are basically two ways in which a budget can be set: from the **top down** (imposed budget) or from the **bottom up** (participatory budget).

Imposed budget

In the top-down approach to budgeting, top management prepare a budget with little or no input from operating personnel which is then **imposed** upon the employees who have to work to the budgeted figures.

The **advantages** of this approach are that strategic plans are likely to be incorporated into planned activities; coordination between the plans and objectives of divisions is enhanced; senior management's awareness of total resource availability is used; the input from inexperienced or uninformed lower-level employees is decreased; the period of time taken to draw up the budgets is decreased.

The **disadvantages** of top-down budgeting are dissatisfaction, defensiveness and low morale amongst employees; the feeling of team spirit may disappear; the acceptance of organisational goals and objectives could be limited; the feeling of the budget as a punitive device could arise; lower-level management initiative may be stifled.

Participatory budget

In the bottom-up approach to budgeting, budgets are developed by lower-level managers who then submit the budgets to their superiors. The budgets are based on the lower-level managers' perceptions of what is achievable and the associated necessary resources.

The **advantages** of participative budgets are they are based on information from employees most familiar with the department; knowledge spread among several levels of management is pulled together; morale and motivation is improved; they increase operational managers' commitment to organisational objectives; in general they are more realistic; co-ordination between units is improved; specific resource requirements are included; senior managers' overview is mixed with operational level details.

There are, on the other hand, a number of **disadvantages** of participative budgets. They consume more time; changes implemented by senior management may cause dissatisfaction; budgets may be unachievable if managers' are not qualified to participate; they may cause managers to introduce budgetary slack; they can support 'empire building' by subordinates; an earlier start to the budgeting process could be required.

Negotiated budget

Many organisations in practice develop a budget setting process that incorporates elements of both approaches, where budgets are agreed by a **process of negotiation**. In the imposed budget approach, operational managers will try to negotiate with senior managers the budget targets which they consider to be unreasonable or unrealistic. Likewise senior management usually review and revise budgets presented to them under a participative approach through a process of negotiation with lower level managers.

Final budgets are therefore most likely to lie between what top management would really like and what junior managers believe is feasible. The budgeting process is hence a **bargaining process** and it is this bargaining which is of vital importance, determining whether the budget is an effective management tool or simply a clerical device.

42 Preparation questions: Happy Hotels

Text references. Zero based budgeting is covered in Chapter 9.

Top tips. This question requires you to discuss various aspects of zero-based budgeting. Make sure you apply your explanations to the specific company in the scenario and don't just write everything you know about ZBB.

The F5 examiner will probably combine discussion questions with calculations such as quantitative analysis.

(a)   **Principles of ZBB**

The principle behind **zero based budgeting** is that the budget for each cost centre should be prepared from 'scratch' or zero. Every item of expenditure must be justified to be included in the budget for the forthcoming period.

ZBB rejects the assumption inherent in incremental budgeting that this year's activities will continue at the same level or volume next year, and that next year's budget can be based on this year's costs plus an extra amount, perhaps for expansion and inflation.

Uses for Happy Hotels

Happy Hotels were aiming to cut costs in order to achieve greater profitability and ZBB is particularly useful when making **rationalisation decisions** as it is possible to identify and remove inefficient or obsolete operations.

ZBB is particularly suitable for **service industries** such as hotels where variable expenses make up a **large proportion** of total expenditures. Alternative levels of provision for each activity are possible and cost and benefits are **separately identifiable**.

ZBB forces employees and individual hotel managers to **avoid wasteful expenditure**. It also ensures that **changes in the business environment** are responded to and challenges the status quo.

(b)   **Implementing ZBB**

The implementation of ZBB involves a number of steps but of greater importance is the **development of a questioning attitude** by all those involved in the budgetary process. Existing practices and expenditures must be challenged and questions asked.

- Does the activity need to be carried out?
- What would be the consequences if the activity were not carried out?
- Is the current level of provision adequate?
- Are there alternative ways of providing the function?
- How much should the activity cost?
- Is the expenditure worth the benefits achieved?

The three steps of ZBB

(1)   **Define decision packages**, comprehensive descriptions of specific organisational activities (decision units) which management can use to evaluate the activities and rank them in order of priority against other activities. There are two types.

- **Mutually exclusive packages** contain alternative methods of getting the same job done. The best option among the packages must be selected by comparing costs and benefits and the other packages are then discarded.

- **Incremental packages** divide one aspect of an activity into different levels of effort. The 'base' package will describe the minimum amount of work that must be done to carry out the activity and the other packages describe what additional work could be done, at what cost and for what benefits.

(2)   **Evaluate and rank each activity (decision package)** on the basis of its benefit to the organisation. This can be a lengthy process. Minimum work requirements (those that are essential to get a job done) will be given high priority and so too will work which meets legal obligations. In the accounting department these would be minimum requirements to operate the payroll, purchase ledger and sales ledger systems, and to maintain and publish a satisfactory set of accounts.

(3)   **Allocate resources** in the budget according to the funds available and the evaluation and ranking of the competing packages.

(c)   **How ZBB can motivate employees**

Employees do not set targets based on historical data, but ones consistent with their **future objectives** and those of the organisation.

The extra work required with ZBB ensures that employees benefit by **re-thinking an activity from scratch**.

As ZBB aims to **eliminate slack**, employees raise the expectations of their own achievement and through increasing job satisfaction enhance their motivation.

If **incentive schemes** are based on the budget setting process it may be argued that ZBB encourages goal congruence through increasing flexibility.

(d)   **Problems with ZBB**

The major problem associated with ZBB is the amount of **management time and paperwork** involved. Each hotel manager would have to spend considerably more time and effort on budgeting and may actively resist the process.

Individual managers may not have the **necessary skills** to construct decision packages and undertake the ranking process. **Training** will be required and this will be **costly**, particularly in view of the geographical spread of the hotels.

Happy Hotel's **information systems** may not be capable of providing suitable information so again more costly investment may be needed.

Short-term benefits such as cost reduction may be emphasised to the detriment of long-term benefits. This is particularly significant in the luxury hotel market where customers have high expectations and reputation is easily lost.

(e)   **The advantages of encouraging employee participation in budgeting**

Employees who are **familiar** with specific operations will provide the information for the budget and **knowledge spread** among several levels of management is **pulled together**.

Morale and motivation is improved as it is hard for people to be motivated to achieve targets set by someone else.

Operational managers' commitment to **organisational objectives** is increased and **co-ordination between units** is improved.

In general budgets should be **more realistic** and more acceptable to employees.

43 Brunti

(a) **Activity based costing**

Step 1   Calculate the rate per cost driver for each of the cost pools

Cost pool	Cost $'000	Quantity of cost drivers	Rate per cost driver $	
Machining services	357	420,000	0.850	per machine hour
Assembly services	318	530,000	0.600	per direct labour hour
Set up costs	26	520	50.000	per set up
Order processing	156	32,000	4.875	per customer order
Purchasing	84	11,200	7.500	per supplier's order

Step 2   Allocate costs to the different products.

	XYI	YZT	ABW
Units produced/sold	50,000	40,000	30,000
Machining services			
Machine hrs/unit	2	5	4
Total machine hours	100,000	200,000	120,000
Cost at $0.85/hr	$85,000	$170,000	$102,000
Assembly services			
Assembly hrs/unit	7	3	2
Total assembly hours	350,000	120,000	60,000
Cost at $0.60/hr	$210,000	$72,000	$36,000
No of set-ups	120	200	200
Cost at $50/set-up	$6,000	$10,000	$10,000
No of customer orders	8,000	8,000	16,000
Cost at $4.875/order	$39,000	$39,000	$78,000
No of suppliers' orders	3,000	4,000	4,200
Cost at $7.50/order	$22,500	$30,000	$31,500

Activity based costing profit statement

	XYI	YZT	ABW	Total
Units produced/sold	50,000	40,000	30,000	120,000
	$'000	$'000	$'000	$'000
Sales	2,250.00	3,800.00	2,190.00	8,240.00
Less:				
Prime cost	1,600.00	3,360.00	1,950.00	6,910.00
Overheads:				
Machining services	85.00	170.00	102.00	357.00
Assembly services	210.00	72.00	36.00	318.00
Set up costs	6.00	10.00	10.00	26.00
Order processing	39.00	39.00	78.00	156.00
Purchasing	22.50	30.00	31.50	84.00
	1,962.50	3,681.00	2,207.50	7,851.00
Profit/(loss)	287.50	119.00	(17.50)	389.00

(b) The traditional approach to setting a budget is based on the current year's results plus an extra amount (an 'increment') for estimated growth or inflation next year. This is known as **incremental budgeting**.

It is an **inefficient** form of budgeting, although **administratively it is fairly easy** to prepare. It **encourages slack** and **wasteful spending** to creep into budgets and to become a normal feature of actual spending. If the increment makes the overall figures unacceptable elements in the new budget may be cut on an arbitrary basis to make the overall total 'reasonable', whether or not this is desirable from a business point of view.

Car manufacturers operate in **a highly competitive environment** with a need for **continuous improvement** and driving down of costs to the minimum possible. It is therefore highly unlikely that incremental budgeting will provide the necessary tools for such an environment.

Traditional incremental budgeting will be sufficient only if current operations are as **effective, efficient and economical** as they can be, without any alternative courses of action available to the organisation. The planning process should take account of alternative options, and look for ways of improving performance: this is something that traditional incremental budgeting simply does not do.

(c) At its simplest, **activity based budgeting** (ABB) is merely the use of costs determined using activity based costing as a basis for preparing budgets.

More formally, activity based budgeting involves **defining the activities** that underlie the financial figures in each function and using the **level of activity** to decide how much resource should be allocated to that function, how well it is being managed and to explain variances from budget.

It is based on the principle that **activities drive costs** and the aim is to **control the causes** (drivers) of costs rather than the costs themselves, with the result that in the long term, costs will be better managed and understood.

Not all activities are value adding and so activities must be examined and split up according to their ability to add value.

Implementing ABC leads to the realisation that the **business as a whole** needs to be managed with far more reference to the **behaviour of activities and cost drivers** identified. For example, set up costs for the assembly line of Brunti are clearly identified and can therefore be budgeted for and controlled.

ABB should ensure that the organisation's **overall strategy** and any actual or likely changes in that strategy will be taken into account, because it attempts to manage the business as the **sum of its interrelated parts.**

Critical success factors will be identified and performance measures devised to monitor progress towards them. A critical success factor is an activity in which a business **must** perform well if it is to succeed, for example controlling costs of car components without sacrificing quality.

Because concentration is focused on the **whole** of an activity, not just its separate parts, there is more likelihood of **getting it right first time**. For example what is the use of being able to produce components in time for their despatch date if the budget provides insufficient resources for the distribution manager who has to deliver them?

44 Cushair Designs

Text references. Quantitative techniques are covered in Chapter 10.

Top tips. This question required quite a lot of computation and the production of a neat graph. When calculations are made under time pressure, errors are very likely. It is therefore essential that you show workings, so that credit can be given for method.

(a, b)

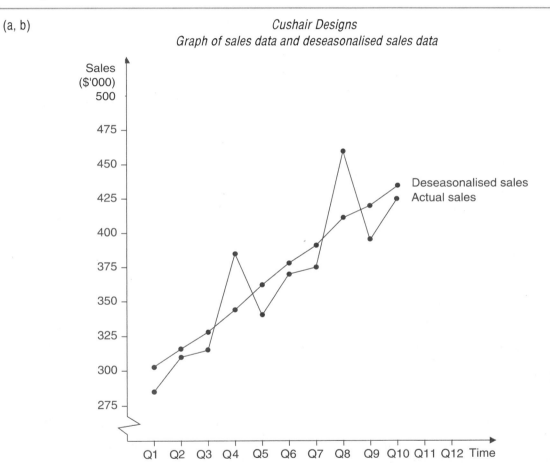

Cushair Designs
Graph of sales data and deseasonalised sales data

It is clear that the **trend** is a **rising** one. **Seasonal adjustments** expressed in terms of dollars of sales, as with the **additive model**, would therefore become **out of date**. Seasonal adjustments need to be expressed as **percentages** of current trend values, so that they **do not fall as proportions of trend** values. The multiplicative model is therefore more appropriate than the additive model.

Deseasonalised data are found by **dividing the data by the seasonal indices** (expressed as proportions). This gives the following values, which are plotted on the graph above.

Quarter	Value of retail sales $'000	Seasonal indices	Deseasonalised sales data $'000
Q1	285	0.94	303
Q2	310	0.98	316
Q3	315	0.96	328
Q4	385	1.12	344
Q5	340	0.94	362
Q6	370	0.98	378
Q7	375	0.96	391
Q8	460	1.12	411
Q9	395	0.94	420
Q10	425	0.98	434

(c) The trend line is to be found by applying least-squares regression to the deseasonalised data. **Time** is the **independent** variable.

x	y	x^2	xy
1	303	1	303
2	316	4	632
3	328	9	984
4	344	16	1,376
5	362	25	1,810
6	378	36	2,268
7	391	49	2,737
8	411	64	3,288
9	420	81	3,780
10	434	100	4,340
55	3,687	385	21,518

For a regression line **y = a + bx**, we have

$$b = \frac{10 \times 21{,}518 - 55 \times 3{,}687}{10 \times 385 - 55^2} = \frac{12{,}395}{825} = 15.02$$

$$a = \frac{3{,}687}{10} - 15.02 \times \frac{55}{10} = 286.09.$$

The **trend line** is therefore y = **15.02x + 286.09**

Sales in $'000 = 286.09 + 15.02 × quarter number.

(d) The **estimated sales for quarter 11** are

$0.96 \times (286.09 + 15.02 \times 11) = 433.2576 = \$433{,}257.60$, say $433,000.

The **estimated sales for quarter 12** are

$1.12 \times (286.09 + 15.02 \times 12) = 522.2896 = \$522{,}289.60$, say $522,000.

(e) The estimates are likely to be **reasonably reliable**, as the period of extrapolation is only **two quarters into the future** and the **trend line** has been **computed** using data from **ten quarters**. However, there is always the possibility that the **trend** or the **pattern of seasonal variations** will **change suddenly** and unexpectedly. It is also possible that the **seasonal indices** used, being based on national averages, are **not entirely appropriate** for this particular business.

Future sales could be affected by **political and economic changes** such as changes in interest rates or taxes affecting demand.

Social changes such as alterations in taste and fashion can also cause forecasting difficulties.

45 Wargrin

Marking scheme

		Marks	
(a)	Lifecycle costing principle:		
	Performance assessment	1	
	Improved decision making	1	
	Cost control	1	
	Relate to Wargrin	1	
	Maximum		3
(b)	Sales	1	
	Variable cost	1	
	Fixed cost	2	
	Marketing cost	1	
	Comments on profit performance	1	
	Consideration of all lifecycle costs	1	
			7
(c)	Why incremental budgeting is common – per idea (max 3)	1	
	Problems of incremental budgets – per idea (max 3)	1	
			6
(d)	Discussion of each component	1	
			4
			20

(a) **Lifecycle costing**

Lifecycle costing tracks and accumulates costs and revenues attributable to each product over the **entire product life cycle**. A product's life cycle costs are incurred from its design stage through development to market launch, production and sales, and finally to its eventual withdrawal from the market.

Lifecycle costing is particularly suited to businesses such as Wargrin who manufacture products with short lifecycles and who have significant research and development costs. In order to compete effectively in today's competitive market, organisations need to **redesign continually their products** with the result that **product life cycles** have become much **shorter**. The **planning, design and development stages of a product's cycle** are therefore **critical** to an organisation's cost management process. Cost reduction at this stage of a product's life cycle, rather than during the production process, is one of the most important ways of reducing product cost.

(b) **Budgeted results**

	Year 1 $	Year 2 $	Year 3 $	Total $
Sales revenue	240,000	480,000	120,000	840,000
Variable cost (W)	(40,000)	(80,000)	(20,000)	(140,000)
Fixed cost (W)	(80,000)	(120,000)	(80,000)	(280,000)
Marketing cost	(60,000)	(40,000)		(100,000)
Profit	60,000	240,000	20,000	320,000

Working

	Units	Cost $
Highest activity level	14,000	150,000
Lowest activity level	10,000	130,000
	4,000	20,000

Variable cost per unit = $20,000/4,000 units = $5

Fixed cost = total cost – variable cost

= 150,000 – (14,000 × 5)

= $80,000

If volumes exceed 15,000 units, fixed costs = $80,000 × 1.5 = $120,000

Assessment

The Stealth will make a **profit** in each of the three years with the highest profit in Year 2. In total, the **net profit margin** is 38% (320,000/840,000 × 100%) which is above the target 35%.

The **contribution rate** is 83% (30 – 5/30 × 100%) which is also above the expected 75%. This indicates that the production process is expected to be under control and reliable.

Wargrin may therefore be satisfied that using **traditional** performance measures, the Stealth will be successful. However, this fails to take into account the **design and development costs** of $300,000. If this is incorporated into the profit forecast, the profit is then only $20,000. This may still be acceptable but it does illustrate the importance of looking at costs throughout the **entire lifecycle**.

(c) **Incremental budgeting**

This is a traditional approach to budgeting which bases the budget on the current year's results plus an extra amount for estimated growth or inflation next year.

Why is it commonly used?

It is a **quick** and **relatively simple** process to prepare an incremental budget and people are usually comfortable and familiar with the technique.

The necessary information is usually **easily available** which again keeps the time needed and costs down.

Incremental budgeting is a reasonable procedure if current operations are as effective, efficient and economical as they can be. It is also appropriate for budgeting for costs such as staff salaries, which may be estimated on the basis of current salaries plus an increment for inflation and are hence administratively fairly easy to prepare.

Problems

In general, however, it is an **inefficient form of budgeting** as it **encourages slack** and **wasteful spending** to creep into budgets. Past inefficiencies are perpetuated because cost levels are rarely subjected to close scrutiny.

In a **rapidly changing** business environment, it is inappropriate as the past is not a reliable indicator of what will happen in the future. It can also be difficult to determine the level of the necessary increment.

(d) **Design and development costs**

Setting a standard cost for this type of cost would be very difficult. Different games will require different amounts of time to design and develop and this timing could be very difficult to predict.

Variable production cost

A game will be produced on a disc in a fairly standard format. Each disc would be identical so setting a standard material cost would be possible. An allowance for waste or faulty discs could be built into the standard.

The discs would be produced using a machine so a standard could be produced for machine time. This should be the same for all items and therefore setting a standard would be valid.

Fixed production cost

The standard fixed production cost of a game would be derived from the time taken to produce the game and the standard fixed overhead absorption rate for the business. It is debateable whether this standard method of absorbing overheads is meaningful.

The time per unit will be fairly standard but a fixed cost per unit implies that costs are variable and this can sometimes confuse non-accountants, causing poor decisions.

Marketing costs

Setting a standard for marketing costs may be difficult as games may have different target audiences and therefore require different marketing strategies. It may be possible to set standards for each marketing media chosen. For example the rates for a page advert in a magazine could be set as a standard.

46 ZBB

Text reference. Budgetary systems are covered in Chapter 9.

Top tips. There are a number of marks available for explanations in this question. Include examples in your answers to maximise your score. Remember to refer back to the view given in your answer to part (d). Aim to include at least three well explained limitations of zero-based budgeting.

Easy marks. There are easy marks available in parts (b) and (c) for simply explaining incremental budgeting and zero-based budgeting and the stages involved in ZBB.

Examiner's comments. Anyone who reads *Student Accountant* would have seen an article in this over the past year and a half on incremental vs. zero based budgeting. These articles are never meant as an indicator of what is going to be examined in a forthcoming session but should be seen as a useful resource, there to supplement the study materials being used. They are there to help broaden your knowledge; if you fail to prepare you prepare to fail.

There were some reasonable attempts to part (a), although too many candidates simply compared the two types of organisation without relating it to budgeting. Similarly, a significant number of candidates were clearly confused about the difference between public sector organisations as opposed to publicly listed companies, and answered the question entirely incorrectly!

The majority of candidates picked up the easy marks available in parts (b) and (c).

There were some reasonable attempts at part (d), although, as with part (a), some answers focused purely on the benefits and drawbacks of both methods without relating it back to the statement.

Marking scheme

		Marks
(a)	Explanation:	
	Difficulty setting objectives quantifiably	2
	Difficulty in saying how to achieve them	1
	Outputs difficult to measure	2
	No relationship between inputs and outputs	2
	Value for money issue	2
		max 5

(a) **Difficulties when budgeting in the public sector**

The main objective for most companies is to **maximise profit**. Effective budgeting can assist in meeting this objective by focussing efforts on reducing certain costs and increasing revenues by a certain amount or percentage. The **objectives of public sector organisations** are more **difficult to define in a quantifiable way**.

The **objectives of public sector organisations** such as hospitals are likely to **be largely qualitative**. For example, ensuring that ambulances reach patients within 20 minutes from an emergency call being received. Such objectives are difficult to define in a quantifiable way, whilst identifying how the objective is actually achieved can also be problematic.

Another problem why budgeting is so difficult in public sector organisations is that outputs in the public sector can seldom be measured in a way that is generally agreed to be meaningful. Whilst outputs for private companies can be measured in terms of sales revenue, outputs in the public sector are harder to pin down. For example in the education sector, are good exam results alone an adequate measure of the quality of teaching? In the public sector, **comparisons are often made between the funds available and the funds actually required**. Therefore, public sector budgeting naturally focuses on inputs, rather than the relationship between inputs and outputs.

Public sector organisations are under constant pressure to prove that they are economical, efficient and effective (offering value for money). **Resources are always kept to a minimum and each item of expenditure must be justified**. This makes the budgeting process more difficult.

(b) **Incremental budgeting**

Incremental budgeting **bases the budget on the current year's results plus an extra amount for estimated growth or inflation next year**. This form of budgeting is a reasonable procedure if current operations are as effective, efficient and economical as they can be. **Zero-based budgeting (ZBB)**

ZBB rejects the assumption that underpins the concept of incremental budgeting; that next year's budget can be based on this year's costs plus an extra amount for estimated growth or inflation. ZBB involves **preparing a budget for each cost centre from a zero base**. Every item of **expenditure must be justified** in its entirety in order to be included in next year's budget.

(c) **Stages in zero-based budgeting**

ZBB involves three main stages.

Define activities (decision packages)

At the first stage, management identify the **key activities** within the organisation. These activities are described within a decision package. The decision package is originally **prepared at a base level** which shows the minimum level of resource required to meet the organisations objectives. **Incremental packages** may be prepared to show any **additional work** that could be done, at what cost and for what benefit.

Evaluate and rank each activity

Management will then rank each activity (decision package) on the basis of its benefit to the organisation. Minimum work requirements (those that are essential to get the job done) will be given high priority and so too will work which meets legal obligations. This process will **help management to decide what to spend and where to spend it**.

Allocate resources

At the final stage, management allocate resources in the budget **according to the funds available and the evaluation and ranking of the competing packages**.

(d) **No longer a place for incremental budgeting and the drawbacks of ZBB**

Incremental budgeting can encourage **slack** and **wasteful spending** as past inefficiencies are perpetuated because cost levels are rarely subjected to close scrutiny. However, the view that there is no longer a place for it in any organisation is rather misleading. Whilst inappropriate for public sector organisations where all expenditure must be justified, to say that it is of no use in any organisation effectively ignores the limitations of zero-based budgeting (ZBB). These limitations are analysed below.

The limitations of ZBB

The major limitation of ZBB is the volume of **extra paperwork** created. Assumptions about costs and benefits in each package must be continually updated and new packages must be developed as new activities occur within the organisation.

ZBB is likely to require **management skills both in constructing decision packages and in the ranking process**. If management do not possess such skills they will require training in ZBB techniques which takes time and money.

The ranking process can also prove problematic. It can be difficult **to rank packages which appear to be equally vital**, for legal or operational reasons. Furthermore, it is difficult to rank activities which have **qualitative rather than quantitative benefits**.

ZBB can **give the impression that all decisions have to be made in the budget**. As a result, management may feel unable to carry out new ideas because they were not approved by a decision package and did not pass through the ranking process.

ZBB in practice

As all costs need to justified under a ZBB system, it would seem inappropriate to use it as the sole system within a private sector organisation where **certain costs will always be incurred in order to meet basic production requirements**. In such a scenario, incremental budgeting is likely to prove more efficient as it is quick and easily understood.

ZBB could be considered more **appropriate for public sector organisations**. The majority of costs in such organisations are **discretionary** and emphasis is placed on obtaining **value for money**. This objective is directly linked to the decision package ranking process within a ZBB system. Furthermore, it is easier to put activities into decision packages in organisations which undertake a number of set definable activities. Hospitals for example have set activities including outpatient wards, children's wards and A&E departments.

Conclusion

Whilst ZBB is more suitable for public sector organisations particularly in the current economic climate, its limitations should not be overlooked. Incremental budgeting can still be of use to organisations.

47 Northland

Text references. Budgeting is covered in Chapters 9 and 10.

Top tips. The expected value calculations in part (b) will need to carefully thought through. There are a number of ways of doing these calculations which are equally acceptable, but do make sure you show your workings clearly.

You must answer the specific requirements of the question in part (c) and apply your answer to the circumstances of a local government organisation.

Easy marks. There are easy marks available for the calculations and some straightforward textbook knowledge.

Examiner's comments. Part (a) was very well done as expected. Part (b) was a little more mixed with candidates getting into a tangle with the expected value calculations. Part (c) was less well done. Candidates can do the calculations but seem to have little idea as to why! The question did not ask for advantages and disadvantages of expected values. Part (d) was poorly done which was surprising and due to a lack of detailed knowledge.

			Marks
(a)	Property cost	1	
	Central wages	1	
	Stationery	1	
			3
(b)	Basic budget	2	
	Contingency included	2	
	Expected value adjustment	2	
			6
(c)	Probability estimates difficult	1	
	Monetary values uncertain	1	
	EV not an actual value	1	
	Easy fall back for managers	1	
	Uncertainty issue	1	
	Weather	1	
	Other outside influences	1	
	Type of repairs variable	1	
			8
(d)	Define the decision package	1	
	Evaluate and rank each design package	1	
	Allocate resources	1	
			3
			20

(a) **Overheads budget for 20X2**

Property cost = $120,000 + 5%
= $120,000 × 1.05
= $126,000

Central wages = ($150,000 + 3%) + $12,000
= ($150,000 × 1.03) + $12,000
= $166,500

Stationery = $25,000 − 40%
= $25,000 × 0.6
= $15,000

(b) **Budget for road repairs**

Expected amount of road repairs = 2,000 metres + 10% contingency
= 2,000 × 1.1
= 2,200 metres

Expected value of weather related repair cost increase = (0.7 × 0%) + (0.1 × 10%) + (0.2 × 25%)
= 6%

After inflation road repair cost = $15,000 + 5% per metre
$$= \$15,000 \times 1.05$$
$$= \$15,750$$

Budget for road repairs = 1.06 × $15,750 × 2,200 metres
$$= \$36,729,000$$

(c) **Problems with using expected values in budgeting**

Probabilities

The probability of different types of weather conditions has been estimated and this is potentially **unreliable**. It is very difficult to accurately forecast long range weather conditions and this could have a major impact on potential budget errors.

Cost estimates

It is also difficult to accurately predict the **effect** of weather conditions on roads. 'Bad' weather could involve a number of different weather conditions such as extreme cold or heavy rain which would affect roads in different ways. Some repairs can be quick and cheap whilst other repairs will involve extensive and expensive work. The resulting **increase in repair costs** could therefore **vary** considerably and unpredictably.

Responsibility

The unpredictable nature of the weather gives managers responsible for road repair budgets a **good excuse** when actual costs are higher to budgeted. This limits the effectiveness of such budgets as a means of **control**.

Need for a contingency

The unpredictability of both weather conditions and the costs of repairs mean that there is a high degree of **uncertainty** associated with a road repair budget. A contingency therefore needs to be added to the budget in order to allow for unexpected increases in costs.

(d) **Zero-based budgeting**

The basic approach of zero-based budgeting has three steps.

Define decision packages

These are comprehensive descriptions of specific organisational activities which management can use to evaluate the activities and **rank** them in order of priority against other activities. A **cost-benefit analysis** will often be conducted at this stage.

Evaluate and rank each activity (decision package)

This is done on the basis of its benefit to the organisation. This can be a lengthy process. Minimum work requirements (those that are essential to get a job done) will be given high priority and so too will work which meets legal obligations.

Allocate resources

These are allocated in the budget according to the funds available and the evaluation and ranking of the competing packages.

BPP
LEARNING MEDIA

Answers 185

48 Velo Racers

(a)   Whenever an individual starts a job which is **fairly repetitive** in nature, and provided that his speed of working is not dictated to him by the speed of machinery (as it would be on a production line), he is likely to become **more confident and knowledgeable** about the work as he gains experience, to become **more efficient**, and to do the work **more quickly**. Eventually, however, when he has acquired enough experience, there will be nothing more for him to learn, and so the **learning process will stop**.

Learning curve theory applies to these situations, where the work force as a whole **improves in efficiency with experience**. The learning effect or learning curve effect describes the speeding up of a job with repeated performance.

Labour time should be expected to get shorter, with experience, in the production of items which exhibit any or all of the following features.

- Made largely **by labour** (rather than by a **highly-mechanised** process)
- Brand **new** or **short lived** (the learning process does not continue indefinitely)
- **Complex** and made in **small quantities** for **special orders**

In learning curve theory, the **cumulative average time per unit produced** is assumed to **decrease by a constant percentage** every time total **output** of the product **doubles**. For instance, where an 80% learning effect occurs, the cumulative average time required per unit of output is reduced to 80% of the previous cumulative average time when output is doubled.

(b)   **Price quotations**

No of bikes		Time per bike Hours	Total time Hours	Incremental time Hours
1		50.0	50.0	50.0
2	@ 80%	40.0	80.0	30.0
4	@ 80%	32.0	128.0	48.0
8	@ 80%	25.6	204.8	76.8
16	@ 80%	20.5	328.0	123.2

Quotation 1

	$	
Materials	1,000	
Labour	300	(30 hours incremental for the second bike)
Fixed overhead	600	
Total cost	1,900	
Profit @ 20%	380	
Selling price	2,280	

Quotation 2

	$	
Materials	2,000	
Labour	480	(48 hours incremental)
Fixed overhead	960	
Total cost	3,440	
Profit @ 20%	688	
Selling price	4,128	
Per bike	2,064	

Quotation 3

	$	
Materials	8,000	
Labour	2,048	(204.8 hours total time taken
Fixed overhead	4,096	
Total cost	14,144	
Profit @ 20%	2,829	
Selling price	16,973	
Per bike	2,122	

Quotation 4

A steady state is reached after the 16th bike so we need the time taken to produce the 16th bike.

For 15 bikes, a = 50 hours (time for first unit)

x = 15

$$b = \frac{\log r}{\log 2}$$

$$= \frac{\log 0.8}{\log 2} = -0.322$$

$$y = 50 \times 15^{-0.322}$$

$$= 20.9 \text{ hours}$$

Cumulative units	Average time per unit	Total time
15	20.9	313.5
16	20.5	328.0
Incremental time for 16th bike		14.5

Total hours for 20 bikes = 328.0 + (4 × 14.5)

= 386

	$
Materials	20,000
Labour	3,860
Fixed overhead	7,720
Total cost	31,580
Profit @ 20%	6,316
Selling price	37,896

(c)   **The relevance of learning curve effects in management accounting**

(i)   **Sales projections, advertising expenditure and delivery date commitments**. Identifying a learning curve effect should allow Velo Racers to plan its advertising and delivery schedules to coincide with expected production schedules. Production capacity obviously affects sales capacity and sales projections.

(ii)   **Budgeting with standard costs**. Companies that use standard costing for much of their production output cannot apply standard times to output where a learning effect is taking place. This problem can be overcome in practice by:

   (1)   Establishing **standard times** for output, once the learning effect has worn off or become insignificant

   (2)   Introducing a **'launch cost'** budget for the product for the duration of the learning period

(iii)   **Budgetary control**. When learning is still taking place, it would be unreasonable to compare actual times with the standard times that ought eventually to be achieved when the learning effect wears off. **Allowance should be made** accordingly when interpreting labour efficiency variances.

(iv)   **Cash budgets**. Since the learning effect reduces unit variable costs as more units are produced, it should be allowed for in **cash flow projections**.

Limitations of learning curve theory

(i)   It assumes **stable conditions** at work which will **enable learning to take place**. This is not always practicable, for example because of **labour turnover**.

(ii)   It must also assume a certain degree of **agreement** and **motivation** amongst employees.

(iii) Breaks between repeating production of an item must not be too long, or workers will **'forget'** and the learning process will have to begin all over again.

(iv)   It might be difficult to **obtain accurate data** to decide what the learning curve is.

49 Q Organisation

Text references. Life-cycle costing is covered in Chapter 2c, pricing in Chapter 5 and the learning curve in Chapter 10.

Top tips. Part (a) of the question requires you to identify the five stages of the product life cycle and the appropriate pricing policies for each stage. Think about the product and apply your knowledge to this specific product.

Part (b)(i) is difficult and requires you to know how to calculate a rate of learning and a learning curve.

Part (b)(ii) should just follow on: once you have total variable costs for each level of demand you can calculate the optimal contribution.

Part (b)(iii) requires a careful reading of the question – you need to calculate the average variable cost for each learning stage after the initial phase identified in part (ii).

Marking scheme

				Marks	
(a)		Policies suitable at each stage	Max per stage	1	
					5
(b)	(i)	Calculation of r		4	
		Calculation of Y		2	
			Max		4
	(ii)	Table to calculate prices			3
	(iii)	Costs 20 – 30,000 units		2	
		30 – 40,000 units		2	
		Sales 20 – 30,000 units		2	
		Sales 30 – 40,000 units		2	
					8
					20

(a)   The product life cycle comprises five stages:

- Development
- Introduction
- Growth
- Maturity
- Decline

In the **introduction stage** the company needs to price the product to achieve its market strategy using either **penetration** or **skimming** pricing policies.

A **penetration policy** is used with the objective of achieving a high level of demand very quickly by using a low price that is affordable to a large number of potential customers.

A **skimming policy** is particularly appropriate to a product that has a novelty value or that is technologically advanced such as the DVD recorder. Such a policy uses a price that is high and this restricts the volume of sales since only high worth customers can afford the product, but the high unit profitability enables the initial supplier to recover their development costs.

Competitors will be attracted to the product by its high price and will seek to compete with it by introducing their own version of the product at much lower development costs (by reverse engineering Q's product) so it is important for Q to **reduce the price** during the **growth stage** of the product's life cycle. There may be many price reductions during this phase so that the product gradually becomes more affordable to lower social economic groups.

As the product enters the **maturity stage** the price will need to be **lowered further**, though a profitable contribution ratio would continue to be earned. Oligopolistic competition is often found in this stage, but provided Q has gained market share and survived until this stage the opportunity to make profit and cash surpluses should exist. However, in this type of market the price will tend to be set by the market and Q will have to accept that price. Thus Q will need to focus on the **control of its costs** to ensure that the product will remain profitable.

When the product enters the **decline phase** a **loyal group of customers** may continue to be prepared to pay **a reasonable price** and at this price the product will continue to be profitable, especially as costs continue to reduce. Eventually the price will be lowered to **marginal cost** or even lower in order to sell off inventories of what is now an obsolete product as it has been replaced by a more technologically advanced item.

(b)   (i)

Cumulative number of units	Total variable cost/unit	Affected by learning	Not affected by learning
	$	$	$
10,000	60.00	30.00	30.00
20,000	56.10 (W2)	26.10	30.00
30,000	54.06 (W3)	24.06	30.00
40,000	52.71	22.71	30.00

Workings

(1)   *Calculation of rate of learning*

At 10,000 units, variable cost affected by learning = $30

At 40,000 units, variable cost affected by learning = $22.71

Let the rate of learning be r.

$$30r^2 = 22.71$$
$$r^2 = 0.757$$
$$r = 0.87$$

(2)   We can now derive the variable cost affected by learning for 20,000 units,

$$= 30r = 30 \times 0.87 = \$26.10$$

The variable cost affected by learning for 30,000 units will require the use of a formula for the learning curve.

$$a = \$30$$
$$= 3$$
$$b = \log 0.87/\log 2$$
$$= -0.201$$

Thus $Y = aX^b$
$$= 30 \times 3^{-0.201}$$
$$= \underline{\underline{24.06}}$$

(ii) Optimum price at which the DVD recorder should be sold.

Demand in Units	Price/unit $	Variable cost /unit $	Contribution/ unit $	Total contribution $
10,000	100	60.00	40.00	400,000
20,000	80	56.10	23.90	478,000
30,000	69	54.06	14.94	448,200
40,000	62	52.71	9.29	371,600

The price which gives the optimum contribution is $80/unit.

(iii) The initial launch phase identified in (b)(ii) is up to a level of at 20,000 units.

The target contribution is $45,000 per month.

To determine unit costs if after the initial phase, total volume is between 20,000 and 30,000 units, the average cost would be:

$$\frac{(30,000 \times 54.06) - (20,000 \times 56.10)}{10,000} = \$49.98$$

Likewise between 30,000 and 40,000 units, the average cost would be:

$$\frac{(40,000 \times 52.71) - (30,000 \times 54.06)}{10,000} = \$48.66$$

Therefore, at between 20,000 and 30,000 units, the required sales level is calculated as:

$45,000/\$(57 - 49.98) = \underline{6,410 \text{ units}}$

Likewise between 30,000 and 40,000 units, required sales are:

$45,000/\$(57 - 48.66)$

$= \underline{5,396 \text{ units}}$

50 BFG

Text references. The learning curve is covered in Chapter 10.

Top tips. This is probably the hardest question on the pilot paper with some quite tricky calculations. Show your workings clearly to gain as many marks as possible. In part (c) make sure you apply your suggestions to BFG and use your business knowledge.

Easy marks. There are some easy calculations at the start of part (a) provided you don't panic! You can use your common sense in part (c) to come up with some useful suggestions.

Marking scheme

				Marks
(a)	Sales		1	
	Direct labour:	First seven months	3	
		Last five months	3	
	Variable overhead		1	
	Decision		1	
				9
(b)	Second unit times:	80%	2	
		90%	2	
	Comment on faster learning		1	
				5

(c)   Actions to improve net cash flow
       (2 marks per explained idea)

$$\frac{6}{20}$$

(a)

	$	$
Sales revenue (1,200 × $1,050)		1,260,000
Direct materials	514,000	
Direct labour (W1)	315,423	
Variable overhead (W2)	126,169	
		955,592
Net cash flow		304,408

Target cash flow is $350,000 so this will not be achieved.

Workings

(1)   *Direct labour*

For first seven hundred units $y = ax^b$
                                  $y = 2,500 \times 700^{-0.3219}$
                                  $y = \$303.461045$

Total cost for first 700 units = $303.461045 × 700 = $212,423

All units after the first 700 will have the same cost as the 700th unit. To calculate the cost of the 700th batch we need to take the cost of 699 units from the cost of 700 units.

For 699 units $y = ax^b$
                     $y = 2,500 \times 699^{-0.3219}$
                     $Y = \$303.600726$

Total cost for first 699 units = $303.600726 × 699 = $212,217

Cost of 700th unit is $212,423 – $212.217 = $206

Total cost for the 12 months of production

$212,423 + ($206 × 500) = $315,423

(2)   *Variable overhead*

Variable overhead is $2 per hour or 40% of direct labour

40% × $315,423 = $126,169

(b)   (i)   **A learning rate of 80%**

	Hours
Time for first unit	500
Average time for two units (500 × 0.8)	400
Total time for two units (400 × 2)	800
Time for second unit (800 – 500)	300

       (ii)   **A learning rate of 90%**

	Hours
Time for first unit	500
Average time for two units (500 × 0.9)	450
Total time for two units (450 × 2)	900
Time for second unit (900 – 500)	400

The 80% learning rate shows the faster learning as the time taken for the second unit is less.

(c)   In order to improve the net cash flow, BFG could undertake the following action.

   (i)   **Increase the price of the product.** A market has been identified for an agreed design specification but the market may accept a higher price. BFG may be able to use **price skimming** which involves charging high prices when a product is first launched. Market research would be useful to find out what price could be charged.

   (ii)   **Reduce the labour cost per unit.** This could be achieved by analysing operations and processes and removing unnecessary aspects. It may also be possible to simplify the design of the product without affecting its potential market.

   (iii)   **Improve the learning rate**. This could be achieved by improving training or the quality of the labour force but it could be costly and time consuming to do so.

   (iv)   **Use cheaper materials.** New suppliers may be able to provide cheaper materials but care must be taken not to damage the quality of the product.

   (v)   **Reduce variable overheads.** There may be ways to save money on some of the expenses involved.

51 HC

Text reference. Learning curves are covered in Chapter 10.

Top tips. The calculations in this question require a logical approach and should be straightforward, provided you have practised this technique. A clear layout is essential and a heading for each point you make in part (a) will help the marker. Part (c) is only worth 2 marks so if you get stuck, move on.

Easy marks. Use your common sense and business knowledge to gain easy marks in part (a).

Examiner's comments. Part (a) was not well done by many. All that was required was sensible ideas about figures that might have to be included in the bid. Part (b) was well done by many candidates despite it being a fairly demanding aspect of learning curves. A scientific calculator is essential and y should not be rounded.

Marking scheme

			Marks
(a)	For each description	2	
			6
(b)	Average time for 199th kitchen	1	
	Total time for 199 kitchens	1	
	Average time for 200th kitchen	1	
	Total time for 200 kitchens	1	
	200th kitchen time	1	
	Cost for first 200	1	
	Cost for next 400	1	
	Variable cost per hour	1	
	Fixed cost per month	1	
	Fixed cost per hour	1	
	Cost for labour	1	
	Cost for variable overhead	1	
	Cost for fixed overhead	1	
	Maximum		12
(c)	Average time per unit	1	
	Explanation	1	
			2
			20

(a) **Competition**

HC has not worked for this builder before and will be competing against other contractors for the bid who may have a prior relationship with the builder. The bid therefore needs to be sufficiently competitive to overcome these issues.

Contingency allowance

The estimates that HC has made are subject to uncertainty and it needs to ensure that the contract will be profitable even if the estimates are over-optimistic. A contingency allowance should be added to the bid to allow for this.

Idle time

It is assumed that the workforce will be able to work at maximum productivity throughout the length of the contract. However construction is often delayed by unexpected late deliveries of materials etc and labour can therefore be unexpectedly idle. This idle time needs to be incorporated into the labour calculations.

(b) **Calculation of total cost**

Cost	Hours	Rate per hour	Total
		$	$
Labour	9,247 (W1)	15	138,705
Variable overhead	9,247	8 (W2)	73,976
Fixed overhead	9,247	4 (W2)	36,988
Total cost			249,669

Workings

1 *Labour hours*

For 199 kitchens $y = ax^b$

$= 24 \times 199^{-0.074}$

$= 16.22169061$

Total time for 199 kitchens $= 199 \times 16.22169061$

$= 3,228.12$ hours

For 200 kitchens $y = ax^b$

$= 24 \times 200^{-0.074}$

$= 16.21567465$

Total time for 200 kitchens $= 200 \times 16.21567465$

$= 3,243.13$ hours

Time for the 200th kitchen $= 3,243.13 - 3,228.12 = 15.01$ hours

	Hours
1st 200 kitchens	3,243.13
Next 400 kitchens (15.01 × 400)	6,004.00
Total time	9,247.13

2 *Overheads*

	Hours	Cost
		$
Highest activity level	9,600	116,800
Lowest activity level	9,200	113,600
	400	3,200

Variable cost per hour = $3,200/400 hours = $8

Fixed cost = total cost – variable cost

= 116,800 – (9,600 × 8)

= $40,000 per month

Annual fixed cost = $40,000 × 12 = $480,000

Fixed overhead absorption rate = $480,000/120,000 hours = $4 per hour

(c)

Number of kitchens	Time taken Hours	Cumulative time Hours	Average time Hours
1	24.00	24.00	24.00
2	21.60	45.60	22.80

When output doubles from 1 to 2, average time reduces from 24.00 hours to 22.80 hours. This **reduction in average time** is 22.80/24.00 × 100% = 95% and this is the **learning rate**.

52 Big Cheese Chairs

Text reference. Target costing is covered in Chapter 2b and learning curves in Chapter 10.

Top tips. The question gives you the value of b and it is important to keep the accuracy by using all of the decimal places given. Show all your workings clearly and make sure you identify in both parts (a) and (b) what the final figures mean. In part (b), you need to apply your answer to the specific circumstances of Big Cheese Chairs and not just write a general description of how to close a cost gap.

Easy marks. There are easy marks available throughout this question.

Examiner's comments. Attempts at part (a) were reasonable. Whilst many candidates correctly identified ways of closing the gap in part (b), a number of answers included a suggestion to increase the selling price! This suggestion goes totally against the whole ideology of target costing and needless to say was not a mark earner!

There were some good attempts to part (c). Some candidates clearly did not understand the difference between a cumulative cost and an incremental cost and simply repeated their calculations from part (a).

Marking scheme

			Marks
(a)	Frame cost	1	
	Leather cost	2	
	Labour average time for 128 units	1	
	Labour total time for 128 units	1	
	Average cost per chair	1	
	Target cost	1	
	Cost gap	1	
			8
(b)	Per suggestion	1½	
			6

(c)

Frame		½
Leather		½
Average time per unit		2
Total time		1
Time for 128th chair		1
Conclusion		1
		6
		20

(a) **Expected cost per unit**

		$ per chair
Frame and massage mechanism		51.00
Leather	2 metres × $10/m × 100/80	25·00
Labour (W)		20·95
Total cost		96·95
Target cost	$120 × 80%	(96.00)
Cost gap		0.95

Working

$$y = ax^b$$
$$y = 2 \times 128^{-0.074000581}$$
$$y = 1.396674595 \text{ hours}$$

Average labour cost of a chair = 1.396674595 × $15
= $20.95

(b) **Closing the cost gap**

The chair's **design** could be looked at again to remove any **unnecessary features** which do not **add value** for the customer. This would reduce costs.

The **raw materials** are leather and the frame and it may be possible to **negotiate with the suppliers** for a better cost, perhaps as a bulk buying discount as volumes increase. However, reduced costs must not be at the expense of **quality**.

Reducing the level of **leather wasted** would save on cost. This could be achieved by better training of workers or improved processes.

Labour costs could be reduced by improving the **rate of learning** with better training and supervision. Alternatively, cheaper labour could be employed perhaps by reducing the skill level expected. This may however have the detrimental effect of quality reduction or increased wastage.

(c) Using the formula, we need to calculate the time taken for the first 127 chairs and deduct that from the time taken for the first 128 chairs.

$$y = ax^b$$
$$y = 2 \times 127^{-0.074000581}$$
$$y = 1.39748546 \text{ hours}$$

Total time for 127 chairs = 127 × 1.39748546 = 177.48 hours
Total time for 128 chairs = 128 × 1.396674592 = 178.77 hours
Time for 128th chair = 178.77 − 177.48 = 1.29 hours

Cost of 128th chair

		$ per chair
Frame and massage mechanism		51.00
Leather	2 metres × $10/m × 100/80	25·00
Labour (W)	1.29 hours × $15	19.35
Total cost		95.35

The target cost is $96 so the target cost is now being achieved.

53 Mermus

Text references. Flexible budgets are covered in Chapter 11 and variance analysis is covered in Chapter 12.

Top tips. If you know your calculation of variances, it is easy to get good marks but you must practise them. You must also be able to explain what variances mean.

Easy marks. In all parts provided you know how to calculate the variances requested.

Examiner's comments. In part (a), many candidates flexed the fixed costs and in part (b), many candidates were able to calculate raw material and direct labour total cost variances.

Fewer were able to calculate the fixed overhead variances and some candidates offered general explanations for the variances in part (c), showing that they failed to understand the basis for their calculation.

Marking scheme

		Marks	
(a)	Sales and raw materials	1	
	Direct labour and variable overheads	1	
	Fixed overheads	1	
	Flexed budget	1	
	Explanation	2	
			6
(b)	Raw material total cost variance	1	
	Direct labour total cost variance	1	
	Fixed overhead absorption rate	1	
	Fixed overhead efficiency variance	2	
	Fixed overhead capacity variance	2	
	Fixed overhead expenditure variance	1	
			8
(c)	Raw material total cost variance	2	
	Fixed overhead efficiency variance	2	
	Fixed overhead expenditure variance	2	
			6
			20

(a) The flexed budget will be based on the activity level of 90,000 units rather than the budgeted level of 95,000 units.

Revised budget

	$	$
Sales ($950,000 × 90/95)		900,000
Cost of sales:		
Raw materials ($133,000 × 90/95)	126,000	
Direct labour ($152,000 × 90/95)	144,000	
Variable production overheads ($100,700 × 90/95)	95,400	
Fixed production overheads	125,400	
		(490,800)
		409,200

A **revised budget** should be prepared because budgets are used for **control purposes** and to **assess performance**. Only those aspects of performance that are **controllable** by the managers should be highlighted. Comparing actual results to a **fixed** budget would result in **meaningless variances** for control purposes.

(b)

	Budget $	Actual $	Variance $
Raw materials total cost variance	126,000	130,500	4,500 (A)
Direct labour total cost variance	144,000	153,000	9,000 (A)

Standard fixed overhead absorption rate
  125,400/28,500 = $4.40 per machine hour
Standard machine hours for actual production
  28,500 × 90/95 = 27,000 hours

Standard fixed overhead for actual production			
27,000 × $4.40	118,800		
Fixed overhead on actual hours			
27,200 × $4.40		119,680	
Fixed overhead efficiency variance			880 (A)
Fixed overhead absorbed on budgeted hours			
28,500 × $4.40	125,400		
Fixed overhead on actual hours			
27,200 × $4.40		119,680	
Fixed overhead capacity variance			5,720 (A)
Fixed overhead expenditure variance	125,400	115,300	10,100 (F)

(c) The **raw materials total cost variance** of $4,500 adverse has arisen because the budgeted cost per unit of $133,000/95,000 units = $1.40 was overtaken by an actual cost of $130,500/90,000 units = $1.45. This may have been due to a supplier price increase, or an increase in the amount of raw material used per unit.

The **fixed overhead efficiency variance** is the difference between the number of hours that actual production should have taken, and the number of hours actually taken (that is, worked) multiplied by the standard absorption rate per hour. A total of 200 more hours than expected were used, maybe because of inaccurate initial planning or operational problems (inexperienced staff, machine breakdown).

The **fixed overhead expenditure variance** is the difference between the budgeted fixed production overhead expenditure and actual fixed production overhead expenditure. The favourable variance could be due to inaccurate budgeting or cost savings being achieved during the period.

54 Ash

Text references. Variance analysis is covered in Chapter 12.

Top tips. If you have practised variance analysis questions and use a standard format you should find this question straightforward but very time pressured. It is unlikely that the F5 examiner will require variance calculations in this much detail but the more practice you can get the better.

You will probably find part (b) more of a struggle. Try to make three points on each section.

Easy marks. Variance analysis questions provide plenty of easy marks provided you are happy with the calculations.

Examiner's comments. This question was very popular with many answers gaining high marks. In part (a), budgeted standard labour hours are given so standard labour hours per unit can be used to find the budgeted sales volume. Fixed overhead variances were a common source of confusion. In part (b) most candidates seemed unaware of the budgetary control cycle and how the operating system fitted into the control process. Most candidates seemed to be unaware that, in the short term, fixed costs are uncontrollable.

Marks

(a) Standard gross profit per unit 1
Budgeted production 1
Budgeted gross profit 1
Sales volume profit variance 1
Sales price variance 1
Material price variances 2
Material usage variances 1
Material mix and yield variances 1
Labour rate variance 1
Labour efficiency variance 1
Variable overhead expenditure variance 1
Variable overhead efficiency variance 1
Fixed overhead expenditure variance 1
Fixed overhead volume variance 2
Fixed overhead efficiency and capacity 1
Actual gross profit 1
Operating statement format 1

Max 15

(b) Controlling variable costs 2-3
Controlling fixed costs 1-2

Max 5
20

(a) **Product RS8**

Standard cost per unit

	$
Direct material M3 (0.6 kg × $1.55)	0.93
Direct material M7 (0.68 kg × $1.75)	1.19
Direct labour (14/60 × $7.20)	1.68
Variable production overhead (14/60 × $2.10)	0.49
Fixed production overhead (14/60 × $9.00)	2.10
Production cost	6.39
Selling price	15.00
Standard gross profit per unit	8.61

Variances

$

Selling price variance
2,100 × $(15 – 14.50) 1,050.00 (A)

Sales volume variance

	Units
Actual sales in units	2,100
Budgeted sales in units (497 × 60/14)	2,130
Variance in units	30(A)
× standard profit per unit	× $8.61

258.30 (A)

Material M3 price variance

1,050 kg should have cost (× $1.55)	1,627.50
but did cost	1,680.00

52.50 (A)

Material M3 usage variance

		$
2,100 units should use (× 0.6 kg)	1,260 kg	
but did use	1,050 kg	
Variance in kgs	210 kg (F)	
× standard cost per kg	× $1.55	
		325.50 (F)

Material M7 price variance

	$	
1,470 kg should have cost (× $1.75)	2,572.50	
but did cost	2,793.00	
		220.50 (A)

Material M7 usage variance

2,100 units should use (× 0.68 kg)	1,428 kg	
but did use	1,470 kg	
Variance in kgs	42 kg (A)	
× standard cost per kg	× $1.75	
		73.50 (A)

Direct labour rate variance

	$	
525 hours should cost (× $7.20)	3,780.00	
but did cost	3,675.00	
		105.00 (F)

Direct labour efficiency variance

2,100 units should take (× 14/60 hrs)	490 hrs	
but did take	525 hrs	
Variance in hours	35 (A)	
× standard rate per hour	× $7.20	
		252.00 (A)

Variable overhead expenditure variance

	$	$
Budgeted variable production overhead (525 × $2.10)	1,102.50	
Actual expenditure	1,260.00	
		157.50 (A)

Variable overhead efficiency variance

2,100 units should take (× 14/60 hrs)	490 hrs	
but did take	525 hrs	
Variance in hours	35 (A)	
× standard rate per hour	× $2.10	
		73.50 (A)

Fixed production overhead expenditure variance

	$	
Budgeted fixed overhead expenditure (497 × $9)	4,473.00	
Actual expenditure	4,725.00	
		252.00 (A)

Fixed production overhead volume variance

Budgeted standard labour hours	497 hrs	
Standard hours for actual production (2,100 × 14/60)	490 hrs	
Variance in hours	7 (A)	
× standard absorption rate per labour hour	× $9.00	
		63.00 (A)

Fixed production overhead capacity variance

Budgeted standard labour hours	497 hrs	
Actual hours of work	525 hrs	
× standard absorption rate	28 (F)	
	× $9.00	
		252.00 (F)

Fixed production overhead efficiency variance

		$
2,100 units should take	490 hrs	
but did take	525 hrs	
	35 (A)	
× standard absorption rate	× $9.00	
		315.00 (A)

Note: Fixed production overhead volume variance = efficiency variance + capacity variance

OPERATING STATEMENT

	$	$
Budgeted gross profit (497 × 60/14 × $8.61)		18,339.30
Sales variances: Price	1,050.00	
Volume	258.30	
		1,308.30
Actual sales minus standard cost of sales		17,031.00

Cost variances	*F*	*A*
	$	$
Material M3 price		52.50
Material M3 usage	325.50	
Material M7 price		220.50
Material M7 usage		73.50
Direct labour rate	105.00	
Direct labour efficiency		252.00
Variable overhead expenditure		157.50
Variable overhead efficiency		73.50
Fixed overhead expenditure		252.00
Fixed overhead volume		63.00
	430.50	1,144.50

		$
		(714.00)
Actual gross profit		16,317.00

	$	$
Direct material M3	1,680.00	
Direct material M7	2,793.00	
Direct labour	3,675.00	
Variable production overhead	1,260.00	
Fixed production overhead	4,725.00	
		14,133.00
Sales revenue (2,100 × $14.50)		30,450.00
Actual gross profit		16,317.00

(b) (i) Costs are controlled by firstly **measuring** actual costs. Variances are then calculated to show the differences between actual costs and budgeted costs. The variances are reported to managers responsible for them who will decide if action needs to be taken. The operating statement provides a **clear format** in which to report relevant variances to management and to enable them to make decisions.

Adverse and favourable variances can be easily identified as can the effect of the volume difference between budgeted and actual sales. This enables managers to concentrate their efforts on the areas where there is a **significant difference** between actual results and planned performance and which will have the greatest effect on correcting operations. Concentrating on areas highlighted by the variances where management action can be taken, controls variable costs. For example, the adverse direct labour efficiency variance of $252 could be reduced by training workers to work more efficiently.

(ii) It is unlikely that fixed production overhead costs can be controlled in the short-term as they are a **sunk cost** and managers will not be able to take corrective action. The adverse fixed production overhead expenditure variance, for example, may be due to poor budget planning and further investigation would be needed to determine whether any of its components were controllable.

The fixed production overhead volume variance shows the effect of actual production being different from planned production and arises due to the process of **absorption costing**. Fixed production overhead variances are included in the operating statement in order to reconcile budgeted profit with actual profit, but they are unlikely to help in controlling costs.

55 Product RYX

Text references. Variance analysis is covered in Chapter 12.

The calculations in (a) should not contain any traps. Remember when discussing the variances, that poor quality labour **and** materials can lead to adverse efficiency variances. An adverse capacity variance arises if the business does not work all its budgeted hours, probably indicating lower output then planned.

(a) (i) **Budgeted fixed overhead absorption rate =**

$22,260 ÷ 8,400 hours = $2.65 per labour hour

Standard labour hours per unit of component RYX =

8,400 hours ÷ 1,200 units = 7 hours per unit

Standard fixed overhead absorbed per unit =

7 hours × $2.65 per hour = $18.55

	$
Fixed production overhead incurred	25,536
Fixed production overhead absorbed (1,100 × $18.55)	20,405
Fixed production overhead cost variance	5,131 (A)
Budgeted expenditure	22,260
Actual expenditure	25,536
Fixed production overhead expenditure variance	3,276 (A)
1,100 units should have taken (× 7 hrs)	7,700 hrs
but did take	7,980 hrs
	280 hrs (A)
× standard rate per hour	× $2.65
Fixed production overhead efficiency variance	$742 (A)
Budgeted hours of work	8,400 hrs
Actual hours of work	7,980 hrs
	420 hrs (A)
× standard rate per hour	× $2.65
Fixed production overhead capacity variance	$1,113 (A)

(ii) **Reconciliation of fixed overhead variances**

	$
Expenditure variance	3,276 (A)
Efficiency variance	742 (A)
Capacity variance	1,113 (A)
Cost variance	5,131 (A)

(b) **Possible reasons for the occurrence of the fixed overhead expenditure, efficiency and capacity variances**

Expenditure variance

This variance represents the difference between actual and budgeted fixed overhead expenditure. An overall adverse variance could arise **if expenditure on one or more categories of fixed overhead was higher than anticipated** (the actual expenditure on other categories either being at the same level as, or not significantly less than, anticipated). There may be a greater than expected rise in buildings insurance premium, for example. Alternatively **global factors**, such as a rate of inflation higher than that allowed for in the budget, will have a more **general adverse effect** on fixed overhead expenditure.

Efficiency variance

This variance shows the effect, at the standard absorption rate per hour, of actual hours worked being more or less than the standard allowance for the actual output. An adverse variance will occur if **actual hours are greater than standard hours**; possible reasons for this are the same as those for an adverse labour efficiency variance and include the following.

(1)   The **use of less skilled labour** than that stipulated in the standard.

(2)   **Higher than anticipated labour turnover**, resulting in more time spent on training than budgeted.

(3)   The **use** of **poor quality materials**, with the result that **production takes longer** than budgeted.

(4)   The **use** of **poor quality materials** leading to a **higher scrap rate** than anticipated and hence more time spent on rectification than planned.

(5)   Problems with **motivation** and **morale**.

(6)   The **standard hours** could have been set **unrealistically low**.

Capacity variance

This component of the volume variance does not take into account the standard hours per unit of production but simply compares the actual number of hours worked with the budgeted number of hours, the difference being multiplied by the standard absorption rate per hour to calculate the variance. An adverse variance arises if **actual hours worked are less than budgeted hours** (because we would expect output to be less than budgeted). Possible reasons for such a variance include the following.

(1)   **Lack of demand** for the **product**

(2)   A **higher than anticipated level of downtime** due to problems with plant and machinery

(3)   **Shortage of labour**

(4)   **Excessive time lost** due to sickness or disputes

(c)   Individual variances should not be looked at in isolation. One variance might be dependent upon another, and much of it might have occurred only because the other inter-dependent variance occurred too. Consider the following examples.

(1)   **Using less skilled workers** than anticipated when standards were set is likely to result in a **favourable labour rate variance** (because the labour rate should be less) but, because the workers are likely to be less efficient and less skilled at using materials, it could also produce **adverse labour efficiency**, **material usage and fixed production overhead efficiency variances**.

(2)   The use of **materials of a higher quality** than required by a standard could produce an **adverse material price variance** (because the material is likely to be more expensive) but, because the material could be easier to use, it could lead to **favourable material usage, labour efficiency and fixed production overhead efficiency variances**.

56 Woodeezer

Text references. Variance analysis is covered in Chapter 12.

Top tips. In part (a) you should make sure you calculate the full range of variances required, including fixed overhead, efficiency and capacity.

In part (b), make sure you relate your answers to the scenario described in the question. Use the information given to help your interpretation as for example the statement that suppliers were changed to improve quality.

Examiner's comments. There were some very good answers to part (a) showing clear understanding of variance analysis. The standard of answers to part (b) was generally disappointing with many candidates failing to relate their answers to the scenario.

(a) **Operating statement**

			$
Budgeted profit ($28 × 4,000)			112,000
Sales volume profit variance			
(3,200 − 4,000) × $28			(22,400) (A)
Standard profit on actual sales			89,600
Selling price variance ($220 − $225) × 3,200			16,000 (F)

			$
			105,600
Cost variances	*Fav*	*Adv*	
Material price		24,000	
Material usage	32,000		
Labour rate	16,000		
Labour efficiency		12,800	
Variable overhead expense	4,000		
Variable overhead efficiency		6,400	
Fixed overhead expense	60,000		
Fixed overhead efficiency		25,600	
Fixed overhead capacity	nil		
	112,000	68,800	
			43,200
Actual profit			148,800

(b) (i) **Motivation and budget setting**

Absorption costing profit has increased from $95,200 (28 × 3,400) to $148,800.

Mr Beach has adopted an **aspirations budget** in order to motivate employees to maximise output. This is a budget that is challenging or difficult but credible. A budget that would present no challenge would not motivate employees to exceed their expectations. However, in choosing an aspirations budget, there is an **implied expectation of adverse planning variances**.

(ii) **Explanations of variances**

The sales volume and sales price variances may be **inter-related** as an increase in price may reduce demand. A favourable sales price variance is consistent with an adverse sales volume variance.

An adverse materials price variances may be consistent with a favourable materials usage variance. This is because with better materials there may be less waste.

Similarly, cheaper labour that has resulted in a favourable labour rate variance may be the reason for lower labour efficiency.

The fixed overhead expenditure variance should be further investigated. The variable overhead efficiency variance is a function of the labour efficiency variable. However, its usefulness is questionable as in practice variable overheads do not normally vary proportionately to labour hours.

57 Carat

Text references. Variance analysis is covered in Chapter 12.

Top tips. This type of question requires practice of the different types of variance so be prepared before you go to the exam and make sure you know how to do these.

Easy marks. In part (a) calculating each variance. In part (d) which is book knowledge.

Examiner's comments. Flaws in answering part (a) included careless reading, and incorrect calculation of variances which weren't asked for. In part (c), answers that offered general explanations of variances which did not relate to calculated variances were given little credit.

Marks

(a) Sales volume contribution variance   1
     Sales price variance   1
     Material price variances   1
     Material mix variances   2
     Material yield variances   2
     Labour rate and efficiency variances   1
     Idle time variances   1
                                              Maximum   7

(b) Budgeted gross profit   1
     Budgeted contribution   1
     Fixed production overhead expenditure variance   1
     Actual gross profit   1
                                                                                   4

(c) Material price, mix and yield variances   3
     Labour rate, efficiency and idle time variances   2
                                                                                   5

(d) Basic standard   1
     Ideal standard   1
     Effect on motivation   2
                                                                                   4
                                                                                  20

(a) Standard sales price   12.00

     Material A $1.70 × 2.5   4.25
     Material B $1.20 × 1.5   1.80
     Labour $6.00 × 0.45   2.70
     Standard contribution   3.25

     Sales volume contribution variance

     Budgeted sales volume   50,000 units
     Actual sales volume   48,000 units
     Sales volume variance in units   2,000 units (A)
     × standard contribution per unit ($3.25)   × $3.25
     Sales volume variance $6,500 (A)

     Sales price variance

                                                                                  $
     Sales revenue for 48,000 units should have been (× $12)   576,000
          but was   580,800
     Selling price variance   4,800 (F)

     Direct material price variances

                                                                                  $
     121,951 kgs of A should have cost (× $1.70)   207,317
          but did cost   200,000
     Material A price variance   7,317 (F)

                                                                                  $
     67,200 kgs of B should have cost (× $1.20)   80,640
          but did cost   84,000
     Material B price variance   3,360 (A)

Material mix variances

			kg
Total quantity used (121,951 + 67,200) kgs			189,151
Standard mix for actual use	2.5/4 A		118,219
	1.5/4 B		70,932

Material	Actual quantity standard mix	Actual quantity actual mix	Variance	Standard cost per kg	Variance
	kgs	kgs	kgs	$	$
A	118,219	121,951	3,732 (A)	1.70	6,344 (A)
B	70,932	67,200	3,732 (F)	1.20	4,478 (F)
	189,151	189,151	–		1,866 (A)

Material yield variances

In total

		$
Each unit of product ZP requires	2.5 kg of A, costing	4.25
	1.5 kg of B, costing	1.80
	4.0 kg	6.05

189,151 kg should have yielded (÷ 4 kg)	47,288 units
But did yield	48,000 units
Yield variance in units	712 units (F)
× standard cost per unit of output	× $6.05
Yield variance	$4,308 (F)

For individual materials

Material	Standard quantity standard mix	Actual quantity standard mix	Variance	Standard cost per kg	Variance
	kgs	kgs	kgs	$	$
A	120,000	118,219	1,781 (F)	1.70	3,028 (F)
B	72,000	70,932	1,068 (F)	1.20	1,282 (F)
	192,000	189,151	2,849 (F)		4,310

Labour rate variance

	$
19,200 hours of work should have cost (× $6 per hr)	115,200
but did cost	117,120
Labour rate variance	1,920 (A)

Labour efficiency variance

48,000 units of ZP should have taken (× 0.45 hrs)	21,600 hrs
but did take	18,900 hrs
Efficiency variance in hours	2,700 hrs (F)
× standard rate per hour	× $6
Efficiency variance	$16,200 (F)

Idle time variance

18,900 hours were worked but 19,200 hours were paid for.
Idle time variance = 300 hours (A) × $6 = $1,800 (A)

(b)

		F	A	$
Budgeted contribution (50,000 × $3.25)				162,500
Sales volume contribution variance			6,500	
Sales price variance		4,800		
		4,800	6,500	(1,700)
				160,800
Cost variances:				
Material A price		7,317		
Material B price			3,360	
Material A mix			6,344	
Material B mix		4,478		
Material A yield		3,028		
Material B yield		1,282		
Labour rate			1,920	
Idle time			1,800	
Labour efficiency		16,200		
		32,305	13,424	
				18,881
Actual contribution				179,681
Budgeted fixed production overhead			62,500	
Fixed production overhead expenditure variance				
($64,000 − $62,500)			1,500 (A)	
Actual fixed production overhead				(64,000)
Actual gross profit				115,681

(c) (i) The **favourable Material A price variance** shows that it cost less than standard. This could have been because of an out of date standard, price changes by the supplier or perhaps a discount.

The **adverse mix variance** shows that more was used as input than had been expected, maybe because it was cheaper.

The **favourable Material A yield variance** indicates that more output was produced than expected. This could be due to better operating processes or a superior workforce.

It should be noted however that any explanation of the mix and yield variances for Material A cannot really be discussed in isolation from those for Material B.

(ii) The **adverse labour rate variance** is because staff were paid more per hour than expected. This may have been because more skilled staff were employed, or there may have been a pay increase since the standard was developed.

The **favourable labour efficiency variance** shows that fewer hours were worked than was expected, maybe as employees benefited from a learning curve effect or additional training.

The **adverse idle time variance** may be due to process problems such as machine breakdowns.

(d) An **ideal standard** is one which can be attained under perfect operating conditions: no wastage, no inefficiencies, no idle time, no breakdowns.

A **basic standard** is a long-term standard which remains unchanged over the years and is used to show trends.

Ideal standards can be seen as **long-term targets** but are not very useful for day-to-day control purposes as they cannot be achieved. It is claimed that they provide employees with an **incentive** to be more efficient. However, they may have an **unfavourable effect** on employee motivation as variances will always be adverse.

Basic standards may have an **unfavourable effect** on motivation as employees discover over time that they are easily able to achieve the standards.

58 Chaff Co

Marking scheme

			Marks
(a)	Assessment of each person:		
	Buyer (poor quality, usage, sales issue)	2	
	Production director (motivation, efficiency)	2	
	Allow flexibility here in interpretation	2	
			6
(b)	*Budget profit calculation*		
	Labour	1	
	Sales	½	
	Rice seed	½	
	Variable overhead	½	
	Fixed cost	½	
	Sales price variance	1	
	Sales volume variance	1	
	Material price variance	1	
	Material usage variance	1	
	Labour rate variance	1	
	Labour efficiency variance	2	
	Idle time variance	2	
	Variable overhead expenditure variance	1	
	Variable overhead efficiency variance	1	
	Fixed overhead expenditure variance	1	
	Format	1	
	Maximum		14
			20

(a) **Purchasing manager**

The purchasing manager believes that he has **performed well** as he has reduced purchase costs by using a new supplier. The **material price variance** is favourable by $48,000 which could be due to good negotiating and buying skills, a reduction in quality or changing market conditions. The market for the purchase of seeds is stable, so the price reduction is not due to market conditions.

The **material usage variance** is significantly adverse at $52,000 indicating that **wastage** has increased. Poorer quality seed could be responsible for this. Alternatively, labour problems may have resulted in increased wastage. However, the **labour efficiency variance** is favourable so this looks less likely to be the cause.

The **sales price variance** is also significantly adverse at $85,000 and this indicates that the price of the product had to be reduced. Again, given that the market for the product is stable, the cause could be assumed to be quality issues caused by the purchase of poorer quality seed. This could also explain the fall in sales resulting in an adverse **sales volume variance** of $21,000.

Therefore, rather than performing well as he believes, it could be argued that the production manager is responsible for a loss amounting to $110,000 (85,000 + 52,000 + 21,000 − 48,000).

Production director

The production director feels unfairly criticised for increasing the labour rate. His actions resulted in an adverse **labour rate variance** of $15,000. This adverse variance can be justified if labour efficiency improved as a result. The **labour efficiency variance** was $18,000 favourable and the **labour idle time variance** was also favourable by $12,000. These variances indicate an improvement in the productivity of the workforce, even though they were working with poorer quality materials.

The total effect of the production director's actions in increasing the wage rate is an increase in profits of $15,000 (18,000 + 12,000 − 15,000). The improvement may however only be temporary, as workers become accustomed to the new wage level and their efficiency and motivation drops again.

(b)
Standard contribution per tonne

	$	$
Sales price		240
Less:		
Rice seed (1.4 tonnes × $60)	84	
Labour (2 hours × $18 × 10/9)	40	
Variable overhead (2 hours × $30)	60	
Marginal costs of production		184
Standard contribution		56

Variances

		$
Selling price variance		
8,000 × $(1,800,000/8,000 − 240)		120,000 (A)
Sales volume variance	*Tonnes*	
Actual sales in tonnes	8,000	
Budgeted sales in tonnes	8,400	
Variance in tonnes	400 (A)	
× standard contribution per unit	× $56	
		22,400 (A)
Material price variance		
12,000 tonnes should have cost (× $60)	720,000	
but did cost	660,000	
		60,000 (F)

Material usage variance

		$
8,000 tonnes should use (× 1.4)	11,200 tonnes	
but did use	12,000 tonnes	
Variance in tonnes	800 tonnes	
X standard cost per tonne	× $60	
		48,000 (A)

Labour rate variance

15,800 hours should cost (× $18)	284,400	
but did cost	303,360	
		18,960 (A)

Labour efficiency variance

8,000 tonnes should take (× 2 hours)	16,000 hours	
but did take	15,000 hours	
Variance in hours	1,000 (F)	
× standard rate per hour (× $18/0.9)	× $20	
		20,000 (F)

Idle time variance

Idle time should have been (10% × 15,800)	1,580 hours	
but was (15,800 − 15,000)	800 hours	
Variance in hours	780 (F)	
× standard rate per hour	× $20	
		15,600 (F)

Variable overhead expenditure variance

Budgeted variable production overhead (15,000 × $30)	450,000	
Actual expenditure	480,000	
		30,000 (A)

Variable overhead efficiency variance

8,000 tonnes should take (× 2 hours)	16,000 hours	
but did take	15,000 hours	
Variance in hours	1,000 (F)	
× standard rate per hour	× $30	
		30,000 (F)

Fixed cost expenditure variance

Budgeted fixed costs	210,000	
Actual fixed costs	200,000	
		10,000 (F)

Budgeted profit statement

	$	$
Sales (8,400 tonnes × $240)		2,016,000
Less:		
Rice seed (1.4 tonnes × $60 × 8,400 tonnes)	705,600	
Labour (2 hours × $20 × 8,400 tonnes)	336,000	
Variable overhead (2 hours × $30 × 8,400 tonnes)	504,000	
		1,545,600
Contribution		470,400
Less fixed costs		210,000
Budgeted profit		260,400

Operating statement

		$	$
Budgeted contribution			470,400

Variances	F	A	
Sales price		120,000	
Sales volume		22,400	
			(142,400)
Material price	60,000		
Material usage		48,000	
Labour rate		18,960	
Labour efficiency	20,000		
Idle time	15,600		
Variable overhead efficiency	30,000		
Variable overhead expenditure		30,000	
	125,600	96,960	
			28,640
Actual contribution			356,640
Budgeted fixed cost		210,000	
Less: Fixed cost expenditure variance		10,000	
Actual fixed cost			200,000
Actual profit			156,640

Check		
Sales		1,800,000
Less:		
Rice seed	660,000	
Labour	303,360	
Variable overhead	480,000	
Marginal costs of production		1,443,360
Contribution		356,640
Less: Fixed costs		200,000
Actual profit		156,640

59 AHW Co

Text reference. Flexible budgets are covered in Chapter 11 and budgetary control in Chapter 8.

Top tips. Part (a) is straightforward provided you approached it methodically and did not make an arithmetic error. The trick is to work out a budgeted cost per individual processing activity.

Part (b) emphasises that budgetary control may not work if the system is not used sensitively and efficiently.

(a)

	Original budget cost $'000	Flexed budget costs (W) $'000	Actual costs $'000	Variances $'000
Processing activity W	160	159	158	1 (F)
Processing activity X	130	135	139	4 (A)
Processing activity Y	80	78	73	5 (F)
Processing activity Z	200	206	206	–
	570	578	576	2 (F)

Workings

Budgeted number of processing activities

Costs are expected to be variable in relation to the number of processing activities. We therefore need to calculate the budgeted number of activities for each process.

W $(20 \times 4) + (30 \times 5) + (15 \times 2) + (40 \times 3) + (25 \times 1) = 405$
X $(20 \times 3) + (30 \times 2) + (15 \times 5) + (40 \times 1) + (25 \times 4) = 335$
Y $(20 \times 3) + (30 \times 3) + (15 \times 2) + (40 \times 4) + (25 \times 2) = 390$
Z $(20 \times 4) + (30 \times 6) + (15 \times 8) + (40 \times 2) + (25 \times 3) = 535$

Budgeted cost per processing activity

W $\dfrac{\$160{,}000}{405} = \$395.06$

X $\dfrac{\$130{,}000}{335} = \$388.06$

Y $\dfrac{\$80{,}000}{390} = \$205.13$

Z $\dfrac{\$200{,}000}{535} = \$373.83$

Actual number of processing activities

W $(18 \times 4) + (33 \times 5) + (16 \times 2) + (35 \times 3) + (28 \times 1) = 402$
X $(18 \times 3) + (33 \times 2) + (16 \times 5) + (35 \times 1) + (28 \times 4) = 347$
Y $(18 \times 3) + (33 \times 3) + (16 \times 2) + (35 \times 4) + (28 \times 2) = 381$
Z $(18 \times 4) + (33 \times 6) + (16 \times 8) + (35 \times 2) + (28 \times 3) = 552$

Budgeted cost for actual number of processing activities

W $\$395.06 \times 402 = \$158{,}814.12$
X $\$388.06 \times 347 = \$134{,}656.82$
Y $\$205.13 \times 381 = \$78{,}154.53$
Z $\$373.83 \times 552 = \$206{,}354.16$

(b)   (i)   **How budgetary control might act as an incentive in achieving maximum performance**

       (1)   **Target to direct management actions**
            If management do not know what is expected of them, their actions may tend to lack direction with **no real incentive to achieve maximum performance**.

       (2)   **Rewards for good performance and penalties for poor performance**
            These need not necessarily be financial; psychological awareness in the form of **self esteem** and **management recognition** can be just as effective.

       (3)   **Information on actual performance**
            If managers know what results they are achieving, they are more likely to feel that there is an **incentive to achieve maximum performance**.

  (ii)   **How budgetary control might act as a disincentive in achieving maximum performance**

       (1)   **Strict targets**
            If targets are set at unrealistically high levels, or at performance levels which are too low to encourage maximum achievement.

       (2)   **Management imposition**
            If **budgets** are **imposed** by an authoritarian senior management.

       (3)   **Lack of communication**
            If **budgets** are not **communicated** clearly to those who are responsible for achieving them.

Control reports
If **control reports** are **received too late** for effective management action to be taken, or if **control reports do not contain appropriate information** to assist management to monitor their actions.

Actions that might be taken to overcome the disincentive effects

(1)   **Set targets which are neither too high nor too low**
Past performance can be a **good indicator** of what is achievable, but should never be automatically accepted as a reasonable target.

(2)   **Operate a participative system of budget preparation**
Management are much more likely to want to work to achieve a budget when they have been consulted in its preparation.

(3)   **Communicate budgets in clear terms, in plenty of time**
Managers should be able to take appropriate action to achieve the targets contained therein.

(4)   **Provide for rapid feedback of actual results**
Management action can be taken quickly to correct any variances.

(5)   **Prepare control reports with sufficient information**
This will aid management control, without cluttering the reports with so much data they are rejected and ignored.

60 Linsil

Text references. Variance analysis is covered in Chapter 12 and planning and operational variances in Chapter 13.

Top tips. The variance calculations in this question are advanced and you should make sure that you have practised them thoroughly. Make sure that you can also explain and discuss variances as you can expect an exam question to involve written elements as well as calculations.

(a)

Revised standard costs

Direct material price	2.30×1.03	2.369	$/kg
Direct material usage	$3.00 \times 95\%$	2.85	kg/unit
Direct labour rate	12.00×1.04	12.48	$/hr
Direct labour hours	$1.25 \times 100/90$	1.39	hrs/unit

(b)

Material	$
Actual material costs (for 122,000 units)	
$(122{,}000 \times 2.80 \text{ kg} \times \$2.46)$	840,336
Revised standard cost (for 122,000 units)	
$(122{,}000 \times 2.85 \text{ kg} \times \$2.369)$	823,701
Total operational variance	16,635 (A)
Revised standard cost	823,701
Original standard	
$(122{,}000 \times 3.00 \text{ kg} \times £2.30)$	841,800
Total planning variance	18,099 (F)

Labour	$
Actual labour costs	
$(122{,}000 \times 1.30 \text{ hrs} \times \$12.60)$	1,998,360
Revised standard cost	
$(122{,}000 \times 1.39 \text{ hrs} \times \$12.48)$	2,116,358
Total operational variance	117,998 (F)
Revised standard cost	2,116,358
Original standard cost	
$(122{,}000 \times 1.25 \text{ hrs} \times \$12.00)$	1,830,000
Total planning variance	286,358 (A)

(c)   The planning and operational variance approach attempts to divide a total variance into a group of variances which have arisen because of inaccurate planning or faulty standards (**planning variances**) and a group of variances which have been caused by adverse or favourable operational performance (**operational variances**).

A **planning variance** compares an original standard with a revised standard that should or would have been used if planners had known in advance what was going to happen. Planning variances are **uncontrollable** (see below) by managers.

An **operational variance** compares an actual result with the revised standard. Operational variances are **controllable** by managers.

Planning and operational variances are based on the principle that variances ought to be reported by taking as the main starting point a standard which can be seen, in hindsight, to be the **optimum** that should have been achievable. For example, in the example given in the question, the standard direct labour rate should have been $12.48 rather than $12.00.

Exponents of this approach argue that the monetary value of variances ought to be a **realistic reflection** of what the causes of the variances have cost the organisation. In other words they should show the cash (and profit) gained or lost as a consequence of operating results being different to what should have been achieved. Variances can be valued in this way by comparing actual results with a realistic standard or budget.

Planning variances arise because the original standard and revised (more realistic) standards are different, and these have nothing to do with operational performance. In most cases, it is unlikely that anything could be done about planning variances: they are not controllable by operational managers but by senior management.

Problems

The reasons behind **why planning variances arise** may need to be investigated. It needs to be understood how certain pieces of information get missed or otherwise omitted from the standard setting process.

It can also be too easy to justify **all** the variances are being due to bad planning, so no operational variances ill be highlighted.

It is difficult to **decide in hindsight** what the realistic standard should have been and establishing the standards is time consuming.

61 Simply Soup

Text references. Variance analysis is covered in Chapter 12 and behavioural aspects of standard costing in Chapter 13.

Top tips. In your explanations of the meanings of variances in part (a) do not forget to state the simple, more obvious points and make sure you apply your explanations to Simply Soup. This question demonstrates that you need to **understand** what variances mean and not just concentrate on being able to do the calculations.

Easy marks. Part (a)(i) is worth 6 marks for some quite simple explanations. The calculations in part (b) get progressively more difficult but there are some easy marks available if you have practised variance calculations.

Marks

(a) (i) For each variance
Explanation of meaning of variance   1
Brief discussion of controllability   1

Max 6

(ii) Comment on cost variances
Price:
Outside production manager's control   1
Rising prices pressure   1
Mix: Cheaper mix and comments   1
Yield: High yield results and comment   1
Quality: Comment on quality implications   1

5

(b) Variance calculations
Price: 1 mark for each ingredient   3
Mix: 3
Yield   3
Method marks should be awarded as appropriate   9

20

(a) (i) **Material price variance**

This is the difference between what the materials did cost and what they were expected to cost. The expected cost is the **standard** that was set for the period. If the variance is **adverse**, a higher price than expected was paid and if it is **favourable,** a lower price than expected was paid. Either variance could occur, for example, if a new supplier was used.

The choice of supplier is controllable and therefore some of the price variance may be controllable. However, vegetables are one of the materials used and they are seasonal and affected by weather conditions. Their prices are therefore subject to changes beyond the control of Simply Soup.

It would not usually be expected that the production manager would be responsible for material purchases. Price control would usually be carried out by a purchasing manager.

Material mix variance

A material mix variance occurs when the material are not mixed or blended in **standard proportions** and it is a measure of whether the actual mix is cheaper or more expensive than the standard mix. For example, more butter and less stock could be used than the standard mix and this will be more expensive so there will be an adverse variance. However, the soup will probably taste better and be of a higher quality.

The mix is controlled by the production manager so he is responsible for any variances.

Material yield variance

A yield variance arises because there is a difference between what the input should have been for the output achieved and the actual input. It shows the **productivity** of the manufacturing process. If more soup (the output) is produced than expected from the ingredients (the input), there is a favourable variance. This could happen due to greater operational efficiency or a change in the mix of ingredients.

An adverse yield variance could result from increased spillage or wastage or from poor quality ingredients.

The production manager is responsible for **operational efficiency**, quality of ingredients and the control of spillage. The yield variance is therefore controllable by the production manager.

(ii) **Cost variances**

The total material variance is **significantly favourable** and has risen from $4,226 to $10,352 in three months. This is 7.1% of the standard monthly material cost of $145,000.

The material price variance has **deteriorated** indicating that prices of ingredients have been rising. This is probably out of the control of the production manager but may have led to pressure to change the mix of ingredients to absorb the price increase. For example, using less butter and more stock. This is demonstrated by the **favourable mix variances** but there may be implications in the form of lower quality soup.

The yield variance has shown the most dramatic improvement so the new mix is more **productive**. Again, this could indicate good performance by the production manager, provided quality is not suffering.

Quality

The Sales Director is concerned that sales are significantly down and this could be as a result of poorer quality soup. It is a competitive market and consumers will soon switch to an alternative producer if quality and taste deteriorates.

In conclusion, the cost variances indicate that **more** is being produced at a lower cost, but this could be at the **expense of quality** resulting in a decline in sales. Cost control and efficiency are important but not at the expense of customer satisfaction and quality.

(b) **Material price variances**

	$
82,000 litres of liquidised vegetables should have cost ($\times$ $0.80)	65,600
but did cost	69,700
Material price variance	4,100 (A)

	$
4,900 litres of melted butter should have cost ($\times$ $4)	19,600
but did cost	21,070
Material price variance	1,470 (A)

	$
122,000 litres of stock should have cost ($\times$ $0.50)	61,000
but did cost	58,560
Material price variance	2,440 (F)

Material mix variances

Total quantity used = 82,000 + 4,900 + 122,000 = 208,900 litres
Standard total input per litre of soup = 0.9 + 0.05 + 1.1 = 2.05 litres
Standard mix of actual use:

Vegetables	0.9/2.05 $\times$ 208,900 = 91,712.2 litres
Melted butter	0.05/2.05 $\times$ 208,900 = 5,095.12 litres
Stock	1.1/2.05 $\times$ 208,900 = 112,092.68 litres

	Actual quantity Actual mix	Actual quantity Standard mix	Variance	Standard cost per litre	Variance
	Litres	Litres	Litres	$	$
Vegetables	82,000	91,712.20	9,712.20	0.80	7,770 (F)
Melted butter	4,900	5,095.12	195.12	4.00	780 (F)
Stock	122,000	112,092.68	9,907.32	0.50	4,954 (A)
Total mix variance					3,596 (F)

Material yield variance

The standard inputs of 2.05 litres are expected to produce 1 litre of soup.

	Litres
The actual quantity of inputs are expected to yield (208,900 /2.05)	101,902.44
Actual output	112,000.00
Yield variance in litres	10,097.56 (F)
× standard cost per litre of output ($1.47)	$14,843 (F)

Alternative method

	Standard quantity Standard mix Litres	Actual quantity Standard mix Litres	Variance Litres	Standard cost per litre $	Variance $
Vegetables	100,800	91,712	9,088	0.80	7,270 (F)
Melted butter	5,600	5,095	505	4.00	2,020 (F)
Stock	123,200	112,093	11,107	0.50	5,553 (F)
					14,843 (F)

62 Spike Limited

Text reference. Revised budgets and planning and operational sales variances are covered in Chapter 13.

Top tips. Part (a) does not require detailed technical knowledge but should be based on your knowledge of how budgets and control systems can operate effectively. Argue your points clearly and try not to waffle!

The variance calculations in part (b) are very straightforward but you may need to think a little more about the variances in part (c). The key is to consider what is controllable and what is not. This will also help you in part (d).

Easy marks. The variance calculations should provide some easy marks.

Examiner's comments. Part (a) was often very poorly done. Candidates seemed to have avoided any understanding of the practical problems involved in planning and operational variances.

Part (a) needed arguments in favour and against with points separated and a consistent conclusion.

In part (c) candidates often provided a discussion rather than the required analysis. In part (d) weaker candidates seemed totally unaware of the meanings and implications of the data.

Candidates must understand what the numbers tell them about the business performance.

Marking scheme

			Marks
(a)	Materials discussion	3	
	Conclusion	1	
	Labour discussion	3	
	Conclusion	1	
			8
(b)	Sales price variance	2	
	Sales volume variance	2	
			4
(c)	Market size variance	2	
	Market share variance	2	
			4
(d)	Comment on sales price	2	
	Comment on sales volume	2	
			4
			20

(a)   **Materials**

Arguments for a revision

The problem arose due to a liquidation of a supplier which is **outside the control** of the buyer who is unlikely to have been aware it was going to happen.

The buyer will expect this revision to be allowed as it is outside his control and is likely to be demoralised and demotivated if it is refused.

Arguments against a revision

The buyer accepted the deal with the new supplier **without attempting to negotiate**. This may have been a panicked reaction to the immediate problem which has increased Spike Limited's costs.

The buyer is responsible for sourcing the cheapest materials and this could have been achieved with an alternative local supplier. A more **considered, careful approach** would have achieved a better deal.

A buyer should also have a good knowledge of his supplier's circumstances and it could be argued that some advance knowledge of liquidity problems could have been expected.

Conclusion

The budget revision should not be allowed. Although the liquidation was outside the control of the buyer, he could have achieved a better price.

Labour

Arguments for a revision

The Board made the decision to change the recruitment policy and this decision was outside the control of the departmental manager. The departmental manager is therefore not responsible for the extra cost.

Arguments against a revision

The **organisation as a whole** is in control of this decision so the cost is controllable.

The departmental manager **requested** a change in recruitment so is responsible for the extra cost involved.

The **productivity increases** have benefited the department involved so it should also be charged with the costs involved.

Conclusion

This was an **operational decision** that the departmental manager requested and agreed to. It has had the desired effects so no budget revision should be allowed.

(b)   **Total sales price variance**

	$
Sales revenue for 176,000 units should have been (× $17.00)	2,992,000
but was	2,886,400
Variance	105,600 (A)

Total sales volume variance

Budgeted sales volume	180,000 units
Actual sales volume	176,000 units
Variance in units	4,000 units (A)
× standard contribution per unit	× $7.00
Variance	$28,000 (A)

(c)   **Market size variance**

Revised sales volume (1.6/1.8 × 180,000)	160,000 units
Budgeted sales volume	180,000 units
Variance in units	20,000 units (A)
× standard contribution per unit	× $7.00
Variance	$140,000 (A)

Market share variance

Revised sales volume	160,000 units
Actual sales volume	176,000 units
Variance in units	16,000 units (F)
× standard contribution per unit	× $7.00
Variance	$112,000 (F)

(d) **Sales performance of the business**

Sales price

Spike Limited has **reduced the price** of the diaries from $17.00 to $16.40 which has resulted in an adverse price variance of $105,600. The price reduction was probably in response to **increased competitive pressures** from electronic substitutes. The reduction in price was aiming to sustain rather than increase sales volumes, given that the market is declining.

Sales volume

The sales volume variance is also adverse so it could be assumed that the price reduction strategy did not work. However, the break down of this variance into **planning and operational** variances provides a better insight.

The **fall in market size** is uncontrollable by the management of Spike Limited and therefore results in an adverse **planning variance**.

The **increase in market share** is controllable and results in a favourable **operational variance**. This has been achieved by reducing prices but the improved capabilities and performance of the support staff may also have contributed.

This means that Spike Limited has done well to hold on to the level of sales that have been achieved, but management should still be concerned that the market for Spike's products is shrinking.

63 Crumbly Cakes

Text references. Variance analysis is covered in Chapters 12 and 13.

Top tips. You may find part (a) quite tricky. You need to plan a structured answer using the headings suggested by the question. Make some sensible, common sense suggestions and if you run out of ideas, move on to part (b) where easier marks are available. Read the information very carefully in part (b) and layout your workings clearly.

Easy marks. There are some easy variance calculations in part (b) as well as some trickier mix and yield variances.

Examiner's comments. Many candidates completely missed the point in part (a). If a business fundamentally changes its business process without altering the standard costs of the process, it renders the variances that are produced meaningless. Some candidates tried to discuss each variance in turn rather than carry out a performance assessment of each manager. This is not as effective a method. Motivation is a complex topic and credit was given for any sensible comments.

Part (b) was well done with many candidates scoring good marks.

			Marks
(a)	Production manager assessment	2	
	Sales manager assessment	2	
	Bonus scheme comment	3	
			7
(b)	Price variance	3	
	Mix variance	3	
	Yield variance	3	
	Sales price variance	2	
	Sales volume variance	2	
			13
			20

(a) **Production manager**

The production manager instigated the new organic cake production approach and this has **fundamentally changed** the nature of the business. Before the new system started, there were **favourable material variances** for price and yield and the production manager would have received a bonus as a result.

Organic ingredients are **more expensive** and this results in **adverse** material price and mix variances in March. The **material yield** variance is favourable but not by enough to compensate for the adverse variances. This means that the production manager would not receive a bonus under the current scheme.

Sales of the cakes have improved significantly so customers presumably appreciate the new flavour and mix of ingredients. The production manager does not receive any credit for the favourable sales variances and that does not seem fair.

Sales manager

In contrast, the **sales variances** that the sales manager is responsible for have moved from adverse in February to favourable in March. The new organic approach has therefore been a **success** with customers. The sales manager will have had to sell the new organic cakes to customers and is therefore **partly responsible** for the improvement, but the original impetus came from the production manager.

Bonus scheme

The bonus scheme does not seem to be fair as it will **not reward** the two managers fairly for their efforts. They are both responsible for the improved sales but it is very difficult to **fairly allocate responsibility** in this situation. Some form of **sharing** of responsibility and reward is required.

The **standards** that the variances are based on need to be changed to reflect the new approach that the business is taking. For example, the standard price of the materials needs to be increased.

(b) **Variance calculations**

Material price variances

	$
5,700 kg of flour should have cost ($\times$ $0.12)	684
but did cost	741
Material price variance	57 (A)

	$
6,600 kg of eggs should have cost ($\times$ $0.70)	4,620
but did cost	5,610
Material price variance	990 (A)

					$
6,600 kg of butter should have cost (× $1.70)					11,220
but did cost					11,880
Material price variance					660 (A)

					$
4,578 kg of sugar should have cost (× $0.50)					2,289
but did cost					2,747
Material price variance					458 (A)

					$
Total material price variance					2,165 (A)

Material mix variances

Total quantity used = 5,700 + 6,600 + 6,600 + 4,578 = 23,478 kg

Standard mix of actual use of each ingredient is in equal proportions = 23,478/4 = 5,869.5 kg

	Actual quantity Actual mix Kg	Actual quantity Standard mix Kg	Variance Kg	Standard cost per kg $	Variance $
Flour	5,700	5869.5	169.5	0.12	20.34 (F)
Eggs	6,600	5869.5	730.5	0.70	511.35 (A)
Butter	6,600	5869.5	730.5	1.70	1,241.85 (A)
Sugar	4,578	5869.5	1,291.5	0.50	645.75 (F)
	23,478	23,478			1,087.11 (A)

Material yield variance

Standard cost of a cake

		$
Flour	0.1 kg × $0.12	0.012
Eggs	0.1 kg × $0.70	0.070
Butter	0.1 kg × $1.70	0.170
Sugar	0.1 kg × $0.50	0.050
		0.302

	Cakes
The actual quantity of inputs are expected to yield (23,478/0.4)	58,695
Actual output	60,000
Yield variance in cakes	1,305 (F)
× standard cost per cake ($0.302)	$394.11 (F)

Alternative method

	Standard quantity Standard mix Kg	Actual quantity Standard mix Kg	Variance Kg	Standard cost per kg $	Variance $
Flour	6,000	5869.5	130.5	0.12	15.66
Eggs	6,000	5869.5	130.5	0.70	91.35
Butter	6,000	5869.5	130.5	1.70	221.85
Sugar	6,000	5869.5	130.5	0.50	65.25
	24,000	23,478			394.11 (A)

Sales price variance

60,000 × $(0.99 − 0.85) = $8,400 (F)

Sales contribution volume variance

Actual sales of cakes	60,000
Budgeted sales of cakes	50,000
Variance in cakes	10,000
× standard contribution per cake	× $0.35
	$3,500 (F)

64 Secure Net

Text reference. Planning and operational variances are covered in Chapter 13.

Top tips. Part (a) should not cause any problems. In part (b) the examiner has stated that any methods applied consistently would score full marks. This answer shows the BPP approach and the approach used in the article previously written by the examiner. If you get stuck on the details of which numbers to use where, make an attempt at something sensible and move on.

Part (c) is a straightforward discussion of the production manager's performance. Even if you struggled with the calculations in part (b), you should be able to pick up on the clues given in the scenario for factors that would have been controllable and uncontrollable.

Easy marks. Part (a) should be an easy 4 marks and there are easy marks available in part (c) just from describing factors in the scenario.

Examiner's comments. Part (a) was where the easy marks were but many candidates did not manage to score them. It shows a serious lack of work if a candidate walks into a F5 exam unable to calculate basic variances. These are a fundamental tool for performance management, which is, after all, what the paper is about!

Unsurprisingly, then, answers for part (b) could have been better. As we know from articles that have been written on operational and planning variances in the past, there are often different approaches to calculating some of them. Candidates should remain assured that, whichever approach they adopted, full credit would be given if they were consistent.

Part (c) produced some mixed answers. Candidates need to be reminded to state the obvious points: operational variances are deemed to be within the control of the production manager, planning variances are not; the net effect of usage and price variances must be considered when assessing the production manager's performance.

Marking scheme

			Marks
(a)	Price variance	2	
	Usage variance	2	
			4
(b)	Planning price variance	2	
	Planning usage variance	2	
	Operational price variance	2	
	Operational usage variance	2	
			8
(c)	Explanation of external problems beyond control of manager	4	
	Assessment of factors within the control of the manager	4	
	Conclusion	1	
	Maximum		8
			20

(a)   **Total material price variance**

Amount of material purchased = 100,000 cards × 0.035kg = 3,500 kg

		$
3,500 kg should have cost (× $4.00)	14,000	
but did cost ($5.25 × 3,500)	18,375	
		4,375 (A)

Total material usage variance

100,000 cards should use (× 0.04 kg)	4,000 kg	
but did use	3,500 kg	
Variance in kgs	500 kg (F)	
× standard cost per kg	× $4.00	
		2,000 (F)

(b)   **Total materials planning variance**

		$
Original flexed budget cost	(100,000 × $4 × 0.04kgs)	16,000
Revised flexed budget cost	(100,000 × $4.80 × 0.042kgs)	20,160
		4,160 (A)

Planning price variance

Actual units × revised standard usage × (original standard price − revised standard price)

= 100,000 units × 0.042 kgs × ($4.00 − $4.80) = $3,360 (A)

Planning usage variance

Actual units × original standard price × (original standard usage − revised standard usage)

= 100,000 units × $4.00 × (0.04 kgs − 0.042 kgs) = $800 (A)

Planning price variance + planning usage variance = total planning variance

$3,360 + $800 = $4,160 (A)

Total materials operational variance

	$
Actual cost (for 100,000 units)	18,375
Revised standard cost (for 100,000 units) (0.042 kgs × $4.80)	20,160
Total operational variance	1,785 (F)

Operational price variance

	$
Actual price of actual materials (3,500 kg)	18,375
Revised standard price of actual materials ($4.80 × 3,500 kg)	16,800
Operational price variance	1,575 (A)

Operational usage variance

Actual quantity should have been	4,200 kgs
but was	3,500 kgs
Operational usage variance in kgs	700 kgs (A)
× revised standard cost per kg	× $4.80
Operational usage variance in $	$3,360 (F)

(c)   **Worldwide standard size**

The size of the security card has to fit the reader of that card and if the **industry specification changes** there is nothing that the production manager can do about it. This is **beyond his control** and therefore a planning error and should not be used to assess his performance.

Oil prices

World-wide oil prices have increased which have **increased plastic prices** and again the production manager **cannot control** that. This is another planning error and should be ignored in an assessment of his performance.

New supplier

The decision to use a new supplier cost an extra $1,575 which is the **operational price variance** and could be regarded as **poor performance** by the production manager. However, the manager seems to have agreed to the higher price on the promise of **better quality** and **reliabilit**y.

The **operational usage variance** is $3,360 favourable and this could be as a result of improved quality.

Increase in production and sales

Production levels increased significantly from 60,000 to 100,000 which could potentially have caused problems for the production manager. However, the ability to increase production suggests that the new suppliers' reliability was good.

The total materials operational variance shows a saving of $1,785 which reflects well on the performance of the production manager. The ability to react and be flexible can often form a part of a performance assessment.

In **conclusion** the manager could be said to have performed well.

65 Sticky Wicket

Text references. Variance analysis is covered in Chapter 12.

Top tips. Ensure that you comment on each April 20X0 variance given to you in the question in your answer to part (a).

Easy marks. There are 13 marks available for calculating variances in part (b). Ensure that you are familiar with each type of variance.

Examiner's comments. It was good to see an improvement in the variance analysis discussion that was performed in part (a) of the question this time round, compared to December 2009's variance analysis question. Fewer candidates made meaningless comments such as "the material price variance is favourable, which is good." Good comments tended to be along the lines of "whilst there has been a favourable material price variance, this is because cheaper, lower quality materials were used, which, in turn, has led to an adverse material usage variance" (although admittedly, few answers were quite as succinctly constructed as this, but the understanding was there!)

Part of the skill in part (b) was in identifying the variances that needed to be calculated. It was good to see that most candidates were able to do this, although a few missed the labour idle time variance. The calculations were performed with a reasonable degree of accuracy as well, showing that candidates were far better prepared than in previous sitting.

		Marks
(a)	Assessment of wood decision	2½
	Assessment of labour decision	2½
	Sales consequences	2
		7

13
20

(a) The performance of the production director can be analysed by looking at each decision in turn.

Lower grade of labour employed

SW usually employs a skilled workforce due to **the traditional manual techniques involved** in manufacturing the cricket bats. Using a lower grade of staff has saved the company $43,600 in wages. However, the idle time and efficiency variances total $54,200 meaning that the **new workforce** actually **cost** the company more money over the first month.

The adverse efficiency variance shows that it **took the new workforce longer** to make the bats than expected, possibly due to their lower skill level. As this is the first working month, it is reasonable to assume that the variance will improve at the end of May 20X0 as staff gain experience and take less time to manufacture each bat (the **learning curve** principle).

New wood supplier

Purchasing wood from the new supplier saved the company $5,100 on the standard cost. However the wood from the new supplier may be of **lower quality**. The adverse material usage variance of $7,500 shows that **waste levels are worse** than standard.

The total material variance ($2,400 adverse) would suggest that the decision to switch suppliers was a bad one. As the skill level of the new workforce increases there is a chance that waste levels may be reduced.

Sales for April 20X0 were down 10% on budget and returns were up 20% on the previous month. This could be due to the poor quality wood that has been purchased from the new supplier, reducing the overall quality of the finished product. This is likely to have a negative impact on the SW brand.

(b) **Variances for May 20X0**

	$
Material price variance	
40,000kg of wood *should* cost (× $5)	200,000
40,000kg of wood *did* cost	196,000
	4,000 (F)

	Kg
Material usage variance	
19,200 cricket bats *should* use (× 2kg)	38,400
19,200 cricket bats *did* use	40,000
Difference	1,600
Valued at $5/kg std cost (1,600 × $5)	$8,000 (A)

	$
Labour rate variance	
62,000 hours *should* cost (× $12)	744,000
62,000 hours *did* cost	694,000
	50,000 (F)

	Hrs
Labour efficiency variance	
19,200 cricket bats *should* take (× 3 hrs)	57,600
19,200 cricket bats *did* take	61,500
Efficiency variance in hours	(3,900)(A)
Valued at $12/hr std cost ((3,900) × $12)	46,800 (A)

Labour idle time variance	Hrs
Hours *paid*	62,000
Hours *worked*	61,500
Difference	(500)
Valued at $12/hr std cost ((500) × $12)	$6,000 (A)

Sales price variance	$
Budgeted selling price per bat	68
Actual selling price per bat	65
Difference	3
Difference x Actual sales ($3 × 18,000 units)	54,000 (A)

Sales volume contribution variance	Units
Budgeted unit sales	19,000
Actual unit sales	18,000
Sales volume variance in units	(1,000)
Difference x Std contribution ((1,000) × $22)	$22,000 (A)

66 Carad Co

Text reference. Sales, labour and planning and operational variances are covered in Chapter 12.

Top tips. In part (a) the examiner has stated that any methods applied consistently would score full marks. This answer shows the BPP approach. If you get stuck on the details of which numbers to use where, make an attempt at something sensible and move on.

Part (b) is a straightforward discussion of planning and operational variances. Even if you struggled with the calculations in part (a), you should be able to explain a few reasons why Carad would be interested in planning and operational variances.

Easy marks. Part (a)(ii) should be an easy 2 marks and there are easy marks available in part (b) just for explaining planning and operational variances and relating your answer to the scenario.

Examiner's comments. There were plenty of easy marks in this question, but if anyone didn't understand variances properly, they would have struggled with the labour variances, which required a little bit of thought. The sales and materials variance calculations were thankfully well performed by candidates, but the attempts at the labour variances were poor.

The question clearly stated that the labour variance related solely to the temporary workers. This meant that it was necessary to work out exactly how many hours the temporary workers had worked for. The calculation was not particularly difficult, but it did require an understanding of the scenario. Since permanent workers only had the capacity to work 2,200 hours and a total of 2,475 hours was needed for production, the initial calculation required was that there was a shortfall of 275 hours. However, the question stated that temporary workers took twice as long as permanent workers and therefore the temporary workers would be needed for 550 hours. Approximately one fifth of candidates worked this out and went on to calculate the variances correctly.

The most common error in part (b) was that candidates didn't read the requirement properly. They expected it to be asking them how the manager had performed and this was what they wrote about. Every exam sitting, this proves a problem – candidates pre-empting the question and not reading it properly. It should not be assumed that every single variance question will give you some variances, maybe ask you to calculate some more, and then ask for a discussion of management's performance. Exam papers cannot be allowed to become that predictable as examinees would then start to only partly prepare for them, on the basis that they know what will be examined, more or less. Candidates that did read the question, however, tended to make a reasonable attempt at this part.

			Marks
(a)	(i)	Sales price variance	3
		Sales volume variance	3
			6
	(ii)	Purchasing planning variance	1
		Purchasing efficiency variance	1
			2
	(iii)	Actual hours worked	3
		Labour rate variance	2
		Labour efficiency variance	2
			7
(b)		1 mark per valid reason	5
			20

(a) **(i)** **Sales price variance**

	$
Sales revenue for 750 Plasma TVs ($350) and 650 LCD TVs ($300) should have been	457,500
but was (Plasma TVs actual selling price $330, LCD TVs actual selling price $290)	436,000
	21,500 (A)

Sales volume contribution variance

	Actual sales volume (units)	Budgeted sales volume (units)	Difference (units)	× Standard margin	Sales volume variance
				$	$
Plasma TVs	750	590	160	190	30,400 (F)
LCD TVs	650	590	60	180	10,800 (F)
	1,400	1,180			41,200 (F)

(ii) **Material price planning variance**

	$
Standard cost of component X ($60.00 × 1,400 components)	84,000
Market price of component X ($85.00 × 1,400 components)	119,000
	35,000 (A)

Material price operational variance

	$
Market price at time of purchase ($85.00 × 1,400 components)	119,000
Actual price paid ($80.00 × 1,400 components)	112,000
	7,000 (F)

(iii) **Labour rate variance**

	$
550 hours (w1) should have cost (× $14)	7,700
but did cost (× $18)	9,900
	2,200 (A)

Working

Actual hours worked by temporary workers:

Total hours required if staff are fully efficient = (750 × 2) + (650 × 1.5) = 2,475

Total capacity of permanent workforce is 2,200 hours, therefore excess = 2,475 − 2,000 = 275

Temporary workers take twice as long, therefore hours worked = 275 × 2 = 550 hours

The labour rate variance relates solely to temporary workers, therefore ignore permanent staff in the calculation.

Labour efficiency variance

	Hours
Based on temporary workers, actual production should have taken	275
but did take (275 × 2)	550
	275 (A)
Difference valued at standard rate per hour (275 × $14)	$3,850 (A)

(b)   **Material price variance**

The adverse material price variance could arise due to a number of **controllable** and **uncontrollable factors**. For this reason, it is important to analyse the variance in further detail to provide a true and fair assessment of the efficiency of the purchasing department.

Splitting the total variance into planning and operational components will enable Carad to distinguish between variances that have arisen due **to inaccurate planning and faulty standards** (planning variances) and those which have been caused by **adverse or favourable operational performance** (operational variances).

Material price planning variance

Planning variances arise because the **original standard and revised standards are different**. It is unlikely that the purchasing department could do anything to alter the planning variance as it is not controlled by operational functions, but by senior management. The material price planning variance shows how skilled management are in estimating future prices.

Material price operational variance

Operational variances **compare actual results with a realistic standard or budget**. The material price operational variance measures the purchasing department's efficiency given the market price at the time that materials were purchased.

The operational variance ignores factors that the purchasing department cannot control and is likely to gain greater acceptance as a performance measure as staff know that **they will not be held responsible for poor planning and faulty standard setting**.

67 Noble

Text references. Flexed budgets are covered in Chapter 9. Sales mix and quantity variances are covered in Chapter 12. Planning and operational variances are covered in Chapter 13.

Top tips. When you prepare a flexed budget, remember its format should replicate the original budget to which it relates. For example, if the original budget totals up variable costs, so should the flexed budget. This makes it easier to compare like with like.

Easy marks. There are 12 marks available for preparing a flexed budget in part (a). The steps involved in preparing a flexed budget should be familiar to you from your earlier studies.

Examiner's comments. Many candidates answered part (a) well and easily scored 9 out of the 12 marks available, tripping up only on staff wages and energy costs calculations.

Many candidates confused the sales mix variance with the materials mix variance and talked about the latter in part (b). Also many candidates could not describe the quantity variance or identify why it had arisen. There is clearly a lack of understanding about variances, with candidates perhaps learning formulae in order to churn out calculations but not really understanding what variances mean to a business. This area needs more work by the majority of students.

In part (c) only a few candidates were able to show that planning and operational variances needed to be calculated, so that the manager would only be assessed on results that were within his control.

ACCA examiner's answers. The ACCA examiner's answer to this question can be found at the back of this kit.

Marking scheme

			Marks
(a)	Flexed budget:		
	Food sales	1	
	Drink sales	1	
	Total revenue	1	
	Staff wages	1½	
	Food costs	1	
	Drink costs	1	
	Energy costs	1½	
	Variable costs total	1	
	Contribution	1	
	Manager's and chef's pay	½	
	Rent & rates	½	
	Operating profit	1	
			12
(b)	Explanation of variances	2	
	Suggestions of reason for variances	2	
			4
(c)	Discussion of variance 1	Max 2	
	Discussion of variance 2	Max 2	
			4
			20

(a) **Flexed budget**

Number of meals 1,560

	$	$
Revenue:		
Food sales (W1)	62,400	
Drink sales (W1)	15,600	
		78,000
Variable costs:		
Staff wages (W2)	(12,672)	
Food costs (W3)	(7,800)	
Drink costs (W4)	(3,120)	
Energy costs (W5)	(4,234)	
		(27,826)
Contribution		50,174
Fixed costs:		
Manager's and chef's pay	(8,600)	
Rent, rates and depreciations	(4,500)	
		(13,100)
Operating profit		37,074

Workings

1   *Revenue*
    Food revenue = 1,560 × (($45 + $35)/2) = $62,400
    Drinks revenue = 1,560 × ($2.50 × 4) = $15,600

2   *Staff wages*
    Average number of orders per day = 1,560/(6 days × 4 weeks) = 65 orders per day
    Therefore extra orders = 15 per day (65 – 50). 15/5 = 3 therefore, 3 × 0.5 hours (1.5 hours) of
    overtime must be paid.
    8 staff × 1.5 hours × 6 days × 4 weeks = 288 extra hours
    Extra wages = 288 extra hours × $12 = $3,456 extra wages
    Total flexed wages = $9,216 + $3,456 = $12,672

3   *Food costs*
    Food costs = 12.5% × $62,400 = $7,800

4   *Drink costs*
    Drink costs = 20% × $15,600 = $3,120

5   *Energy costs*
    Standard total hours worked = (8 staff × 6 hours) × 6 days × 4 weeks = 1,152 hours
    Extra hours worked = 288 (W2)
    Total hours = 1,152 + 288 = 1,440
    Total energy costs = 1,440 hours × $2.94 per hour = $4,234

(b)   **Sales mix contribution variance**

The sales mix contribution variance measures the effect on profit when the proportions of products sold are different from those in the standard mix.

The sales mix variance is adverse. Meal B generates a higher contribution than meal A. This means that more of meal A must have been sold, relative to meal B, than budgeted.

Sales quantity contribution variance

The sales quantity contribution variance shows the difference in contribution/profit because of a change in sales volume from the budgeted number of sales.

The sales quantity variance is favourable. This means that the total number of meals sold (in the standard mix) was higher than expected. Indeed, 1,560 meals were sold (budget was 1,200 meals).

(c)   **Food sales**

The half-price drinks promotion has attracted more customers to the restaurant. Calculating variances such as the sales volume variance for food sales would help to show how the promotion on drinks has impacted upon the number of meals sold.

Drink sales

The sales volume variance could also be calculated for drinks sales. This will compare the standard number of drinks sold (1,560 × 4 drinks) to the actual number of drinks sold as a result of the drinks promotion (1,560 × 6 drinks). The sales volume variance will be favourable as the variance is calculated by applying the increase in volume to the standard margin per unit.

The restaurant manager should only be held accountable for matters within his control. As such, the total sales margin price variance could be split into a planning and an operational variance.

The restaurant manager is only accountable for any operational variance and should not be held accountable for any part of the sales margin price variance that relates to bad planning.

68 Heighway

(a)   **Financial ratios**

			20X3	20X4
Return on capital employed	$\dfrac{\text{Profit before interest and tax}}{\text{Capital employed}}$ %		$\dfrac{18}{105.6}$ = 17%	$\dfrac{16.5}{123.2}$ = 13.4%
Net profit margin	$\dfrac{\text{Profit before interest and tax}}{\text{Sales}}$ %		$\dfrac{18}{180}$ = 10%	$\dfrac{16.5}{185.0}$ = 8.9%
Asset turnover	$\dfrac{\text{Sales}}{\text{Capital employed}}$		$\dfrac{180}{105.6}$ = 1.7 times	$\dfrac{185}{123.2}$ = 1.5 times
Current ratio	$\dfrac{\text{Current assets}}{\text{Current liabilities}}$		$\dfrac{13.6}{8.4}$ = 1.6 : 1	$\dfrac{11.9}{9.2}$ = 1.3 : 1

(b)   **Profitability**

Return on capital employed has fallen from 20X3 to 20X4, caused by a **decrease in operating profit** and an **increase in capital employed**. The fall in operating profit may have been caused by an **increase in costs**, whilst the **new investment programme** will have caused an increase in capital employed.

Asset turnover has fallen. Sales have only increased by 2.8% between 20X3 and 20X4 so the new investment programme may not yet have had a significant effect upon sales.

In the **short term**, the investment programme has increased assets and costs but has not yet influenced sales.

Liquidity

The **current ratio** has deteriorated so the firm's ability to meet its short-term obligations from its short-term resources has been reduced. The expenditure on the investment programme may have decreased the cash balance between 20X3 and 20X4, causing the deterioration in liquidity.

(c)   *(Note that only three indicators are required)*

Non financial performance indicator	Importance
% of trains on time	Punctuality is important to passengers and a well-understood target
% of trains cancelled	Reliability is important to passengers
Accidents per 1,000,000 passengers	Safety is vital in any form of travel, and an important PR issue for railways in recent times
Customer rating of cleanliness of trains	Passengers require good quality service facilities
% utilisation of rolling stock profits	Underused assets do not earn maximum profits

% utilisation of staff	Underused staff do not help to grow profits
% of new customers	New customers are vital for sustained growth
Employee morale	Happy employees (particularly those who deal with customers), are vital for success in a service business

(d) **Short-termism** is when there is a bias towards short-term rather than long-term performance.

Organisations often have to make a trade-off between short-term and long-term objectives. Decisions which involve the **sacrifice of longer-term objectives** include the following.

(i) Postponing or abandoning capital expenditure projects, which would eventually contribute to growth and profits, in order to protect short term cash flow and profits.

(ii) Cutting R&D expenditure to save operating costs, and so reducing the prospects for future product development.

(iii) Reducing quality control, to save operating costs (but also adversely affecting reputation and goodwill).

(iv) Reducing the level of customer service, to save operating costs (but sacrificing goodwill).

(v) Cutting training costs or recruitment (so the company might be faced with skills shortages).

Managers may also **manipulate** results, especially if rewards are linked to performance. This can be achieved by changing the timing of capital purchases, building up inventories and speeding up or delaying payments and receipts.

Steps that could be taken to encourage managers to take a **long-term view**, so that the 'ideal' decisions are taken, include the following.

(i) **Making short-term targets realistic**. If budget targets are unrealistically tough, a manager will be forced to make trade-offs between the short and long term.

(ii) **Providing sufficient management information** to allow managers to see what trade-offs they are making. Managers must be kept aware of long-term aims as well as shorter-term (budget) targets.

(iii) **Evaluating managers' performance** in terms of contribution to long-term as well as short-term objectives.

(iv) **Link managers' rewards to share price**. This may encourage goal congruence.

(v) **Set quality based targets** as well as financial targets. Multiple targets can be used.

69 Preparation question: Accounting for business

Text references. The balanced scorecard is covered in Chapter 14 and ROI in Chapter 15.

Top tips. This is a completely written question, which is unlikely in the exam, but it does give you excellent practice at applying techniques to a specific organisation. Make sure your answers do not simply regurgitate textbook theories but relate to AFB.

(a) **Problems with using ROI**

The use of a single financial measure to judge the performance of branches has the following problems.

- Because the measure is **short-term** and looks at the results of a single year, there is **no incentive** for branches to improve. They will not invest in long-term projects and will be inclined to hold on to assets too long so that their carrying amount reduces and ROI increases.

- No consideration is given to other **non-financial measures** which will be critical to the company's success, such as customer satisfaction, staff motivation etc.

- The **costs** of each branch will generally be **fixed**: controlling the costs will not necessarily make the branches more successful. For example costs could be cut by using less experienced staff or cheaper teaching materials, but this is likely to harm the long-term success of the business.

- Because the branches rent their premises, they will have **very few non-current assets** (desks, chairs, screens, etc) and therefore ROI will always be high. The managers will therefore not be **motivated** to improve performance further.
- The use of a national target ROI will not take account of **local environmental factors** which will be different for each branch (such as the level of competition, power of customers, etc).
- Managers may not introduce **profitable courses** if the ROI on the course is below their existing ROI, even though the course may provide a return above the company's overall target ROI.

Overall, the use of ROI as the company's sole performance indicator will not help the business to obtain its goals of **development** and **growth**.

(b) **The balanced scorecard approach**

The balanced scorecard approach will help the business because it recognises the importance of both **financial** and **non-financial** performance. It sets performance indicators and targets for both these areas.

The balanced scorecard looks at four areas which are crucial to the success of the business.

- **Financial perspectives**. It will be important that the company is performing well enough both to satisfy shareholder requirements and to fund future growth. It will also need to compete effectively in its markets to ensure it can maintain its current market position.

- **Customer perspectives**. One of the critical success factors for the business will be how it is perceived by its customers. There will be four key areas here – customer satisfaction, customer loyalty, customer acquisition, and market awareness of the company. It needs to be measured whether branches are performing well in these areas.

- **Internal business perspectives**. If AFB is to be market leader, then in order to satisfy customers and shareholders an internal structure and framework need to be in place which allows this to happen. This will include having adequate facilities for customers, motivated staff and quality services.

- **Innovation and learning perspectives**. For the company to satisfy its development and growth goals it will need to be innovative (introduce new products etc) and encourage staff to keep up to date with technical changes within their area of expertise (tax law changes, etc). This will be needed in order both to maintain customer satisfaction and to create value for other stakeholders in the business, such as Jim Buxton and his staff.

It can be seen that the balanced scorecard examines many different stakeholder requirements which are **critical to the success** of the business. It does not concentrate solely on financial measures but recognises the importance of customer satisfaction, staff motivation, innovation etc.

The business should develop **performance measures** which can gauge the success of each branch in satisfying these other goals, so that targets can be set and performance monitored.

This should ensure that the branch managers concentrate more on what is important to the business. They should be encouraged by the balanced scorecard to take a **longer term approach** to their management. For example, whereas upgrading their premises and facilities may harm their financial perspectives, it should lead to better customer and internal perspectives.

Managers will also not be able to take it easy at their branch because the financial performance is above target – they will also need to consider how things can be further improved and developed in order to satisfy the other sectors of their scorecard. This should remove many of the problems induced by using only ROI as a sole measure of performance.

(c) **Performance measures**

The following is an outline of how the balanced scorecard could be implemented by AFB.

Financial perspective

Critical success factors	Performance measures
Return to shareholders	ROI
Course profitability	Margins per course
Grow/prosper	Sales growth

Customer perspective

Critical success factors	*Performance measures*
Satisfaction	Individual customer course appraisals (using a ranking system)
Loyalty	% of repeat business
Acquisition	% of queries turned into customers

Internal business perspective

Critical success factors	*Performance measures*
Motivated staff	Staff turnover ratio
Adequate facilities	Individual customer course appraisals (using a ranking system)
Efficient use of assets	Staff/lecture room utilisation%

Innovation and learning perspective

Critical success factors	*Performance measures*
Introduce new products	% of new to old courses
Keep staff up to date	Average staff hours on training courses
Adapt to customer needs	% of bespoke to standard courses

70 Brace Co

Text references. The balanced scorecard approach to performance measurement is covered in Chapter 14. Return on investment and residual income are covered in Chapter 15.

Top tips. Make your answer to part (a) easy to mark. Start with a short introduction then write a little bit about each perspective under seperate headings.

Easy marks. Although it is based in the context of a company, the requirement in part (a) is really generic. You should score highly providing your answer covers all four perspectives of the balanced scorecard.

Examiner's comments. There were some really good answers to part (a), although the structure of answers could have been better. It is really hard to mark a question like this where candidates' answers include no headings and often not even any paragraphs.

About 50% of candidates scored full marks on the calculations in part (b) but some had no idea how to calculate ROI/RI. As for the commentary, most answers were poor, showing that there is little understanding of what these figures actually mean.

ACCA examiner's answers. The ACCA examiner's answer to this question can be found at the back of this kit.

Marking scheme

			Marks
(a)	Balanced scorecard approach:		
	Stating what it is	2	
	Financial perspective	2	
	Customer perspective	2	
	Internal perspective	2	
	Learning and growth perspective	2	
			10
(b)	ROI/RI:		
	ROI for A	1	
	ROI for B	1	
	RI for A	2	
	RI for B	2	

Comments:	
A rejects, B accepts under ROI	1
Both accept under RI	1
ROI produces wrong decision for company	1
RI produces right decision	1
Manager right	1
Other factors to consider	1

Max 10

20

(a) **Balanced scorecard**

The **balanced scorecard** approach to performance measurement emphasises the need to provide management with a set of information which covers all relevant areas of performance in an objective and unbiased fashion.

The information provided may be both financial and non-financial and cover areas such as profitability, customer satisfaction, internal efficiency and innovation.

The balanced scorecard focuses on **four different perspectives**, as follows.

Customer perspective

The customer perspective considers how new and existing customers view the organisation. This perspective should identify targets that matter to customers such as cost, quality, delivery, inspection and so on.

The customer perspective is linked to revenue/profit objectives in the financial perspective. If customer objectives are achieved, it is likely that revenue/profit objectives will also be achieved.

Internal perspective

The internal perspective makes an organisation consider what processes it must excel at in order to achieve financial and customer objectives.

The perspective aims to improve internal processes and decision making.

Innovation and learning perspective

The innovation and learning perspective requires the organisation to consider how it can continue to improve and create value.

Organisations must seek to acquire new skills and develop new products in order to maintain a competitive position in their respective market(s) and provide a basis from which the other perspectives of the balanced scorecard can be accomplished.

Financial perspective

The financial perspective considers whether the organisation meets the expectations of its shareholders and how it creates value for them.

This perspective focuses on traditional measures such as growth, profitability and cost reduction.

(b) **Division A**

Return on investment (ROI):
Net profit = $44.6m × 28% = $12.488m
ROI = (profit / capital employed) × 100%
  = $12.488m / $82.8m = 15.08%

Residual income (RI):
Net profit = $12.488m
Capital employed = $82.8m
Imputed interest charge = $82.8m × 12% (cost of capital for both divisions) = $9.936m
RI = net profit − imputed interest charge
  = $12.488m − $9.936m = $2.552m

Division B

Return on investment (ROI):
Net profit = $21.8m × 33% = $7.194m
ROI = $7.194m / $40.6m = 17.72%

Residual income (RI):
Net profit = $7.194m
Capital employed = $40.6m
Imputed interest charge = $40.6m × 12% = $4.872m
RI = $7.194m − $4.872m = $2.322m

Comments

The current return on investment (ROI) of each division is 16%. It is likely that the manager of Division A will reject any proposal based solely on ROI as the Division A investment only has a ROI of 15.08%. The proposed investment would reduce Division A's ROI by 0.92 percentage points.

In contrast, the manager of Division B is likely to accept the proposal as the Division B investment has an ROI of 17.72%. The proposed investment would increase Division B's ROI by 1.72 percentage points.

Both divisions are likely to accept the proposal based on residual income as both have a healthy RI ($2.552m and $2.322m respectively).

The views of the new manager of Division A are correct. The use of ROI as the sole decision tool in the past has led to a lack of goal congruence between Division A and the company as a whole.

It is clear that the use of RI as an investment measure will help the divisions to make decisions that are in the best interests of the company.

71 Investment group

Text references. Performance measurement is covered in Chapters 14 and 15.

Top tips. This question required calculation, explanation and discussion. However, while you should of course have paid careful attention to the first word of each requirement you should also have noted that in (b) and (c) you had to reach specific conclusions. In part (b), you had to decide which of two measures was superior, and in (c) you had to specify additional information. Such requirements should be answered as specifically as possible: the examiner wants to see whether you can actually make decisions. In part (d) make sure you refer to H investment group in your explanation.

(a) **Return on investment**

	CS	HE	LE
	$'000	$'000	$'000
Profit	220	1,073	240
Capital employed	150	5,650	925
ROI	147%	19%	26%
Residual income			
Profit	220	1,073	240
Less group finance charge @ 12%	18	678	111
Residual income	202	395	129

Return on investment figures indicate that the CS sector is the most successful but this reflects the much **lower level of capital employed** in a consultancy business compared to manufacturing companies. **Residual income** figures indicate that the HE sector is the most successful, reflecting the high level of profits that it generates.

(b) **ROI v RI**

(i) Return on investment (ROI) is intended to measure the **efficiency** with which assets are being used, by taking the profit as a proportion of the net assets. Residual income (RI) on the other hand, is simply the **profit reduced** by a **financing charge** which is based on the net assets. RI is an absolute, not a relative measure.

(ii) **ROI** has the major advantage of taking full account of the size of the business, so that **businesses of different sizes can be compared. Residual income**, on the other hand, may be **less distorted by inappropriate values for investment**.

(c) The problem is to decide which sector to expand. While recent results are of course relevant to such a decision, the **information given in the question is inadequate** for the following reasons.

(i) **Results for earlier years are not given**. Some of the results for 20X1 could be out of line with normal results.

(ii) Non-current and current assets are **not analysed** by type of asset, nor is any indication given of the remaining lives of non-current assets.

(iii) A **single rate** is used **for the group finance charge**, without any account being taken of the business risk of each sector.

(iv) All the information provided comes from the group's accounting system. It makes **no reference to the open market values** of whole businesses or of individual assets.

The following further information would be useful.

(i) An **analysis of non-current assets** by type and by likely time to replacement.

(ii) An **analysis of current assets** into inventory, receivables and cash.

(iii) **Results for at least the two previous years**, adjusted for inflation so as to be comparable with the 20X1 results.

(iv) **Expected results for 20X2,** together with a clear statement of the assumptions used in preparing the forecasts.

(v) The **market share of each sector**.

(vi) The extent to which the results include **intra-group transactions**, and the bases on which prices for such transactions are determined.

(d) Fitzgerald and Moon's **building blocks** for **dimensions, standards** and **rewards** attempt to overcome the problems associated with performance measurement of service businesses. They would therefore be particularly useful for the CS sector. Certain elements may also be worth considering for HE and LE.

Performance measurement in **service businesses** has sometimes been perceived as difficult because of factors such as the intangibility, inseparability, heterogeneity and perishability of services.

The modern view is that if something is difficult to measure this is because it has not been clearly enough defined. Hence Fitzgerald & Moon provide **building blocks** for performance measurement systems in service businesses.

Three questions are asked: What **dimensions** of performance should be measured? How should **standards** be set for those measures? What **rewards** should be associated with the achievement of these standards?

Three issues need to be considered if the performance measurement system is to operate successfully: **clarity, motivation** and **controllability.**

(i) The organisation's objectives need to be **clearly understood** by those whose performance is being appraised ie they need to know what goals they are working towards.

(ii) Individuals should be **motivated** to work in pursuit of the organisation's strategic objectives. Goal clarity and participation have been shown to contribute to higher levels of motivation to achieve targets, providing managers accept those targets. Bonuses can be used to motivate.

(iii) Managers should have a certain level of **controllability** for their areas of responsibility. For example they should not be held responsible for costs over which they have no control.

The building block framework will therefore be particularly useful for the CS sector but aspects can also be used throughout the group to measure how well corporate objectives are being achieved and highlighting where improvements are needed.

72 Boats and cladding

> **Text references.** Performance measures are covered in Chapters 14,15 and 16.
>
> **Top tips.** Use information provided in the question to illustrate your answer as necessary.

(a)   **Possible counter-productive behaviour resulting from using the current ROCE calculation for performance appraisal**

Under the current method of performance appraisal, managers are judged on the basis of the **ROCE** that their divisions earn, the ROCE being calculated using the net book value of non-current assets. The use of ROCE as a method of appraising performance has disadvantages, whilst there are additional disadvantages of using ROCE based on the net book value of non-current assets.

(i)   As managers are judged on the basis of the ROCE that their divisions earn each year, they are likely to be **motivated** into taking decisions which increase the division's short-term ROCE and rejecting projects which reduce the short-term ROCE even if the project is in excess of the company's target ROCE and hence is desirable from the company's point of view.

Suppose that the manager of the Boats division was faced with a proposed project which had a projected return of 21%. He would be likely to reject the project because it would reduce his division's overall ROCE to below 24%. The investment would be desirable from Cordeline Co's point of view, however, because its ROCE would be in excess of the company's target ROCE of 20%. This is an example of **sub-optimality** and a **lack of goal congruence** in decision making.

(ii)   A similar misguided decision would occur if the manager of the Cladding division, say, was worried about the low ROCE of his division and decided to reduce his investment by scrapping some assets not currently being used. The reduction in both depreciation charge and assets would immediately improve the ROCE. When the assets were eventually required, however, the manager would then be obliged to buy new equipment.

(iii)   The current method bases the calculation of ROCE on the **net book value of assets**. If a division maintains the same annual profits and keeps the same asset without a policy of regular asset replacement, its ROCE will increase year by year as the assets get older. Simply by allowing its non-current assets to depreciate a divisional manager is able to give a false impression of improving performance over time.

The level of new investment in non-current assets by the Cladding division was over three times that of the Boats division in 19X3 and nearly 13 times that of the Boats division in 19X4. The Boats division is using old assets that have been depreciated to a much greater extent than those of the Cladding division and hence the basis of the ROCE calculation is much lower. Consequently it is able to report a much higher ROCE.

(iv)   The method used to calculate ROCE therefore also provides a **disincentive** to divisional mangers to **reinvest** in new or replacement assets because the division's ROCE would probably fall. From the figures provided it is obvious that the Cladding division has replaced assets on a regular basis, the difference between original and replacement costs of its assets being small. The manager of the Boats division, on the other hand, has not replaced assets, there being a marked difference between original and replacement cost of the division's assets.

(v)   A further disadvantage of measuring ROCE as profit divided by the net book value of assets is that it is not easy to **compare fairly** the performance of one division with another. Two divisions might have the same amount of working capital, the same value of non-current assets at cost and the same profit. But if one division's assets have been depreciated by a much bigger amount, perhaps because they are older, that division's ROCE will be bigger.

In some respects this is the case with the Boats and Cladding divisions. Both the profit and the original asset cost of the Cladding division are about the same proportion of the Boats division's profit and original asset cost but the ROCE of the Boats division is twice that of the Cladding division.

(b) **A revised ROCE measure**

Instead of using the net book value of non-current assets to calculate ROCE, it could be calculated using the gross book value of non-current assets. This would remove the problem of ROCE increasing over time as non-current assets get older and will enable comparisons to be made more fairly.

Using the alternative method, the ROCE for the two divisions in the two years would be as follows.

Boats	20X3	13.8%
	20X4	10.6%
Cladding	20X3	11.7%
	20X4	9.7%

Although the Boats division still has a greater ROCE, the difference between the ROCE of the two divisions is much less.

(c) **An alternative financial performance measure**

The board could consider using **residual income (RI)** as an alternative financial performance measure. RI will increase when investments earning above the cost of capital are undertaken or when investments earning below the cost of capital are eliminated.

RI will increase for even **'marginally profitable'** investments and hence such investments are likely to be undertaken by a divisional manager if RI is used as the basis of performance appraisal. In contrast, when a manger is judged by ROCE, a marginally profitable investment would be less likely to be undertaken because it would reduce the average ROCE earned by the division as a whole.

Although RI does not always point to the right decision, it is more likely than ROCE to improve when managers make correct investment/divestment decisions and so is probably a 'safer' basis than ROCE on which to measure performance.

73 Pasta division

Text references. Return on investment and residual income are covered in Chapter 15.

Top tips. You should have found this question very straightforward. Set out your workings clearly in parts (a) and (b). Underline the key words such as the need to do the calculations 'before' and 'after' in parts (a) and (b).

(a)

	Before expansion $m	Additions $m	After proposed expansion $m
Investment in non-current assets	1.5	+0.75	2.25
Investment in working capital	1.0	+0.35	1.35
Net divisional assets	2.5		3.60
Operating profit	0.5	+0.198	0.698
Return on investment	20.0%		19.4%

(b)

	Before expansion		After proposed expansion	
		$m		$m
Operating profit		0.500		0.698
Imputed interest on net divisional assets	($2.5m × 15%)	0.375	($3.6m × 15%)	0.540
Residual income		0.125		0.158

(c) Using **return on investment (ROI)** as a performance measure, the divisional manager would not be happy to accept the proposed expansion. The ROI would reduce if the expansion went ahead, indicating a **deterioration** in the division's performance, and because bonuses are paid as a percentage on this basis, the manager would receive a lower bonus.

If **residual income (RI)** was used as a performance measure the manager would be happy to accept the proposed expansion. This is because the RI would increase as a result of the expansion. This indicates an **improvement in the division's performance** and so the manager would receive a higher bonus.

(d) **ROI** has the obvious advantages of being compatible with accounting reports and is easier to understand.

There are a number of **disadvantages** associated with both ROI and RI, however.

(i) Both methods suffer from disadvantages in measuring profit (how should inventory be valued, how should arbitrary allocations of head office charges be dealt with) and investment (what basis to use).

(ii) It is questionable whether a single measure is appropriate for measuring the complexity of divisional performance.

(iii) If a division maintains the same annual profit, keeps the same assets without a policy of regular non-current asset replacement and values assets at net book value, ROI and RI will increase year by year as the assets get older, even though profits may be static. This can give a false impression of improving performance over time and acts to discourage managers from undertaking new investments.

In addition, **ROI** suffers from the following **disadvantages**.

(i) The need to **maintain ROI** in the **short-term** can discourage managers from investing in new assets (since the average ROI of a division tends to fall in the early stages of a new investment) even if the new investment is beneficial to the group as a whole (because the investment's ROI is greater than the group's target rate of return). This focuses attention on **short-run performance** whereas investment decisions should be evaluated over their full life. RI can help to overcome this problem of **sub-optimality** and a **lack of goal congruence** by highlighting projects which return more than the cost of capital.

(ii) It can be **difficult to compare** percentage ROI results of divisions if their activities are very **different**. RI can overcome this problem through the use of different interest rates for different divisions.

There are also a number of **disadvantages associated with RI**: it does not facilitate comparison between divisions; neither does it relate the size of a division's income to the size of the investment. In these respects ROI is a better measure.

The disadvantages of the two methods have a number of **behavioural implications**. Managers tend to favour proposals that produce excellent results in the short term (to ensure their performance appears favourable) but which, because they have little regard for the later life of their division's projects, are possibly unacceptable in the longer term. They will therefore disregard proposals that are in the best interests of the group as a whole. ROI and RI can therefore produce **dysfunctional decision making**.

74 Preparation question: Transfer pricing

Text references. Transfer pricing is covered in Chapter 15.

Top tip. This question covers key issues on the topic of transfer pricing which you must understand. It is likely to form part of a question rather than an entire written question.

As we say in the front pages of the kit, make sure you do what the question says, so 'explain' does not mean a bulleted list.

(a)   **Advantages of divisionalisation**

(i)   Divisionalisation can **improve** the **quality of decisions** made because divisional managers (those taking the decisions) know local conditions and are able to make more informed judgements. Moreover, with the personal incentive to improve the division's performance, they ought to take decisions in the division's best interests.

(ii)   **Decisions should be taken more quickly** because information does not have to pass along the chain of command to and from top management. Decisions can be made on the spot by those who are familiar with the product lines and production processes and who are able to react to changes in local conditions quickly and efficiently.

(iii) The authority to act to improve performance should **motivate divisional managers**.

(iv)   Divisional organisation **frees top management** from detailed involvement in day-to-day operations and allows them to devote more time to strategic planning.

(v)   Divisions provide **valuable training grounds for future members of top management** by giving them experience of managerial skills in a less complex environment than that faced by top management.

(vi)   In a large business organisation, the **central head office will not have the management resources or skills to direct operations closely enough itself**. Some authority must be delegated to local operational managers.

(b)   (i)   **Marginal cost**

With such an approach, variable cost is usually assumed to be equivalent to the marginal cost of the unit being transferred.

Supplying division. A transfer price at marginal cost means that the supplying division does not cover its fixed costs and so makes no contribution on the transfer. The division would therefore have no incentive to provide the service internally.

Receiving division. Provided the variable cost of the service is less than the market price (which it should be if the supplying division is efficient), the receiving division would be keen on such an approach to setting transfer prices.

SK. Given that the manager of the supplying division would prefer to transfer externally, head office are likely to have to insist that internal transfers are made.

(ii)   **Total cost**

Supplying division. If the supplying division operates at normal levels of activity, internal transfers at total cost means that the division makes no profit on the transfers. The manager of the division would therefore prefer to transfer externally to earn a profit, regardless of whether or not internal transfers would be in the best interests of SK plc as a whole. If internal transfers cause activity levels above normal levels, however, the division will earn a profit on the transfers. The supplying division will thus make internal transfers provided it has spare capacity.

Receiving division. Provided full cost is less than market price (which it should be if the supplying division is operating efficiently), the receiving division will be better off if it uses internally-provided services.

SK. Unless the supplying division has spare capacity, head office is likely to have to force the supplying division to transfer internally.

(iii) **Cost plus**

Supplying division. The 'plus' acts as an incentive for the division to transfer internally, although external transfers will still be preferable if the 'plus' on external transfers is greater than that on internal transfers.

Receiving division. The 'plus' causes an increase in cost for the receiving division but the division will still prefer internal transfers to external purposes if the cost is less than the market price.

SK. Unless the supplying division has spare capacity, it will prefer external transfers to internal transfers if the internal 'plus' is less than the external 'plus', and will transfer less internally. This may or may not be in the best interests of SK.

(iv)   **Opportunity cost**

With this approach, the transfer price is set at the standard variable cost per unit in the supplying division plus the opportunity cost to the organisation as a whole of supplying the unit internally instead of externally.

The transfer price will be either the maximum contribution foregone by the supplying division in transferring internally rather than selling externally, or the contribution foregone by not using the same facilities in the supplying division for their next best alternative use.

If there is no external market for the service being transferred and no alternative uses for the supplying division's facilities, the method will give a transfer price of variable (marginal) cost, with its accompanying consequences.

If resources are limited, however:

(1)   The **supplying division** will be indifferent between internal and external sales as the transfer price will be market price.

(2)   The **receiving division** will be indifferent between purchasing internally and eternally (unless internal transfers are accompanied by a far higher level of service).

(3)   The transfer price should ensure that available resources are used in a way which will maximise the benefit to **SK** as a whole. An organisational policy will be needed, however, to ensure that internal transfers are accompanied by savings in administration and distribution costs.

(c)   (i)   **Actual cost versus standard cost**

When a transfer price is based on cost, **standard cost should be used**, not actual cost. A transfer at **actual cost** would give the **supplying division** no **incentive to control costs** because all of the costs could be passed on to the receiving division. **Actual cost** plus transfer prices might even **encourage** the manager of the supplying division to **overspend**, because this would increase divisional profit, even though the organisation as a whole (and the receiving division) suffers.

Standard cost based transfer prices should **encourage** the supplying division to become **more efficient** as any variances that arise would affect the results of the supplying division (as opposed to being passed on to the receiving division if actual costs were used).

The problem with the approach, however, is that it **penalises** the **supplying division** if the standard cost is **unattainable**, while it **penalises** the **receiving division** if it is **too easily attainable**.

(ii)   A transfer price based on **marginal cost** is the **theoretically correct transfer price** to encourage total organisational profitability when there is **no external market** for the item being transferred and **no capacity constraints** affecting production (so that there is no opportunity cost associated with the transfer). If there is no external market for the product, marginal cost would be an appropriate transfer price provided that there is no relevant capacity constraints.

A transfer price at marginal cost means that **the supplying division does not cover its fixed costs,** however, and so makes **no contribution on the transfer**, and no profit. There is therefore **no incentive** for the division to make the transfer. **Head office** would therefore be likely to have to **insist** that the transfers were made, thereby **undermining divisional autonomy**.

There are a number of ways in which the **problem of not covering fixed costs can be overcome,** however, such as **dual pricing** and a **two-part tariff system**, although these may also **undermine divisional autonomy**.

75 FP Photocopiers and SW Ltd

Text references. Transfer pricing is covered in Chapter 15.

Top tips. Part (a) requires the candidate to identify the impact of different approaches to transfer pricing on company profitability. Although a great deal of information is given, a methodical approach could easily help score full marks.

Parts (b) and (c) require an explanation and discussion of divisional structures for performance measurement and management control.

(a)

	Per repair	For 500 repairs
	$	$
Parts	54	
Labour (3 hrs × $15 per hour)	45	
Variable overheads (3 hrs × $10 per labour hour)	30	
Marginal cost	129	64,500
Fixed overheads (3 hrs × $22 per labour hour)	66	33,000
Total cost	195	97,500
Mark-up (40% of total cost)	78	39,000
Selling price	273	136,500

Transfers at 40% mark up

	Sales department	Service department	FP
	$	$	$
Sales	120,000	136,500	120,000
Costs	(136,500)	(97,500)	(97,500)
Profits	(16,500)	39,000	22,500

Transfers at marginal cost

	Sales department	Service department	FP
	$	$	$
Sales	120,000	64,500	120,000
Costs	64,500	97,500	97,500
Profits	55,500	(33,000)	22,500

Repairs carried out by RS

	Sales department	Service department	FP
	$	$	$
Sales	120,000	–	120,000
Repair costs ($180 per repair × 500)	90,000	–	(90,000)
Fixed overheads		33,000	33,000
Profit/(loss)	30,000	(33,000)	(3,000)

(b) (i) **Full cost plus transfer pricing** may not be appropriate because it is likely to **build the inefficiencies** of the Service Department.

It may lead to implied **poor performance** by the Sales Department. The performance measures and reward system would lead to sub-optimal decisions by the manager of the Sales Department.

(ii) Other issues to consider include:

- Why is the quote by RS lower than the cost of the Services Department?
- Are fixed costs committed?
- What is the standard quality of the repairs by RS?

- Is the offer by RS a short-term offer? Is the price likely to remain stable or rise in the long term?
- Why are the costs of the Service Department higher than the price charged by RS?
- Are the fixed costs avoidable?
- Can the Services Department find other work to take up the capacity released if RS do the guaranteed repairs?

(c) **Overall group policy**

The group transfer pricing policy should ensure the maximisation of group profits. This is achieved by the inclusion in the transfer price of any opportunity costs associated with internal transfer.

Policy up to January 20X2

In the period up to January 20X2, SW Limited will **have spare capacity**: 500,000 litres per week can be produced and so production of 100,000 litres for internal transfer will have no effect on our ability to produce 350,000 litres for external customers.

There is therefore **no opportunity cost** associated with the internal transfers as they do not cause a reduction in contribution from external sales.

The transfer price should therefore be set at **variable cost**.

Internal transfers are often **cheaper** than external sales, however (due to savings in selling, administration, delivery costs and so on), and so it would seem reasonable for AL Limited to expect a discount on variable cost.

The transfer price might therefore be set **at slightly less than variable cost** so that the two divisions can share the cost savings from internal transfers compared with external sales.

Note that **standard** variable cost should be used because actual costs vary with volume, seasonal and other factors and because, if used as a basis for transfer prices, any inefficiency in SW Limited could be passed on to AL Limited in the form of an increased transfer price.

Given that **SW Limited** earns no contribution on transfers at variable cost, it will be **indifferent** between **making the transfers and producing no output**. **Head office intervention** may therefore be required to ensure that transfers take place.

Policy from January 20X2

From January 20X2, SW Limited will have **insufficient capacity** to meet both internal and external demand.

If SW Limited were to supply AL Limited with 250,000 litres per week, it would be unable to meet 100,000 litres of external demand and would lose the contribution on these sales. The transfer price must therefore take the **opportunity cost** of this lost contribution into account.

A **two-tier transfer pricing system** is required.

150,000 litres should have a transfer price of (adjusted) **variable cost** (as above) as there is no external demand for this output.

100,000 litres should have a transfer price of **external selling price**, adjusted for any savings on internal transfers as necessary.

76 Hammer

Text references. Transfer pricing is covered in Chapter 15.

Top tips. Do not forget to exclude fixed costs from your calculations in part (a). The question states that the current pricing policy is variable cost plus 30%.

Easy marks. Six marks are available in part (d) for discussing factors to consider when purchasing from outside suppliers.

Marking scheme

		Marks
(a)	Steel	1
	Other material	1
	Labour	1
	Variable overhead	1
	Delivery	1
	Margin	1
		6
(b)	Fixed cost	2
	Margin	2
		4
(c)	Covers all cost	1
	Risk	1
	Fixed cost accounting	1
	Converts a FC to VC	2
		max 4
(d)	Market price may be temporary	1
	Brand	1
	Profitability	1
	Flexibility	1
	Control	1
	Motivation	1
	Performance assessment	1
		max 6
		20

(a) **Price Nail would charge under existing policy (cost plus 30%)**

	$
Steel (0.4kg/0.95 (5% steel loss)) × $4.00	1.68
Other materials ($3.00 × 0.9 × 0.1)	0.27
Labour ($10 × 0.25)	2.50
Variable overhead ($15 × 0.25)	3.75
Delivery	0.50
Total variable cost	8.70
Mark-up (30%)	2.61
Transfer price	11.31

(b) **Price Nail would charged under total cost plus 10%**

	$
Total variable cost from part (a)	8.70
Extra fixed cost (0.25 × $15 × 0.8)	3.00
Total cost	11.70
Mark up (10%)	1.17
Transfer price	12.87

The increase in price if the pricing policy switches to total cost plus 10% is $1.56 per unit ($12.87 - $11.31).

(c) Fixed costs can be accounted for in a number of ways. As such, including the fixed cost within the transfer price could lead to **manipulation of overhead treatment**. For example employing absorption costing or activity based costing.

Including the fixed costs in the transfer price will benefit the manufacturer who can ensure that **all costs** incurred during the manufacturing process are **covered**. Assuming the fixed overhead absorption calculations are accurate, the manufacturing division should be **guaranteed a profit**.

The main **problem** with this pricing strategy is **fixed costs** are **effectively treated as variable costs** from the perspective of the stores, as they are included within the variable buy-in price. This could lead to **poor decision-making** from a **group perspective**.

(d) Managers of the retail stores are likely to be more **motivated** if they are given **freedom** in which to **operate** and are able to purchase from outside suppliers if prices are cheaper.

In addition, the performance of **store managers will be easier to assess** in an environment in which managers are able to control greater elements of the business.

Price differences are perhaps to be expected given that products are rarely identical. There is a **risk** that store managers purchase cheaper shears of **inferior quality** to those produced internally (whilst claiming they are comparable) in order to achieve a greater margin. Such scenarios jeopardise the **reputation** of the brand for the benefit of individual stores.

Allowing store managers to purchase from cheaper suppliers could result in Hammer **losing control** of its business as retail stores could potentially stock different shears and other products from a range of different suppliers. On the other hand **flexibility is increased** and profits could increase as store managers find bargain prices.

In a competitive market, it is unlikely that suppliers will offer products significantly cheaper to Hammer for a sustained period of time. Any cheap prices accessed by store managers are likely to be the result of a sale or special promotion. If this is the case, it would not be advisable for Hammer to grant store managers the power to purchase from cheaper external suppliers in the long term.

Overall profitability of the company is key. The retail stores and Nail should be working in a way that is best for the company overall. This is known as **goal congruence**.

77 All Premier Services

Text references. Performance measures for not-for profit organisations are covered in Chapter 16.

Top tips. This question covers a number of areas in the F5 syllabus and you should be prepared for this in the exam. In (a) we have set out all our workings clearly, although you might not have time to do this in the exam. You should however make clear the basis of the calculations even if you do not set them out in full.

Examiner's comment. In (a) not many candidates got the cost per bed calculations correct. Many candidates failed to change the fixed overhead apportionment despite the change in the number of beds. In (b) many candidates confused responsibility accounting with financial accounting.

(a) (i) **Budgeted income statement for wards**

	Workings	X	Y	Z	Total
		$	$	$	$
Fees	1	61,425	44,800	53,550	159,775
Fixed overheads	2	(52,676)	(35,117)	(39,507)	(127,300)
Variable overheads	3	(16,305)	(11,892)	(14,215)	(42,412)
(Loss)		(7,556)	(2,209)	(172)	(9,937)
Cost per occupied bed	4	$1,769	$1,469	$1,194	

Workings

1 *Fees*

Fees = No of beds × Budgeted fee × Budgeted occupancy rate × 7

X Fees = $60 \times 225 \times 0.65 \times 7 = 61,425$

Y Fees = $40 \times 200 \times 0.8 \times 7 = 44,800$

Z Fees = $45 \times 170 \times 1 \times 7 = 53,550$

2 *Fixed overheads*

Fixed overhead absorption rate = $\dfrac{127,300}{\text{No. of beds}}$

$= \dfrac{127,300}{60+40+45}$

$= \$877.93$

Ward fixed overheads = No of beds × Absorption rate

X Fixed overheads = $60 \times \$877.93$
= $\$52,676$

Y Fixed overheads = $40 \times \$877.93$
= $\$35,117$

Z Fixed overheads = $45 \times \$877.93$
= $\$39,507$

3 *Variable overheads*

Variable overhead absorption rate = $\dfrac{42,412}{159,775}$

$= \$0.26545$

Ward variable overheads = Fees × Absorption rate

X variable overheads = $61,425 \times 0.26545$
= $\$16,305$

Y variable overheads = $44,800 \times 0.26545$
= $\$11,892$

Z variable overheads = $53,550 \times 0.26545$
= $\$14,215$

4 *Cost per occupied bed*

X = $\dfrac{52,676 + 16,305}{60 \times 0.65}$

= $\$1,769$

Y = $\dfrac{35,117 + 11,892}{40 \times 0.8}$

= $\$1,469$

Z = $\dfrac{39,507 + 14,215}{45 \times 1}$

= $\$1,194$

(ii) **Budgeted income statement for wards**

	Workings	X $	Y $	Z $	Total $
Fees	1	75,600	53,200	89,250	218,050
Fixed overheads	2	(43,646)	(29,097)	(54,557)	(127,300)
Variable overheads	3	(20,068)	(14,122)	(23,691)	(57,881)
Profit		11,886	9,981	11,002	32,869
Cost per occupied bed	4	$1,327	$1,137	$1,043	

Workings

1   *Fees*

Fees   = No of beds $\times$ Budgeted fee $\times$ Budgeted occupancy rate $\times$ 7
X Fees = $60 \times 225 \times 0.80 \times 7 = 75,600$
Y Fees = $40 \times 200 \times 0.95 \times 7 = 53,200$
Z Fees = $75 \times 170 \times 1 \times 7 = 89,250$

2   *Fixed overheads*

$$\text{Fixed overhead absorption rate} = \frac{127,300}{\text{No. of beds}}$$

$$= \frac{127,300}{60 + 40 + 75}$$

$$= \$727.43$$

Ward fixed overheads   = No of beds $\times$ Absorption rate
X Fixed overheads   = $60 \times \$727.43$
                         = $\$43,646$
Y Fixed overheads   = $40 \times \$727.43$
                         = $\$29,097$
Z Fixed overheads   = $75 \times \$727.43$
                         = $\$54,557$

3   *Variable overheads*

$$\text{Variable overhead absorption rate} = \frac{57,881}{218,050}$$

$$= \$0.26545$$

Ward variable overheads   = Fees $\times$ Absorption rate
X variable overheads   = $75,600 \times 0.26545$
                          = $\$20,068$
Y variable overheads   = $53,200 \times 0.26545$
                          = $\$14,122$
Z variable overheads   = $89,250 \times 0.26545$
                          = $\$23,691$

4   *Cost per occupied bed*

$$X = \frac{43,646 + 20,068}{60 \times 0.8}$$

$$= \$1,327$$

$$Y = \frac{29,097 + 14,122}{40 \times 0.95}$$

$$= \$1,137$$

$$Z = \frac{54,557 + 23,691}{75 \times 1}$$

$$= \$1,043$$

(b) (i) **Characteristics of responsibility accounting system**

Responsibility accounting is a system of **control** and **reporting** that segregates revenues and costs into areas of **personal responsibility** in order to monitor and assess the performance of each part of an organisation.

Budgets

Budgets will be set to establish the parameters within which managers must work and against which their performance will be **measured**.

Responsibility centres

Units of organisations headed by managers who have **direct responsibility** for their performance are called **responsibility centres.** These include:

(1) **Cost centres**
With cost centres, managers have control over **controllable costs**, and their performance is measured by **variance analysis.**

(2) **Profit centres**
With profit centres, managers have control over **controllable costs, sales volumes and sales prices,** and their performance is measured by the **profits** that their centre makes.

(3) **Investment centres**
Here managers have control over controllable costs, sales prices, output volumes and investment in fixed and current assets, and their performance is measured by return on investment and residual income.

Characteristics of non-profit making organisations

Objectives

Non-profit making organisations may primarily exist to **provide a service**. However in order to provide an **acceptable service**, **costs** may have to exceed budget in which managers may face a **conflict of objectives**.

In addition in some organisations the objectives may **not** be **defined clearly**. There may therefore be **no obvious link between inputs and outputs**. Responsibility may then be hard to define.

Budget holders not able to control costs

The majority of costs in many not-profit-organisations may be apportioned central overheads, leaving many managers with **few controllable costs**. The fixed costs that are apportioned may be **difficult to change**.

In addition budget holders may be responsible for **monitoring costs** rather than **controlling costs**. For example budget holders in a hospital are often not medical staff, but medical decisions control the extent to which costs are incurred.

Surpluses and return for investment

Many areas of the not-for-profit sector will be expected to reach certain financial targets, for example charity appeals being expected to raise certain sums, and expenses of those appeals being a set maximum percentage of the income. However **setting targets** can be difficult – there may be limited data available about **average returns** in the sector in which the organisation operates.

Other significant targets

The performance of managers in many non-profit making organisations will be judged by how well they fulfil **quality and effectiveness targets**. However performance measurement in these terms may be **difficult** and rather **subjective** – what for example are acceptable levels of unsolved crimes for police or pupil/teacher ratios in education.

(ii) **Alternative ward performance measures**

All Premier Services is a fee charging hospital so **customer satisfaction** will be a factor to consider, perhaps measured using a **survey** to be completed by patients on discharge.

Mortality rates are a typical hospital performance measure and the **number of infections contracted by patients** is of topical interest. Some measure of **cleanliness** would therefore be very useful.

Average rates of recovery following specific operations could also be useful especially as this will impact on the length of time patients will need to spend in Ward Z.

78 Woodside

Text reference. Operating statements are covered in Chapter 12 and not-for-profit organisations in Chapter 16.

Top tips. In part (a), fixed costs do not relate to any particular activity of the charity and so a marginal costing approach has to be used in analysing the budgeted and actual information provided. Remember to apply your discussion to the specific entity. As the organisation is a charity, adverse variances do not necessarily equate to poor performance.

Part (b) is a straightforward discussion using knowledge that you should be familiar with for this exam but again, you must specifically refer to the issues that Woodside faces.

(a) **Operating statement**

	Favourable $	Adverse $	$
Budgeted surplus (W1)			98,750
Funding shortfall (W3)			(80,000)
			18,750
Free meals (W4)			
Price variance		4,000	
Usage variance		8,750	
Overnight shelter (W5)			
Price variance		4,380	
Usage variance	31,000		
Advice centre (W6)			
Price variance		9,100	
Usage variance		7,500	
Campaigning and advertising (W7)			
Expenditure variance		15,000	
Fixed cost (W8)			
Expenditure variance		18,000	
	31,000	66,730	(35,730)
Actual shortfall (W2)			(16,980)

Workings

1 **Budgeted figures**

	$	
Free meals provision	91,250	(18,250 meals at $5 per meal)
Overnight shelter (variable)	250,000	(10,000 bed-nights at $30 – $5 per night)
Advice centre (variable)	45,000	(3,000 sessions at $20 – $5 per session)
Fixed costs	65,000	$(10,000 \times \$5) + (3,000 \times \$5)$
Campaigning and advertising	150,000	
	601,250	
Surplus for unexpected costs	98,750	
Fundraising target	700,000	

2   **Actual figures**

		$	
	Free meals provision	104,000	(20,000 meals at $5·20 per meal)
	Overnight shelter	223,380	(8,760 bed-nights $25·50 per night)
	Advice centre	61,600	(3,500 sessions at $17·60 per session)
	Fixed costs	83,000	
	Campaigning and advertising	165,000	
		636,980	
	Shortfall	16,980	
	Funds raised	620,000	

3   Funding shortfall = 700,000 – 620,000 = $80,000 (A)

4   Free meals price variance = (5·00 – 5·20) × 20,000 = $4,000 (A)
Free meals usage variance = (18,250 – 20,000) × 5·00 = $8,750 (A)

5   Overnight shelter price variance = (25·00 – 25·50) × 8,760 = $4,380 (A)
Overnight shelter usage variance – (10,000 – 8,760) × 25 = $31,000 (F)

6   Advice centre price variance = (17·60 – 15·00) × 3,500 = $9,100 (A)
Advice centre usage variance = (3,000 – 3,500) × 15·00 = $7,500 (A)

7   Campaigning and advertising expenditure variance = 150,000 – 165,000 = $15,000 (A)

8   Fixed cost expenditure variance = 65,000 – 83,000 = $18,000 (A)

There was a **fundraising shortfall** of $80,000 compared to the target and **costs were over budget** in all areas except overnight shelter provision.

Provision of free meals cost 14% (104,000 – 91,250/91,250) more than budgeted with most of the variance due to the extra 1,750 meals that were provided. However $4,000 of the variance was due to an increase of 20c (5.20 – 5.00) in the average cost of a meal.

Overnight shelter cost $26,620 (250,000 – 223,380) less than expected. $31,000 was saved because there were 1,240 bed nights less of the service used than expected, but the average unit cost of the provision increased by 50c, leading to an adverse price variance of $4,380.

Advice centre costs were also above budget by 37% (61,600 – 45,000/45,000). There were two factors contributing to this increase. **Usage of the service** increased by 17% (3,500 – 3,000/3,000) and **average costs** also increased by 17% (17.60 – 15/15).

Fixed costs of administration and centre maintenance were $18,000 (28%) above budget and **campaigning and advertising** were $15,000 (10%) above budget.

The shortfall identified in the operating statement may initially cause concern and individual adverse variances could be investigated to determine if **future cost increases could be controlled**. However, the **objective** of a charity such as Woodside is not to make money but to provide help to homeless people.

The figures demonstrate that this **objective was achieved** in terms of advice and free meals provided. It appears that the demand for overnight shelter has fallen so resources could be switched from this area if it is believed that this is a long-term trend. Further investigation of the reason for the fall in demand would be useful.

(b)   Financial management and control in a not-for-profit organisation (NFPO) such as the Woodside charity needs to recognise that such organisations often have **multiple objectives** that can be **difficult to define** and are usually **non-financial**.

Performance of such organisations is judged in terms of inputs and outputs and hence the **value for money** criteria of economy, efficiency and effectiveness.

Economy means that inputs should be obtained at the lowest cost. **Efficiency** involves getting as much as possible for what goes in ie using the charity's resources as efficiently as possible to provide the services offered by the charity. **Effectiveness** means ensuring the outputs ie the services provided, have the desired impacts and achieve the charity's objectives.

Performance measures to determine whether objectives have been achieved can be difficult to formulate for an organisation such as Woodside.

Measures such as the number of free meals served, number of advice sessions given and number of bed-nights used, show that quantitative measures can be used to demonstrate that the charity is meeting a growing need.

Financial management and control in this organisation will primarily be concerned with preparing budgets and controlling costs.

Preparing budgets

Budgets rely on **forecasting** and accurate forecasts can be difficult to prepare for a charity such as Woodside. The level of activity is driven by the needs of the homeless and therefore **difficult to predict**. A high degree of **flexibility** is required to meet changing demand so provision needs to be built into budgets for this.

It is unlikely that Woodside has carried out a **detailed analysis of costs** and they have probably used an **incremental** approach to budgeting. This will limit the accuracy of their forecasts but staff may not have the necessary financial skills to use more advanced techniques.

Controlling costs

This is a key area of financial management due to the need for efficiency and economy. Inputs such as food, drink, bedding etc can be sourced as cheaply as possible and expenses such as electricity and telephone usage can be kept to an absolute minimum through careful use.

The responsibility for cost control would probably be the responsibility of the full-time members of staff but a culture of economy and efficiency can be encouraged amongst the volunteers.

Woodside will also need to provide **annual accounts** in order to retain charitable status and to show the providers of funds that their donations are being used as they intended.

79 Trenset Co

> **Text references.** Variance analysis is covered in Chapter 12 and behavioural aspects of performance management in Chapter 16.
>
> **Top tips.** You need to be prepared to answer questions on more complex variances as well as their implications for performance management and behaviour.
>
> This question illustrates how various areas of the syllabus can be combined.

(a) **Idle time**

A workforce that is expected to work at a particular level of efficiency may not always be able to achieve this. **Idle time** may be caused by machine breakdowns or not having enough work to give to employees, perhaps because of bottlenecks in production or a shortage of orders for customers. Trenset incurs idle time through having to re-work products.

Idle time can be built into an **attainable labour hours standard** and/or adjustments can be made to the **labour budget.** If idle time is built into a budget, a greater number of hours will need to be paid than the standard time in order to produce the required number of units.

(b) **Excess idle time**

Idle time should have been (3,800 × 10%)	380	hrs
but was	430	hrs
Variance	(50)	hrs (A)
× standard rate	× $270	
Variance in $	$(13,500)	(A)

Expenditure

	$	
Expenditure should have been (3,800 × $270)	1,026,000	
but was	1,070,000	
Variance	(44,000)	(A)

(c) **Use of learning curve**

The **learning curve** can be used for forecasting production time and labour costs in certain circumstances where the workforce as a whole improves in efficiency with experience.

Impact of learning curve

Companies that use standard costing for much of their production output cannot apply standard times to output where a learning effect is taking place. This problem can be overcome in practice by:

(i) Establishing **standard times** for output, once the learning effect has worn off or become insignificant; and

(ii) Introducing a **'launch cost'** budget for the product for the duration of the learning period.

Accounting for learning effect

When learning is still taking place, it would be unreasonable to compare actual times with the standard times that ought eventually to be achieved so **allowances must be made** when interpreting labour efficiency variances. Standard costs should reflect the point that has been reached on the learning curve. When learning has become **insignificant**, standards set on the basis of this **'steady state'** will be different to when learning was taking place. If the learning rate has been wrongly calculated, this must be allowed for in the variance calculations.

(d) Cost driver rate = $28,000/500 orders = $56 per order

Order handling costs charged to products = 380 × $56 = $21,280

Actual handling costs = $27,360

Expenditure variance = $6,080 (A)

Traditional costing

Traditionally, the view has been that a fair share of overheads should be added to the cost of units produced. This fair share will **include a portion of all production overhead expenditure** and possibly administration and marketing overheads too. This is the view embodied in the principles of **absorption costing.** Fixed overheads are absorbed on the basis of a pre-determined **overhead absorption rate** which, for Trenset would probably be per machine hour. A **variance** will occur if fixed overheads are greater or smaller than the budgeted amount and/or the number of machine hours is less or more than budgeted.

Traditional costing systems, which assume that all products consume all resources in proportion to their production volumes, tend to **allocate too great a proportion of overheads to high volume products** (which cause relatively little diversity and hence use fewer support services) and **too small a proportion of overheads to low volume products** (which cause greater diversity and therefore use more support services).

ABC

All overheads within an **ABC system** are **treated as variable costs**, varying either with production levels in the short term or with some other activity such as the number of orders in this case.

Variances produced using activity based costs will allow better control of overheads which vary with activities other than the volume of production.

(e) **Controllability principle**

The **controllability principle** is that managers of responsibility centres should only be held accountable for costs over which they have some influence. From a **motivation** point of view this is important because it can be very demoralising for managers who feel that their performance is being judged on the basis of something over which they have no influence. It is also important from a **control** point of view in that control reports should ensure that information on costs is reported to the manager who is able to take action to control them.

The controllability principle can be **implemented** either by removing the uncontrollable items from the areas that managers are accountable for, or producing reports which calculate and distinguish between controllable and uncontrollable items.

For Trenset, the controllability principle means that production managers should only be held responsible for **excess** idle time, above that which is expected. For example, better training programmes could achieve a lower volume of products needing to be re-worked.

The order processing department have handled less orders than expected and this could be due to inefficiency within this department or a lower level of sales, which would not be under the control of the manager of this department.

80 The Western

Text reference. Forecasting is covered in Chapter 10 and incremental budgeting in Chapter 9.

Top tips. You should find the calculations in this question straightforward if you have practised these techniques. Don't forget to increase the costs that you calculate in part (b) by the expected inflation. Show your workings clearly and use a table to ensure you gain the maximum marks, even if you make an error in the calculations.

There are 1½ marks available per advantage and disadvantage in part (c) so make sure you make four clear points.

Easy marks. There are plenty of easy marks available throughout this question.

Examiner's comments. The most common mistake in part (a) was the use of quarter numbers 1, 2, 3 & 4 in the formula rather than 5, 6, 7 & 8.

The main problem with answers to part (b) was that a significant number of candidates used the high-low method rather than regression analysis.

Answers to part (c) were generally fine, although they would have been better if they had linked the advantages and disadvantages to local government organisations specifically, rather than writing in general terms.

Marking scheme

			Marks
(a)	Calculation of trend figures	1	
	Adjustment for seasonal variation	2	
	Total tonnage for budget	1	
			4
(b)	Completion of table with X, Y, WY and X²	4	
	Calculation of (b)	2	
	Calculation of (a)	2	
	Allowance for inflation	2	
			10
(c)	Per advantage/disadvantage	1½	
	Add marks where necessary		6
			20

(a) **Expected tonnes of waste in 20X2**

Quarter 1 20X1, Q = 1

Quarter 1 20 X 2	Q = 5, T = 2,000 + (25 x 5) = 2,125 tonnes
Quarter 2 20 X 2	Q = 6, T = 2,000 + (25 x 6) = 2,150 tonnes
Quarter 3 20 X 2	Q = 7, T = 2,000 + (25 x 7) = 2,175 tonnes
Quarter 4 20 X 2	Q = 8, T = 2,000 + (25 x 8) = 2,200 tonnes

With seasonal adjustments:

Quarter 1 20 X 2	2,125 − 200 =	1,925 tonnes
Quarter 2 20 X 2	2,150 + 250 =	2,400 tonnes
Quarter 3 20 X 2	2,175 + 150 =	2,325 tonnes
Quarter 4 20 X 2	2,200 − 100 =	2,100 tonnes
Total tonnes of waste		8,750

(b) **Regression analysis**

Tonnes x	Total cost y $'000	xy	x^2
2,100	950	1,995,000	4,410,000
2,500	1,010	2,525,000	6,250,000
2,400	1,010	2,424,000	5,760,000
2,300	990	2,277,000	5,290,000
9,300	3,960	9,221,000	21,710,000

$y = a + bx$

where a = fixed operating cost

b = variable operating cost

$$b = \frac{n\Sigma xy - \Sigma x\Sigma y}{n\Sigma x^2 - (\Sigma x)^2} \text{ and } a = \frac{\Sigma y}{n} - \frac{b\Sigma x}{n}$$

$$= \frac{(4 \times 9,221,000) - (9,300 \times 3,960)}{(4 \times 21,710,000) - (9,300)^2}$$

$$= \frac{56,000}{350,000}$$

$$= 0.16$$

$$= \$160 \text{ per tonne}$$

$$a = \frac{3,960}{4} - \frac{(0.16 \times 9,300)}{4}$$

$$= 990 - 372$$

$$= 618$$

$$= \$618,000$$

Inflation is expected to be 5%

Variable operating cost expected in 20X2 = $160 × 1.05 = **$168** per tonne

Fixed operating cost expected in 20X2 = $618,000 × 1.05 = **$648,900**

(c) **Advantages of incremental budgeting**

Incremental budgeting is a **simple approach** to a budget that everyone in the organisation should be able to understand. Local government organisations tend to be **complex** and this simplicity may be attractive.

Incremental budgeting is **less time consuming** than many other budget processes, which again may help in a complex local government organisation.

Disadvantages of incremental budgeting

Incremental budgeting encourages **slack** and **wasteful spending** to creep into budgets. A local government organisation may make sure it uses up all of this year's budget in order to ensure that next year's budget will be as high as possible. This builds in an element of **flexibility** to cope with unpredictable public service requirements.

Past inefficiencies are perpetuated because cost levels are rarely subjected to scrutiny. This can mean that taxpayers do not get **value for money**.

81 Preston Financial Services

Marking scheme

		Marks	
(a)	Financial commentary		
	Turnover growth	1	
	Profitability	1	
	Cash position	1	
	Credit management	1	
	Overall comment	1	
			5
(b)	Future performance		
	General explanation with example	2	
	Comment on each area	3	
			5
(c)	Assessment of future prospects		
	Internal business processes		
	Error rates	2	
	Not revealed to clients	1	
	Customer knowledge		
	Retention	1	
	Fee levels	1	
	Market share/size	1	
	Learning and growth		
	Lack of product range	2	
	Employee retention	2	
			10
			20

(a) **Turnover** has increased by 5%, which is higher than the 3% rate of inflation, indicating that the business has grown in real terms.

Net profits have risen by 3.9% ((187 – 180)/180 × 100%) and net profits of $187,000 for a sole practitioner look very healthy.

Net profit margin has however fallen from 20% (180/900 × 100%) to 19.8% (187/945 × 100%). This suggests either that costs have risen disproportionately or that the profit margin on fees charged has declined, perhaps due to increased competition.

Average cash balances have increased by 5% ((21 – 20)/20 × 100%) indicating that liquidity has improved and the business has a healthy cash balance.

Average trade receivables days have fallen by 4 days indicating that the business has become more efficient at collecting amounts owing from customers. The industry average is 30 days so the working capital management must be particularly effective. However, Richard Preston is apparently dominant and aggressive and the methods used to collect debts may upset customers and lose business.

In conclusion, the business is healthy and successful with just some minor concerns over margins and low growth.

(b)   **Financial performance indicators** will generally only give a measure of the **past success** of a business. There is no guarantee that a good past financial performance will lead to a good **future** financial performance. Clients may leave and costs may escalate turning past profits to losses in what can be a very short time period.

Non financial measures are often termed 'indicators of future performance'. Good results in these measures can lead to a good financial performance. For example if a business delivers good quality to its customers then this could lead to more custom at higher prices in the future.

Specifically the information in appendix 2 relates to the non financial measure within the balanced scorecard.

Internal business processes are a measure of internal efficiency. Interestingly these measures can indicate current cost efficiency as much as any future result.

Customer knowledge measures how well the business is dealing with its external customers. A good performance here is very likely to lead to more custom in the future.

Innovation and learning measures the way the business develops. New products would be reflected here along with indicators of staff retention. Again this is much more focused on the future than the present.

Measuring performance by way of non-financial means is much more likely to give an indication of the **future success** of a business.

(c)   **Internal business processes**

Error rates in jobs done have increased from 10% to 16%, possibly as a result of the reduction in the average job completion time. This is unacceptable as accuracy is a primary concern for clients of an accounting practice. Such errors could cause clients to have problems with the tax authorities, banks etc and the clients may well sue Richard for negligence.

Customer knowledge

The number of customers has fallen dramatically by 18.7% ((1,500 − 1,220)/1,500 × 100%) and this is a serious cause for concern. Existing clients are obviously not happy with the service that has been provided and the repeat work that an accountancy practice relies on has suffered.

Average fees have increased dramatically by 29% ((775 − 600)/600 × 100%) and this could explain why clients have been lost. It does also explain the increase in the turnover figure.

Market share has fallen from 20% to 14% so competitors are offering a better service and taking clients from Preston Financial Services.

Learning and growth

The percentage of revenue from non-core work is considerable lower than the industry average and has fallen from 5% to 4% compared to a growth in the industry average from 25% to 30%. It would appear that clients are wanting a wider range of services from their accountants which Richard is failing to provide.

The employee retention rate has fallen indicating that staff have become more dissatisfied and have left the business. Clients of accountancy practices like to have continuity of service and may resent having to deal with different people each year, especially as information is often private and confidential. Staff may be leaving more frequently as they have been put under pressure to complete jobs more quickly or because they want to develop their knowledge and experience in non-core work.

Conclusion

The non-financial information indicates that there are fundamental problems with the business which need to be addressed. Future prospects for growth do not look good unless Richard responds to changes in his business environment. In particular, he needs to improve the quality of the work being done and offer a wider range of services to clients.

82 Ties Only Limited

Marking scheme

			Marks
(a)	Sales	2	
	Gross profit	2	
	Website development	2	
	Administration	2	
	Distribution	1	
	Launch marketing	2	
	Overall comment	2	
	Maximum		10
(b)	Future profits comment		3
(c)	Number of tie sales	1	
	Tie price calculation	2	
	On time delivery	2	
	Returns	2	
	System down time	1	
	Summary comment	1	
	Maximum		7
			20

(a)   **Financial performance**

Sales growth

Ties Only Limited appear to have made an excellent start with initial sales of $420,000 growing by 62% ((680,000 − 420,000)/420,000 × 100%) to Quarter 2. This is particularly impressive given the acknowledged competitiveness of this business sector.

Gross profit

The gross profit margin in Quarter 1 was 52% (218,400/420,000 × 100%) and 50% (339,320/680,000 × 100%) in Quarter 2. The level of margin may be as expected for this business sector but we would need industry average data for comparison.

However, a **fall in margin** needs to be investigated. It could be that Ties Only was initially able to source cheaper ties but the rapid growth meant that alternative, more expensive suppliers had to be found. Alternatively, competitors quickly responded to this new entrant and lowered their prices in response. This pressure could have forced Ties Only to lower their prices.

Website Development

All website development costs are being **written off as incurred** so we would expect costs to be higher in the initial quarters. The website costs are over a third of total expenses, so the initial loss is mostly explained by this write-off and does not therefore give any major cause for concern.

Administration costs

Although administration costs have risen in absolute terms, as a **percentage of sales** they have **fallen** from 23.9% (100,500/420,000 × 100%) to 22.2% (150,640/680,000 × 100%). Administration costs are the second biggest expense so very important to control.

This could indicate that administration costs are being **effectively controlled** which is good news. It could also be because fixed overheads are being **spread over a larger volume** and this will continue to improve as the business grows.

Distribution costs

These costs form the **smallest proportion** of total expenses (about 6%) and the proportion of distribution costs to sales has **remained constant** at 4.9% (20,763/420,000 × 100%). These costs will be subject to external influences such as a general rise in postage costs.

Launch marketing

This is similar to the website costs as it is expected to fall once the business is established. Ties Only will need to **continue to market** their website but this is likely to be cheaper than the initial big launch marketing campaign. The negative impact on profitability will therefore reduce over time.

Other variable expenses

These have again increased in line with the sales volume and are 11.9% of sales (50,000/420,000 × 100%).

(b) **Current and future profits**

An initial look at the accounts would identify a worrying total loss of $188,303 in the first two quarters.

However, much of this loss is due to the website development costs which will not be incurred again. Websites do need to be maintained and continually improved but this cost will be much lower. Launch marketing is another initial cost which will fall rapidly. If we deduct these expenses, the business made an **underlying profit** of $47,137 in Quarter 1 and $75,360 in Quarter 2, an encouraging **upward trend**.

The initial impact of the business has been very good. There is a threat from falling margins to consider but cost control looks effective so the future is promising.

These figures illustrate that a short-term view of a new business is not necessarily a good indicator of future performance.

(c) **Non-financial performance indicators**

Average price of ties

Quarter 1: $420,000/27,631 = $15.20
Quarter 2: $680,000/38,857 = $17.50

In part (a) it was suggested that **the fall in gross profit margin** might be due to a price reduction. This data provides evidence that this is **not** the case. There must therefore be an alternative explanation.

On time delivery

This has dropped significantly from 95% to 89% and this is worrying. The service provided to customers is a **key differentiator**, especially if the company is competing on quality not price. Customers will go elsewhere if their expectations are not met. Action will need to be taken to remedy this problem.

Sales returns

This is again a key indicator of **quality** and whether **customers' expectations** are being met. Returns have risen from 12% to 18% and are now above the industry average of 13%. Returns are to be expected on Internet sales where the product may look different in reality, but a higher than average rate means that the internet is **not adequately describing and illustrating** the products. Again, quality may be less than customers expect.

Alternatively, the **pressure to dispatch orders** may be resulting in **errors** or packaging problems. Either of these reasons does not bode well for the business and action must be taken to remedy the problem.

System downtime

Customers who use shopping websites are usually **time pressured** individuals who will not react well to delays in loading pages. It is all too easy to immediately switch to a competitor's website so it is essential that system downtime is kept to an absolute minimum to **avoid lost sales**.

It would be useful to compare the figures with an **industry average** but the important point is that system downtime has **doubled**. This could be due to **pressure on the website** as a result of the volume of demand. As the website development has been such a costly and important part of the business set-up, the owners of Ties Only should have an urgent discussion with the website developers to come up with a solution.

Conclusion

Ties Only are doing well in terms of sales growth and potential profitability for a brand new business. However the owners need to focus their attention on the accuracy of order delivery, website reliability and the quality of the product. Further investigation needs to be made of the fall in gross profit margin.

83 Jump

Text references. Performance measurement is covered in Chapter 14.

Top tips. Ensure that your answer to part (b) supports both arguments. Use headings in your answer, one for each target.

Easy marks. Part (c) is relatively straight forward and is worth five marks.

Examiner's comments. Answers to part (a) were good on the whole. For a narrative requirement, part (b) was fairly well answered overall. Part (c) asked for a description of ways in which the manager could manipulate the situation in order to make sure he gets his bonus. Again, there were some good answers here, with only a minority of candidates talking about manipulating profits, which wasn't relevant to a business where profit based targets weren't being used.

Marking scheme

			Marks
(a)	Per target	2	
			6
(b)	For each target – supporting controllability	1½	
	For each target – denying controllability	1½	
			9
(c)	For each idea of manipulation	2½	
			5
			20

(a) **Bonus calculation**

	Qtr to 30 June 20X9	Qtr to 30 September 20X9	Qtr to 31 December 20X9	Qtr to 31 March 20Y0	Bonus hits
Staff on time?					
On-time %	95.5% (430/450)	94.2% (452/480)	94.0% (442/470)	95.8% (460/480)	
Bonus earned?	Yes	No	No	Yes	2

	Qtr to 30 June 20X9	Qtr to 30 September 20X9	Qtr to 31 December 20X9	Qtr to 31 March 20Y0	Bonus hits
Member visits					
Target visits	21,600 ($60\% \times 3,000 \times 12$)	23,040 ($60\% \times 3,200 \times 12$)	23,760 ($60\% \times 3,300 \times 12$)	24,480 ($60\% \times 3,400 \times 12$)	
Actual visits	20,000	24,000	26,000	24,000	
Bonus earned?	No	Yes	Yes	No	2

	Qtr to 30 June 20X9	Qtr to 30 September 20X9	Qtr to 31 December 20X9	Qtr to 31 March 20Y0	Bonus hits
Personal training					
Target visits	300 ($10\% \times 3,000$)	320 ($10\% \times 3,200$)	330 ($10\% \times 3,300$)	340 ($10\% \times 3,400$)	
Actual visits	310	325	310	339	
Bonus earned?	Yes	Yes	No	No	2

Total number of bonus hits from table above = 6

The earned by the manager is 6 x $400 = $2,400. This represents 50% of the total bonus available.

(b) It is essential that the targets set are based on elements of the job that the local managers are able to control. Targets that are based on elements that local managers are unable to influence will be seen as pointless and unrealistic and could **demotivate staff** at the local manager level.

Staff on time

Individual members of staff may be late for work as a result of external factors including home pressures or delayed public transport. Such factors cannot be controlled by the local manager. However if such problems occur on a regular basis to certain members of staff, the local manager does have the power **to amend their contract of employment**.

The way in which the local manager manages staff will impact upon how **motivated** they are to work and to arrive on time. The **local manager** has the power to **devise shift patterns** that best their team and can **reward** them accordingly through their ability to amend employment contracts.

In summary, **lateness** to work **can be controlled** by the local manager.

Personal training sessions

The local manager has control over prices charged to customers. If demand for personal training sessions falls he/she can reduce prices or make special offers in a bid to increase customer numbers.

A number of potential customers may view personal training sessions as a luxury, particularly in the current economic climate. Also, the personal training market is particularly competitive which may make it difficult for the local managers to increase sales. Local managers can take steps to improve the service offered by the sports club but any significant expenditure requires approval at Board level.

In summary, the local manager can only **partly control** the number of **personal training sessions** that are booked.

Member use of facilities

The local manager controls the staff and hence the level of customer service. It is likely that a **high level of customer service** could encourage some **members to use** the facilities **more often**. The local manager also has the ability to influence member numbers by **adjusting membership prices**.

However, external factors such as **work pressures** and level of **health** may prevent some members from visiting the club as often as they would like.

In summary, the local manager can only **partly control** the **number of member visits**.

(c) **Reduce prices**

The targets are largely volume driven and local managers have the power to **adjust membership fees** and **prices for personal training sessions**. Local managers could therefore reduce prices to ensure that they meet the targets and therefore obtain their bonus. Such a scenario would **harm** Jump's **overall profitability**.

Recording of transactions

A local manager with access to the accounting records could deliberately record visits to the club in the **incorrect period** in order to ensure that he/she achieves a bonus. For example, in Q2 the target for personal training sessions was not met by 5 sessions. The manager could record the first 5 transactions of Q3 in Q2 to ensure that he/she obtains an extra $400 bonus.

84 The Accountancy Teaching Co

Text reference. Performance measurement is covered in Chapter 14.

Top tips. At first glance, you may not know where to begin with this question! Take care to structure your answer around the headings given in the requirement and set out your workings clearly to maximise your score in each area.

Be sure to explain what your calculations mean for AT Co, to add depth to your answer. Finally, do not forget to comment on each of the non-financial performance indicators.

Easy marks. There are easy marks available throughout this question (providing you spend enough time on each heading provided in the question requirement!)

Examiner's comments. This was a typical performance measurement question. There was quite a lot of information to absorb but I strongly believe that, unless you are given plenty of information to work with, it is only possible to make very generalised, insipid comments. This is not what F5 is all about. I want candidates to be able to handle information and make some quality analysis about it. It requires common sense and ability to link information. Needless to say, answers were poor. Anyone who had read my article on this area, or indeed my predecessor's article on this area, would know that insipid comments such as 'turnover decreased by 8.3%, which is poor' will score only a calculation mark, for working out the 8.3%. Is this decrease in turnover poor? Well, it depends on the market in which the company is operating. You have to read the scenario. When you take into account the fact that there has been a 20% decline in the demand for accountancy training, AT Co's 8.3% looks relatively good. You must link information; this is an essential skill for any accountant. Nothing is ever what it seems...ask any auditor!

Let me also take the opportunity to distinguish between an acceptable comment, which might earn one mark, compared to a good point, which might earn two marks. Cost of sales fell by $10.014m in the year. Part of this reduction was down to a fall in freelance lecture costs. A good candidate would have commented that, whilst the company requested that freelance lecturers reduce their fees by 10%, the actual fee reduction gained was 15%, a strong performance. A comment such as this would have earned two marks. A less observant comment, earning one mark, would have been that the reduction in cost of sales was partly due to the fact that the company requested freelance lecturers to reduce their fees by 10%.

I hope that this question will serve as a good revision question to future examinees of F5. The information given is there to help you make worthwhile comments. When planning the question, you should annotate it carefully, cross-referencing different parts of the question, linking financial and non-financial information etc.

		Marks
Turnover:		
8.3% decrease	½	
Actual turnover 14.6% higher	½	
Performed well CF market conditions	1	
Transfer of students	1	
		3
Cost of sales:		
19.2% decrease	½	
63.7% of turnover	½	
15% fee reduction from freelance staff	2	
Other costs of sale fell by $3.555m	2	
Online marking did not save as much as planned	1	
		Max 5
Gross profit – numbers and comment	1	
Indirect expenses:		
Marketing costs:		
42.1% increase	½	
Increase necessary to reap benefits of developments	1	
Benefits may take more than one year to be felt	½	
Property costs – stayed the same	½	
Staff training:		
163.9% increase	½	
Necessary for staff retention	1	
Necessary to train staff on new website etc	1	
Without training, staff would have left	1	
Less student complaints	1	
Interactive website and student helpline:		
Attracted new students	1	
Increase in pass rate	1	
Enrolment costs:		
Fall of 80.9%	½	
Result of electronic system being introduced	1	
Reduced number of late enrolments	1	
		Max 9
Net operating profit:		
Fallen to $2.106	½	
Difficult market	1	
Staff training costs should decrease in the future	1	
Future increase in market share	1	
Lower advertising cost in future	1	
Charge for website	1	
		Max 3
		20

Turnover

Turnover has decreased by 8.3% from $72·025 million in 20X9 to $66·028 million in 20Y0. Given the 20% **decline in demand for accountancy training**, AT Co's turnover would have been expected to fall to $57·62m in line with market conditions. As such, it would appear that **AT has performed well in a tough market as it's actual turnover is 14·6% higher than expected**.

Non-financial performance indicators show that the number of students who transferred to AT from an alternative training provider in has increased to 20% in 20Y0 (from 8% in 20X9). This **increase in market share** is likely to be directly linked to **the improved service provided to students** as a result of the new student helpline and interactive website as well as other developments.

Cost of sales

Cost of sales has decreased by 19·2% from $52.078m in 20X9 to $42.056m in 20Y0. In 20X9, cost of sales represented 72·3% of turnover and in 20Y0 this figure was 63·7%. The reasons for this substantial decrease are considered below.

Freelance costs in 20X9 were $14·582m. Given that a minimum 10% reduction in fees had been requested to freelance lecturers and the number of courses run by them was the same year on year, the expected cost for freelance lecturers in 20Y0 was $13·124m. The **reduction in costs was successful** as actual costs were $12·394m (a reduction of 15%).

Prior to any cost cuts and **assuming a consistent cost of sales to turnover ratio**, costs of sales for 20Y0 were expected to be $47·738m. The actual cost of sales was $5·682m lower at $42.056m. Freelance lecturer costs fell by $2·188m, meaning that the remaining $3·494m is made up of decreases in other costs of sale.

Employees were told they would not receive a pay rise for at least one year and the average number of employees hardly changed year on year. As such, **the decreased costs are unlikely to be related to staff costs**.

The introduction of the **electronic marking system was expected to save the company $4m**. It is possible that the system did not save as much as predicted, hence the $3·494m fall. Alternatively, the saved marking costs may have been partially counteracted by an increase in another cost included in cost of sales.

Gross profit

As a result of the increased market share and cost savings discussed above, the **gross profit margin has increased** in 20Y0 from 27·7% to 36·3%.

Indirect expenses

Marketing costs

AT Co has increased spend on marketing campaigns to make students aware of the improved service and the range of facilities that the company offer. As such, marketing costs have increased by 42·1% in 20Y0. It would appear that the marketing campaigns have been a success, with higher student numbers relative to the competition in 20Y0. It is important to recognise the time lag between the cost outlay and the benefit received from such campaigns. It is likely that many of the benefits will not be felt until 20Y1.

Property costs

Property costs have remained in line with 20X9, indicating no significant investment in company premises.

Staff training

Training costs have increased dramatically from $1.287m in 20X9 to $3.396m in 20Y0, an increase of 163.9%. In 20X9 and before, AT Co had experienced problems with staff retention which resulted in a lower quality service being provided to students.

Considerable time and money is likely to have been spent on training staff to use the new interactive website as well as the electronic enrolment and marking systems. If the company had not spent this money on essential training, the quality of service would have deteriorated further and more staff would have left as they became increasingly dissatisfied with their jobs.

The number of student complaints has fallen dramatically in 20Y0 to 84 from 315, indicating that the staff training appears to have improved the quality of service being provided to students.

Interactive website and the student helpline

Interactive website and student helpline costs have not been incurred in previous years and have arisen from the drive towards providing students with an improved service and to increase pass rates. The percentage of students passing exams first time increased from 48% in 20X9 to 66% in 20Y0 which would suggest that the developments have improved the student learning environment.

Enrolment costs

Enrolment costs have fallen by $4.072m (80.9%), largely due to the new electronic enrolment system that was launched in 20Y0. It is likely that the new system has contributed to the reduction in late enrolments from 297 in 20X9 to106 in 20Y0.

Net operating profit

Net operating profit has fallen from $3.635m to $2.106m (42%). Whilst this is a significant decrease, AT Co has been operating in tough market conditions in 20Y0. The company may have considered charging students a fee to use the interactive website in order to recoup some of the funds invested. This would have increased net operating profit.

Going forward, staff training costs are likely to decrease as staff become familiar with the new developments and staff retention improves. Higher pass rates are likely to attract more students in the coming years which will further increase market share.

As the AT brand becomes established in the market, it is likely that fewer advertising campaigns will take place, resulting in lower marketing costs.

Workings (Note: All workings are in $'000)

1   *Turnover*

Decrease in turnover = $72,025 – $66,028/$72,025 = 8.3%

Expected 20Y0 turnover given 20% decline in market = $72,025 x 80% = $57,620

Actual 20Y0 turnover CF expected = $66,028 – $57,620/$57,620 = 14.6% higher

2   *Cost of sales*

Decrease in cost of sales = $42,056 – $52,078/$52,078 = 19.2%

Cost of sales as percentage of turnover: 20X9 = $52,078/$72,025 = 72.3%

20Y0 = $42,056/$66,028 = 63.7%

3   *Freelance staff costs*

In 20X9 = $41,663 × 35% = $14,582

Expected cost for 2010 = $14,582 × 90% = $13,124

Actual 20Y0 cost = $12,394

$12,394 – $14,582 = $2,188 decrease

$2,188/$14,582 = 15% decrease in freelancer costs

4   *Expected cost of sales for 20Y0*

Before costs cuts, = $66,028 × 72.3% = $47,738

Actual cost of sales = $42,056

Difference = $5,682, of which $2,188 relates to freelancer savings and $3,494 relates to other savings.

5   *Gross profit margin*

20X9: $19,947/$72,025 = 27.7%

20Y0: $23,972/$66,028 = 36.3%

6   *Increase in marketing costs*

$4,678 – $3,291/$3,291 = 42.1%

7   *Increase in staff training costs*

$3,396 – $1,287/$1,287 = 163·9%

8   *Decrease in enrolment costs*

$960 – 5,032/5,032 = 80·9%

9   *Net operating profit*

Decreased from $3,635 to $2,106. This is fall of 1,529/3,635 = 42·1%

85 Bridgewater Co

Text references. Performance measurement is covered in Chapter 14.

Top tips. The key to success in this type of question is reading the information in the question very carefully and making full use of it. When the examiner asks for 'comment', he requires an opinion not simply a re-statement of the proposals.

Easy marks. For half marks in part (a) all that was expected was a statement (with simple supporting calculations) of whether or not the manager would meet each of the targets.

Examiner's comments. Candidates must be able to assess performance which means interpret financial and other data and make sensible comments on it. Few candidates realised that the division's improving performance in Quarters 3 and 4 came too late for the promotion at the end of Quarter 2. Many only commented on the profits of the division and ignored all the other targets. Many also assessed the performance more generally, calculating amongst other things % margins and ignored the targets altogether. This was very disappointing.

Part b) was also poorly performed and misreading the question was common. Candidates must learn to read performance management questions more carefully.

For Part c) candidates answers primarily consisted of a re-statement of the different steps being proposed with little or no comment at all. A comment requires opinion and anything sensible scored marks.

Candidates should prepare themselves to assess the performance of a business, both financially and non-financially if they want to pass.

Marking scheme

			Marks
(a)	Per target discussed	2	
			8
(b)	Revised forecasts		
	Voucher sales effect	1	
	Vista sales effect	2	
	Extra trainer cost	1	
	Extra room hire cost	1	
	Staff training increase	½	
	Software cost	½	
	Overall revised profit calculation	1	
	Maximum		6
(c)	Per idea commented on	2	
			Max 6
			20

(a) **Each quarter, sales should grow and annual sales should exceed budget**

In the Northwest division, sales are forecasted to fall by 10% ($4/40 \times 100\%$) from Quarter 1 to Quarter 2 but then start to grow. Average growth per quarter over the year is 14.5% ($\sqrt[3]{(60/40) - 1}$). Annual sales are forecast to exceed the sales budget by $6,000 ($186 - 180$).

It would therefore appear that the annual **target will be met**. However, the promotion decision is to be taken in Quarter 3 and the **slow start** to the year may not reflect well on the manager of the Northwest division.

Trainer costs should not exceed $180 per teaching day

The manager is paying $200 ($8,000/40$) per teaching day in trainer costs which **exceeds the target**. He believes in quality and therefore appears to be paying more to attract better teaching staff. This may well improve sales in the long-term as the reputation for quality delivery becomes known, but it is at the expense of increased costs in the short-term.

Room hire costs should not exceed $90 per teaching day

The manager of this division is also **spending more** on room hire costs than the target. He is spending $100 per teaching day rather than $90. This could be again part of his quality improvement policy as he is hiring better facilities, but it could also be due to poor negotiation and buying strategy.

Each division should meet its budget for profit per quarter and annually

The achievement of this target suffers from the same problem as the sales target. The manager will meet the target for the year by $2,500, but is **below target** in the first two quarters.

This again will impact on his promotion prospects which overall are not looking good. He is failing to meet any of the targets in the first two quarters and will have to hope that the senior managers agree with his **long-term** rather than **short-termist** approach.

(b) **Revised forecasts**

	Q1 $'000	Q2 $'000	Q3 $'000	Q4 $'000	Total $'000
Existing sales	40.0	36.0	50.0	60.0	186.0
Voucher sales ($125 \times 80/4$)	2.5	2.5	2.5	2.5	10.0
Software training			10.0	12.0	22.0
	42.5	38.5	62.5	74.5	218.0
Less:					
Existing trainer costs	8.0	7.2	10.0	12.0	37.2
Additional training costs ($200 \times$ teaching days)			2.0	2.4	4.4
Room hire	4.0	3.6	5.0	6.0	18.6
Additional room hire ($100 \times$ teaching days)			1.0	1.2	2.2
Staff training	1.0	1.0	1.0	1.0	4.0
Additional staff training	0.5	0.5			1
Other costs	3.0	1.7	6.0	7.0	17.7
Software	1.8				1.8
Forecast net profit	24.2	24.5	37.5	44.9	131.1
Original budget profit	25.0	26.0	27.0	28.0	106.0

(c) **Voucher scheme**

The voucher scheme looks like a good idea as the manager is confident that the take-up would be good and customers would follow his advice to attend one session per quarter. This will **increase revenue** without incurring additional costs as customers would attend existing planned courses. However, some additional unforeseen costs may still be incurred.

The additional revenue and profit will help, but targets for Quarters 1 and 2 will still not be met so the voucher scheme will not necessarily improve the manager's promotion prospects.

There is always the danger with offering a discount that **existing customers** will be disgruntled, particularly if they have already paid a higher price for a course that is now being offered at a discount. The vouchers are however only being offered to **new** customers so the manager should be able to offer this promotion without upsetting existing customers.

Software upgrade

It is essential that a software training company uses the **latest software technology** on its courses. The investment in software and staff training is therefore a **necessity** and cannot be avoided.

The courses will generate **extra revenue** but not until Quarters 3 and 4. This software upgrade will therefore further damage the achievement of targets in Quarters 1 and 2, as costs will rise but the extra revenue will be too late for the promotion assessment.

It is to be hoped that the senior managers will recognise the essential long-term planning being undertaken.

Delaying payments to trainers

This is not a good idea. None of the performance targets will be affected, as the plan will not affect costs or profits. The only positive impact will be on **cash flow**. The worrying aspect is the negative impact it may have on **relationships with trainers**. Software training is a competitive market and good trainers will be in demand by a number of training providers. If the company is to offer quality training, it must have the best trainers and this is not the way to retain them.

In conclusion, if all the proposals were taken together, they will **not improve** the manager's chance of promotion as any benefits will accrue after Quarter 2.

86 PC

Text reference. Performance measurement is covered in Chapters 14 and 15.

Top tips. This is the style of performance measurement question that we have come to expect from this examiner with a financial performance measure giving a misleading picture of a company's performance. Use a clear layout for your calculations and headings to give a structure to your discussions and explanations. Each part of the question can be answered separately so if you get stuck or are unsure what is required, move on.

Easy marks. The calculations are straightforward provided you are happy with calculating ROI and there are plenty of marks available for common sense explanations.

Examiner's comments. Many candidates scored reasonable marks in part (a) but in part (b) few candidates understood how performance can be manipulated with most only suggesting depreciation. Far too few suggested accruals and tampering with sales timing. Part (c) was reasonably attempted but layout was not always in columnar format or neatly done.

Marking scheme

			Marks
(a)	Sales calculation	1	
	Sales revenue assessment	1	
	Gross margin calculation	1	
	Gross margin assessment	1	
	Overhead control and flexibility	1	
	ROI calculation	1	
	ROI comment	2	
			8
(b)	Timing of decision problem	1	
	Revenue acceleration	1	
	Delay of cost (½ per example)	1	
	Manipulation of accounting policy	1	
			4

(c)
Sales volume	1
Sales price	1
Sales revenue	1
Gross profit Year 1	½
Gross profit Year 2	½
Gross profit Year 3	½
Gross profit Year 4	½
Overhead included	1
Investment values	1
ROI calculations	1

$$\frac{8}{20}$$

(a) **Calculation of performance measures**

	20X5	20X6	20X7	20X8
ROI (net profit/net assets × 100%)	13.0%	17.5%	16.7%	20.0%
Gross profit margin (gross profit/sales × 100%)	40%	35%	35%	30%
Net profit margin (net profit/sales × 100%)	6.5%	7.0%	5.6%	4.7%
Change in sales	–	0%	-10%	-5.6%
Overheads (Gross – net profit)	$67,000	$56,000	$53,000	$43,000

ROI

The **target ROI** is 15% and this has been achieved every year apart from 20X5. This looks impressive but it is **not due** to increasing profits. **Net assets have fallen in value** each year due to depreciation. It is this fall which has compensated for the fall in net profits and enabled the target ROI to be achieved.

Change in sales

The market in which PC operates has been growing steadily but **sales revenues have been declining** in store W. This is a worrying sign and indicates that PC is either failing to compete effectively or is reducing selling prices.

Gross profit margin

PC's stores typically generate a 40% gross profit margin and this has only been achieved in 20X5. This could be due to reduced selling prices or an increase in the cost of sales, for example increased labour costs. As sales revenue has fallen, it looks like **sales prices have been reduced** in an effort to improve sales.

Overheads

Overheads have been **reducing** year on year and this is usually considered to be positive, especially as sales have fallen. However, the cost cutting could have damaged customers' experiences in the store and contributed to the decline in sales.

Net profit margin

Even though overheads have been reduced, net profit margin has still been **falling**. This is again primarily due to the fall in gross margin.

Conclusion

The positive ROI information **fails to reflect** the true performance of store W. Profitability and sales revenue have declined and it seems hard to justify awarding a bonus to the manager of store W based on an inappropriate performance measure.

(b) The manager's aim would be to **just hit** the target 15% each year rather than exceed the target in one year and fail to meet it in another.

The manager would not have been awarded a bonus in 20X5 because ROI was below the target. In order to gain the bonus in 20X5 he would have had to manipulate the results so that $2,000 less profit was made in 20X6 and more in 20X5.

Manipulation methods

Accelerate revenue by allocating sales made early in 20X6 to 20X5. This could be achieved by dating an invoice when an order is received in late 20X5 but not actually sending it to the customer until delivery is made in 20X6.

Delay costs by not recording suppliers' invoices until 20X6, even though goods were received in 20X5.

Manipulate provisions and accruals so that less costs are charged in 20X5.

Manipulate accounting policies such as inventory values or depreciation charges so that more profit is made in 20X5. For example, closing inventory could be overstated.

(c)

	Year 1 $	Year 2 $	Year 3 $	Year 4 $
Sales revenue (W1)	216,000	237,600	248,292	235,877
Variable costs (W2)	129,600	142,560	156,816	156,816
Gross profit	86,400	95,040	91,476	79,061
Overheads	70,000	70,000	80,000	80,000
Net profit	16,400	25,040	11,476	(939)
Non-current assets (W3)	100,000	75,000	50,000	25,000
ROI	16.4%	33.4%	23.0%	-3.8%

Workings

1 Sales

	Year 1	Year 2	Year 3	Year 4
Sales volume (units)	18,000	$18,000 \times 1.1 = 19,800$	$19,800 \times 1.1 = 21,780$	21,780
Sales price ($)	12.00	12.00	$12.00 \times 0.95 = 11.40$	$11.40 \times 0.95 = 10.83$
Sales revenue ($)	216,000	237,600	248,292	235,877

2 *Variable costs*

In 20X5:

Gross profit = 40% × $216,000 = $86,400

Sales – variable costs = gross profit

$216,000 – variable costs = $86,400

Variable costs = 216,000 – 86,400 = 129,600

Variable cost per unit = 129,600/18,000 = $7.20

	Year 1	Year 2	Year 3	Year 4
Sales volume (units)	18,000	19,800	21,780	21,780
Variable cost (× $7.20)	129,600	142,560	156,816	156,816

3 *Non-current assets*

Depreciate by 25% of cost per annum = $25,000

87 Oliver's Salon

Text references. Performance measurement is covered in Chapter 14.

Top tips. This is quite a long scenario with lots of information to deal with. In part (a) you need to use the sales value and the number of client visits to calculate the average price. Part (b) relates only to financial performance so a range of ratios need to be calculated and explained. The approach to use is to calculate a ratio (½ mark), make a qualitative statement (1 mark) and suggest a cause or some other comment (1 mark).

Part (c) gives you the headings to give a structure to your answer. Quality and resource utilisation are two of the dimensions in the Building Block Model. The question does not ask for recommendations for Oliver so make sure you stick to the requirements of the question.

Easy marks. The ratio analysis in part (b) has plenty of easy marks available but make sure you do more than just calculate the ratios.

Examiner's comments. A significant number of candidates could not calculate the prices for female and male clients in the two years in question. In part (b) there was some improvement in candidate's ability to assess performance. There were problems however: Mathematical descriptions are not performance assessments; simply stating the % increases in numbers is not enough; indicating the absolute change in a cost is rarely that useful; too narrow a range of figures considered, virtually all the numbers in the question carry marks.

In part (c) answers on quality dealt with the complaints issue well, but very few talked about the new members of staff and how their performance might be suspect. The lack of a pay rise can be de-motivating and so quality might suffer, this too was rarely picked up.

On resource utilisation candidates had a mixed result. The male throughput per specialist was very high but this was perhaps due to the fact that male hair tends to be easier (quicker) to cut. The female situation was different, with fewer clients for more staff. Many candidates recognised this. Very few talked about the property utilisation at all.

Marking scheme

			Marks
(a)	Average price for male customers	1	
	Average price for female customers	2	
			3
(b)	Sales growth	3	
	Gross margin	3	
	Rent	1½	
	Advertising spend	1	
	Staff costs	1½	
	Electricity	1	
			11
(c)	Quality – single gender	1	
	Quality – wage levels	1	
	Quality – other	1	
	Resource utilisation – property	1	
	Resource utilisation – staff	1	
	Resource utilisation – other	1	
			6
			20

(a) **Average price for hair services per female client**

    20X8: Sales = $200,000
             Number of female client visits = 8,000
             Average price = 200,000/8,000
                            = $25

    20X9: Prices were not increased so average price is still $25

Average price for hair services per male client

    20X8: No male clients

    20X9: Sales = $238,500

             Female sales = $25 × 6,800 visits
                         = $170,000

             Male sales = 238,500 – 170,000
                   = $68,500

             Average price = 68,500/3,425
                             = $20

(b) **Financial performance**

Sales growth

Sales have grown by 19.25% ((238,500 – 200,000)/200,000 × 100%) from 20X8 to 20X9. This is particularly impressive as Oliver's Salon experiences high levels of competition.

This growth has come from the new **male hairdressing** part of the business as female sales have fallen by 15% ((200,000 – 170,000)/200,000 × 100%). There was **no price increase** during this time so this fall is due to less female client visits.

Gross profit

The gross profit margin in 20X8 was 53% (106,000/200,000 × 100%) and in 20X9 had **fallen** to 47.2% (112,500/238,500 × 100%). This is predominantly due to a 40% ((91,000 – 65,000)/65,000 × 100%) in **staff costs** as a result of the recruitment of two new staff.

The new specialist hairdresser for male clients is on a salary of $17,000 (91,000 – 65,000 – 9,000) whereas the female hairdressers were paid an average of $16,250 (65,000/4) in 20X8.

However it is the **female client** business which has been responsible for the drop in gross profit margin.

	20X8 Female $	20X9 Female $	20X9 Male $
Sales	200,000	170,000	68,500
Less cost of sales:			
Hairdressing staff	(65,000)	(74,000)	(17,000)
Hair products – female	(29,000)	(27,000)	
Hair products – male			(8,000)
Gross profit	106,000	69,000	43,500
Gross profit margin	106/200 × 100% = 53%	69/170 × 100% = 40.6%	43.5/68.5 × 100% = 63.5%

The gross profit margin from male clients is higher than for female clients.

Rent

This has not changed so is a **fixed cost** at the moment.

Administration salaries

These have increased by only 5.6% ((9,500 – 9,000)/9,000 × 100%) which is impressive given the expansion in the business.

Electricity

This has increased by 14.3% ((8,000 − 7,000)/7,000 × 100%. More clients would involve more electricity so it is a **semi-variable cost**. There may also have been a **general increase** in electricity prices which would be beyond the control of Oliver.

Advertising

This has increased by 150%((5,000 − 2,000)/2,000 × 100%) which could be expected at the **launch of a new service**. Provided the advertising has generated new clients, it should not be a cause for concern.

Net profit

Net profit has only increased by 2.6% ((80,000 − 78,000/78,000 × 100%) which is disappointing compared to a 19.25% increase in sales.

(c)   **Non-financial performance**

Quality

The number of complaints has increased significantly by 283% ((46 − 12)/12 × 100%). This is not just due to the increase in client numbers.

Complaints per customer visit have increased from 0.15% (12/8,000 × 100%) to 0.44%. This is a cause for concern in a service business, especially as many customers will not actually complain but will just not come back.

The complaints could be from the new male clients who are not happy with the new hairdresser, or they could be from female clients who do not like having men in the salon. More information is needed and action to be taken to reduce the complaints.

Resource utilisation

The resources in Oliver's Salon are the **salon** itself and the **staff**. The salon is being utilised more as a result of the increase in clients from 8,000 in 20X8 to 10,225 (6,800 + 3,425) in 20X9. This is a 27.8% ((10,225 − 8,000)/8,000 × 100%) increase. This increase in utilisation has not however resulted in a proportionate increase in profit.

The **female specialist hairdressers** served 2,000 (8,000/4) clients per specialist in 20X8 and this fell to 1,360 (6,800/50) in 20X9, following the recruitment of two new staff. Oliver may be prepared to accept this reduction in resource utilisation in order to boost service levels and reduce complaints.

This contrasts with the higher figure of 3,425 clients per **male specialist** in 20X9. The time taken per male client is much less so this should be expected.

88 Thatcher International Park

Text reference. Performance measurement is covered in Chapter 13.

Top tips. This is a classic performance measurement question from this examiner with a contrast between the picture painted by financial indicators and that given by non-financial indicators. Start with the ratio calculations and then make sure that you fully analyse what the numbers are telling you. Use headings for each indicator to make it easy for the marker.

Easy marks. This type of question should be familiar to you by now and give plenty of opportunities to score easy marks.

Examiner's comments. Overall, I would say that the quality of answers to this question were poor. Too often, candidates made all their points about the non-financial factors in part (a) to the detriment of ignoring some of the financial factors and then simply repeated themselves in part (b).

Many candidates did not read the requirement to part (b) carefully and never got as far as mentioning the risks properly.

		Marks	
(a)	Sales growth	3	
	Maintenance	3	
	Directors pay	2	
	Wages	2	
	Net profit	2	
	Return on assets	2	
			14
(b)	Reliability of rides	2	
	Average queuing time	2	
	Each risk (1 mark per risk)	2	
			6
			20

(a) **Financial analysis**

	20X1	20X2
Average admission price	$5,250,000/150,000 = $35 per person	$5,320,000/140,000 = $38 per person
Return on assets	1,045/13,000 × 100% = 8.03%	1,372/12,000 × 100% = 11.4%

Sales growth

Sales have **increased** by 1·3% ((5,320 – 5,250)/5,250 × 100%)) which is a little **above** the rate of inflation of 1%. However, **average admission prices** have increased by 8·6% ((38 – 35)/35 × 100%) and the **numbers of visitors** have fallen by 6.7% ((150,000 – 140,000)/150,000) indicating there are problems. The increases in admission prices have been **unpopular with customers** so it is unlikely that the rate of increase is sustainable or even justifiable.

Maintenance and repairs

A decision has been made to **reduce routine maintenance** where possible and costs have fallen by 12.5% ((80,000 – 70,000)/80,000 × 100%). This has impacted on costs of repairs which have increased by 23% ((320,000 – 260,000)/260,000 × 100%). This approach is therefore **not saving any money** as the combined cost of maintenance and repair is **higher** in 20X2 than in 20X1.

Directors' remuneration

Directors' salaries have increased by 6·7% ((160,000 – 150,000)/150,000 × 100%) which is well above inflation. **Bonus levels** have also increased in absolute terms by 20% ((18,000 – 15,000)/15,000 × 100%) and also as a percentage of turnover. The directors have some form of **profit related pay scheme** which has rewarded them for the improved profit performance.

Wages

Wages have **fallen** by 12% ((2,500 – 2,200)/2,500 × 100%). If at least part of the wages cost is **variable**, this may be due to reduced customer numbers. It may also be that the directors are reducing staff levels **beyond** the fall in the level of customers to enhance short-term profit and directors' bonuses. This could have a detrimental effect on customer service and possibly safety.

Net profit

Net profit has **increased** by 31·3% ((1,372 – 1,045)/1,045 × 100%). This is a significant increase which the owners are probably pleased with. Net profit is a very **traditional measure** of performance and most would say this was a sign of good performance.

Return on assets

The return on assets has **increased** considerably from 8% to 11·4%. This measures profit relative to the assets that are being used to generate the profit. The increase is therefore partly due to the significant rise in profit and partly due to the fall in asset value. TIP has **cut back** on new development so the fall in asset value is probably due to depreciation being charged with little being spent during the year on assets.

It is therefore questionable whether this indicates good performance, particularly in the long-term.

(b) **Quality of service**

Reliability of the rides

The **hours lost to breakdown** of rides has increased significantly from 9,000 to 32,000 hours. The capacity of the park in terms of rides is 180,000 hours (360 days × 50 rides × 10 hours per day). The **percentage of capacity lost due to breakdowns** has increased from 5% in 20X1 (9,000/180,000 × 100%) to 17·8% in 20X2 (32,000/180,000 × 100%).

This increase in unreliability will inevitably lead to **customer dissatisfaction and disappointment**. The fixed admission price becomes even less value for money when some rides are not available.

Average queuing time

Theme park customers will usually accept they have to queue for certain rides at peak times. However an increase of 10 minutes (or 50%) in queuing time is likely to be **noticeable** and will not please customers.

The increase is probably due to the high number of hours lost due to breakdown as there are fewer rides to choose from.

Risks

The **lack of routine maintenance** could lead to an accident or injury to a customer. This could result in an expensive compensation payment and damage to the theme park's reputation.

Customers could become disgruntled at the increased prices without the excitement of new thrill rides and general deterioration in their enjoyment of the theme park. They could choose to go to **alternative** theme parks or leisure attractions. If customer numbers fall then so will profit and the **long- term result** of the policies could be a fall in bonuses for directors and rewards for the owners.

Mock exams

ACCA

Paper F5

Performance Management

Mock Examination 1

Question Paper	
Reading and planning	*15 minutes*
Writing	*3 hours*
ALL FIVE questions are compulsory and MUST be attempted	

DO NOT OPEN THIS PAPER UNTIL YOU ARE READY TO START UNDER EXAMINATION CONDITIONS

ACCA

Paper F5

Performance Management

Mock Examination 1

Question paper		
Time allowed		
Reading and planning		15 minutes
Writing		3 hours

ALL FIVE questions are compulsory and MUST be attempted.

All FIVE questions are compulsory and MUST be attempted

Question 1

Admer owns several home furnishing stores. In each store, consultations, if needed, are undertaken by specialists, who also visit potential customers in their homes, using specialist software to help customers realise their design objectives. Customers visit the store to make their selections from the wide range of goods offered, after which sales staff collect payment and raise a purchase order. Customers then collect their self-assembly goods from the warehouse, using the purchase order as authority to collect. Administration staff process purchase orders and also arrange consultations.

Each store operates an absorption costing system and costs other than the cost of goods sold are apportioned on the basis of sales floor area.

Results for one of Admer's stores for the last three months are as follows:

Department	Kitchens	Bathrooms	Dining Rooms	Total
	$	$	$	$
Sales	210,000	112,500	440,000	762,500
Cost of goods sold	63,000	37,500	176,000	276,500
Other costs	130,250	81,406	113,968	325,624
Profit	16,750	(6,406)	150,032	160,376

The management accountant of Admer is concerned that the bathrooms department of the store has been showing a loss for some time, and is considering a proposal to close the bathrooms department in order to concentrate on the more profitable kitchens and dining rooms departments. He has found that other costs for this store for the last three months are made up of:

	$	Employees
Sales staff wages	64,800	12
Consultation staff wages	24,960	4
Warehouse staff wages	30,240	6
Administration staff wages	30,624	4
General overheads (light, heat, rates, etc.)	175,000	
	325,624	

He has also collected the following information for the last three months:

Department	Kitchens	Bathrooms	Dining Rooms
Number of items sold	1,000	1,500	4,000
Purchase orders	1,000	900	2,500
Floor area (square metres)	16,000	10,000	14,000
Number of consultations	798	200	250

The management accountant believes that he can use this information to review the store's performance in the last three months from an activity-based costing (ABC) perspective.

Required

(a) Produce a profit statement using activity based costing from the information provided. **(8 marks)**

(b) Evaluate and discuss the proposal to close the bathrooms department. **(6 marks)**

(c) Discuss the advantages and disadvantages that may arise for Admer from introducing activity-based costing in its stores. **(6 marks)**

(Total = 20 marks)

BPP
LEARNING MEDIA

Question 2

(a) A large manufacturing company is investigating the cost of sickness amongst production workers who have been employed by the company for more than one year. The following regression equation, based on a random sample of 50 such production workers, was derived for 20X5.

$$y = 15.6 - 1.2x$$

y represents the number of days absent in a year because of sickness and x represents the number of years employment with the company.

Required

(i) Explain the meaning of each component of the regression equation **(2 marks)**

(ii) Predict the number of days absence through sickness to be expected of an employee who has been with the company for eight years. **(2 marks)**

(iii) Discuss any limitations or problems of using this equation in practice. **(4 marks)**

(b) A statistician is carrying out an analysis of a company's production output. The output varies according to the season of the year and, from the data, she has calculated the following seasonal variations, in units of production.

	Spring	Summer	Autumn	Winter
Year 1			+ 11.2	+ 23.5
Year 2	− 9.8	− 28.1	+ 12.5	+ 23.7
Year 3	− 7.4	− 26.3	+ 11.7	

Required

(i) Calculate the average seasonal variation for each season and explain what this means.

(ii) If the trend output in the winter of Year 3 is expected to be 10,536 units, what is the forecast output? **(4 marks)**

(c) The Valuation Department of a large firm of surveyors wishes to develop a method of predicting its total costs in a period. The following past costs have been recorded at two activity levels.

	Number of valuations (V)	Total cost (TC)
Period 1	420	82,200
Period 2	515	90,275

Required

(i) Derive a formula for the total cost model for a period. **(4 marks)**

(ii) Evaluate the usefulness of the high low method. **(4 marks)**

(Total = 20 marks)

Question 3

(a) A major information source within many businesses is a system of standard costing and variance analysis.

Required

(i) Describe briefly four purposes of a system of standard costing. **(4 marks)**

(ii) Comment on whether standard costing applies in both manufacturing and service businesses and how it be may be affected by modern initiatives of continuous performance improvement and cost reduction. **(4 marks)**

PS Co manufactures two products, the W and the S.

The accountant of the company has provided the following commentary on the results for the last accounting period.

'To produce a W we use 5 kg of X and our plans were based on a cost of X of $3 per kg. Due to market movements the actual price changed and if we had purchased efficiently the cost would have been $4.50 per kg.

Production of W was 2,000 units and usage of X amounted to 10,800 kg at a total cost of $51,840.

An S uses raw material Z but again the price of this can change rapidly. It was thought that Z would cost $30 per tonne but in fact we only paid $25 per tonne and if we had purchased correctly the cost would have been less as it was freely available at only $23 per tonne. It usually takes 1.5 tonnes of Z to produce one S but our production of 500 S used only 700 tonnes of Z.'

Required

(b)   Analyse the material variances for both products, utilising the following.

   (i)   Traditional variance analysis.
   (ii) An approach which distinguishes between planning and operational variances.   **(12 marks)**

                                                                                   (Total = 20 marks)

Question 4

Lewisville is a town with a population of 100,000 people. The town council of Lewisville operates a bus service which links all parts of the town with the town centre. The service is non-profit seeking and its mission statement is 'to provide efficient, reliable and affordable public transport to all the citizens of Lewisville.' Attempting to achieve this mission often involves operating services that would be considered uneconomic by private sector bus companies, due either to the small number of passengers travelling on some routes or the low fares charged. The majority of the town council members are happy with this situation as they wish to reduce traffic congestion and air pollution on Lewisville's roads by encouraging people to travel by bus rather than by car.

However, one member of the council has recently criticised the performance of the Lewisville bus service as compared to those operated by private sector bus companies in other towns. She has produced the following information:

Lewisville bus service
SUMMARISED INCOME AND EXPENDITURE ACCOUNT
YEAR ENDING 31 MARCH 20X6

	$'000	$'000
Passenger fares		1,200
Staff wages	600	
Fuel	300	
Depreciation	280	
		1,180
Surplus		20

SUMMARISED STATEMENT OF FINANCIAL POSITION AS AT
31 MARCH 20X6.

	$'000	$'000
Non-current assets (net)		2,000
Current assets		
Inventory	240	
Cash	30	
	270	
Less creditors (suppliers) due within one year	60	
Net current assets		210
Total assets less liabilities		2,210
Ordinary share capital ($1 shares)		2,000
Reserves		210
		2,210

OPERATING STATISTICS FOR THE YEAR ENDED
31 MARCH 20X6

Total passengers carried	2,400,000 passengers
Total passenger miles traveled	4,320,000 passenger miles

Private sector bus companies industry average ratios
Year ended 31 March 20X6.

Return on capital employed	10%
Return on sales (net margin)	30%
Asset turnover (revenue)	0.33 times
Average cost per passenger mile	37.4c

Required

(a)   Calculate four ratios to compare the performance of Lewisville bus service with industry averages.

(4 marks)

(b)   Explain the meaning of each ratio you have calculated. Comment on the performance of the Lewisville bus service using the four ratios.   **(9 marks)**

(c)   Another council member suggests that the performance of the bus service should be assessed on the basis of economy, effectiveness and efficiency.

Required

Explain the meaning of the following terms in the context of performance measurement and suggest a measure of each one appropriate to a bus service.

(i)   Economy.
(ii)   Effectiveness.
(iii)   Efficiency.   **(3 marks)**

(d)   Suggest two non-financial indicators that could be useful in measuring the performance of a bus service and explain why your chosen indicators are important.   **(4 marks)**

(Total = 20 marks)

Question 5

Metallica Co is an engineering company that manufactures a number of products and components, using a team of highly skilled workers and a variety of different metals.

Metallica has developed a new product that it will manufacture in its workshop. The product is highly specialised and initially will be produced to order only. The product will be manufactured in batches. The estimated labour time required for the first batch is 40 hours, but due to the nature of the product and the manufacturing method to be used, it is expected that an 80% learning curve will apply.

Required

(a) Calculate the expected time for the eighth batch. **(3 marks)**

(b) When production commenced the first batch took 45 hours. The actual learning rates observed were as follows.

Month	Total batches produced to date	Actual learning rate
1	1	
2	2	75%
3	4	75%
4	8	90%

For each of months 2 and 4, state possible reasons why the actual learning rates differed from the expected rates. **(3 marks)**

One of Metallica's suppliers has announced that the amount of M1, one of the materials it currently supplies, will be limited to 1,000 square metres in total for the next three-month period because there will be insufficient M1 to satisfy demand.

The only items manufactured using M1 and their production costs and selling prices (where applicable) are shown below.

	Product P4 $/unit	Product P6 $/unit	Component C3 $/unit	Component C5 $/unit
Selling price	125	175	n/a	n/a
Direct materials:				
M1*	15	10	5	10
M2	10	20	15	20
Direct labour	20	30	16	10
Variable overhead	10	15	8	5
Fixed overhead**	20	30	16	10
Total cost	75	105	60	55

* Material M1 is expected to be limited in supply during the next three months. These costs are based on M1 continuing to be available at a price of $20 per square metre.

** Fixed overhead is absorbed on the basis of direct labour cost.

Products P4 and P6 are sold externally. Components C3 and C5 are used in other products made by the company. These other products do not require any further amounts of material M1.

The estimated total demand for these products and components during the next three months is as follows.

P4	2,000 units
P6	1,500 units
C3	500 units
C5	1,000 units

Components C3 and C5 are essential components. They would have to be bought in if they could not be made internally. They can be purchased from external suppliers for $75 and $95 per unit respectively The bought in components are of the same quality as those manufactured by the company. The product they are used in have sufficient margins to remain financially worthwhile if C3 and C5 are bought in at these prices.

Required

(c) (i)   Prepare calculations to show the most profitable course of action for the company for the next three months, assuming that there are no other suppliers of material M1.   **(11 marks)**

(ii) Outline **three** other factors that Metallica should consider before making its decision.   **(3 marks)**

(Total = 20 marks)

Answers

**DO NOT TURN THIS PAGE UNTIL YOU HAVE
COMPLETED THE MOCK EXAM**

A PLAN OF ATTACK

We've already established that you've been told to do it 101 times, so it is of course superfluous to tell you for the 102nd time to **Take a good look at the paper before diving in to answer questions.** You are going to remember aren't you; good!

Which order to do the questions

Having **looked through** the **paper in detail,** you need to have worked out the **order** in which to attempt the questions. You will probably have decided which question looks the easiest and started with that one. Answer plans will help you to decide how to approach each question.

The next step

You're probably thinking that you don't know where to begin or you could answer all of the questions in two hours!

Option 1 (Oh dear)

If you are challenged by this paper, do the **questions in the order of how well you think you can answer them.**

- **Question 1** has some detailed calculations that you may find tricky but there are plenty of marks available for straightforward explanations.
- **Question 2** may look tricky if you are not confident with forecasting but parts (a) (iii) and (c) (ii) can be attempted independently.
- **Question 3** has difficult planning and operational variances but part (b)(i) involves straightforward traditional variance calculations so don't panic!
- **Question 4** may look daunting with a lot of information but read it through carefully and remember to use your common sense.
- The calculations in **Question 5** may look difficult but there are plenty of straightforward marks available throughout this question.

Option 2 (This one's definitely easier)

Are you **sure** it is? If you are then that's encouraging but don't forget to do answer plans to make sure you don't miss the point of the questions.

- Don't just concentrate on the calculations in **Question 1.** Make sure you also write full answers to the discussion parts.
- Again, the explanations are worth half the marks in **Question 2**, so plan your answer carefully to gain the maximum marks.
- Timing is going to be crucial in **Question 3**. Make sure you allow yourself enough time to write detailed explanations and do the complicated calculations.
- **Question 4** requires you to really think about the needs of the specific organisations. Don't just write everything you know about performance measures.
- **Question 5** contains lots of detail so make sure you give yourself enough time to read it through carefully.

Once more for the road

You must must must **allocate your time** according to the marks for the question in total, and for the parts of the questions. And you must must must also **follow the requirements exactly.**

Finished with fifteen minutes to spare?

Looks like you slipped up on the time allocation. However if you have, make sure you don't waste the last few minutes; go back to **any parts of questions that you didn't finish** because you ran out of time.

Forget about it!

Forget about what? Excellent, you already have.

Question 1

Marking scheme

			Marks
(a)	Analysis of cost drivers	4	
	Activity-based profit statement	5	
		max	8
(b)	Evaluation and discussion of closure proposal		6
(c)	Up to 2 marks for each detailed advantage	6	
	Up to 2 marks for each detailed disadvantage	4	
		max	6
			20

(a)

Cost drivers	Kitchens	Bathrooms	Dining Rooms	Total
Items sold	1,000	1,500	4,000	6,500
Purchase orders	1,000	900	2,500	4,400
Floor area	16,000	10,000	14,000	40,000
Number of consultations	798	200	250	1,248

Cost analysis using the cost drivers above:

Sales staff wages	64,800
Items sold	6,500
Per item sold	9.97
Consultation staff wages	24,960
Number of consultations	1,248
Per consultation	20.00
Warehouse staff wages	30,240
Items sold	6,500
Per item sold	4.65 (there may be more than one item per purchase order that needs handling)
Administration staff wages	30,624
Purchase orders plus consultations	5,648 (they process and arrange both tasks)
Per task	5.42
General overheads	175,000
Floor space	40,000
Per square metre	4.38

ABC profit statement

	Kitchens	Bathrooms	Dining Rooms	Total	
	$	$	$	$	
Sales	210,000	112,500	440,000	762,500	
Cost of goods sold	(63,000)	(37,500)	(176,000)	(276,500)	
Contribution	147,000	75,000	264,000	486,000	
Sales staff wages	(9,970)	(14,955)	(39,880)	(64,805)	items sold × $9.97
Consultation staff wages	(15,960)	(4,000)	(5,000)	(24,960)	consultations × $20.00
Warehouse staff wages	(4,650)	(6,975)	(18,600)	(30,225)	items sold × $4.65
Administration staff wages	(9,745)	(5,962)	(14,905)	(30,612)	total 'tasks' × $5.42
General overheads	(70,080)	(43,800)	(61,320)	(175,200)	floor area × $4.38
Profit	36,595	(692)	124,295	160,198	

(b) The bathrooms department does appear to be making a loss. Even using the suggested ABC profit statement, that is still the case although it is interesting to note that if sales staff wages had been apportioned on the basis of purchase orders rather than on actual items sold, then the sales staff wages apportioned to bathrooms would have been around $13,000. This would have converted the loss into a small profit, and demonstrates how the use of cost drivers can influence results.

As can be seen, the bathroom department makes a contribution of $75,000 and a profit before general overheads (which were also apportioned on a fairly arbitrary basis) of about $43,000. These general overheads would still need to be met even if the department was closed down. It is therefore not clear cut that the department should be closed down.

Further investigation is needed, such as a close analysis of individual product lines to determine the strong sellers and those which could be discontinued. A better use for the space might be found, such as expansion into a totally new product area. This would of course need to be thoroughly investigated, and would need the approval of the entire organisation rather than just one individual store. Strategically, Admer's management might prefer to retain the bathrooms department as it is complementary to kitchens in the field of home improvements and customers might expect to see the company continuing to offer a range of options.

(c) Once the necessary information has been obtained, ABC is similar to traditional absorption costing. This simplicity is part of its appeal, although some apportionment of certain overhead costs may need to be done on an **arbitrary basis**.

The **complexity** of the business has increased, with wider product ranges, shorter product life cycles and more complex processes. ABC recognises this complexity with its **multiple cost drivers**, and so provides an adaptable tool for Admer to use by highlighting the activities that generate costs. As can be seen in the example, there was a high cost for consultation staff in the kitchens department, but this was not matched by sales. Consultations in the kitchen department might be costing more than is necessary.

In a more **competitive environment**, companies must be able to assess product profitability realistically. ABC can facilitate a good understanding for companies such as Admer of what drives overhead costs. This enables **better decision making**, for example by providing more information on whether or not to close the bathrooms department, or how to price certain products.

In modern systems, overhead functions include a lot of **non-factory-floor activities** such as product design, quality control, production planning and customer services. ABC is concerned with all overhead costs and so it takes management accounting beyond its 'traditional' factory floor boundaries, helping Admer to understand more clearly the origins of its costs.

It should also be noted that the introduction and maintenance of an ABC system might be **time consuming** to set up. The information needed by the new system may not currently be available. Also the costs of **introducing** and **maintaining** an activity-based costing system may exceed the benefits of such a costing system.

Question 2

Marking scheme

			Marks
(a)	Explanation of each component of the regression equation	2	
	Calculation of number of days absence	2	
	Limitations of using the equation – 1 mark per point	4	
			8
(b)	Calculation and explanation of average seasonal variation for each season	2	
	Calculation of forecast output for Year 3	2	
			4
(c)	Formula for total cost model	4	
	Evaluation of the high-low method	4	
			8
			20

(a) (i) We have **negative correlation** here, as **shown by the negative coefficient of x in the regression line**. That is, as the number of years employed with the company rises, so the number of days absent in a year through sickness falls.

$y = 15.6 - 1.2x$

The **15.6** represents the numbers of days absence through sickness that an employee with zero years service is expected to suffer, so it is the number of days that an employee will need off through sickness in their first year of employment. The **−1.2** represents the gradient of the regression line, meaning that for each extra year's service with the company, an employee will take 1.2 fewer days off sick per year.

(ii) $y = 15.6 - (1.2 \times 8) = 15.6 - 9.6 = 6$ days.

An employee who has been with the company for eight years is expected to require six days sick leave per year.

(iii) **Limitations and problems of using this equation in practice**

(1) The regression line approach presupposes that there is a **linear relationship** between the two variables: a sample of 50 workers has given us quite strong correlation, but still a strict **linear relationship seems unlikely**.

(2) A linear relationship may hold good within a small relevant range of data within which the equation may be useful in practice. But **extrapolating** outside this range will **lead to serious inaccuracies**. Thus the equation would predict that an employee with more than 15.6/1.2 = 13 years' service would have less than zero sick leave.

(3) If we use the equation to predict the future, we will use **historical data to forecast the future**, which is always **risky**.

(4) The regression line shows the expected number of days sick for a given employment period. But it is **unlikely that all categories of workers will experience the same sickness pattern**. The equation would be most useful if there were many employees all doing the same job in the same work conditions.

(b) (i)

	Spring	Summer	Autumn	Winter	Total
Year 1			+11.2	+23.5	
Year 2	−9.8	−28.1	+12.5	+23.7	
Year 3	−7.4	−26.3	+11.7		
Average variation	−8.6	−27.2	+11.8	+23.6	−0.4
Adjust total variation to nil	+0.1	+0.1	+0.1	+0.1	+0.4
Estimated seasonal variation	−8.5	−27.1	+11.9	+23.7	0.0

Seasonal variations are short-term fluctuations in recorded values, due to different circumstances which affect results at different times of the year, on different days of the week, at different times of day, or whatever. For example, sales of ice cream will be higher in summer than in winter.

In this data, the highest output can be expected to be in the winter and the lowest in the summer.

(ii) Forecast output = Trend + Seasonal variation
= 10,536 + 23.7
= 10,559.7 units

(c) (i)

	Valuations V	Total cost $
Period 2	515	90,275
Period 1	420	82,200
Change due to variable cost	95	8,075

∴ Variable cost per valuation = $8,075/95 = $85.

Period 2: fixed cost = $90,275 − (515 × $85)
= $46,500

The total cost model can therefore be represented as TC = $46,500 + $85V

(ii) The high-low method is a **simple** and **easy** to use method of estimating fixed and variable costs. However there are a number of problems with it.

- The method **ignores** all cost information apart from at the highest and lowest volumes of activity and these may not be **representative** of costs at all levels of activity
- **Inaccurate** cost estimates may be produced as a result of the assumption of a constant relationship between costs and volume of activity
- Estimates are based on **historical** information and conditions may have changed

Question 3

Text references. Standard costing is covered in Chapter 11 and variance analysis in Chapters 12 and 13.

Top tips. This was a fairly straightforward question, especially part (a)(i), although you would have had to take care not to spend too long on this part of the question.

A useful check on your calculations is shown in the summary at the end of (b): operational variance plus planning variance = total variance.

Easy marks. The traditional variance calculations in part (b)(i) are very straightforward.

			Marks
(a)	One mark for each purpose described		4
	One mark for each point discussed		4
(b)	Traditional variance analysis	5	
	Planning and operational variances	7	
			12
			20

(a) (i) **Uses of standard costing**

Standard costing is the **preparation of standard costs to be used in a number of circumstances**, including the following.

(1) **To value inventory and cost production for cost accounting purposes**. It is an alternative method of valuation to methods like FIFO and LIFO.

(2) **To act as a control device** by establishing standards (expected costs) and **comparing actual costs with the expected costs**, thus highlighting areas of the organisation that may be out of control.

(3) **To assist in setting budgets**; standards are the building blocks of periodic budgets.

(4) **To motivate staff and management** by the provision of challenging targets.

(ii) **Standard costing situations**

Standard costing can be used in a **variety of costing situations**, such as batch and mass production, process manufacture and jobbing manufacture (where there is standardisation of parts). It can also be used in **service industries if a realistic cost unit can be established**. For example, banks may have standard processes for, say, processing cheques, while fast food restaurants will use standard recipes for the preparation of burgers, pizzas and so on and cleaning firms will have standard times to clean a certain area of office space.

Benefits of using standard costing

The **greatest benefit** from the use of standard costing, however, can be gained if there is a degree of **repetition** in the production process so that average or expected usage of resources can be determined. It is therefore **most suited** to mass production and repetitive assembly work and **less suited** to organisations that produce to customer demand and requirements.

Problems with standard costing

It has been argued that standard costing is unhelpful and potentially misleading in the modern organisation and causes management to focus their attention on the wrong issues. **Continuous improvement and cost reduction programmes** are widespread but can they **co-exist** with systems of standard costing?

Standard costing and efficiency improvements

Efforts to improve the efficiency of operations or reduce costs will alter quantities of inputs, prices and so on whereas standard costing is best suited, as discussed above, to stable, standardised, repetitive environments. In fact, predetermined standards **conflict** with a philosophy of continual improvement and standard costs often incorporate a planned level of scrap in material standards which is at odds with the aim of 'zero defects' inherent in continuous improvement programmes.

Review of standards

If standard costing is to be adopted in conjunction with cost reduction and continuous improvement programmes, it is therefore vital that management **review standards on a regular basis** and **revise them** if necessary.

(b) (i) **Traditional variance analysis**

2,000 W should use (× 5 kg)	10,000 kg
but did use	10,800 kg
Material X usage variance in kgs	800 kg (A)
× standard cost per kg	× $3
Material X usage variance in $	$2,400 (A)

	$
10,800 kg of X should cost (× $3)	32,400
but did cost	51,840
Material X price variance	19,440 (A)
500 S should use (× 1.5 tonnes)	750 tonnes
but did use	700 tonnes
Material Z usage variance in tonnes	50 tonnes (F)
× standard cost per tonne	× $30
Material Z usage variance in $	$1,500 (F)

	$
700 tonnes of Z should cost (× $30)	21,000
but did cost (× $25)	17,500
Material Z price variance	3,500 (F)

Summary	Material X variances $	Material Z variances $	Total $
Price variance	19,440 (A)	3,500 (F)	15,940 (A)
Usage variance	2,400 (A)	1,500 (F)	900 (A)
	21,840 (A)	5,000 (F)	16,840 (A)

(ii) **Planning and operational variances**

W: the revised standard was 5 kg at $4.50 per kg

	$
10,800 kg of X should have cost (× $4.50)	48,600
but did cost	51,840
Material X price variance (**operational variance**)	3,240 (A)

Material X usage variance = 800 kg (A) × $4.50 = (**operational variance**)	$3,600 (A)

The **planning variance** is calculated as follows.

	$
Original standard (using X) 2,000 units × 5 kg × $3 =	30,000
Revised standard (using X) 2,000 units × 5 kg × $4.50 =	45,000
Planning variance ($1.50 (A) per kg) or	15,000 (A)

S: the revised realistic standard is 1.5 tonnes of Z at $23

	$
700 tonnes of Z should cost (× $23)	16,100
but did cost (× $25)	17,500
Material Z price variance (**operational variance**)	1,400 (A)

Material Z usage variance = 50 tonnes (F) × $23 = (**operational variance**)	$1,150 (F)

The **planning variance** is calculated as follows.

		$
Original standard 500 units × 1.5 tonnes × $30 per tonne =		22,500
Revised standard 500 units × 1.5 tonnes × $23 per tonne =		17,250
Total planning variance ($7 per tonne (F)) or		5,250 (F)

Summary

	Material X	Material Z	Total
	$	$	$
Price variance	3,240 (A)	1,400 (A)	4,640 (A)
Usage variance	3,600 (A)	1,150 (F)	2,450 (A)
Operational variances	6,840 (A)	250 (F)	7,090 (A)
Planning variances	15,000 (A)	5,250 (F)	9,750 (A)
Total variances	21,840 (A)	5,000 (F)	16,840 (A)

Question 4

Text references. Performance measures are covered in Chapter 14 and not-for-profit organisations in Chapter 16.

Top tips. In part (a), the first three ratios are well-known financial performance measures. You might find average cost per passenger mile a bit difficult to work out at first. However, the information is in the question so you just need to read carefully.

Part (b) asks for knowledge and application. Make sure you can make at least one point on each measure as it applies to the bus service.

You must know what each of the '3 Es' means. Candidates often mix these up. Think about an example in your own workplace and apply the measures. This will help you remember them better.

In part (d) make sure that the measures you suggest are indeed non-financial. Probably the most common fault in answers to this section will be confusion between what is to be measured (for example customer satisfaction) and the performance measure (level of complaints).

Easy marks. The ratio calculations should be mostly straightforward and the meaning of the 3E's is text book regurgitation.

(a) (i) **Return on capital employed (ROCE)** (also called return on investment (ROI)) is calculated as (profit/capital employed) × 100%. This shows how much profit has been made in relation to the amount of resources invested. In the case of the bus service, the measure is calculated by using the surplus figure as profit.

Profit = $20,000

Capital employed (or total assets less liabilities) = $2,210,000

Therefore ROCE = (20,000/2,210,000) × 100% = 0.9% = 1%

(ii) **Return on sales.** The profit margin (profit to sales ratio) is calculated as (profit ÷ sales) × 100%. For the bus service, taking the surplus figure as above and using income from passenger fares as sales:

Return on sales = (20,000/1,200,000) × 100% = 1.7%

(iii) **Asset turnover** is a measure of how well the assets of a business are being used to generate sales. It is calculated as (sales ÷ capital employed). Sales are passenger fares and capital employed is as stated in (a)(i) above

Asset turnover = 1,200,000/2,210,000 = 0.54 times.

(iv) **Average cost per passenger mile**. When service organisations are being measured, the cost unit needs to be relevant to the service and reflect what is being provided.

For the bus service, take the cost of providing the service as $1,180k and divide by the number of passenger miles travelled:

Average cost per revenue mile = $1,180,000/4,320,000 = 27.3c

(b) (i) **Return on capital employed (ROCE)**. This is a measure of how much profit has been made in relation to the amount of resources invested. The bus service appears to have a very low return compared to private bus companies. However the bus service does not have investors nor does it have the same profit maximisation objectives as private operators. As a public service, it operates to provide a public good and has public service requirements such as availability to all, unlike private companies. It also has low fares and so could be unable to increase profitability. The Lewisville bus service is only generating an annual profit of 0.9 cents for every $1 invested. Private bus companies are showing a return of 10 cents or 10%.

(ii) **Return on sales**. This is a simple measure of performance, which calculates the profit margin and thus alerts managers to excessive costs when compared to industry averages. The bus service has low margins compared to the private sector. Once again, this may be partly explained by its public service ethos and lack of discretion in charging fares. Of course it also means that costs will have to be looked at in case these are excessive.

The Lewisville bus service is making a return on sales of 1.7% or 1.7 cents per $1 of sales. Its private sector equivalents are making a return of 30 cents per $1 of sales.

(iii) **Asset turnover**. This is a measure of how well the assets of the business are being used to generate sales. The figure for the bus service is better than that for the private sector. However this may also mean that capital employed is lower and so less investment has been made which is not necessarily ideal.

The Lewisville bus service manages to generate sales of 54 cents for every $1 of capital employed compared to 33 cents for every $1 among the private bus companies.

(iv) **Average cost per passenger mile**. This is a measure of the costs of transporting passengers per mile travelled. Based on this measure the public service is more economic than its comparators.

The Lewisville bus service is cheaper on this measure than the private bus companies. It has a cost of 27.3 cents per passenger mile compared to 37.4 cents per mile in these companies.

In conclusion, the bus service performs better than its comparators on some measures and worse on others. However as it does not have the same objectives, it would be more sensible to compare the bus service with operators who have similar objectives.

(c)   Performance is often judged in terms of inputs and outputs. This ties in with the **'value for money'** criteria often used to assess non-profit-making organisations.

     (i)   **Economy** (spending money frugally). This is a measure of **input**, which is normally based on expenditure.

     (ii)   **Efficiency** (getting out as much as possible for what goes in). This is a measure of input in relation to output. This measure links economy to effectiveness.

     (iii)   **Effectiveness** (getting done, by means of (economy) and (efficiency), what was supposed to be done). This is an **output measure** and measures what the organisation achieves in relation to its objectives.

So effectiveness is the relationship between an organisation's **outputs** and its **objectives**, efficiency is the relationship between **inputs** and **outputs**, and economy means **controlling expenditure**.

Interpreting these for a bus service:

Economy would mean spending as little money as possible to provide an adequate service. This would be measured by, say, total expenditure compared to budget. **Efficiency** would mean providing the best service for the money available, so for instance cost per passenger mile travelled. **Effectiveness** would be providing the service that is supposed to be provided for the best price, and so could be measured by the number of passengers or miles travelled.

(d)   *(Note that only two indicators are required)*

Non financial performance indicator	*Importance*
% of buses on time	Punctuality is important to passengers and a well-understood target
% of buses cancelled	Reliability is important to passengers
Accidents per 1,000,000 passengers	Safety is vital in any form of travel.
Customer rating of cleanliness of facilities	Passengers require good quality service
% utilisation of staff	Underused staff are a waste of resources
% of new customers	New customers are vital for sustained growth
Employee morale	Happy employees (particularly those who deal with customers), are vital for success in a service business

Question 5

Text references. Learning curves are covered in chapter 10 and limiting factor analysis is revised in Chapter 4.

Top tips. Part (a) requires a straightforward use of the learning curve formula but you need to really think about what the theory means in part (b).

Part (c) uses brought forward knowledge to calculate the contribution per unit of the limiting factor. Use a clear layout to show the marker how you arrived at your conclusions.

Easy marks. There are some straightforward calculations in parts (a) and (c).

			Marks
(a)	Cumulative average time per 8th batch	1	
	Cumulative average time per 7th batch	1	
	Expected time for 8th batch	1	
			3
(b)	1 mark per reason		3
(c) (i)	Calculation of contribution per unit	4	
	Calculation of contribution per m²	2	
	Ranking	1	
	Production plan	4	
			11
(ii)	1 mark per factor		3
			20

(a) **Expected time for the eighth batch**

$Y_x = aX^b$

$Y_8 = 40 \times 8^{-0.32193}$
   $= 40 \times 0.512$
   $= 20.48$ hours (average time per batch)

$Y_7 = 40 \times 7^{-032193}$
   $= 40 \times 0.534$
   $= 21.36$ hours (average time per batch)

Cumulative batches	Cumulative average time Per batch (hours)	Total time (hours)
8	20.48	163.84
7	21.36	149.52
		14.32

The expected time for the eighth batch is therefore 14.32 hours

(b) **Possible reasons why actual learning rates differed from expected rules**

The learning rates for months 2 and 3 are better than expected. This may be due to management underestimating the ability of the workforce to master the new techniques. The workforce may also have been initially enthusiastic about learning new skills.

The learning rate in month 4 deteriorated. Possible reasons for this could be changes in the workforce, lack of motivation or potential long periods between production of batches (as batches are only produced to order).

(c) (i) The most profitable course of action can be determined by ranking the products and components according to **contribution per unit of the limiting factor**. Direct material M1 is the limiting factor in this case, therefore the highest rank will be given to the product/component with the greatest contribution per m² of this material.

	Product P4	Product P6	Component C3	Component C5
	$	$	$	$
Selling price	125	175	–	–
Opportunity cost			75	95
Direct materials:				
M1	15	10	5	10
M2	10	20	15	20
Direct labour	20	30	16	10
Variable overhead	10	15	8	5
Total direct costs	55	75	44	45
Contribution/unit	70	100	31	50
m² of M1/unit	0.75	0.5	0.25	0.5
Contribution/m²	$93.33	$200	$124	$100
Ranking	4	1	2	3

Optimal production schedule

Material available	1,000 m²
Produce: 1,500 units of P6	750 m²
	250 m²
500 units of C3	125 m²
	125 m²
$\dfrac{125 \text{ m}^2}{0.5} = 250$ units of C5	125 m²
	NIL

Optimal production plan is therefore:

P4	No units
P6	1,500 units
C3	125 units
C5	250 units

(ii) **Other factors to be considered** (only three are required).

- Will the non-production of P4 have an effect on the sales of other products?

- What is the likelihood of the price of Material M1 remaining at $20 per m²?

- Is there a possibility of replacing Material M1 with another material that is in more plentiful supply?

- What are the future prospects for product P4? Should production be terminated completely? Would this affect the company's overall market position?

ACCA

Paper F5

Performance Management

Mock Examination 2

Question Paper	
Reading and planning Writing	15 minutes 3 hours
ALL FIVE questions are compulsory and MUST be attempted	

DO NOT OPEN THIS PAPER UNTIL YOU ARE READY TO START UNDER EXAMINATION CONDITIONS

ACCA

Paper F5

Performance Management

Mock Examination 2

Question Paper

Reading and planning		15 minutes
Writing		3 hours

ALL FIVE questions are compulsory and MUST be attempted

All FIVE questions are compulsory and MUST be attempted

Question 1

Mr G and Mrs H have recently formed a consultancy business, and have sought your advice concerning costs and fees. Mr G and Mrs H each wish to receive a salary of $20,000 in the first year of trading. They have purchased two cars at a cost of $13,000 each and expect to use them for three years. At the end of this time each of the cars has an expected resale value of $4,000. Straight-line depreciation is to be applied.

Mr G and Mrs H each expect to work for eight hours per day, five days per week for 45 weeks per year. They refer to this as *available time*. 25% of the available time is expected to be used dealing with administrative matters related to their own business, and in the first year it is expected that there will be idle time which will average 22.5% of the available time. The remainder of the available time is expected to be chargeable to clients.

Mr G and Mrs H agreed that their fee structure should comprise the following.

An hourly rate for productive client work

An hourly rate for travelling to/from clients

A rate per mile travelled to/from clients

They expect that the travelling time will equal 25% of their chargeable time, and will amount to a total of 18,000 miles. They have agreed that this time should be charged at one-third of their normal hourly rate.

Apart from the costs referred to above, Mr G and Mrs H have estimated their other costs for the first twelve months as follows.

	$
Electricity	1,200
Fuel for vehicles	1,800
Insurance – professional liability and office	600
Insurance – vehicles	800
Mobile telephones	1,200
Office rent and rates	8,400
Office telephone/facsimile	1,800
Postage and stationery	500
Secretarial costs	8,400
Servicing and repairs of vehicles	1,200
Vehicle road tax	280

Required

(a) In order that the consultancy business breaks even after paying the required salaries, classify the costs between professional services and vehicle costs, and then analyse the available time into travelling time and productive time. Using this data, calculate the following.

  (i)   An hourly rate for productive client work
  (ii) An hourly rate for travelling to/from clients
  (iii) A rate per mile travelled to/from clients   **(13 marks)**

(b) Explain how Mr G and Mrs H may monitor their income and costs during the year to see if they are achieving their objectives.   **(4 marks)**

(c) Mr G and Mrs H are considering implementing an activity-based costing system to ensure that each of their clients is charged correctly for the services provided. Briefly outline the main principles of activity-based costing and explain why it may <u>not</u> be appropriate for the business.   **(3 marks)**

(Total = 20 marks)

Question 2

KL manufactures three products, W, X and Y. Each product uses the same materials and the same type of direct labour but in different quantities. The company currently uses a cost plus basis to determine the selling price of its products. This is based on full cost using an overhead absorption rate per direct labour hour. However, the managing director is concerned that the company may be losing sales because of its approach to setting prices. He thinks that a marginal costing approach may be more appropriate, particularly since the workforce is guaranteed a minimum weekly wage and has a three month notice period.

Required

(a)   Given the managing director's concern about KL's approach to setting selling prices, discuss the advantages and disadvantages of marginal cost plus pricing **AND** total cost plus pricing.   **(6 marks)**

The direct costs of the three products are shown below:

Product	W	X	Y
Budgeted annual production (units)	15,000	24,000	20,000
	$ per unit	$ per unit	$ per unit
Direct materials	35	45	30
Direct labour ($10 per hour)	40	30	50

In addition to the above direct costs, KL incurs annual indirect production costs of $1,044,000.

Required

(b)   Calculate the full cost per unit of each product using KL's current method of absorption costing.

(4 marks)

An analysis of the company's indirect production costs shows the following:

	$	Cost driver
Material ordering costs	220,000	Number of supplier orders
Machine setup costs	100,000	Number of batches
Machine running costs	400,000	Number of machine hours
General facility costs	324,000	Number of machine hours

The following additional data relate to each product:

Product	W	X	Y
Machine hours per unit	5	8	7
Batch size (units)	500	400	1,000
Supplier orders per batch	4	3	5

Required

(c)   Calculate the full cost per unit of each product using activity based costing and briefly comment on the contrast to your results in part (b).   **(10 marks)**

(Total = 20 marks)

Question 3

Kybosh manufactures road humps for Local Authorities. It operates a standard absorption costing system, with fixed overheads absorbed on the basis of direct labour hours. As assistant management accountant you are responsible for preparing the monthly operating statements. Data from the budget and the standard product cost for the month ended 31 January 20X9 are given below.

Budget data

Budgeted sales and production for the month   100 units

Standard cost for each unit of product

		$
Direct materials	6 kg @ $25 per kilo	150
Direct labour	16 hours @ $4.50 per hour	72
Variable overhead	16 hours @ $0.625 per hour	10
Fixed overhead	16 hours @ $5.25 per hour	84
Selling price		500

Actual data for month ended 31 January 20X9

Production	95 units sold at a price of 15% higher than that budgeted
Direct materials consumed	584 kgs at a cost of $14,454
Direct wages incurred	1,840 hours @ $4.20 per hour (although due to late deliveries of some of the raw materials, 340 hours were idle time)
Fixed production overhead incurred	$9,000
Variable overheads	$1,200

Required

(a)   Using the data given, prepare the operating statement for the month ended 31 January 20X9 to show the budgeted profit, all relevant variances and the actual profit/loss.   **(8 marks)**

The company has just employed a new senior management accountant who has never worked in a manufacturing environment before. He has said that he expects profits this month to be lower than planned due to the lower level of sales and high level of idle time. He has also had a quick review of the fixed production overhead account and was shocked by the amount under absorbed. 'Why is it so high? The actual fixed overheads this month were not that much over budget.'

Required

(b)   Discuss the comments made by the management accountant.   **(7 marks)**

(c)   The following cost information relates to product ZIM 3A, which is produced in one continuous process by Chemacca.

	$
Actual quantity of materials at standard price	103,500
Actual quantity of materials at actual price	103,250
Actual yield at standard materials cost	102,500
Standard yield from actual input of materials at standard cost	100,000

Required

(i)   Calculate and present the following material cost variances.

    (1)   Price
    (2)   Usage
    (3)   Mix and yield

(ii)   Comment briefly on your findings.   **(5 marks)**

(Total = 20 marks)

Question 4

Colour Co is a paint manufacturer with a number of divisions. Brief details of the Green and Blue divisions are set out below for the year ended 30 September 20X8.

	Green $m	Blue $m
Net profit for year ended 30 September 20X8	4.2	5.6
Net book value of non-current assets at 1 October 20X7	20.0	32.0
Additions to non-current assets on 2 October 20X7	4.5	
Depreciation for year ended 30 September 20X8	(4.0)	(6.2)
Net book value of non-current assets at 30 September 20X8	20.5	25.8
Net current assets	11.5	10.2
Total net assets at 30 September 20X8	32.0	36.0

There were no sales of non-current assets during the year. Depreciation has been charged on the basis of assets in use. The cost of capital used by Colour plc is 12%.

The budgeted assets and profits for Green and Blue for the year ended 30 September 20X9 are identical to those in use at the end of the previous year. A new investment in computerised mixing equipment is available to either Green or Blue at the beginning of the year 20X9. This investment would increase total net assets by $25m and produce annual net profits of $3.5m for many years.

Required

(a)   Calculate for Green and Blue, using 'net assets in use' as a basis:

   (i)   Return on investment (ROI) for year ended 30 September 20X8;
   (ii)   Residual income (RI) for year ended 30 September 20X8.   **(4 marks)**

(b)   Comment briefly on the performance of Blue and Green in 20X8.   **(2 marks)**

(c)   Discuss whether Blue or Green would want to take the new investment opportunity in the year 20X9 described above. Provide calculations to support your comments.   **(8 marks)**

(d)   Describe how the balanced scorecard is used as a performance measure and explain its relevance to assessing the performance of the Green and Blue divisions.   **(6 marks)**

(Total = 20 marks)

Question 5

The bank Barklods is reviewing the bank account it offers to its business customers and the charges it makes for routine transactions (for example paying into the account, writing cheques, making electronic payments and transfers). Currently, Barklod's charges to its business customers are $0.60 per routine transaction. The bank pays interest to the customer at 0.1% per year on any balance in the account.

According to the Barklod's records, there are currently one million business customers. Each customer makes one thousand routine transactions each year; 45% of business customers maintain an average balance of $2,000 in their account. The accounts of the other 55% of business customers are overdrawn with an average overdraft balance of $4,000. Interest on overdrawn accounts is charged at 20% per year. Interest on overdrawn accounts is charged at 20% per year.

In addition, the bank has a number of savings account customers which, together with the bank's business customers, result in a balance of net funds that are invested by the bank and yield an annual return of 3% per year.

Barklod is concerned about a growing tendency for its competitors to provide routine transactions free of charge to their business customers. As a result the bank is considering two account options.

Triple F Account

An account that charges the business customer a fixed fee of $10 per month, with no further charges for any routine transactions. Interest would be paid to the business customer at 0.5% per year on any balances in the account. The bank expects that if it adopts this charging structure, it will increase the number of business customers by 5% from its present level.

Zero Account

An account that does not charge the customer for any routine transactions, but pays no interest on any balances in the account. The bank expects that if it adopts this charging structure this will increase the number of business customers by 10% from its present level.

The bank does not expect the profile of new business customers to be different from existing business customers in terms of the balances in their account or the number of routine transactions they make. Interest will continue to be charged at 20% per year on overdrawn accounts. The bank does not expect that either of these options will result in any changes to its existing staffing or other resources.

The bank also expects that if it takes no action and continues with its existing bank account the number of business customers will decrease by 20%. The bank also predicts that net profits will be $831,280,000 if no action is taken.

Required

(a)   Recommend which course of action the bank should take by preparing calculations to show the annual profits from each of the two account options described above.   **(7 marks)**

The bank is also reviewing its policy with regard to small loans. Currently, the bank charges an arrangement fee of $500 per loan and interest on the average loan balance. The profit the bank makes on the interest it charges is 5% of the average loan balance. The bank's records show that there are 200,000 small loans in issue at any one time. The average loan balance is $5,000.

Market research undertaken by the bank has shown that if it were to carry out an advertising campaign that specifically targeted the small loans market, the number of loans would increase, though the amount of the increase is uncertain. It is predicted that the advertising campaign may increase the number of loans in issue at any one time to 250,000, 280,000 or 300,000.

Furthermore, it is believed that the advertising campaign would increase the value of the loans. The amount of the increase is uncertain, but it is believed that the average loan balance may increase to $7,500; or that they may increase by $9,000; or that they may increase by $10,000.

The expected total cost of the advertising campaign and the associated administrative costs are $112 million.

Required

(b)   (i)   Prepare a two-way data table that shows profit that would be earned by the bank for each of the **nine** possible outcomes that are expected to arise as a result of the advertising campaign.   **(8 marks)**

(ii)   State any other factors the bank could consider before making its decision and advise the bank on whether or not it should carry out the advertising campaign.   **(5 marks)**

(Total = 20 marks)

Answers

A PLAN OF ATTACK

We've already established that you've been told to do it 102 times, so it is of course superfluous to tell you for the 103rd time to **Take a good look at the paper before diving in to answer questions.** You are going to remember aren't you; good!

Which order to do the questions

Having **looked through** the **paper in detail,** you need to have worked out the **order** in which to attempt the questions. You will probably have decided which question looks the easiest and started with that one. Answer plans will help you to decide how to approach each question.

The next step

You're probably thinking that you don't know where to begin or you could answer all of the questions in two hours!

Option 1 (Oh dear)

If you are challenged by this paper, do the **questions in the order of how well you think you can answer them.**

- **Question 1** contains lots of information and may appear daunting, but a careful, methodical approach will enable you to calculate the required performance measures.
- **Question 2** may look daunting but there are a number of parts where marks can be scored independent of your ability to do every section.
- **Question 3** is a wide ranging variance analysis question which may again look daunting. You can however gain plenty of easy marks if you show all your workings, use a logical layout and don't panic!
- **Question 4** requires you to be able to calculate and explain RI and ROI which may be tricky. There are however easier marks available for a more general discussion of the balanced scorecard.
- **Question 5** has lots of detail to read through but a logical approach will earn plenty of marks.

Option 2 (This one's definitely easier)

Are you **sure** it is? If you are then that's encouraging but don't forget to do answer plans to make sure you don't miss the point of the questions.

- Don't just concentrate on the calculations in **Question 1.** Make sure you also write full answers to the discussion parts.
- Don't just do a brain dump of everything you know in **Question 2.** Make sure you apply your discussions to the organisation in the question.
- Time management is going to be important in **Question 3** as there are a lot of calculations to get through. Make sure you leave enough time for the written parts of the question which have equal marks.
- **Question 4** answers need to be sufficiently detailed and applied to the organisation in the question.
- **Question 5** has some tricky calculations and is time pressured so don't spend too long on part (a).

Once more for the road

You must must must **allocate your time** according to the marks for the question in total, and for the parts of the questions. And you must must must also **follow the requirements exactly.**

Finished with fifteen minutes to spare?

Looks like you slipped up on the time allocation. However if you have, make sure you don't waste the last few minutes; go back to **any parts of questions that you didn't finish** because you ran out of time.

Forget about it!

Forget about what? Excellent, you already have.

Question 1

Marking scheme

		Marks
(a)	Allocation of costs to correct headings (½ marks for each to max of 6½)	6½
	Calculation of:	
	Depreciation	½
	Available hours	½
	Chargeable time	1
	Travelling time	½
	Productive time	½
	Weighted chargeable time	½
	Hourly rate: productive client work	1
	Hourly rate for travelling	1
	Rate per mile travelled	1
		13
(b)	Budget preparation	1
	Cost collection	1
	Time recording	1
	Comparisons with budgets	1
	Variances	1
		Max 4
(c)	Explanation of activity-based costing	2
	Explanation of why ABC would not be appropriate for a consultancy business	1
		3
		20

(a)   **Classification of costs**

	Professional services costs $	Vehicle costs $
Electricity	1,200	
Fuel for vehicles		1,800
Insurance: professional liability and office	600	
vehicles		800
Mobile telephones (note 1)	1,200	
Office rent and rates	8,400	
Office telephone/fax	1,800	
Postage and stationery	500	
Secretarial costs	8,400	
Servicing and repair of vehicles		1,200
Vehicle road tax		280
Vehicle depreciation (note 2)		6,000
Salaries	40,000	
	62,100	10,080

Notes

(1)   It is assumed that the mobile telephones are used in providing professional services and that their use is not consequent upon travelling.

(2)   Annual depreciation = $\dfrac{\$13,000 - \$4,000}{3} \times 2 \text{ cars} = \$6,000$

Analysis of available time

Total hours per annum ((8 × 5 × 45) × 2 people)		3,600 available hours
Less: administration	25.0%	
idle time	22.5%	
	47.5% × 3,600 =	(1,710) hours
Chargeable time		1,890 hours
Travelling time (25%)		472.5 hours
Productive time (75%)		1,417.5 hours

Travelling time is to be charged at one third of the normal hourly rate.

'Weighted' chargeable time	=	1,417.5 + (472.5/3)
	=	1,575 hours
∴ Rate per productive hours	=	$62,100/1,575
Hourly rate for productive client work	=	$39.43 per hour
Hourly rate for travelling (÷ 3)	=	$13.14 per hour
Rate per mile travelled	=	$10,080/18,000
	=	$0.56 per mile

(b)   (i)   **Preparation of budgets**

Costs and income should be budgeted on a monthly basis, allowing for any seasonal fluctuations. Cost behaviour patterns should be taken into account, so that fixed and variable costs can be analysed separately in each month's budget.

(ii)   **Cost collection system**

An efficient cost collection system must be established. All costs should be analysed between professional services and vehicle costs so that the hourly rate can be carefully monitored.

(iii)   **Time recording system**

An efficient time recording system will also be required. Mr G and Mrs H must record how they use all of their time, analysing it between the categories of idle time, travelling time, productive time and so on. Efficient time recording will obviously be necessary so that clients can be charged quickly and correctly.

(iv)   **Comparison with budgets**

Actual costs and income can then be compared with the budget for the month. If variable costs are significant and there are wide variations in activity levels, the budget allowance can be flexed to give a realistic control target for the actual activity level achieved.

(v)   **Use of variances**

Any variances can be highlighted and remedial action can be taken to ensure that Mr G and Mrs H achieve their objectives.

(c)   **Activity-based costing (ABC)**

Under an ABC system, Mr G and Mrs H would need to **identify factors (cost drivers)** which cause the costs of the business's major activities. Support overheads are charged to products on the basis of their usage of an activity.

For costs that vary with activity levels in the short term, the cost driver will be volume related (labour hours). Overheads that vary with some other activity (and not volume of production) should be traced to products using transaction-based cost drivers such as number of orders received.

By definition, **consultancy services are tailored to meet the needs of each individual client**. ABC is not really appropriate in a consultancy business as it is **difficult to define cost units**. Job or contract costing may be considered more appropriate.

Question 2

Text references. ABC is covered in Chapter 2a. Pricing is covered in Chapter 5.

Top tips. Part (a) wants you to **compare and contrast** marginal cost plus pricing and total cost plus pricing. We start off with a definition of each. Then we discuss their advantages and disadvantages. Don't panic – we have made more points in our answer than you would need to in the real exam. Don't do a mind dump and write all you know, as this will not be rewarded. Make concise points and keep to short paragraphs to make it easier for the marker to read your script.

Part (b) is asking for a **short calculation of full cost** per unit using absorption costing data from the question. There shouldn't be anything tricky for you to consider here.

In (c) you need to calculate the **full cost using activity costing**. The best approach is to break your answer down into manageable workings as we have done and follow these through to the ultimate unit cost calculation asked for.

A **quicker approach** would be to allocate overhead across the products directly on the basis of the drivers rather than calculating the costs per driver.

Don't forget to comment on your results.

Easy marks. Parts (a), (b) and (c) are self-contained so you could answer then in any order. Part (b) is very straight forward and should be able to be answered using information you have brought forward from your earlier studies.

		Marks
(a)	Marginal cost plus pricing	3
	Total cost plus pricing	3
		6
(b)	Calculation of overhead absorption rate	2
	Calculation of cost per unit	2
		4
(c)	Calculation of unit costs	8
	Comment	2
		10
		20

(a) **Marginal cost pricing and total cost plus pricing**

Full cost plus pricing is a method of determining the sales price by calculating the full cost of the product and adding a percentage mark-up for profit.

Marginal cost plus pricing/mark-up pricing is a method of determining the sales price by adding a profit margin on to either marginal cost of production or marginal cost of sales.

The managing director has observed that labour costs are **fixed** over the short term. Currently KL uses full cost plus pricing based on a full cost which incorporates labour cost as a variable or marginal cost. The MD has noted that labour costs are actually fixed in the short-term, however, and hence should be included as part of overheads. This should result in a different full cost. Thus he believes that the absorption rate for overheads may be distorted as it doesn't reflect true activity. Marginal costing would exclude these overheads from costs.

Problems with and advantages of full cost-plus pricing

There are several **problems** with relying on a full cost approach to pricing.

(i) It fails to recognise that since demand may be determining price, there will be a profit-maximising combination of price and demand.

(ii) There may be a need to adjust prices to market and demand conditions.

(iii) Budgeted output volume needs to be established. Output volume is a key factor in the overhead absorption rate.

(iv) A suitable basis for overhead absorption must be selected, especially where a business produces more than one product.

However, it is a **quick, simple and cheap** method of pricing which can be delegated to junior managers (which is particularly important with jobbing work where many prices must be decided and quoted each day) and, since the size of the profit margin can be varied, a decision based on a price in excess of full cost should ensure that a company working at normal capacity will **cover all of its fixed costs and make a profit**.

The advantages and disadvantages of a marginal cost-plus approach to pricing

Here are the **advantages**.

(i) It is a **simple and easy** method to use.

(ii) The **mark-up percentage can be varied**, and so mark-up pricing can be adjusted to reflect demand conditions.

(iii) It **draws management attention to contribution**, and the effects of higher or lower sales volumes on profit. In this way, it helps to create a better awareness of the concepts and implications of marginal costing and cost-volume-profit analysis. For example, if a product costs $10 per unit and a mark-up of 150% is added to reach a price of $25 per unit, management should be clearly aware that every additional $1 of sales revenue would add 60 pence to contribution and profit.

In practice, mark-up pricing is **used** in businesses **where there is a readily identifiable basic variable cost**. Retail industries are the most obvious example, and it is quite common for the prices of goods in shops to be fixed by adding a mark-up (20% or 33.3%, say) to the purchase cost.

There are, of course, **drawbacks** to marginal cost-plus pricing.

(i) Although the size of the mark-up can be varied in accordance with demand conditions, it does not ensure that sufficient attention is paid to demand conditions, competitors' prices and profit maximisation.

(ii) It ignores fixed overheads in the pricing decision, but the sales price must be sufficiently high to ensure that a profit is made after covering fixed costs.

(b) **Calculate the full cost per unit of each product using absorption costing**

The full cost of each product will include indirect costs allocated to each product using a predetermined overhead absorption rate. In the case of KL, this is based on **direct labour hours**.

	W $	X $	Y $
Variable cost per unit			
Direct materials	35.00	45.00	30.00
Direct labour	40.00	30.00	50.00
Production overhead (W)	18.00	13.50	22.50
Full cost per unit	93.00	88.50	102.50

Working

Total overheads = $1,044,000.

	W	X	Y	Total
Total labour hours				
Hrs per unit	4	3	5	
Budgeted annual production	15,000	24,000	20,000	
Total annual direct labour hrs	60,000	72,000	100,000	232,000

Overhead absorption rate (OAR) = $1,044,000/232,000

OAR per direct labour hour = $4.50/hr per direct labour hour

	W	X	Y
Hrs per unit	4	3	5
Production overhead absorbed per unit	18.00	13.50	22.50

(c) **Calculate the full cost per unit of each product using ABC**

We have listed the steps taken to calculate the unit costs using an ABC system of costing. The references to workings are to the workings below.

Step 1   Work out the annual activity for each cost driver.

Working

Annual activity

	W	X	Y	Total
Batches				
Batch size (units)	500	400	1,000	
Annual units	15,000	24,000	20,000	
Annual number of batches	30	60	20	110
Supplier orders				
Per batch	4	3	5	
Annual number of batches	30	60	20	
Annual supplier orders	120	180	100	400
Machine hours				
Per unit	5	8	7	
Annual units	15,000	24,000	20,000	
Annual machine hours	75,000	192,000	140,000	407,000

Step 2   Use this information to calculate the **activity cost driver rates** in **working below**. You should also be able to use information provided in the table in the question.

Working

Cost driver rates

Material ordering costs $220,000 ÷ 400 supplier orders = $ 550 per supplier order
Machine setup costs $100,000 ÷ 110 batches = $ 909 per batch
Machine running costs $400,000 ÷ 407,000 machine hours = $ 0.98 per machine hour
General facility costs $324,000 ÷ 407,000 machine hours = $ 0.80 per machine hour

Step 3   **Apply these cost driver rates** to the **supplier orders, batch sizes and machine hours** for **each product.** This will give you the **unit cost** for each product for each cost pool. See **workings 1, 2,3 and 4.**

Workings

1		W	X	Y
	Supplier orders per batch	4	3	5
	Batch size	500	400	1,000
	Cost driver (supplier orders) per unit	= 4/500	= 3/400	= 5/1,000
	Activity cost driver rate (per order) $	550	550	550
	Unit cost $	4.40	4.125	2.75

2		W	X	Y
	Batch size in units	500	400	1,000
	Activity cost driver rate (per batch) $	909	909	909
	Unit cost $	1.82	2.27	0.91

3		W	X	Y
	Machine hours per unit	5	8	7
	Activity cost driver rate $ (per machine hour)	0.98	0.98	0.98
	Unit cost $	4.90	7.84	6.86

4		W	X	Y
	Machine hours per unit	5	8	7
	Activity cost driver rate $ (W5)	0.80	0.80	0.80
	Unit cost $	4.00	6.40	5.60

Step 4   You should now be able to calculate the **full unit cost** using the information you have already calculated slotted into a table as below.

Using **activity based costing**, unit costs for the three products would be as follows.

	W	X	Y
	$/unit	$/unit	$/unit
Direct material	35.00	45.00	30.00
Direct labour	40.00	30.00	50.00
Material ordering costs (W1)	4.40	4.13	2.75
Machine set-up costs (W2)	1.82	2.27	0.91
Machine running costs (W3)	4.90	7.84	6.86
General facility costs (W4)	4.00	6.40	5.60
	90.12	95.64	96.12

The unit costs calculated using ABC differ to those calculated under full cost. These are summarised in the table below.

	W	X	Y
	$	$	$
Full cost per unit	93.00	88.50	102.50
ABC cost per unit	90.12	95.64	96.12
Difference	2.88	(7.14)	6.38

Profit

The differences in unit costs between full cost, and ABC cost shown in the table show that management need to consider a few actions from the results of ABC costing. Should they increase the price of X which has a higher ABC cost than full cost?

On the other hand should management reduce the price of Y which has a lower ABC cost than full cost?

Question 3

Text references. Variance analysis is covered in Chapter 12.

Top tips. This question covers all of the **basic variances** examinable in Paper F5. If you found it difficult you must revise this **crucial area** of the syllabus. You must also ensure that you can deal with the written part of the question.

For part (a), first write out the **proforma operating statement**, cross-referencing to workings. Then set-up **workings** for each variance, calculating the ones you are happiest with first. The efficiency variance should be calculated in hours, then valued according to the appropriate standard cost per hour for labour, variable and fixed overheads, giving you three variances quite quickly.

In part (b), this type of discussion question needs to be broken down to become manageable, so look at the profit level and fixed overheads separately.

Profit. Discuss the impact on profit due to variances, noting particularly the favourable sales price variance and the adverse idle time and sales volume variances.

Fixed overheads. It is essential that you **distinguish** between **actual overheads and absorption of overheads**. The rest of the solution can be padded out with explanations of the analysis of the under absorption (illustrated with the variances calculated in part (a)).

Part (c) tests the calculation of **materials variances including mix and yield** variances.

Easy marks. A logical layout to your answer will help you pick up marks even if you do not completely finish the question.

Marking scheme

		Marks
(a)	Budget profit	½
	Selling price variance	½
	Sales volume variance	1
	Material price variance	½
	Material usage variance	½
	Labour rate variance	½
	Labour idle time variance	½
	Labour efficiency variance	½
	Variable overhead expenditure variance	½
	Variable overhead efficiency variance	½
	Fixed overhead expenditure variance	½
	Fixed overhead efficiency variance	1
	Fixed overhead capacity variance	1
	Actual profit	½
	Max	8
(b)	Profit overview	2
	Fixed overheads	5
		7

(c)

Calculation of price variance		½
Calculation of usage variance		½
Calculation of mix variance		1
Calculation of yield variance		1
Comments (1 mark per point up to max of 2)		2
		5
		20

(a) OPERATING STATEMENT – JANUARY 20X9

	$	$	$
Budgeted profit (100 × $184)			18,400
Sales price variance (W1)		7,125 (F)	
Sales volume variance (W2)		920 (A)	
			6,205 (F)
			24,605

Cost variances	F	A	
Material price (W3)	146.00		
Material usage (W4)		350.00	
Labour rate (W5)	552.00		
Labour idle time (W6)		1,530.00	
Labour efficiency (W7)	90.00		
Variable overhead expenditure (W8)		262.50	
Variable overhead efficiency (W9)	12.50		
Fixed overhead expenditure (W10)		600.00	
Fixed overhead efficiency (W11)	105.00		
Fixed overhead capacity (W12)		525.00	
	905.50	3,267.50	
			2,362 (A)
Actual profit			22,243

Actual profit proof

		$	$
Sales (95 × 500 ×1.15)			54,625
Less:	Direct materials	14,454	
	Direct labour (1,840 × $4.20)	7,728	
	Variable overhead	1,200	
	Fixed overhead	9,000	
Actual profit			32,382
			22,243

Workings

1 *Selling price variance*

	$
Sales revenue should have been (95 × $500)	47,500
but was (95 × $500 × 115%)	54,625
	7,125 (F)

2 *Sales volume variance*

Actual sales in units	95 units
Budgeted sales in units	100 units
Variance in units	5 units (A)
× standard profit per unit	×$184
	$920 (A)

BPP
LEARNING MEDIA

3   *Material price variance*

	$
584 kg should have cost ($\times$ $25)	14,600
but did cost	14,454
	146 (F)

4   *Material usage variance*

95 units should have used ($\times$ 6kg)	570 kgs
but did use	584 kgs
Variance in kgs	14 kgs (A)
$\times$ standard cost per kg	$\times$ $25
	$350 (A)

5   *Labour rate variance*

	$
1,840 hrs should have cost ($\times$ $4.50)	8,280
but did cost ($\times$ $4.20)	7,728
	552 (F)

6   *Idle time variance*

340 hours at $4.50 per hour	$1,530 (A)

7   *Labour efficiency variance*

95 units should have taken ($\times$ 16 hours)	1,520 hrs
but did take	1,500 hrs
Variance in hrs	20 hrs (F)
$\times$ standard rate per hour	$\times$ $4.50
	$90 (F)

8   *Variable overhead expenditure variance*

	$
1,500 hours should have cost ($\times$ $0.625)	937.50
but did cost	1,200.00
	262.50 (A)

9   *Variable overhead efficiency variance*

As per labour efficiency variance	
20 hours (F) at $0.625 per hour	$12.50 (F)

10   *Fixed production overhead expenditure variance*

	$
Budgeted fixed overhead expenditure (100 $\times$ $84)	8,400
Actual fixed overhead expenditure	9,000
	600 (A)

11   *Fixed production overhead efficiency variance*

Saving in time taken (as for labour efficiency)	
20 hours (F) $\times$ $5.25 per hour	$105 (F)

12   *Fixed production overhead capacity variance*

Budgeted hours of work (16 hours $\times$ 100 units)	1,600 hrs
Actual hours of work	1,500 hrs
Variances in hours	100 hrs (A)
$\times$ absorption rate per hr	$\times$ $5.25
	$525 (A)

(b)   **Profit overview**

At $22,243 **profits** are $3,843 **higher than those budgeted**. This is primarily due to a **favourable sales price variance** of $7,125 arising from a **sales price increase** of 15%. This has possibly caused the **lower volumes of sales** and given rise to an adverse volume variance of $920. The **cost variances** have eroded the remaining benefit of the price increase. In particular, **idle time** of $1,530 and **under absorption of fixed overheads** of $1,020 have had a significant impact.

Fixed overheads

A pre-determined fixed overhead absorption rate (FOAR) is calculated by dividing budgeted overheads by budgeted activity (ie direct labour hours). The fixed production overheads are absorbed on this direct labour hour basis at the rate of $84 per unit (16 hours × $5.25), hence the $7,980 ($84×95) absorbed in January. The **under absorption** of $1,020 is the **difference between the amount absorbed** and the **actual overhead** incurred of $9,000.

Analysis of the under absorption

	$	
Under absorption	1,020	(A)
Expenditure variance	(600)	(A)
Volume variance	420	(A)

Volume and expenditure

The volume variance is made up on an efficiency variance of $105 (F) and a capacity variance of $525 (A).

The **expenditure variance** has arisen because overheads for January were $600 greater than the budgeted figure of $8,400.

The balance of the under absorption ($420) is a **volume variance** arising from production being only 95 units compared to the original budget of 100 units.

Efficiency and capacity

This can be further analysed between efficiency and capacity.

(i)   When calculating the FOAR it was assumed that the company would have **a capacity** for 1,600 hours of direct labour and that it would take 16 hours to make each unit. In fact, only 1,500 hours were worked. The standard cost of working under capacity amounts to the $525 capacity variance.

(ii)   In addition, the workforce were more **efficient** than budgeted, producing the 95 units in 20 hours less than standard. This accounts for the efficiency variance of $105 (F).

Conclusion

Given that the pre-determined FOAR is based on two variables, budgeted expenditure and budgeted activity level (direct labour hours), it is not unusual to see such variances.

(c)   (i)

			$
(1)	Actual quantity of materials should have cost		103,500
	but did cost		103,250
	Price variance		250 (F)
(2)	Output should have used (at standard price)		102,500
	but did use (at standard price)		103,500
	Usage variance		1,000 (A)
(3)	Mix should have been		100,000
	but was (at standard price)		103,500
			3,500 (A)
	Yield should have been		100,000
	but was		102,500
			2,500 (F)

(ii) **Reasons for adverse variance**

The overall material cost variance is the sum of the price and the usage variances ($750 adverse). Chemacca has therefore not achieved its raw material budget, mainly due to the occurrence of the **large adverse usage variance**. The **two components of this** are the mix and the yield variance, **both** of which **need to be investigated**. Possible causes include the use of a greater proportion of an expensive constituent that has improved the yield but has led to an increase in the overall cost, or the use of poor quality materials.

Question 4

Text reference. Performance measures are covered in Chapters 14 and 15.

Top tips. Parts (a) to (c) are fairly standard calculations on ROI and RI, involving a comparison between different divisions and calculating the effect of a changed situation. The superiority of residual income as a measure will always need to be discussed in answers.

Part (d) is a good test of your knowledge of the balanced scorecard. The six marks available required you to go into detail about the various aspects it covers.

Easy marks. The calculations in part (a) should be straightforward if you can remember the methods involved.

Marking scheme

				Marks
(a)	1 mark for each correct calculation			4
(b)	1 mark for each relevant comment			2
(c)	1 mark for each correct calculation		4	
	1 mark for each relevant comment about the results shown by ROI and RI			
		max	3	
	Comment on superiority of RI		1	
				8
(d)	Limitations of traditional measures		1	
	Perspectives of balanced scorecard		2	
	Uses of balanced scorecard		1	
	Relevance of balanced scorecard to Colour Co		2	
				6
				20

(a) In the case of Blue division, the **value of net assets** should exclude the non-current assets purchased on 29 September 20X8, because these were bought at the end of the year and so have not yet been able to make any contribution to the division's profitability.

(i) **ROI**

	Green	Blue
Net profit	$4.2 m	$5.6 m
Net assets	$32.0 m	$36.0 m
Return on investment (ROI)	13.1%	15.6%

(ii) **RI**

	Green	Blue
	$m	$m
Net profit	4.20	5.60
Notional interest (12% of net assets)	3.84	4.32
	0.36	1.28

(b)   **ROI and RI values**

Both Green and Blue have achieved a return on investment that is higher than the company's cost of capital, and so both have a positive residual income.

Comparison of divisions

Blue division has achieved a higher ROI and a higher residual income than Green division, suggesting that it has achieved the better performance. In the case of Green division, a fall in profitability by more than $360,000 would mean that its ROI would be less than the cost of capital, and the residual income would be negative.

(c)   **Assumptions**

The ROI and residual income of Green and Blue can be calculated, on the assumption that the new investment is undertaken and other results in 20X9 will be the same as in 20X8.

		Green		*Blue*
Net profit	(4.2 + 3.5)	$7.7 m	(5.6 + 3.5)	$9.1 m
Net assets	(32 + 25)	$57.0 m	(36 + 25)	$61.0 m
ROI		13.5%		14.9%

	Green	*Blue*
	$m	$m
Net profit	7.70	9.10
Notional interest (12% of net assets)	6.84	7.32
RI	0.86	1.78

Green division

The manager of Green division would want to undertake the investment, because it would result in an **increase in both the ROI** and the **residual income** of the division. This is because the ROI of the investment is (3.5/25) = 14%, higher than the ROI currently achieved by the division, and there is an addition to residual income because the extra net profit of $3.5 million exceeds the extra notional interest charge of (12% of $25 million) = $3 million.

Blue division

If the performance of Blue division is judged by **ROI**, the manager would be reluctant to undertake the investment. The ROI of the investment is 14%, which is higher than the company's cost of capital, but lower than the ROI currently being achieved by Blue. As a result, the division's ROI would fall, and reported performance would be worse. If on the other hand the performance of Blue is judged by **residual income**, the manager would want to undertake the investment. The return from the investment would exceed the company's cost of capital, and so residual income would rise (by $500,000).

Conclusion

This situation illustrates the **advantage** of **residual income** over ROI as a measure of divisional performance. Unlike ROI, residual income as a measure of performance will 'reward' divisional managers who invest in projects that earn an annual return in excess of the company's cost of capital.

(d)   **Limitations of traditional measures**

Traditional financial accounting measures such as return on investment and earnings per share have been criticised as giving misleading signals for **continuous improvement** and **innovation** – activities which today's competitive environment demands. The **balanced scorecard** is a way of measuring performance which integrates traditional financial measures with operational, customer and staff issues which are vital to the long-term competitiveness of an organisation.

Balanced scorecard perspectives

The balanced scorecard allows managers to look at their business from four important perspectives.

(i) **Customer perspective**

What do existing and new customers value from us?

The DIY market is subject to trends and customers expect new products and paint colours on a regular basis. Quality is often a key factor in customer decisions.

(ii) **Internal business perspective**

Measures from the customer's perspective need to be translated into the actions the organisation must take to meet these expectations. The internal business perspective of the balanced scorecard identifies the business processes that have the greatest impact on customer satisfaction, such as quality and employee skills.

(iii) **Innovation and learning perspective**

The organisation needs to learn, innovate and improve to satisfy future needs. It must produce new products, reduce costs and add value. Performance measures must emphasise continuous improvement in meeting customer needs. Examples of measures might be the length of time it takes to create new products or the percentage of revenue which comes from new products.

(iv) **Financial perspective**

This includes traditional measures such as profitability and growth but the measures are set through talking directly to shareholders. The financial perspective looks at whether the other three perspectives will result in financial improvement.

The success of the balanced scorecard approach lies in viewing all of the measure as a whole.

Use of balanced scorecard

Once those factors that are important to the organisation's success have been established, **performance measures** and **targets for improvement are set**. The measures and targets must be clearly communicated to all levels of management and employees so that they understand how their efforts can impact upon the targets set. The balanced scorecard can then become the most important monthly management report.

If the company takes a balanced scorecard approach, it will judge the performance of Blue and Green divisions on a mixture or balance of financial and non-financial measures. These could include impact on the customer and on internal processes and decision-making, and measures relating to innovation and learning, as well as financial targets.

Question 5

Marking scheme

			Marks
(a)	Triple F account net profit	3	
	Zero account net profit	3	
	Conclusion	1	
			7
(b)(i)	Layout of table	1	
	Average loan balances	1	
	Profit calculations	6	
			8
(b)(ii)	Current profit calculation	1	
	Compairson to outcomes in (b)	1	
	Factors to consider	3	
			5
			20

(a) **Triple F Account**

		$
Number of business customers		
(1,000,000 × 1.05)	1,050,000	
Fixed fees (1,050,000 × $10 × 12)		126,000,000
Customers with positive balances		
(1,050,000 × 45%)	472,500	
Interest paid ($2,000 × 472,500 × 0.5%)		(4,725,000)
Customers with overdrafts (1,050,000 × 55%)	577,500	
Interest charged		
($4,000 × 577,500 × 20%)		462,000,000
Business customers' account balances		
($2,000 × 472,500) + (577,500 × (4,000))	(1,365,000,000)	
Investment income foregone		
(1,365,000,000 − 1,040,000,000 (W1)) × 3%		(9,750,000)
Net profit from Triple F option		573,525,000

Zero Account

		$
Number of business customers		
(1,000,000 × 1.1)	1,100,000	
Number of transactions	1,100,000,000	
Transaction charges		Nil
Fixed fees		Nil
Customers with positive balances		
(1,100,000 × 45%)	495,000	
Interest paid		Nil
Customers with overdrafts (1,100,000 × 55%)	605,000	
Interest charged ($4,000 × 605,000 × 20%)		484,000,000
Business customers' account balances		
(495,000 × $2,000) + (605,000 × (4,000))	(1,430,000,000)	
Investment income foregone		
($1,430,000,000 − 1,040,000,000 (W1)) × 3%		(11,700,000)
Net profit under Zero Account Option		472,300,000

Conclusion

The bank should maintain its existing account structure with an estimated net profit of $831,280,000 as the other options would result in a reduction in profit.

Working

(1) **Investment income from account under current terms**

	$
1,000,000 business customers x (1,000 transactions x $0.60 transaction fee)	600,000,000
550,000 overdrawn business customers x (4,000 av overdraft x 0.2 (20% interest))	440,000,000
	1,040,000,000

(b) (i) **Two way data table**

There are two items of uncertainty: number of loans in issue and average loan balance.

Average loan balance	$7,500	$14,000	$15,000
Number of loans in issue			
250,000	106.75m	188.00m	200.50m
280,000	133.00m	224.00m	238.00m
300,000	150.50m	248.00m	263.00m

Profit calculation

Arrangement fee: $500 × number of loans

+ Interest charged: Average loan balance × 5% × number of loans

− Incremental advertising $112 million

(ii) **Other factors to be taken into consideration.**

Before the bank can make a decision about whether or not it should carry out the advertising campaign, it must determine any **additional profit** it would make for doing so.

Current profit

	$
Arrangement fee ($500 × 200,000)	100,000,000
Interest charged ($5,000 × 200,000 × 5%)	50,000,000
	150,000,000

Of the nine possible outcomes shown in the two-way data table, there are several that would give higher profits than the current $150 million.

The advertising campaign has the potential to increase the bank's **small loans' business**. It must consider if its **current resources** would cope with this potential increase in business. If additional resources are required the incremental profits may decline.

Another issue is the bank's **attitude towards risk**. Although profits are increased in seven out of the nine possible outcomes there is still a chance that profits will fall.

Finally, the bank should consider the **probability** of each of the outcomes occurring. The greater the likelihood of the outcomes with negative incremental profits, the greater the risk.

However, the advertising campaign would appear likely to result in higher profits for the bank. As a result, it should undertake the campaign.

ACCA

Paper F5

Performance Management

Mock Examination 3
December 2011

Question Paper	
Reading and planning Writing	15 minutes 3 hours
ALL FIVE questions are compulsory and MUST be attempted	

DO NOT OPEN THIS PAPER UNTIL YOU ARE READY TO START UNDER EXAMINATION CONDITIONS

ACCA

Paper F5

Performance Management

Mock Examination 3
December 2011

Question Paper		
Time allowed	Reading and planning	15 minutes
	Writing	3 hours

ALL FIVE questions are compulsory and MUST be answered

DO NOT OPEN THIS PAPER UNTIL YOU ARE READY TO START UNDER EXAMINATION CONDITIONS

BPP LEARNING MEDIA

All FIVE questions are compulsory and MUST be attempted

Question 1

The Telephone Co (T Co) is a company specialising in the provision of telephone systems for commercial clients. There are two parts to the business:

- installing telephone systems in businesses, either first time installations or replacement installations;
- supporting the telephone systems with annually renewable maintenance contracts.

T Co has been approached by a potential customer, Push Co, who wants to install a telephone system in new offices it is opening. Whilst the job is not a particularly large one, T Co is hopeful of future business in the form of replacement systems and support contracts for Push Co. T Co is therefore keen to quote a competitive price for the job. The following information should be considered:

(1) One of the company's salesmen has already been to visit Push Co, to give them a demonstration of the new system, together with a complimentary lunch, the costs of which totalled $400.

(2) The installation is expected to take one week to complete and would require three engineers, each of whom is paid a monthly salary of $4,000. The engineers have just had their annually renewable contract renewed with T Co. One of the three engineers has spare capacity to complete the work, but the other two would have to be moved from contract X in order to complete this one. Contract X generates a contribution of $5 per engineer hour. There are no other engineers available to continue with Contract X if these two engineers are taken off the job. It would mean that T Co would miss its contractual completion deadline on Contract X by one week. As a result, T Co would have to pay a one-off penalty of $500. Since there is no other work scheduled for their engineers in one week's time, it will not be a problem for them to complete Contract X at this point.

(3) T Co's technical advisor would also need to dedicate eight hours of his time to the job. He is working at full capacity, so he would have to work overtime in order to do this. He is paid an hourly rate of $40 and is paid for all overtime at a premium of 50% above his usual hourly rate.

(4) Two visits would need to be made by the site inspector to approve the completed work. He is an independent contractor who is not employed by T Co, and charges Push Co directly for the work. His cost is $200 for each visit made.

(5) T Co's system trainer would need to spend one day at Push Co delivering training. He is paid a monthly salary of $1,500 but also receives commission of $125 for each day spent delivering training at a client's site.

(6) 120 telephone handsets would need to be supplied to Push Co. The current cost of these is $18·20 each, although T Co already has 80 handsets in inventory. These were bought at a price of $16·80 each. The handsets are the most popular model on the market and frequently requested by T Co's customers.

(7) Push Co would also need a computerised control system called 'Swipe 2'. The current market price of Swipe 2 is $10,800, although T Co has an older version of the system, 'Swipe 1', in inventory, which could be modified at a cost of $4,600. T Co paid $5,400 for Swipe 1 when it ordered it in error two months ago and has no other use for it. The current market price of Swipe 1 is $5,450, although if Push Co tried to sell the one they have, it would be deemed to be 'used' and therefore only worth $3,000.

(8) 1,000 metres of cable would be required to wire up the system. The cable is used frequently by T Co and it has 200 metres in inventory, which cost $1·20 per metre. The current market price for the cable is $1·30 per metre.

(9) You should assume that there are four weeks in each month and that the standard working week is 40 hours long.

Required:

(a) Prepare a cost statement, using relevant costing principles, showing the minimum cost that T Co should charge for the contract. Make DETAILED notes showing how each cost has been arrived at and EXPLAINING why each of the costs above has been included or excluded from your cost statement. **(14 marks)**

(b) Explain the relevant costing principles used in part (a) and explain the implications of the minimum price that has been calculated in relation to the final price agreed with Push Co. **(6 marks)**

(Total = 20 marks)

Question 2

Bath Co is a company specialising in the manufacture and sale of baths. Each bath consists of a main unit plus a set of bath fittings. The company is split into two divisions, A and B. Division A manufactures the bath and Division B manufactures sets of bath fittings. Currently, all of Division A's sales are made externally. Division B, however, sells to Division A as well as to external customers. Both of the divisions are profit centres.

The following data is available for both divisions:

Division A

Current selling price for each bath	$450
Costs per bath:	
Fittings from Division B	$75
Other materials from external suppliers	$200
Labour costs	$45
Annual fixed overheads	$7,440,000
Annual production and sales of baths (units)	80,000
Maximum annual market demand for baths (units)	80,000

Division B

Current external selling price per set of fittings	$80
Current price for sales to Division A	$75
Costs per set of fittings:	
Materials	$5
Labour costs	$15
Annual fixed overheads	$4,400,000
Maximum annual production and sales of sets of fittings (units)	200,000
(including internal and external sales)	
Maximum annual external demand for sets of fittings (units)	180,000
Maximum annual internal demand for sets of fittings (units)	80,000

The transfer price charged by Division B to Division A was negotiated some years ago between the previous divisional managers, who have now both been replaced by new managers. Head Office only allows Division A to purchase its fittings from Division B, although the new manager of Division A believes that he could obtain fittings of the same quality and appearance for $65 per set, if he was given the autonomy to purchase from outside the company. Division B makes no cost savings from supplying internally to Division A rather than selling externally.

Required

(a) Under the current transfer pricing system, prepare a profit statement showing the profit for each of the divisions and for Bath Co as a whole. Your sales and costs figures should be split into external sales and inter-divisional transfers, where appropriate. **(6 marks)**

(b) Head Office is considering changing the transfer pricing policy to ensure maximisation of company profits without demotivating either of the divisional managers. Division A will be given autonomy to buy from external suppliers and Division B to supply external customers in priority to supplying to Division A.

Calculate the maximum profit that could be earned by Bath Co if transfer pricing is optimised. **(8 marks)**

(c)   Discuss the issues of encouraging divisional managers to take decisions in the interests of the company as a whole, where transfer pricing is used. Provide a reasoned recommendation of a policy Bath Co should adopt.

(6 marks)

(Total = 20 marks)

Question 3

You have recently been appointed as an assistant management accountant in a large company, PC Co. When you meet the production manager, you overhear him speaking to one of his staff, saying:

'Budgeting is a waste of time. I don't see the point of it. It tells us what we can't afford but it doesn't keep us from buying it. It simply makes us invent new ways of manipulating figures. If all levels of management aren't involved in the setting of the budget, they might as well not bother preparing one.'

Required

(a)   Identify and explain SIX objectives of a budgetary control system.   **(9 marks)**

(b)   Discuss the concept of a participative style of budgeting in terms of the six objectives identified in part (a).

(11 marks)

(Total = 20 marks)

Question 4

Fit Co specialises in the manufacture of a small range of hi-tech products for the fitness market. They are currently considering the development of a new type of fitness monitor, which would be the first of its kind in the market. It would take one year to develop, with sales then commencing at the beginning of the second year. The product is expected to have a life cycle of two years, before it is replaced with a technologically superior product. The following cost estimates have been made.

	Year 1	Year 2	Year 3
Units manufactured and sold		100,000	200,000
Research and development costs	$160,000		
Product design costs	$800,000		
Marketing costs	$1,200,000	$1,000,000	$1,750,000
Manufacturing costs:			
Variable cost per unit		$40	$42
Fixed production costs		$650,000	$1,290,000
Distribution costs:			
Variable cost per unit		$4	$4·50
Fixed distribution costs		$120,000	$120,000
Selling costs:			
Variable cost per unit		$3	$3·20
Fixed selling costs		$180,000	$180,000
Administration costs	$200,000	$900,000	$1,500,000

Note: You should ignore the time value of money.

Required

(a)   Calculate the life cycle cost per unit.   **(6 marks)**

(b)   After preparing the cost estimates above, the company realises that it has not taken into account the effect of the learning curve on the production process. The variable manufacturing cost per unit above, of $40 in year 2 and $42 in year 3, includes a cost for 0·5 hours of labour. The remainder of the variable manufacturing cost is not driven by labour hours. The year 2 cost per hour for labour is $24 and the year 3 cost is $26 per hour. Subsequently, it has now been estimated that, although the first unit is expected to take 0·5 hours, a learning curve of 95% is expected to occur until the 100th unit has been completed.

Calculate the revised life cycle cost per unit, taking into account the effect of the learning curve.

Note: the value of the learning co-efficient, b, is –0·0740005. **(10 marks)**

(c)   Briefly discuss the benefits of life cycle costing for pricing, performance management and decision-making.

(4 marks)

(Total = 20 marks)

Question 5

Choc Co is a company which manufactures and sells three types of biscuits in packets. One of them is called 'Ooze' and contains three types of sweeteners: honey, sugar and syrup. The standard materials usage and cost for one unit of 'Ooze' (one packet) is as follows:

		$
Honey	20 grams at $0·02 per gram	0·40
Sugar	15 grams at $0·03 per gram	0·45
Syrup	10 grams at $0·025 per gram	0·25
		1·10

In the three months ended 30 November 20X1, Choc Co produced 101,000 units of 'Ooze' using 2,200 kg of honey, 1,400 kg of sugar and 1,050 kg of syrup. Note: there are 1,000 grams in a kilogram (kg).

Choc Co has used activity-based costing to allocate its overheads for a number of years. One of its main overheads is machine set-up costs. In the three months ended 30 November 20X1, the following information was available in relation to set-up costs:

Budget

Total number of units produced	264,000
Total number of set ups	330
Total set-up costs	$52,800

Actual

Total number of units produced	320,000
Total number of set ups	360
Total set-up costs	$60,000

Required

(a)   Calculate the following variances for materials in Ooze:

    (i)   Total materials usage variance; **(4 marks)**

    (ii)   Total materials mix variance; **(4 marks)**

    (iii)   Total materials quantity (yield) variance. **(4 marks)**

(b)   Calculate the following activity-based variances in relation to the set-up cost of the machines:

    (i)   The expenditure variance; **(3 marks)**

    (ii)   The efficiency variance. **(3 marks)**

(c)   Briefly outline the steps involved in allocating overheads using activity based costing. **(2 marks)**

(Total = 20 marks)

Formulae Sheet

Learning curve

$Y = ax^b$

Where y = cumulative average time per unit to produce x units

      a = the time taken for the first unit of output

      x = the cumulative number of units produced

      b = the index of learning (log LR/log2)

      LR = the learning rate as a decimal

Regression analysis

$y = a + bx$

$$b = \frac{n\sum xy - \sum x \sum y}{n\sum x^2 - (\sum x)^2}$$

$$a = \frac{\sum y}{n} - \frac{b\sum x}{n}$$

$$r = \frac{n\sum xy - \sum x \sum y}{\sqrt{n\sum x^2 - (\sum x)^2 \left(n\sum y^2 - (\sum y)^2 \right)}}$$

Demand curve

$P = a - bQ$

$$b = \frac{\text{change in price}}{\text{change in quantity}}$$

a = price when Q = 0

$MR = a - 2bQ$

Answers

**DO NOT TURN THIS PAGE UNTIL YOU HAVE
COMPLETED THE MOCK EXAM**

A PLAN OF ATTACK

If this were the real Performance Management exam and you had been told to turn over and begin, what would be going through your mind?

An important thing to say (while there is still time) is that it is vital to have a good breadth of knowledge of the syllabus because the question requirements for each question will relate to different areas of the F5 syllabus. However, don't panic. Below we provide guidance on how to approach the exam.

Which order to do the questions

Use the 15 minutes reading time to **look through** the **paper in detail** and establish the **order** in which to attempt the questions. You will probably have decided which question looks the easiest and started with that one. Answer plans will help you to decide how to approach each question.

It is vital that you attempt all the questions in the paper to increase your chances of passing. The best way to do this is to make sure you stick to the time allocation for each question – both in total and for each of the question parts. The worst thing you can do is run over time in one question and then find that you don't have enough time for the remaining questions.

The next step

You're probably thinking that you don't know where to begin or you could answer all of the questions in three hours!

Option 1 (Oh dear)

If you are challenged by this paper, do the **questions in the order of how well you think you can answer them.**

- **Question 1** covers relevant costing. It requires you to prepare a cost statement, explaining why each cost is included or excluded. There are a number of easy marks available.
- **Question 2** looks at transfer pricing. You may find this area of the syllabus challenging. Make sure you give yourself enough time to attempt each of the three requirements.
- **Question 3** is a discursive question on budgeting and offers a number of easy marks, providing you can remember the objectives of a budgetary control system.
- **Question 4** looks at life cycle costing and learning curves. You may find the calculations in parts (a) and (b) challenging, but you should be able to score well in part (c) by discussing the benefits of life cycle costing on pricing, performance measurement and decision-making.
- **Question 5** covers variance analysis in an activity-based costing environment. You are required to calculate a number of materials variances as well as expenditure and efficiency variances.

Option 2 (This one's definitely easier)

Are you **sure** it is? If you are then that's encouraging but don't forget to do answer plans to make sure you don't miss the point of the questions.

- Address each cost in turn in **question 1.** Show all workings and remember to explain *why* the cost is included or excluded from the cost statement. Ensure you relate your answer to part (b) to the scenario.
- **Question 2** requires a number of calculations so once again, remember to show all your workings. Include headings for each working and split your answer to part (c) into short, punchy paragraphs to make it easy to mark.
- Discuss each objective under a separate heading in **question 3**. The questions asks for <u>six</u> objectives of a budgetary control system so do not waste time writing about more than six!
- **Question 4** contains some tricky calculations. There are easy marks on offer in part (c) so you may decide to answer this requirement first.

- **Question 5** requires a number of variance calculations so make sure you set your answer out clearly and remember to show all workings.

Once more for the road

You must must must **allocate your time** according to the marks for the question in total, and for the parts of the questions. And you must must must also **follow the requirements exactly.**

Finished with fifteen minutes to spare?

Looks like you slipped up on the time allocation. However if you have, make sure you don't waste the last few minutes; go back to **any parts of questions that you didn't finish** because you ran out of time.

Forget about it!

Forget about what? Excellent, you already have.

Question 1

Marking scheme

			Marks
(a)	Costing statement:		
	Lunch	1	
	Engineer costs	4	
	Technical advisor	1	
	Site visits	1	
	Training costs	1	
	Handsets	2	
	Control system	3	
	Cable	1	
			14
(b)	Explanation:		
	Relevant costing	1	
	Future cost / sunk cost	1	
	Cash flow not accounting adjustment	1	
	Incremental	1	
	Committed	1	
	Opportunity cost	1	
		max 4	
	Price to be charged:		
	Doesn't incorporate profit	1	
	Doesn't cover all costs	1	
	Ignores fixed costs	1	
	Contract X – engineer's time	1	
	Starting point only	1	
	Need to make a profit	1	
	Need to attract future work	1	
		max 4	max 6
			20

(a)   **Cost statement for T Co**

	Note	$
Demonstration & complimentary lunch	1	Nil
Engineers	2	500
Technical advisor	3	480
Site inspector visits	4	Nil
Training costs	5	125
Telephone handsets	6	2,184
Computerised control system	7	7,600
Cable costs	8	1,300
		12,189

(1) Demonstration & complimentary lunch

The salesman has already been to visit Push Co to demonstrate the new system. The associated costs are sunk costs (they have already been incurred) and are therefore excluded from the cost statement.

Relevant cost = $Nil

(2) Engineers

One of the three engineers has spare capacity to complete the installation and his/her salary will be paid regardless of whether they work on the contract for Push Co. The relevant cost is therefore $Nil.

The other two engineers are currently fully utilised and earn a contribution of $5 per hour each on Contract X. The engineers could be temporarily taken off of Contract X to work on the contract for Push Co. Work on Contract X would recommence in one week's time when there is no other scheduled work for the engineers.

Delaying the work on Contract X would result in T Co missing the contractual completion deadline and having to pay a one-off penalty of $500.

Relevant cost = $500

(3) Technical advisor

The technical advisor is working at full capacity so would need to work 8 hours overtime on the contract for Push Co. All overtime is paid at a premium of 50% above his usual hourly rate of $40 ($40 × 1.5 = $60).

Relevant cost = $60 × 8 hours = $480

(4) Site inspector visits

The site inspector is an independent contractor who is not employed by T Co and charges Push Co directly for the work.

Relevant cost = $Nil

(5) Training costs

The system trainer is paid a monthly salary of $1,500. This is not a relevant cost, as it is not incremental. The trainer is also paid $125 commission for each day spent delivering training at a client's site. This cost will arise as a direct result of the decision and is therefore included.

Relevant cost = $125 per day × 1 day = $125

(6) Handsets

120 handsets would need to be supplied to Push Co. Though 80 handsets are already in inventory, the handsets are frequently requested by T Co's customers and so would need to be replaced if supplied to Push Co. The current cost of a handset is $18.20.

Relevant cost = $18.20 × 120 handsets = $2,184

(7) Computerised control system

The current market price of Swipe 2 is $10,800.

The original cost of Swipe 1 ($5,400) is a sunk cost and not relevant to the decision.

The current market price of Swipe 1 ($5,450) is also not relevant to the decision as T Co has no intention of replacing Swipe 1.

The company could sell Swipe 1 for $3,000 if it does not use it for this contract. This represents an opportunity cost.

In addition to the $3,000, Swipe 1 could be modified at a cost of $4,600, bringing the total cost of converting Swipe 1 to $7,600.

The total cost of converting Swipe 1 ($7,600) is significantly less than purchasing Swipe 2 ($10,800). It is assumed that the company would choose the cheaper option.

Relevant cost = $7,600

(8) Cable costs

1,000 metres of cable is required. Although T Co has 200 metres of cable in inventory, it is used frequently and so would need to be replaced. All 1,000 metres should be valued at the current market rate ($1.30 per metre). The original purchase cost of $1.20 per metre is a sunk cost and is not relevant to the decision.

Relevant cost = 1,000 metres × $1.30 per metre = $1,300

(b)   **Relevant costing principles**

Relevant costs are future cash flows arising as a direct consequence of a decision.

Future costs

A cost that has been incurred in the past is totally irrelevant to any decision that is being made 'now'. Such costs are **past costs** or **sunk costs**.

Cash flows

Relevant costs are cash flows. This means that costs or charges such as **depreciation** or **notional rent** which do not reflect additional cash spending, should be ignored for the purpose of decision-making.

Direct consequence

The cash flow must be **incremental** if it is to be relevant to the decision-making process. For example, the $125 commission paid to the system trainer is an incremental cost – his monthly salary of $1,500 will be paid regardless of the decision that is made.

Opportunity cost

Opportunity cost is the **benefit sacrificed** by choosing one opportunity rather than the **next best alternative**. By using the Swipe 1 system for this contract, Push Co will forego sales proceeds of $3,000. This represents an opportunity cost which is **relevant** to the decision.

Implications of the minimum price

The cost calculated in part (a) represents the **minimum cost** that could be charged to the customer. If T Co charged this price for the contract it would make **no profit or loss** and so would not be rewarded for the **risk** it takes in completing the job. A suitable mark-up should be added to the cost.

T Co should also seek to recover costs that have **already been incurred**, such as costs attributed to the system demonstration and complimentary lunch.

In addition, none of T Co's **overhead costs** have been considered in the cost statement. These would need to be covered in the long term.

The cost statement assumes that engineers will delay work on Contract X for one week to work on the contract for Push Co. Another opportunity could arise in the week in which engineers are due to complete the work on Contract X. Any such opportunities would be rejected to ensure completion of Contract X, potentially giving rise to further **opportunity costs**.

In summary, the cost calculated in part (a) is only a **starting point**. T Co should price the contract so as to attract **future business** from Push Co whilst also making a profit, thus **increasing shareholder wealth**.

Question 2

Text reference. Transfer pricing is covered in Chapter 15.

Top tips. You may find part (a) particularly time pressured. Ensure your profit statement is neatly presented and remember to split sales and costs figures into external sales and inter-divisional transfers. If you are struggling with the calculations in parts (a) and (b), move on to the discussion requirement (part (c)).

Easy marks. There are easy marks available in part (c) for discussing the autonomy of managers and recommending a suitable transfer pricing policy for Bath Co.

Marking scheme

			Marks
(a)	Profit statement:		
	Sales revenue:		
	External	1	
	Inter-divisional transfers	½	
	External material costs	1	
	Inter-divisional transfers	½	
	Labour costs	1	
	Fixed costs	1	
	Profit	1	
			6
(b)	Revised profit:		
	External sales	1	
	Inter-divisional transfers	1	
	Material costs	2	
	Internal transfers (materials)	1	
	Labour costs	1	
	Fixed costs	1	
	Profit	1	
			8

(c) Transfer price difficulties and policy:

Each well-explained point on difficulties (1 mark per point)   max 4

Well reasoned recommendation   max 4

max 6

20

(a) **Profit statement**

	Division A $'000	Division B $'000	Company $'000
Sales revenue:			
External (W1)	36,000	9,600	45,600
Inter-divisional transfers	0	6,000	–
	36,000	15,600	45,600
Variable costs:			
External material costs (W2)	(16,000)	(1,000)	(17,000)
Inter-divisional transfers (W3)	(6,000)	0	–
Labour costs (W4)	(3,600)	(3,000)	(6,600)
	(25,600)	(4,000)	(23,600)
Fixed costs	(7,440)	(4,400)	(11,840)
Profit	2,960	7,200	10,160

Workings ($'000)

(1) **External sales**

Division A: 80,000 units × $450 = $36,000

Division B: 120,000 units × $80 = $9,600

Division B: 80,000 units × $75 = $6,000

(2) **External material costs**

Division A: 80,000 units × $200 = $16,000

Division B: 200,000 units × $5 = $1,000

(3) **Inter-divisional transfers**

Division A: 80,000 units × $75 = $6,000

(4) **Labour costs**

Division A: 80,000 units × $45 = $3,600

Division B: 200,000 units × $15 = $3,000

(b) **Bath Co's profit is transfer pricing is optimised**

	Division A $'000	Division B $'000	Company $'000
Sales revenue:			
External sales (W1)	36,000	14,400	50,400
Internal sales (W2)	0	1,300	–
	36,000	15,700	50,400
Variable costs:			
External material costs (W3)	(19,900)	(1,000)	(20,900)
Inter-divisional transfers (W2)	(1,300)	0	–
Labour costs	(3,600)	(3,000)	(6,600)
	(24,800)	(4,000)	(27,500)
Fixed costs	(7,440)	(4,400)	(11,840)
Profit	3,760	7,300	11,060

Note: The above statement has been prepared on the assumption that Bath Co will introduce the policy discussed in part (c). Assuming that the transfer price is set between Division B's marginal cost ($20) and the cost to Division A of buying from outside the group ($65), the actual transfer price is irrelevant in this calculation. The overall profit of the company will be the same.

Workings ($'000)

(1) **External sales**

Division A: 80,000 units × $450 = $36,000

Division B: 180,000 units × $80 = $14,400

(2) **Internal sales**

20,000 units × $65 = $1,300

(3) **External material costs**

Division A: 60,000 units × $265 + (20,000 units × $200) = $19,900

Division B: 200,000 units × $5 = $1,000

(c) **Issues**

Divisional profits will affect all common performance metrics that may be used by Bath Co such as return on capital employed (ROCE), profit for the period and residual income. As such, divisional managers will be keen to **maximise the profits** of their respective divisions.

By focussing on divisional profit, there is a risk that managers may make decisions that improve the performance of a division, but are not in the **best interests of the company** as a whole.

A **'dual transfer pricing system'** could be introduced to ensure that divisional managers act in the interest of the company.

The calculations in part (b) show that the best decision for the company is as follows.

To ensure that Division B is working at full capacity, Division A should buy 60,000 sets of fittings from an external supplier and the remaining 20,000 sets of fittings from Division B.

Division B should sell to the external market at $80 per set. As the maximum external demand is 180,000 units, the remaining 20,000 sets of fittings should be sold to Division A. As it has spare capacity, the minimum transfer price that would be acceptable to Division B is $20 (the **marginal cost per unit**). The maximum price that Division A will be willing to pay is $65 per unit (the price at which it can buy from **external suppliers**).

Recommended policy

Bath Co's transfer pricing policy should ensure that Division B is prepared to sell sets of fittings to Division A at a price of $65 per set. The manager of Division B should agree to this – it is in the division's best interest to work to full capacity and it is clear that Division A can obtain fittings for $65 per set from an **external supplier**.

The company also needs to have a policy whereby divisions **buy internally first**, where this would be in the best interests of the overall profitability of the company. This will ensure that Division A buys 20,000 sets of fittings from Decision B.

A policy of **negotiated transfer pricing** may help to agree a price that both divisional managers believe is fair. This will maximise the overall profit of the company and ensure that both divisional managers are **motivated**.

Question 3

> **Text reference**. Objectives of budgetary control are covered in Chapter 8. Budgetary systems are covered in Chapter 9.
>
> **Top tips**. Use the objectives identified in part (a) to structure your answer to part (b). Address each objective under a separate heading.
>
> **Easy marks**. There are plenty of easy marks available in part (a).

Marking scheme

			Marks
(a)	Objectives:		
	Each objective - 1½ marks per objective		max 9
(b)	Participative style of budgeting:		
	Explanation of participative budgeting	2	
	Each objective discussed in relation to it – 1½ marks per objective	9	
			11
			20

(a) Objectives of a budgetary control system

To compel planning

Budgeting forces management to look ahead and to set out detailed plans for **achieving targets** for each department, operation and (ideally) each manager within the organisation. It thus prevents management from relying on ad hoc or uncoordinated planning which may be detrimental to the performance of the organisation.

To communicate ideas and plans

A formal budgeting system is necessary to ensure that each person affected by management plans is aware of what he or she is supposed to be doing. Communication might be **one-way** with managers giving orders to subordinates, or there may be a **two-way dialogue** and exchange of ideas (participative budgeting).

To coordinate activities

Budgetary control systems help to coordinate the activities of different departments or sub-units of the organisation, ensuring **maximum integration** of effort towards common goals. The concept of coordination implies, for example, that the purchasing department should base its budget on production requirements

and that the production budget should in turn be based on sales expectations. Coordination is difficult to achieve and there is often **conflict** between departmental plans in the budget so that the efforts of each department are not fully integrated into a combined plan to achieve the company's **best targets**.

To provide a framework for responsibility accounting

Budgetary planning and control systems require that managers of **budget centres** are made responsible for the achievement of **budget targets** for the operations under their personal control.

To establish a system of control

A budget is a **benchmark** against which actual performance is **measured** and **assessed**. Control over actual performance is provided by the comparisons of actual results against the budget plan. Departures from budget can then be **investigated** and the reasons for the departures can be divided into controllable and uncontrollable factors.

To motivate employees to improve their performance

Employees can be motivated via a system of **feedback** of actual results, which lets them know how well or badly they are performing. The identification of controllable reasons for departures from budget with managers responsible provides an incentive for **improving future performance**.

Top tips. The question asks you to identify and explain SIX objectives of a budgetary control system. Other possible objectives include the following.

To ensure the achievement of the organisation's objectives

Objectives can be set for individual departments and operations as well as the organisation as a whole. Quantified expressions of these objectives are then drawn up as **targets** to be achieved within the timescale of the **budget plan**.

To evaluate performance

Performance can be evaluated by **comparing actual results against the budget**. Employees are often rewarded with bonuses if performance **exceeds budget**. This makes more sense than simply comparing actual results against the previous year as economic conditions can change and events happen that may not be expected to reoccur.

(b) **Participative budgeting**

Under a participative style of budgeting budgets are developed by **lower-level managers** who then submit the budgets to their superiors. The budgets are based on the lower-level managers' perceptions of what is achievable and the associated necessary resources.

Each of the objectives from part (a) is addressed below, considering the extent to which participate budgeting hopes to achieve this.

To compel planning

Participative budgeting (bottom-up budgeting) will compel planning. Under this style of budgeting, participation starts at the **lowest level of management** and goes all the way up to the top. In this way, planning takes place at **all levels** within the organisation. As a result, plans should be **more accurate** as they will be based on information from employees who are most familiar with day-to-day operations.

To communicate ideas and plans

Communication of **ideas and plans** will be particularly effective with participative budgeting. If all levels of management actively participate in the budgeting process then they will all know what the plan is. However, budgets may be updated during the **review process** to conform with the expectations of top level management. If this happens, lower-level management will have to work towards budgets that differ from those that were originally submitted.

To coordinate activities

Co-ordination of activities is likely to take **significantly longer** under a style of participative budgeting. For everyone to know what the plan is, not only does there need to be co-ordination between departments but there also has to be co-ordination between the **different levels of management** within each department.

To provide a framework for responsibility accounting

Participative budgeting is likely to **improve morale** amongst lower-level management and motivate them to work towards the budget targets under their control. However, there is a risk that lower-level management will introduce **budgetary slack** to make targets more achievable.

To establish a system of control

As stated above, budgets are likely to be more accurate if a participative style of budgeting is used, thus providing a solid **benchmark** against which to monitor actual results. However, the type of budgeting style used is largely irrelevant in establishing an effective **system of control**. Actual results should be compared against budget on a regular basis and any significant differences should be investigated, regardless of the budgetary system in place.

To motivate employees to improve their performance

Managers are more likely to think that a budget is **realistic** if they have been involved in the budget-setting process. They will therefore work harder to achieve the targets set. However, lower-level management may become disillusioned if top management make **significant changes** to the budget. They may be deliberately unproductive so that the final budget is not achieved and to prove that the budget they initially submitted was **more realistic / accurate**.

Question 4

> **Text reference.** Life cycle costing is covered in Chapter 2c. The learning curve is covered in Chapter 10.
>
> **Top tips.** Part (a) requires you to calculate the life cycle cost *per unit*. Do not forget to divide the total life cycle cost by the number of units.
>
> Ensure you remove the labour cost included in part (a) when calculating the revised life cycle cost in part (b).
>
> **Easy marks.** You should be able to score well in part (c) by briefly discussing the implications of life cycle costing on pricing, performance management and decision-making.

		Marks
(a)	Life cycle cost:	
	R&D costs	½
	Product design costs	½
	Marketing costs	½
	Fixed production costs	½
	Fixed distribution costs	½
	Fixed selling costs	½
	Administration costs	½
	Variable selling costs	½
	Variable manufacturing costs	½
	Variable distribution costs	½
	Total costs	½
	Cost per unit (correct figure)	½
		6

(b) Revised life cycle cost:

Cost per unit for 100 units	1
Total cost of 100 units	1
Cost per unit for 99 units	1
Total cost of 99 units	1
Cost of 100th unit	1
Total labour cost year 2	1
Total labour cost year 3	1
Carry forward life cycle costs from (a)	1
Deduct original labour cost in (a)	1
Revised cost per unit	1

10

(c) Benefits of life cycle costing:
Per valid point made - 1½ marks per point   max 4
20

(a) **Life cycle cost per unit**

	$
R&D costs	160,000
Product design costs	800,000
Marketing costs	3,950,000
Fixed production costs	1,940,000
Fixed distribution costs	240,000
Fixed selling costs	360,000
Administration costs	2,600,000
Variable manufacturing costs (W1)	12,400,000
Variable distribution costs (W2)	1,300,000
Variable selling costs (W3)	940,000
	24,690,000

Life cycle cost per unit = $24,690,000 / 300,000 units = $82.30

Workings

(1) **Variable manufacturing costs**

(100,000 units × $40) + (200,000 units × $42) = $12,400,000

(2) **Variable distribution costs**

(100,000 units × $4) + (200,000 units × $4.50) = $1,300,000

(3) **Variable selling costs**

(100,000 units × $3) + (200,000 units × $3.20) = $940,000

(b) **New life cycle cost per unit**

$Y = ax^b$

Where Y = cumulative average time per unit to produce x units

    a = the time taken for the first unit of output

    x = the cumulative number of units produced

    b = the index of learning (log LR / log2)

    LR = the learning rate as a decimal

b = − 0.0740005 (given in question)

The question states that a learning curve of 95% is expected to occur until the 100th unit has been completed.

Total labour time for first 100 units

x = 100

The question states that the first unit is expected to take 0.5 hours (a = 0.5)

$Y = 0.5 \times 100^{-0.0740005}$

= 0.3556 labour hours per unit

Therefore, labour time for 100 units = 0.3556 × 100 = 35.56 hours

Total labour time for 99 units

$Y = 0.5 \times 99^{-0.0740005}$

= 0.3559 labour hours per unit

Therefore, labour time for 99 units = 0.3559 × 99 = 35.23 hours

Therefore, time for 100th unit = 35.56 hours − 35.23 hours = 0.33 hours

Total labour cost over life of product

Year 2

	Hours
100 units × 0.3556 hours per unit	36
99,900 units × 0.33 hours per unit	32,967
	33,003
@ $24 per hour	$792,072

Year 3

	Hours
200,000 units × 0.33 hours per unit	66,000
@ $26 per hour	$1,716,000

Total revised life cycle cost

	$
Total labour cost ($792,072 + $1,716,000)	2,508,072
Life cycle costs from (a)	24,690,000
Less: Labour cost included in (a) (W1)	(3,800,000)
	23,398,072

Therefore, life cycle cost per unit = $23,398,072 / 300,000 units = $77.99

Working

(1)   **Labour cost included in (a)**

(100,000 units × 0.5 hours × $24) + (200,000 units × 0.5 hours × $26) = $3,800,000

(c)   **The benefits of life cycle costing**

Life cycle costing **tracks and accumulates actual costs and revenues** attributable to each product over the entire product life cycle.

The total profitability of any given product can be determined, meaning that **prices can be set** with better knowledge of the **true costs**.

Life cycle costing shows **all costs** relating to a product rather than costs relating to a single period, thus providing more **accurate information for decision making**.

The costs of researching, developing and designing products are also taken into account. This will allow for more accurate analysis when **measuring the performance** of new products.

Question 5

Marking scheme

		Marks
(a)	Material variances:	
	(i) Usage variance	4
	(ii) Mix variance	4
	(iii) Yield variance	4
		12
(b)	Overhead variances:	
	(i) Expenditure variance	3
	(ii) Efficiency variance	3
		6
(c)	ABC:	
	Each step – ½ mark	max 2
		20

(a) (i) **Usage variance**

	Std usage for actual output (W1)	Actual usage	Variance	Standard cost per kg (W2)	Variance
	Kgs	kgs	kgs	$	$
Honey	2,020	2,200	180 (A)	20	3,600 (A)
Sugar	1,515	1,400	115 (F)	30	3,450 (F)
Syrup	1,010	1,050	40 (A)	25	1,000 (A)
	4,545	4,650			1,150 (A)

Workings

(1) **Std usage for actual output**

There are 1,000 grams in a kilogram (kg).

Honey	20 grams per unit / 1,000	= 0.02 kg	× 101,000 units	= 2,020 kg
Sugar	15 grams per unit / 1,000	= 0.015 kg	× 101,000 units	= 1,515 kg
Syrup	10 grams per unit / 1,000	= 0.010 kg	× 101,000 units	= 1,010 kg

(2) **Std cost per kg**

Honey	$0.02 per gram × 1,000	= $20 per kg
Sugar	$0.03 per gram × 1,000	= $30 per kg
Syrup	$0.025 per gram × 1,000	= $25 per kg

(ii) Mix variance

	Actual quantity standard mix (W3)	Actual quantity actual mix	Variance	Standard cost per kg (W2)	Variance
	kgs	kgs	kgs	$	$
Honey	2,066.67	2,200	133.33 (A)	20	2,666.60 (A)
Sugar	1,550.00	1,400	150.00 (F)	30	4,500.00 (F)
Syrup	1,033.33	1,050	16.67 (A)	25	416.75 (A)
	4,650.00	4,650			1,416.65 (F)

Workings

(3) Actual quantity standard mix

	kg
Total quantity used:	
Honey	2,200
Sugar	1,400
Syrup	1,050
	4,650

Standard mix:	
Honey (20 grams / 45 grams per unit) × 4,650	2,066.67
Sugar (15 grams / 45 grams per unit) × 4,650	1,550.00
Syrup (10 grams / 45 grams per unit) × 4,650	1,033.33
	4,650.00

(iii) Yield variance

	Std quantity standard mix (W1)	Actual quantity standard mix (W3)	Variance	Standard cost per kg (W2)	Variance
	kgs	kgs	kgs	$	$
Honey	2,020.00	2,066.67	46.67 (A)	20	933.40 (A)
Sugar	1,515.00	1,550.00	35.00 (A)	30	1,050.00 (A)
Syrup	1,010.00	1,033.33	23.33 (A)	25	583.25 (A)
					2,566.65 (A)

Alternative solution

You may find the above method easier for calculating the mix and yield variances than the one shown below. However, in the method shown below, the individual variances for each material are also meaningful whereas they are not in the method shown above. Since the question only asks for the total variances, candidates were given credit for either method.

(ii) Mix variance

	Actual quantity actual mix	Actual quantity standard mix (W3)	Variance	Budgeted WAC per kg (W4)	Standard cost per kg (W2)	Diff	Variance
	kgs	kgs	kgs		$		$
Honey	2,200	2,066.67	133.33 (A)	24.44	20	(4.44)	591.99 (F)
Sugar	1,400	1,550.00	150.00 (F)	24.44	30	5.56	834.00 (F)
Syrup	1,050	1,033.33	16.67 (A)	24.44	25	0.56	9.34 (A)
	4,650	4,650.00					1,416.65 (F)

(iii) Yield variance

	Std usage actual output	Actual quantity actual mix	Variance	Budgeted WAC per kg	Variance
	kgs	kgs	kgs		$
Honey	2,020	2,200	180 (A)	24.44	4,399.20 (A)
Sugar	1,515	1,400	115 (F)	24.44	2,810.60 (F)
Syrup	1,010	1,050	40 (A)	24.44	977.60 (A)
	4,545	4,650			2,566.20 (A)

Working

(4) Budgeted weighted av cost

	Actual quantity standard mix (W3)	Standard cost per kg (W2)	Total cost
	kgs	$	$
Honey	2,066.67	20	41,333.40
Sugar	1,550.00	30	46,500.00
Syrup	1,033.33	25	25,833.25
	4,650.00		113,666.65

WAC = $113,666.65 / 4,650 kg = $24.44

(b) (i) Expenditure variance

	$
Budgeted expenditure (W1)	57,600
Actual expenditure	60,000
Expenditure variance	2,400 (A)

Workings

(1) Budgeted expenditure

Cost driver rate = Total set-up costs / number of set ups
= $52,800 / 330 = $160 per set up

Budgeted cost = $160 × 360 (actual set ups) = $57,600

(ii) Efficiency variance

Budgeted no. of set ups (W2)	400
Actual no. of set ups	360
Difference	40 (F)
× standard rate per set up	× $160
Volume efficiency variance	$6,400 (F)

Workings

(2) Budgeted no. of set ups

Budgeted no. of units per set up = Total no. of units produced / Total no. of set ups

= 264,000 / 330 = 800

Therefore, budgeted no. of set ups for 320,000 units = 320,000 / 800 = 400 set ups

(c) **Steps involved in allocating overheads using activity based costing (ABC)**

The first stage in allocating overheads using ABC is to identify the organisation's **major activities**.

Next, production overheads associated with each activity should be grouped into **cost pools**.

The third stage is to identify **cost drivers** for each activity, ie what causes these activity costs to be incurred.

Costs should then be **charged to products** on the basis of the cost driver.

ACCA examiner's answers:
June 2011 and December 2011

Note. The ACCA examiner's answers are correct at the time of going to press but may be subject to some amendments before the final versions are published.

1   Cement Co

(a)   Pay off table

				SUPPLY (no. of bags)		
			Prob.*	350,000	280,000	200,000
	Weather			$'000	$'000	$'000
	Good	$'000	0·25	1,750 (1)	1,400	1,000
DEMAND	Average	$'000	0·45	1,085 (2)	1,400	1,000
	Poor	$'000	0·3	325	640	1,000

* The probability column is only shown so as to help in part (b) (iii)'s calculations.

Profit per bag sold in coming year = $9 – $4 = $5
Loss per bag disposed of = $4 + $0·50 = $4·50

(1)   350,000 x $5 = $1,750,000

(2)   [280,000 x $5] – [70,000 x $(4·50)] = $1,085,000 etc

(b)   (i)   Maximin – identify the worst outcome for each level of supply and choose the highest of these worst outcomes.

	SUPPLY (no. of bags)		
	350,000	280,000	200,000
	$'000	$'000	$'000
Worst	325	640	1000

The highest of these is $1,000,000 therefore choose to supply only 200,000 bags to meet poor conditions.

(ii)   Maximax – identify the best outcome for each level of supply and choose the highest of these best outcomes.

	SUPPLY (no. of bags)		
	350,000	280,000	200,000
	$'000	$'000	$'000
Best	1,750	1,400	1,000

The highest of these is $1,750,000 therefore choose to supply 350,000 bags to meet good conditions.

(iii) Expected value – use the probabilities provided in order to calculate the expected value of each of the supply levels.

Good   (0·25 x $1,750,000) + (0·45 x $1,085,000) + (0·30 x $325,000) = $1,023,250
Average   (0·7 x $1,400,000) + (0·3 x $640,000) = $1,172,000
Poor   1 x $1,000,000 = $1,000,000

The expected value of producing 280,000 bags when conditions are average is the highest at $1,172,000, therefore this supply level should be chosen.

(c)   Maximin and expected value decision rules

The 'maximin' decision rule looks at the worst possible outcome at each supply level and then selects the highest one of these. It is used when the outcome cannot be assessed with any level of certainty. The decision maker therefore chooses the outcome which is guaranteed to minimise his losses. In the process, he loses out on the opportunity of making big profits. It is often seen as the pessimistic approach to decision-making (assuming that the worst outcome will occur) and is used by decision makers who are risk averse. It can be used for one-off or repeated decisions.

The 'expected value' rule calculates the average return that will be made if a decision is repeated again and again. It does this by weighting each of the possible outcomes with their relative probability of occurring. It is the weighted arithmetic mean of the possible outcomes.

Since the expected value shows the long run average outcome of a decision which is repeated time and time again, it is a useful decision rule for a risk neutral decision maker. This is because a risk neutral person neither seeks risk or avoids it; they are happy to accept an average outcome. The problem often is, however, that this rule is often used for decisions that only occur once. In this situation, the actual outcome is unlikely to be close to the long run average. For example, with Cement Co, the closest actual outcome to the expected value of $1,172,000 is the outcome of $1,085,000. This is not too far away from the expected value but many of the others are really different.

2 The Energy Buster

(a) Profit

In order to ascertain the optimum price, you must use the formula $P = a - bQ$

Where P = price; Q = quantity; a = intersection (price at which quantity demanded will be nil); b = gradient of the demand curve.

The approach is as follows:

(i) Establish the demand function

b = change in price/change in quantity = $15/1,000 = 0\cdot015$.

We know that if price = $735, quantity = 1,000 units.

Establish 'a' by substituting these values for P, Q and b into our demand function:

$735 = a - 0\cdot015Q$
$15 + 735 = a$
Therefore $a = 750$.

Demand function is therefore $P = 750 - 0\cdot015Q$

(ii) Establish marginal cost

The labour cost of the 100th unit needs to be calculated as follows:

Formula = $y = ax^b$.
$a = 1\cdot5$

Therefore, if $x = 100$ and $b = -\cdot0740005$, then $y = 1\cdot5 \times 100^{-0\cdot0740005} = 1\cdot0668178$
Therefore cost per unit = $1\cdot0668178 \times \$8 = \$8\cdot5345$
Total cost for 100 units = $853\cdot45.

If $x = 99$, $y = 1\cdot5 \times 99^{-0\cdot0740005} = 1\cdot0676115$
Therefore cost per unit = $8\cdot5408
Total cost for 99 = $845\cdot55
Therefore cost of 100th unit = $853\cdot45 - \$845\cdot55 = \$7\cdot90$.

Therefore total marginal cost = $42 + \$7\cdot90 = \$49\cdot90$.
Fixed overheads have been ignored as they are not part of the marginal cost.

(iii) Find profit

(1) Establish the marginal revenue function

$MR = a - 2bQ$
$MR = 750 - 0\cdot03Q$

(2) Equate MC and MR

$49\cdot90 = 750 - 0\cdot03Q$
$0\cdot03Q = 700\cdot1$
$Q = 23,337$

(3) Find optimum price

$P = 750 - (0\cdot015 \times 23,337)$
$= \$399\cdot95$

(b) (i) Penetration pricing

With penetration pricing, a low price would initially be charged for the Energy Buster. The idea behind this is that the price will make the product accessible to a larger number of buyers and therefore the high sales volumes will compensate for the lower prices being charged. A large market share would be gained and possibly, the Energy Buster might become accepted as the only industrial air conditioning unit worth buying.

The circumstances that would favour a penetration pricing policy are:

- highly elastic demand for the Energy Buster i.e. the lower the price, the higher the demand. The preliminary research does suggest that demand is elastic.

- if significant economies of scale could be achieved by Heat Co, then higher sales volumes would result in sizeable reductions in costs. This is not the case here, since learning ceases at 100 units.

- if Heat Co was actively trying to discourage new entrants into the market. In this case, new entrants cannot enter the market anyway, because of the patent.

- if Heat Co wished to shorten the initial period of the Energy Buster's life cycle so as to enter the growth and maturity stages quickly. We have no evidence that this is the case for Heat Co, although it could be.

From the above, it can be seen that this could be a suitable strategy in some respects but it is not necessarily the best one.

(ii) **Market skimming**

With market skimming, high prices would initially be charged for the Energy Buster rather than low prices. This would enable Heat Co to take advantage of the unique nature of the product, thus maximising sales from those customers who like to have the latest technology as early as possible. The most suitable conditions for this strategy are:

- the product is new and different. This is indeed the case with the Energy Buster.

- the product has a short life cycle and high development costs that need to be recovered quickly. The life cycle is fairly short and high development costs have been incurred.

- since high prices attract competitors, there needs to be barriers to entry in order to deter competitors. In Heat Co's case, there is a barrier, since it has obtained a patent for the Energy Buster.

- the strength and sensitivity of demand are unknown. Again, this is not the case here.

Once again, the Energy Buster meets only some of the conditions which would suggest that although this strategy may be suitable the answer is not clear cut. The fact that high development costs have been incurred and the life cycle is fairly short are fairly good reasons to adopt this strategy. Whilst we have demand curve data, we do not really know just how reliable this data really is, in which case a skimming strategy may be a safer option.

3   Noble restaurant

(a)   Flexed budget

Number of meals	1,560	
	$	$
Food sales (1)	62,400	
Drink sales (1)	15,600	
Total revenue		78,000
Variable costs:		
Staff wages (2)	(12,672)	
Food costs (3)	(7,800)	
Drink costs (4)	(3,120)	
Energy costs (5)	(4,234)	
		(27,826)
Contribution		50,174
Fixed costs:		
Manager's and chef's pay	(8,600)	
Rent, rates and depreciation	(4,500)	
		(13,100)
Operating profit		37,074

(1) Food revenue
Food revenue = 1,560 x $40 = $62,400
Drinks revenue = 1,560 x ($2·50 x 4) = $15,600.

(2) Staff wages
Average number of orders per day = 1,560/(6 days x 4 weeks) = 65 per day.
Therefore extra orders = 15 per day.
8 staff x 1·5 hours x 6 days x 4 weeks = 288 extra hours.
At $12 per hour = $3,456 extra wages.
Total flexed wages = $9,216 + $3,456 = $12,672.

(3) Food costs
Food costs = 12·5% x $62,400 = $7,800.

(4) Drink costs
Drinks costs = $15,600 x 20% = $3,120.

(5) Energy costs
Standard total hours worked = (8 x 6) x 6 days x 4 weeks = 1,152 hours.
Extra hours worked = 288 (working 2).
Total hours = 1,152 + 288 = 1,440.
At $2·94 per hour = $4,234.

(b) The sales mix contribution variance measures the effect on profit of changing the mix of actual sales from the standard mix. The sales quantity contribution variance measures the effect on profit of selling a different total quantity from the budgeted total quantity.

The mix variance is adverse here. Since meal B generates a higher contribution than meal A, the adverse variance shows that more of meal A must have been sold, relative to B, than budgeted. Since the quantity variance is favourable, this means that the total quantity of meals sold (in the standard mix) was higher than expected, as evidenced by the number of meals sold being 1,560 rather than the budgeted 1,200.

(c) Two other variances

Drink sales

As well as the price variance for drinks sales, the sales margin volume variance could be calculated. This will examine the difference between the standard volume of sales that would ordinarily be expected for this number of customers (1,560 x 4 drinks) compared to the actual volume of drinks sold because of the drinks promotion (1,560 x 6 drinks). Since the variance is calculated by applying the increase in volume to the standard margin, this variance will be favourable.

In addition, the total sales margin price variance for drinks sales could be split into an operational and a planning variance. The manager is only responsible for any operational variance and any part of the sales margin variance that relates to a planning error (i.e. the last minute decision by the owner to run the drinks promotion) should be separated out. This way, the manager will not be held accountable for matters outside of his control.

Food sales

By running the half price drinks offer promotion, more customers have been attracted to the restaurant. Drinks have been treated as a 'loss leader' i.e. sold at a low price in order to entice customers. It would therefore be relevant to calculate some variances in relation to food sales in order to show how the drinks promotion has increased food sales. The most obvious one to calculate would be the sales margin volume variance for food sales.

NOTE: Candidates only needed to mention two variances.

4   Brace Co

(a) Balanced scorecard

The balanced scorecard is a strategic management technique for communicating and evaluating the achievement of the strategy and mission of an organisation. It comprises an integrated framework of financial and non-financial performance measures that aim to clarify, communicate and manage strategy implementation. It translates an organisation's strategy into objectives and performance measurements for the following four perspectives:

Financial perspective

The financial perspective considers how the organisation appears to shareholders. How can it create value for its shareholders? Kaplan and Norton, who developed the balanced scorecard, identified three core financial themes that will drive the business strategy: revenue growth and mix, cost reduction and asset utilisation.

Customer perspective

The customer perspective considers how the organisation appears to customers. The organisation should ask itself: 'to achieve our vision, how should we appear to our customers?'.

The customer perspective should identify the customer and market segments in which the business units will compete. There is a strong link between the customer perspective and the revenue objectives in the financial perspective. If customer objectives are achieved, revenue objectives should be too.

Internal perspective

The internal perspective requires the organisation to ask itself the question – 'what must we excel at to achieve our financial and customer objectives?'. It must identify the internal business processes that are critical to the implementation of the organisation's strategy. Kaplan and Norton identify a generic process value chain consisting of three processes: the innovation process, the operations process and the post-sales process.

Learning and growth perspective

The learning and growth perspective requires the organisation to ask itself whether it can continue to improve and create value.

If an organisation is to continue having loyal, satisfied customers and make good use of its resources, it must keep learning and developing. It is critical that an organisation continues to invest in its infrastructure – i.e. people, systems and organisational procedures – in order to provide the capabilities that will help the other three perspectives to be accomplished.

(b) Divisional performance

ROI:
Division A
Net profit = $44·6m x 28% = $12·488m
ROI = $12·488m/$82·8m = 15·08%

Division B
Net profit = $21·8m x 33% = $7·194m
ROI = $7·194m/$40·6m = 17·72%

Residual income:
Division A
Divisional profit = $12·488m
Capital employed = $82·8m
Imputed interest charge = $82·8m x 12% = 9·936m
Residual income = $12·488m – $9·936m = $2·552m.

Division B
Divisional profit = $7·194m
Capital employed = $40·6m
Imputed interest charge = $40·6m x 12% = $4·872m
Residual income = $7·194 – $4·872 = $2·322m.

Comments

If a decision about whether to proceed with the investments is made based on ROI, it is possible that the manager of Division A will reject the proposal whereas the manager of Division B will accept the proposal. This is because each division currently has a ROI of 16% and since the Division A investment only has a ROI of 15·08%, it would bring the division's overall ROI down to less than it's current level. On the other hand, since the Division B investment is higher than its current 16%, the investment would bring the division's overall ROI up.

When you consider what would actually be best for the company as a whole, you come to the conclusion that, since both investments have a healthy return, they should both be accepted. Hence, the fact that ROI had been used as a decision-making tool has led to a lack of goal congruence between Division A and the company as whole. This backs up what the new manager of Division A is saying. If they used residual income in order to aid the decision-making process, both proposals would be accepted by the divisions since both have a healthy RI. In this case, RI helps the divisions to make decisions that are in line with the best interests of the company. Once again, this backs up the new manager's viewpoint.

It is important to note, however, that each of the methods has numerous advantages and disadvantages that have not been considered here.

5 (a) Throughput accounting ratio (TAR)

TAR is traditionally defined as: return per factory hour/cost per factory hour. In this context, we are dealing with a hospital, so it will be: return per hospital hour/cost per hospital hour.

Since, in throughput accounting, all costs except material costs are treated as fixed costs, total hospital costs will be all the salaries plus the general overheads:

$45,000 + $38,000 + $75,000 + $90,000 + $50,000 + $250,000 = $548,000.

Total hours of bottleneck resource, the surgeon's time, = 40hrs x 47 weeks = 1,880 hours.

Therefore cost per hospital hour = $548,000/1,880 = $291·49.

Return per hospital hour now needs to be calculated.

	$
Selling price per unit	4,250
Materials cost:	
– injection	(1,000)
– anaesthetic	(45)
– dressings	(5·6)
Throughput per unit	3,199·40
Time on BNR in hours	1·25
Return per hour ($)	2,559·52
TAR	$2,559·52/$291·49
	= 8·78

(b) Optimum production plan

Limiting factor analysis can be used to determine the optimum production plan. Each procedure first needs to be ranked according to its TAR, then as many of each procedure should be performed as possible, starting with the most profitable procedure first.

			A $	B $	C $
TAR			8·96	9·11	8·78
Ranking			2	1	3

Name	Number	Hrs each	Total hours	T/P per hour	Total T/P
B	800	1	800	2,654·40	2,123,520
A	600	0·75	450	2,612·53	1,175,638·5
C	504	1·25	630	2,559·52	1,612,497·6
			1,880		4,911,656·1

The optimum production plan is therefore to perform the maximum number of procedures A and B (600 and 800 respectively) and perform only 504 of procedure C.

Total profit will be:

	$
Throughput	4,911,656·1
Less total costs	(548,000)
Profit	4,363,656·1

(c) Profitability increase

At present, if the company adheres to the optimum production plan above, it will be satisfying customer demand for procedures A and B but not for procedure C. The most obvious way to try and increase profit would be to try and exploit demand for procedure C. There are two main factors that would need to be overcome in order for this demand to be exploited. Firstly, another surgeon would need to be employed. Most other members of staff clearly have excess time available, because the surgeon's required time is at least double their required time. The recovery specialist, however, is currently used for 1,292·96 hours [(600 x 0·6) + (800 x 0·7) + (504 x 0·74)]. This staff member therefore has 587·04 spare hours available (1,880 − 1,292·96). This is enough to carry out the additional 696 procedures of C, gvien that each one uses 0·74 hours of the recovery specialist's time (0·74 x 696 = 515·04).

If another surgeon was employed he would be able to meet all of the excess demand for procedure C, which would be 696 procedures (1,200 − 504).

Secondly, the other theatre would need to be equipped with the necessary equipment so that the second surgeon could operate in it. A quick calculation will show that this cost will be more than covered even in the first year (and the theatre cost is capital anyway, and will be benefitted from over many years).

	$
T/P from additional 696 procedures (696 x 1·25 x $2,559·52) =	2,226,782
Cost of equipment	(750,000)
Surgeon's fee	(90,000)
	1,386,782

Without even taking into account future years, on the basis of one year's throughput alone, it is worth equipping the second theatre provided that a suitably qualified second surgeon can be found.

1   T Co

(a)   Cost statement

	$	Note
Lunch	0	1
Engineers' costs	500	2
Technical advisor	480	3
Site visits	0	4
Training costs	125	5
Handsets	2,184	6
Control system	7,600	7
Cable	1,300	8
Total cost	12,189	

Notes

Note 1: Lunch

This past cost is a 'sunk cost' and should therefore be excluded from the cost statement. It has already arisen and is therefore not incremental.

Note 2: Engineers' costs

Since one of the engineers has spare capacity, the relevant cost of his hours is Nil. This is because relevant costs must arise as a future consequence of the decision, and since his wage will be paid regardless of whether he now works on the contract for Push Co, it is not an incremental cost.

The situation for the other two engineers is slightly different. Their time is currently fully utilised and earning a contribution of $5 per hour each. This is after deducting their hourly cost which, given a salary of $4,000 per month each, is $25 per hour ($4,000/4 x 40). However, in one week's time – when they would otherwise be idle – they can complete Contract X and earn the contribution anyway. Therefore, the only relevant cost is the penalty of $500 that will be payable for the delay on Contract X.

Note 3: Technical advisor

Since the advisor would have to work overtime on this contract, the relevant cost is the overtime rate of $60 ($40 x 1·5) per hour. This would total $480 for the whole job.

Note 4: Site visits

This is a cost paid directly by Push Co to a third party. Since it is not a relevant cost for T Co, it has been excluded.

Note 5: Training costs

Since the trainer is paid a monthly salary irrespective of what work he does, this element of his cost is not relevant to the contract, since it is not incremental. However, the commission of $125 will arise directly as a consequence of the decision and must therefore be included.

Note 6: Handsets

Although T Co has 80 of the 120 handsets required already in inventory, they are clearly in regular use in the business. Therefore, if the 80 are used on this contract, they will simply need to be replaced again. Consequently, the relevant cost for both the 40 that need to be bought and the 80 already in inventory is the current purchase price of $18·20 each. 120 x $18·20 = $2,184.

Note 7: Control system

The historic cost of Swipe 1, $5,400, is a 'sunk' cost and not relevant to this decision. However, since the company could sell it for $3,000 if it did not use it for this contract, the $3,000 is an opportunity cost here. The current market price for Swipe 1 of $5,450 is totally irrelevant to the decision as T Co has no intention of replacing Swipe 1, since it was bought in error. In addition to the $3,000, there is a modification cost of $4,600, bringing the total cost of converting Swipe 1 to $7,600. This is still a cheaper option than buying Swipe 2 for $10,800, therefore the company would choose to do the modification to Swipe 1. The cost of $10,800 of a new Swipe 2 system is therefore irrelevant now.

Note 8: Cable

The cable is in regular use by T Co, therefore all 1,000 metres should be valued at the current market price of $1·30 per metre. The $1·20 per metre is a sunk cost and not relevant.

(b)   Relevant costing principles

Relevant costs are those costs that change as a result of making a particular decision. In simple terms, a relevant cost is a future cash flow arising as a direct consequence of a decision. In order for a cost to be relevant to a decision, it must therefore meet all three of these criteria:

Future – any costs which have already been incurred are regarded as 'sunk' costs and will prevent a cost from being considered relevant.

Cash flow – the cost must be a cash flow and not just an accounting adjustment, such as a provision for a debt or depreciation. Also, cash flows that are the same for all alternatives are not relevant.

Direct consequence – this criteria means that the cash flow must be incremental. For example, if a cost has already been committed to, then it will arise irrespective of whether the decision goes ahead. It will not therefore meet the 'direct consequence' criteria.

Opportunity cost – this is the value of the best alternative that is foregone as a result of making a decision. In the case of the telephone system that Push Co needs for the contract, the foregone sales proceeds of $3,000 are an example of an opportunity cost since, by using the system for this contract, Push Co foregoes these sales proceeds.

Note: *candidates would not be required to write all of this for the available marks.*

Significance of minimum price calculated

The cost calculated in part (a) is a starting point only, showing the minimum cost that could be charged to the customer. If T Co charged this price, it would be no better or worse off than if it did not carry out the work, i.e. it would make no profit or loss. This means that T Co would not be rewarded for the risk that it takes in completing the work, unless some kind of a mark-up is also incorporated.

Also, other costs – such as the lunch of $400 – whilst not incremental to the decision now, have been incurred. Ideally, therefore, T Co should seek to recover them.

It could also be that, for example, in one week's time, when the engineers are busy completing the delayed contract X, another opportunity comes up that the company has to reject because the engineers are busy on Contract X. Therefore, with hindsight, it would be seen that there was an opportunity cost associated with using the engineers on this work and delaying contract X.

Furthermore, none of the business's overheads have been considered in the cost statement and, in the long term, these would need to be covered.

It is clear, therefore, that the relevant cost calculated in part (a) is only a starting point for T Co to use when deciding how to price the contract. The purpose of accepting contracts is to make profit and increase shareholder wealth. This will only be done if a price higher than the relevant cost of the contract is charged. In setting this price, however, T Co also needs to give consideration to the fact that it hopes to attract future work from Push Co. The price needs to be attractive enough for the customer to return in the future.

2   Bath Co

(a)   Profit statement

	Division A $'000	Division B $'000	Company $'000
Sales revenue:			
External (1)	36,000	9,600	45,600
Inter-divisional transfers	0	6,000	
Total	36,000	15,600	45,600
Variable costs:			
External material costs (2)	(16,000)	(1,000)	(17,000)
Inter-divisional transfers (3)	(6,000)	0	
Labour costs (4)	(3,600)	(3,000)	(6,600)
Total	(25,600)	(4,000)	(23,600)
Fixed costs	(7,440)	(4,400)	(11,840)
Profit	2,960	7,200	10,160

Workings ($'000)

(1)   **External sales**
        Div A: 80,000 x $450 = $36,000
        Div B: 120,000 x $80 = $9,600
        Div B: 80,000 x $75 = $6,000

(2)   **External material costs**
        Div A: 80,000 x $200 = $16,000
        Div B: 200,000 x $5 = $1,000

(3)   **Inter-divisional transfers**
        Div A: 80,000 x $75 = $6,000

(4) Labour costs
Div A: 80,000 x $45 = $3,600
Div B: 200,000 x $15 = $3,000

(b) Bath Co's profit if transfer pricing is optimised

	Division A $'000	Division B $'000	Company $'000
Sales revenue:			
External (1)	36,000	14,400	50,400
Internal sales (2)		1,300	
Total	36,000	15,700	50,400
Variable costs:			
External material costs (3)	(19,900)	(1,000)	(20,900)
Inter-divisional transfers (2)	(1,300)		
Labour costs	(3,600)	(3,000)	(6,600)
Total	(24,800)	(4,000)	(27,500)
Fixed costs	(7,440)	(4,400)	(11,840)
Profit	3,760	7,300	11,060

Note: *A transfer price of $65 has been used on the assumption that the company will introduce the policy discussed in (c). Provided that the transfer price is set between the minimum of $20 (Division B's marginal cost) and $65 (the cost to Division A of buying from outside the group), the actual transfer price is irrelevant in this calculation. The overall profit of the company will be the same.*

Workings ($'000)

(1) External sales
Div A: 80,000 x $450 = $36,000
Div B: 180,000 x $80 = $14,400

(2) Internal sales/inter-divisional transfers
20,000 x $65 = $1,300

(3) Material costs
Div A: 60,000 x $265 + (20,000 x $200) = $19,900
Div B: 200,000 x $5 = $1,000

(c) Issues and suitable transfer price

Divisional managers' performance is assessed using a metric as decided by the company. This may simply be the profit for the period, or, depending on the type of responsibility centre being used, a metric such as residual income or return on capital employed. Whatever the metric being used, the division's profit figure is going to affect it and divisional managers are therefore going to be keen to maximise their individual profits. By focusing on individual decisions, divisional managers are often not aware of the impact of their decisions on the company as a whole. This would particularly be the case where a decision which is in the best interests of the company actually makes an individual division's performance look worse.

The transfer pricing system in place needs to take into account the behavioural impact of the prices being charged. Sometimes, this can mean that a 'dual transfer pricing system' needs to be introduced in order to ensure that divisional managers act in the interests of the company as a whole.

It can be seen from part (b) that the best decision for the company is that:

– Division A buys 60,000 sets of fittings from an outside supplier and buys the remaining 20,000 sets of fittings from Division B in order to ensure that Division B is working to full capacity.

– Division B sells as many sets of fittings as possible externally, at $80 per set. Since the maximum external demand is 180,000 units, Division B sells the remaining 20,000 sets of fittings to Division A. The minimum transfer price that would be acceptable to Division B is its marginal cost of $20 per unit, since it has spare capacity. However, if this transfer price is used, Division B becomes worse off than before the autonomy was given, and Division B's manager will not like this. As far as Division A is concerned, it will not want to pay more than the $65 that it can buy from outside the group.

Bath Co's policy therefore needs to ensure that, firstly, Division A's manager is prepared to buy 20,000 sets of fittings from Division B and secondly, Division B is prepared to sell them at $65 per set. Since it is in Division B's best interest to work to full capacity and the manager of Division B knows that Division A can obtain fittings for $65 per set, it should not be difficult for B to agree to sell to A at this price. A policy of negotiated transfer prices would achieve this fairly quickly. However, the company also needs to have a policy that divisions buy internally first, where this would be in the best interests of the overall profitability of the company. This would ensure that Division A buys the 20,000 sets of fittings from Division B. This way, the overall profit of the company is maximised whilst also ensuring that divisional managers do not become demotivated.

3 (a) Objectives of a budgetary control system

– **To compel planning**
Budgeting makes sure that managers plan for the future, producing detailed plans in order to ensure the implementation of the company's long term plan. Budgeting makes managers look at the year ahead and consider the changes in conditions that might take place and how to respond to those changes in conditions.

– **To co-ordinate activities**
Budgeting is a method of bringing together the activities of all the different departments into a common plan. If an advertising campaign is due to take place in a company in three months' time, for example, it is important that the production department know about the expected increase in sales so that they can scale up production accordingly. Each different department may have its own ideas about what is good for the organisation. For example, the purchasing department may want to order in bulk in order to obtain bulk quantity discounts, but the accounts department may want to order in smaller quantities so as to preserve cash flow.

– **To communicate activities**
Through the budget, top management communicates its expectations to lower level management. Each department has a part to play in achieving the desired results of the company, and the annual budget is the means of formalising these expectations. The whole process of budget setting, whereby information is shared between departments, facilitates this communication process.

– **To motivate managers to perform well**
The budget provides a basis for assessing how well managers and employees are performing. In this sense, it can be motivational. However, if the budget is imposed from the top, with little or no participation from lower level management and employees, it can have a seriously demotivational effect. This is discussed further in part (b).

– **To establish a system of control**
Expenditure within any organisation needs to be controlled and the budget facilitates this. Actual results are compared to expected results, and the reasons for any significant, unexpected differences are investigated. Sometimes the reasons are within the control of the departmental manager and he/she must be held accountable; at other times, they are not.

– **To evaluate performance**
Often, managers and employees will be awarded bonuses based on achieving budgeted results. This makes more sense than evaluating performance by simply comparing the current year to the previous year. The future may be expected to be very different than the past as economic conditions change. Also, events happen that may not be expected to reoccur. For example, if weather conditions are particularly wet one year, a company making and selling umbrellas would be expected to make higher than usual sales. It would not be fair to assess managers against these historical sales levels in future years, where weather conditions are more normal.

(Other possible objectives include:

– **To delegate authority to budget holders**
A formal budget permits budget holders to make financial decisions within the specified limits agreed, i.e. to incur expenditure on behalf of the organisation.

– **To ensure achievement of the management's objectives**
Objectives are set not only for the organisation as a whole but also for individual targets. The budget helps to work out how these objectives can be achieved.)

(b) Participative budgeting

'Participative budgeting' refers to a budgeting process where there is some level of involvement from subordinates within the organisation, rather than budgets just being set by the top level of management.

There are various views about whether participative budgeting is more effective than other styles. Each of the objectives from part (a) is dealt with below, considering the extent to which participative budgeting helps to achieve this.

– **To compel planning**
Participative budgeting will compel planning. Although participation can take many forms, often it will take the form of bottom-up budgeting, whereby the participation starts at the lowest level of management and goes all the way up to the top. If this is the case, then planning is taking place at many levels, and should be more accurate than if it simply takes place at a high level, by individuals who are not familiar with the day to day needs of the business.

– **To co-ordinate activities**
Co-ordination of activities may become more time consuming if a participative style of budgeting is used. This is because, not only does there need to be co-ordination between departments but there also has to be co-ordination between the different levels of management within each department. The process should be cumbersome but also effective, with everyone knowing exactly what the plan is.

– **To communicate activities**
Communication will be particularly effective with participative budgeting, although how effective depends on the extent of the participation. If all levels of management are involved, from the bottom up, then all levels of management know what the plan is. However, the plan may change as different departments' budgets are reviewed together and the overall

budgeted profit compared to the top level management's expectations. Hence, it may be the case that those people involved in the initial budgets, i.e. lower level management, have to deal with their budgets being changed.

- **To motivate managers to perform well**

  If managers play a part in setting the budget, they are more likely to think that the figures included in them are realistic. Therefore, they are more likely to try their best to achieve them. However, it may be that managers have built budgetary slack into their budgets, in an attempt to make themselves look good. Therefore, managers could end up performing less well than they would do had tougher targets been set by their superiors.

- **To establish a system of control**

  In terms of establishing a system of control, it is largely irrelevant whether the budget setting process is a participative one or not. What is important is that actual results are compared to expected, and differences are investigated. This should happen irrespective of the budget setting process. Having said that, control is only really effective if the budgeted figures are sound. As stated above, whilst they are more likely to be realistic if a participative style of budgeting is used, the system is open to abuse in the form of budgetary slack.

- **To evaluate performance**

  Managers will be appraised by comparing the results that they have achieved to the budgeted results. A participative budget will be an effective tool for this provided that participation is real rather than pseudo and provided that the managers have not built slack into their figures, which has gone uncorrected.

Note: *candidates would not be required to write all of this for the available marks.*

4 (a) Life cycle cost per unit

	$
R & D costs	160,000
Product design costs	800,000
Marketing costs	3,950,000
Fixed production costs	1,940,000
Fixed distribution costs	240,000
Fixed selling costs	360,000
Administration costs	2,600,000
Variable manufacturing costs	12,400,000
(100,000 x $40 + 200,000 x $42)	
Variable distribution costs	1,300,000
(100,000 x $4 + 200,000 x $4·50)	
Variable selling costs	940,000
(100,000 x $3 + 200,000 x $3·20)	
Total costs	24,690,000

Therefore cost per unit = $24,690,000/300,000 = $82·30

(b) New life cycle cost

Total labour time for first 100 units:
$y = ax^b$
$b = -0.0740005$

If $x = 100$, then $y = 0.5 \times 100^{-0.0740005}$
= 0·3556 hours per unit.
Therefore total hours for 100 units = 35·56 hours

Time for 99th unit
$y = 0.5 \times 99^{-0.0740005}$
= 0·3559 hours per unit.
Therefore total hours for 99 units = 35·23 hours.

Therefore, time for 100th unit = 35·56 hours – 35·23 hours = 0·33 hours

Total labour cost over life of product:

Year 2

100 units at 0·3556 per unit	36	hours
99,900 at 0·33 hours per unit	32,967	hours
	33,003	hours
at $24 per hour	$792,072	

Year 3

200,000 at 0·33 per unit	66,000	hours
at $26 per hour	$1,716,000	

Total revised life cycle cost

	$
Therefore total labour cost	2,508,072
Other life cycle costs from (a)	24,690,000
Less labour cost included in (a)	(3,800,000)
(100,000 x 0·5 x $24) + (200,000 x 0·5 x $26)	
Total revised life cycle costs	23,398,072

Therefore cost per unit = $23,398,072/300,000 = $77·99

(c) Benefits of life cycle costing

- The visibility of ALL costs is increased, rather than just costs relating to one period. This facilitates better decision-making.

- Individual profitability for products is more accurate because of this. This facilitates performance appraisal and decision-making, and means that prices can be determined with better knowledge of the true costs.

- More accurate feedback can take place when assessing whether new products are a success or a failure, since the costs of researching, developing and designing those products are also taken into account.

Note: *Other valid benefits would also be awarded marks.*

5 (a) (i) Usage variance

	Std usage for actual output kgs	Actual usage kgs	Variance kgs	Std cost per kg $	Variance $
Honey	2,020	2,200	(180)	20	(3,600)
Sugar	1,515	1,400	115	30	3,450
Syrup	1,010	1,050	(40)	25	(1,000)
					(1,150) A

(ii) Mix variance

	Actual qnty std mix kgs	Actual qnty actual mix kgs	Variance kgs	Std cost per kg $	Variance $
Honey	2,066·67	2,200	(133·33)	20	(2,666·60)
Sugar	1,550	1,400	150	30	4,500
Syrup	1,033·33	1,050	(16·67)	25	(416·75)
					1,416·65 F

(iii) Yield variance

	Std quantity std mix kgs	Actual qnty std mix kgs	Variance kgs	Std cost per kg $	Variance $
Honey	2,020	2,066·67	(46·67)	20	(933·40)
Sugar	1,515	1,550	(35)	30	(1,050)
Syrup	1,010	1,033·33	(23·33)	25	(583·25)
					(2,566·65) A

The method used above is a more simple method for calculating the mix and yield variances than the one shown below. However, in the method shown below, the individual variances for each material are also meaningful, whereas they are not in the method shown above. Since the question only asks for the total variances, students will be given credit for either method.

(ii) Mix variance

	Actual qnty std mix kgs	Actual qnty actual mix kgs	Variance kgs	budgeted WAC per kg	Std cost per kg $	Difference	Variance $
Honey	2,066·67	2,200	(133·33)	24·44	20	(4·44)	592·59
Sugar	1,550	1,400	150	24·44	30	5·56	833·33
Syrup	1,033·33	1,050	(16·67)	24·44	25	0·56	(9·26)
							1,416·66 F

(iii) Yield variance

	Std usage for actual output kgs	Actual qnty actual mix kgs	Variance kgs		Variance $
Honey	2,020	2,200	(180)	24·44	(4,400·00)
Sugar	1,515	1,400	115	24·44	2,811·11
Syrup	1,010	1,050	(40)	24·44	(977·78)
					(2,566·67) A

Budgeted weighted average cost

Honey	2,066·67	20	41,333·4
Sugar	1,550	30	46,500
Syrup	1,033·33	25	25,833·25
	4,650	113,666·65	24·44

WAC = $113,666·65/4,650 kg = $24·44

(b) (i) Expenditure variance

Cost driver rate = $52,800/330 = $160
Expected cost therefore = 360 x $160 $57,600
Actual cost $60,000

Variance $2,400 A

(ii) Efficiency variance

Expected no. of units per set up
264,000/330 = 800

Therefore expected no. of set ups for
320,000 = 320,000/800 =   400
Actual number of set ups   360

Difference   40 F

x standard rate per set up $160

Variance $6,400 F

(c) Steps involved in activity based costing

- Identify the organisation's major activities.
- Collect the costs associated with each activity into cost pools.
- Identify the cost drivers i.e. those factors which give rise to the costs.
- Charge the costs to the products on the basis of the cost driver.

Review Form – Paper F5 Performance Management (01/12)

Name: _____ **Address:** _____

_____

_____

_____

How have you used this Kit?
(Tick one box only)

☐ Home study (book only)

☐ On a course: college _____

☐ With 'correspondence' package

☐ Other _____

Why did you decide to purchase this Kit?
(Tick one box only)

☐ Have used the complementary Study text

☐ Have used other BPP products in the past

☐ Recommendation by friend/colleague

☐ Recommendation by a lecturer at college

☐ Saw advertising

☐ Other _____

During the past six months do you recall seeing/receiving any of the following?
(Tick as many boxes as are relevant)

☐ Our advertisement in *Student Accountant*

☐ Our advertisement in *Pass*

☐ Our advertisement in *PQ*

☐ Our brochure with a letter through the post

☐ Our website www.bpp.com

Which (if any) aspects of our advertising do you find useful?
(Tick as many boxes as are relevant)

☐ Prices and publication dates of new editions

☐ Information on product content

☐ Facility to order books off-the-page

☐ None of the above

Which BPP products have you used?

Text	☐	*Success CD*	☐	*Learn Online*	☐
Kit	☑	*i-Learn*	☐	*Home Study Package*	☐
Passcard	☐	*i-Pass*	☐	*Home Study PLUS*	☐

Your ratings, comments and suggestions would be appreciated on the following areas.

	Very useful	Useful	Not useful
Passing F5			
Planning your question practice			
Questions			
Top Tips etc in answers			
Content and structure of answers			
Mock exam answers			

Overall opinion of this Kit	*Excellent* ☐	*Good* ☐	*Adequate* ☐	*Poor* ☐

Do you intend to continue using BPP products?   *Yes* ☐   *No* ☐

The BPP author of this edition can be e-mailed at: ianblackmore@bpp.com

Please return this form to: Ian Blackmore, ACCA Publishing Manager (Fundamentals papers), BPP Learning Media Ltd, FREEPOST, London, W12 8BR

✂

Review Form (continued)

TELL US WHAT YOU THINK

Please note any further comments and suggestions/errors below.